THE CAKE MIX DOCTOR GOES CHOCOLATE

• • •

This colorful display of moist, incredible cakes, cookies, cupcakes, and bars is all chocolate, all cake mix, all easy. Take your pick—dark, white, or some chocolate deliciously in between—then turn to the recipe page, gather your favorite add-ins, and heat up your oven. Now if only these photos were scratch and sniff!

THE PERFECT CHOCOLATE CAKE
p. 34

EVER-SO-MOIST CHOCOLATE
CAKE p. 37

MY FAVORITE BIRTHDAY CAKE
p. 39

EASY AND ELEGANT DEVIL'S
FOOD CAKE p. 43

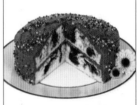

CHOCOLATE SOUR CREAM
MARBLE CAKE p. 46

OLD-FASHIONED DEVIL'S FOOD
CAKE p. 48

EBONY AND IVORY CAKE
p. 50

WHITE-ON-WHITE CAKE
p. 51

CHOCOLATE SNICKERDOODLE
CAKE p. 53

CHOCOLATE MIDNIGHT CAKE
p. 55

CHOCOLATE CINNAMON BANANA
CAKE p. 58

COOKIES AND CREAM CAKE
p. 61

PEANUT BUTTER CAKE p. 63

GERMAN CHOCOLATE CAKE p. 66

GERMAN CHOCOLATE SPICE CAKE
p. 69

CHOCOLATE COCONUT ICEBOX
CAKE p. 72

TRIPLE-DECKER RASPBERRY
CHOCOLATE CAKE p. 75

MARTHA'S CHOCOLATE CHERRY
ICE CREAM CAKE p. 78

CHOCOLATE ORANGE CAKE p. 81

NATALIE'S CHOCOLATE CAFÉ AU
LAIT CAKE p. 83

BUTTERMILK CHOCOLATE SPICE
CAKE p. 86

DEBBIE'S DAZZLING RED VELVET
CAKE p. 88

WHITE CHOCOLATE PEACH CAKE
p. 90

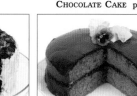

LEMON LOVERS' WHITE
CHOCOLATE CAKE p. 93

QUICK TUNNEL OF FUDGE CAKE
p. 98

CHOCOLATE CHIP PECAN COFFEE
CAKE p. 101

CHOCOLATE CREAM CHEESE
POUND CAKE p. 103

CHOCOLATE-ORANGE CREAM
CHEESE POUND CAKE p. 105

MINT CHOCOLATE CREAM CHEESE
POUND CAKE p. 107

A LIGHTER CHOCOLATE POUND
CAKE p. 109

GOOD-FOR-YOU CHOCOLATE
POUND CAKE p. 111

INCREDIBLE MOCHA MELTED ICE
CREAM CAKE p. 114

DARN GOOD CHOCOLATE CAKE
p. 116

KATHY'S CHOCOLATE CHOCOLATE
CHIP CAKE p. 118

CHOCOLATE MACAROON RING
CAKE p. 120

MILK CHOCOLATE CHERRY POUND
CAKE p. 122

EASY HERSHEY BAR SWIRL CAKE
p. 125

AMAZING GERMAN CHOCOLATE
CAKE p. 128

CHOCOLATE BANANA POUND
CAKE p. 130

GERMAN CHOCOLATE CHIP POUND
CAKE p. 132

BOSTON CREAM PIE CAKE
p. 135

ALMOND MARBLED CHOCOLATE
POUND CAKE p. 137

MILKY WAY SWIRL CAKE p. 139

WHITE CHOCOLATE POUND CAKE
WITH STRAWBERRIES p. 141

PUMPKIN CHOCOLATE CHIP CAKE
p. 143

WHITE CHOCOLATE POUND CAKE
WITH RICOTTA p. 145

LIBBIE'S CHOCOLATE AMARETTO
CAKE p. 148

RICK'S CHOCOLATE RUM BUNDT
CAKE p. 151

CHOCOLATE KAHLÚA CAKE
p. 153

BLACK RUSSIAN CAKE p. 155

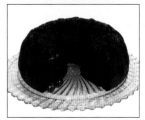

CHOCOLATE FOUR-SEASONS WINE
CAKE p. 157

GERMAN CHOCOLATE UPSIDE-
DOWN CAKE p. 162

WHITE CHOCOLATE PINEAPPLE
UPSIDE-DOWN CAKE p. 165

CHOCOLATE COCONUT CREAM
CAKE p. 167

GERMAN CHOCOLATE CHIP
ZUCCHINI CAKE p. 169

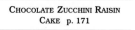

CHOCOLATE ZUCCHINI RAISIN
CAKE p. 171

GERMAN CHOCOLATE VELVET
CRUMB CAKE p. 174

CHOCOLATE CARROT CAKE p. 177

GERMAN CHOCOLATE SHEET
CAKE p. 180

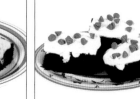

EASY CHOCOLATE POKE CAKE
p. 182

MARCIA'S EASY CHOCOLATE TOFFEE
CRUNCH POKE CAKE p. 184

THE WATERGATE CAKE p. 186

CHOCOLATE RUM RAISIN CAKE
p. 188

CHOCOLATE APRICOT CAKE
p. 190

CHOCOLATE EGGNOG CAKE
p. 192

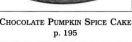

CHOCOLATE PUMPKIN SPICE CAKE
p. 195

DARK CHOCOLATE SHEET CAKE
p. 197

BANANA SPLIT FUDGE CAKE
p. 199

CHOCOLATE SYRUP COFFEE CAKE
p. 201

CHOCOLATE TIRAMISÙ p. 203

CHOCOLATE POTLUCK CAKE
p. 205

WHITE CHOCOLATE WEDDING
CAKE p. 207

CHOCOLATE STRAWBERRY
CHEESECAKE p. 212

WHITE CHOCOLATE BANANA-
MACADAMIA CHEESECAKE p. 215

KEY LIME CHOCOLATE
CHEESECAKE p. 217

DOUBLE-CHOCOLATE LIME
CHEESECAKE p. 220

MOCHA BROWNIE CHEESECAKE
p. 222

PUMPKIN SPICE GERMAN
CHOCOLATE CHEESECAKE p. 225

ORANGE-GINGER GERMAN
CHOCOLATE CHEESECAKE p. 227

MOLTEN CHOCOLATE PUDDING
CAKE p. 230

CHOCOLATE-CINNAMON BANANA
PUDDING CAKE p. 233

CHOCOLATE SOUFFLÉ PUDDING
CAKE p. 235

GUATEMALAN WEDDING CAKE
p. 237

PEAR AND CHOCOLATE TERRINE
p. 241

LUSCIOUS LEMON WHITE
CHOCOLATE TERRINE p. 244

CHOCOLATE LOVE CAKE p. 248

BROWNIE CHOCOLATE MOUSSE
TRIFLE p. 251

STRAWBERRY BROWNIE TORTE
p. 254

DARK CHOCOLATE ROULADE
p. 256

CHOCOLATE KAHLÚA ROULADE
p. 258

CREAM CHEESE BROWNIE PIE
p. 261

KENTUCKY BOURBON PECAN
FUDGE PIE p. 264

BARBARA'S CHOCOLATE MARBLE
ANGEL FOOD CAKE p. 268

CHOCOLATE-ORANGE ALMOND
MARBLE ANGEL FOOD CAKE p. 271

CHOCOLATE PINEAPPLE ANGEL
FOOD CAKE p. 274

CHOCOLATE-SWIRLED APRICOT
ANGEL FOOD CAKE p. 276

CHOCOLATE COFFEE ANGEL FOOD
CAKE p. 278

DEEP CHOCOLATE ALMOND
ANGEL ICEBOX CAKE p. 280

FROZEN CHOCOLATE NEAPOLITAN
CAKE p. 283

WHITE CHOCOLATE ANGEL FOOD
MOUSSE CAKE p. 286

CAPPUCCINO ANGEL FOOD
MOUSSE TORTE p. 289

CHOCOLATE COCONUT MACAROON
CAKE p. 291

WHITE CHOCOLATE CHIFFON
CAKE p. 293

RASPBERRY SWIRL WHITE
CHOCOLATE CHIFFON CAKE p. 295

CHOCOLATE CHIFFON CAKE
p. 298

TRIPLE CHOCOLATE TO-LIVE-FOR
MUFFINS p. 302

PUMPKIN GERMAN CHOCOLATE
CHIP MUFFINS p. 305

MEXICAN CHOCOLATE CINNAMON
MUFFINS p. 307

CHOCOLATE SURPRISE MUFFINS
p. 309

LOADED GERMAN CHOCOLATE
CREAM CHEESE MUFFINS p. 312

CHOCOLATE PEANUT BUTTER
MUFFINS p. 314

CINNAMON-CHOCOLATE ANGEL
FOOD MUFFINS p. 317

WHITE CHOCOLATE MUFFINS WITH
CINNAMON STREUSEL p. 319

CHOCOLATE CHERRY CHIP
CUPCAKES p. 321

CHOCOLATE SOUR CREAM
CUPCAKES p. 324

CHOCOLATE BANANA CUPCAKES
p. 327

ORANGE SWIRL CHOCOLATE
CUPCAKES p. 329

RED VELVET CUPCAKES p. 331

RASPBERRY-PEACH WHITE
CHOCOLATE CUPCAKES p. 333

LITTLE WHITE CHOCOLATE POUND
CAKES p. 336

LITTLE CHOCOLATE ALMOND
CREAM CHEESE CAKES p. 338

LITTLE WHITE CHOCOLATE
LEMON DRIZZLE CAKES p. 340

BABY CHOCOLATE PISTACHIO
CAKES p. 343

STACY'S MINI CHOCOLATE CHIP
LOAVES p. 346

MINI GERMAN CHOCOLATE
BANANA LOAVES p. 348

FUDGE SNOWTOPS p. 352

ALMOND CHOCOLATE CHIP FUDGE
SNOWTOPS p. 354

CHOCOLATE CHUNK WALNUT
CHEWIES p. 357

CHOCOLATE CINNAMON CHIP
CHEWIES p. 359

QUICK PEANUT BUTTER KISS
COOKIES p. 361

DEVIL'S FOOD HEARTS p. 363

CHOCOLATE COOKIE SANDWICHES
p. 366

CHUNKY CHOCOLATE PEANUT
BUTTER BARS p. 368

JOY OF ALMOND BARS
p. 370

GERMAN CHOCOLATE LEMON
CRUMB SQUARES p. 372

CHOCOLATE HELLO DOLLIES
p. 374

SARAH'S CHOCOLATE PEPPERMINT
STICKS p. 376

ORANGE-CHOCOLATE BISCOTTI
WITH ALMONDS p. 379

CHOCOLATE BISCOTTI p. 381

CHOCOLATE CINNAMON BISCOTTI
p. 383

PECAN CHIP BUTTERMILK
BROWNIES p. 385

JESSICA'S CARAMEL CHOCOLATE
BROWNIES p. 387

CHERRY CHEESECAKE BROWNIES
p. 390

MARBLED CREAM CHEESE AND
KAHLÚA BROWNIES p. 392

CHOCOLATE WALNUT BROWNIES
p. 394

SUNDAY FUDGE CAKE WITH CREAMY
CHOCOLATE FROSTING p. 397

TEXAS SHEET CAKE p. 399

CHOCOLATE MINT BROWNIES
p. 401

BANANA BLACK WALNUT
BROWNIES p. 403

RASPBERRY SWIRL BROWNIES
p. 405

CHOCOLATE

from the Cake mix Doctor...

BY ANNE BYRN

Photographs by Anthony Loew

Workman Publishing • New York

Library of Congress Cataloging-in-Publication Data
Byrn, Anne.
Chocolate from the cake mix doctor/by Anne Byrn; photographs by
Anthony Loew
p. cm.
Includes index.
ISBN 0-7611-2538-8 (hc) — ISBN 0-7611-2271-0 (pb)
1. Cake. 2. Cookery (Chocolate) I. Title.
TX771.B98 2001
641.8'653—dc21 2001026781

Cover design by Paul Hanson
Cover cake baked by Ulli Stachl
Book design by Lisa Hollander and Adriana Cordero
Cakes baked by Lauren Huber

Workman books are available at special discounts when purchased
in bulk for premiums and sales promotions as well as
for fund-raising or educational use. Special editions or book excerpts
can be created to specification. For details, contact the
Special Sales Director at the address below.

Workman Publishing Company, Inc.
708 Broadway
New York, NY 10003-9555
www.workman.com

First printing October 2001
10 9 8 7 6 5

For John ...
and in loving memory of
Poppy and Spires

Acknowledgments

• • •

t just doesn't seem possible that *The Cake Mix Doctor* was published less than two years ago. I am still amazed at the overwhelming response I have received from family, friends, and people I didn't even know.

One of my Web page readers said in an e-mail that she never dreamed she would be able to chat with a cookbook author. I, too, am astounded that I can chat with readers! And to these devoted readers, I offer my sincere thanks. Your keen observations, intelligent questions, creative ideas, and heartwarming stories have opened my eyes.

At home, this sequel would not have been possible without my husband, John. Thanks for taking charge again—feeding, bathing, reading to, hiking with, and driving our children through the snow for quesadillas and new shoes while I retreated upstairs to write. Thanks to my

children, Kathleen, Litton, and John, for understanding that cake would not permanently be on your mother's mind. A warm hug goes to my mother, Bebe, who encourages me with her personal courage. Thanks also to my sisters, Ginger Byrn and Susan Anderson, for just being there. It wasn't easy losing our father just days after Christmas. Poppy, as the grandchildren called him, adored chocolate cake, and he will be forever missed. And while Martha Bowden isn't family, she might as well have been. I found a diligent, caring, and creative cook in Martha, and her recipe testing was invaluable. A big hug goes to Kathy Sellers, who tested pound cakes in the summertime and baked casseroles to feed the troops when I couldn't cook.

To my agent, Nancy Crossman, thank you for believing in me again. For their generous taste buds and honest feedback, I appreciate the teachers of Granbery Elementary School and the employees of AmSouth Bank, both in Nashville. And to Diane Hooper and Dorothy Dearth, thank you for keeping things running smoothly in the midst of joyous chaos!

To my colleagues in the media, thank you for embracing *The Cake Mix Doctor.* They include Candy Sagon, Linda Cicero, Cathy Thomas, Barbara Gibbs Ostmann, Judy Walker, Susan Puckett, Regan Walker, Beverly Mills, Alicia Ross, Janice Okun, Carol Ward, Natalie Haughton, Jo Ellen O'Hara, Allison Campbell, Mary Scourtes, Teresa Gubbins, Beverly Bundy, Judy Evans, Ann Criswell, Barbara Houle, and Jann Malone. It was fun being on the other side for a change! To Linda Wertheimer and Carol Klinger, I offer my heartfelt appreciation. To Margo Baumgart, Wow. To Mary Harrison, come back to Nashville anytime. And to Tim Brennan, thanks for sharing your St. Louis kitchen and your wisdom.

But no one has talked up *The Cake Mix Doctor* and *Chocolate from the Cake Mix Doctor* more than Jim Eber, the cake-crazed publicity director at Workman. Jim says if these books are my babies, then he is their godfather! Jim and his staff have done a stupendous job spreading the word from coast to coast; he even appeared on QVC as what he calls the "cake mix intern." And if Jim is the godfather, then Jenny Mandel in Workman's special markets department is the fairy godmother, for she made QVC happen.

Sincere thanks to Suzanne Rafer, my meticulous and thoughtful editor who continues to teach me well, and to her assistant Beth Doty. Many thanks to Peter and Carolan Workman for their generosity. To design director Paul Hanson, thank you for another delicious cover. And thanks to Lisa Hollander and Adriana Cordero for seeing the design through to the finished book. My warm thanks to Kathie Ness for her copyediting skills. And to David Schiller, Amy Hayworth, and Pat Upton, thanks for your continued hard work on the Web site. To Lauren Huber, who baked these chocolate cakes for photography, and to Anthony Loew, who photographed them so beautifully, a big chocolate hug. And once more, to makeup master Mark Lindsey, thanks for years of experience and concealer!

Harley Blaisdell, Doug Thompson, and Rachel Stevenson made QVC worthwhile and fun. Dave Sweeney at Hershey's, Bonnie West in Denver, Sandy Carpenter and Preston Elliott, formerly with Duncan Hines, radio's Stephen Witzenberg in Des Moines, and Alison Bodor at the Chocolate Manufacturers Association—I thank you all.

To the generous cooks who shared recipes for this book, to the escorts who accompanied me around the country and listened as I rambled, and to booksellers nationwide, I happily offer you this latest slice of cake. It's chocolate, and it's warm from the oven.

Anne Byrn
Nashville, Tennessee

Contents

• • •

*T*he ABCs of baking chocolate cakes from a mix, including preparation tips, pantry essentials, cool baking tools, and a chocolate primer.

*T*here is no dessert more delectable than a mile-high layer cake topped with thick swirls of frosting. Enjoy The Perfect Chocolate Cake, Old-Fashioned Devil's Food Cake, Peanut Butter Cake with Fluffy Chocolate Frosting, and White Chocolate Peach Cake. So rich, so delicious.

*J*ust the cakes to serve with scoops of ice cream and icy cold milk. Pumpkin Chocolate Chip Cake, Amazing German Chocolate Cake, Almond Marbled Chocolate Pound Cake, and Boston Cream Pie Cake are all baked in Bundt or tube pans so there's plenty to go around.

*W*hen you're baking for a chocolate-loving crowd, these are the cakes to turn to. For potlucks and picnics, you can't beat the Easy Chocolate Poke Cake, Chocolate Zucchini Raisin Cake, Banana Split Fudge Cake, or The Watergate Cake.

Chocolate for the Soul

• • •

They say there are smells of childhood, scents so strongly rooted in your soul that decades later a whiff of that aroma immediately takes you back. For me, the strong, profound, and provocative scent of chocolate cake is so deeply etched in my psyche that my mind shifts to the past whenever there's a chocolate cake baking in the oven: My mother has just frosted a chocolate layer cake for my tenth birthday. The cake is warm, the milk is cold, and life is good.

In my house, birthdays, visiting relatives, a sister'coming home from college were all occasions for a dark chocolate layer cake or a buttermilk chocolate sheet cake, coated in chocolate pan frosting and topped with toasted pecans. You want to teach children patience? Leave an impeccably frosted chocolate cake resting on the kitchen counter until dinnertime. For us, it was torturous. My sisters and I would sneak into the kitchen, stick a finger into the frosting, and then run like crazy. What my mother didn't know!

The same unbridled joy I felt as a chocolate-snatching child accompanied me as I tested, wrote, and assembled this book on how to doctor a cake mix to create stupendous chocolate desserts, ranging from dark deep chocolate to pale sweet German to creamy white. If this is work, then I am the luckiest working stiff alive.

What's All the Buzz About Chocolate?

We love chocolate, and chocolate seems to love us back.

It has that smooth and creamy texture once it melts in our mouths, and that rich flavor in our favorite devil's food cake, and that memorable aroma when baking . . . but are there hidden reasons why we're so crazy about it?

According to chemists and sensory researchers, chocolate is a highly concentrated, satisfying, and mysterious food. It contains stimulants: theobromine and caffeine. Theobromine and caffeine dilate our blood vessels and stimulate our heart muscles. And chocolate contains small amounts of anandamide, the same compound the brain normally produces to signal pleasure.

Chocolate also triggers our bodies to produce serotonin and endorphin, neurotransmitters that act as antidepressants and help us feel calm and relaxed. Serotonin production is triggered by eating carbohydrates, and endorphin production by eating fat. Researchers say the lift-your-spirits feeling that endorphins provide is somewhat similar to that pleasurable zone known as "runner's high."

Recently researchers have discovered that chocolate contains flavonoids. Flavonoids are beneficial compounds also found in tea, red wine, fruits, and vegetables that act as antioxidants and reduce the risk of developing cancer and heart disease. In the bloodstream they mop up substances called free radicals, small reactive molecules that can cause damage to the body. You receive the most pronounced effect from unsweetened cocoa, followed by dark chocolate and then milk chocolate. White chocolate contains no flavonoids, however, and thus no antioxidant properties.

If we love chocolate, is it possible that chocolate helps us to love? According to Canadian researcher Joseph Schwarcz, chocolate does contain tiny amounts of phenylethylamine, an amphetamine-like substance known as the "chemical of love." People who are in love have high levels of phenylethylamine in their brains. But chocolate is the food of love, and the food we love, most likely, he says, because we can't resist it.

I have determined which are the best-tasting chocolate cake mixes and which are the best ingredients with which to doctor them. I have discovered that you don't need to use fancy European chocolate to create these desserts—supermarket chocolate works just fine! In the process, I have baked and tasted cakes so memorable that I have a whole new repertoire of favorites: The Ever-So-Moist Chocolate Cake with Chocolate Sour Cream Frosting will be our family's new birthday cake. The humble yet substantial Triple-Chocolate To-Live-For Muffins will be toted on our car trips. The unbelievably moist German Chocolate Sheet Cake with Rocky Road Frosting will be a potluck mainstay. And this is just the beginning!

With devil's food, German chocolate, white, angel food, and a few yellow cake mixes, I have created warm pudding cakes and elegant terrines, chocolate cheesecakes in springform pans, chiffons and cookies, more angels, new mini cakes, scrumptious bars, and easy yet sophisticated brownies. And as always, I have stuck to my mother's advice: "You can get away with a cake-mix cake, but you must make your frostings from scratch." Sample the easy White Chocolate Glaze on chiffon cake, the German Chocolate Cream Cheese Frosting, the Pineapple Cream Cheese Frosting, Martha's Chocolate Icing, and the Warm Lemon Curd Sauce on white chocolate cake, and see what I mean.

For those of you who don't know the story, *The Cake Mix Doctor* began as an article I wrote in the summer of 1998 while working for Nashville's newspaper, *The Tennessean.* I shared family recipes for doctoring cake mixes, and I asked readers to send in their favorites. Within a week, more than 500 recipes arrived. Dumbfounded, I wrote a sequel. Then people wanted more, and I ended up writing a book. Cake mixes are time-saving and reliable, but left alone, prepared using the package instructions and frosted with the canned stuff (heaven forbid!), they are ho-hum. What I proposed in that first book was to doctor mixes with mashed bananas, cinnamon, coffee, yogurt, and myriad other ingredients to make them better: cures for the otherwise common cake. In this sequel I zero in on chocolate cake because so many of us are just plain crazy about chocolate. Whether flavored with sour cream, grated German choco-late, puréed canned apricots, straw-berry preserves, melted white chocolate, crushed pineapple, coffee granules, Kahlúa, frozen raspberries, orange juice, or other ingredients found close at hand, these chocolate cakes are magnificent. And they don't look or taste as if they came from a box.

My mission remains the same as in the first book: to help busy cooks find the time to bake even when company is *not* com-ing. And, to help people who have never baked a cake. In spite of what cooking teachers and many cookbook authors say, scratch cakes are not that easy to pull off. Many people never had a mother or grandmother close by to show them how to bake a cake. They have never attended cooking school. And yet they want to celebrate holidays and special days with terrific-tasting

cakes—not from a bakery, but from their own ovens. The most gratifying part of writing *The Cake Mix Doctor* has been helping these first-timers. In this chocolate book, too, there are recipes to build confidence. But, there are also recipes to challenge.

It isn't surprising that many from-scratch cooks e-mailed me or pulled me aside at a book signing and con-fessed that they had contemplated try-ing the "M" word, but they didn't know which mix to buy. I advise these more accomplished cooks to begin with chocolate cake mix. That's because the choco-late mixes, devil's food in particular, taste the least arti-ficial. It is easy to add a few key ingredi-ents, like sour cream and cinnamon, and turn out fabulous cakes that will please the well-traveled palate. One chapter in particular—Chocolate Cheese-cakes, Pudding Cakes, and So Much More—is perfect for these cooks. The Guatemalan Wedding Cake, Pear and Chocolate Terrine, Luscious Lemon White Chocolate Terrine, the roulades, and Key Lime Chocolate Cheesecake

> ℞
> *the Cake Mix Doctor says*
>
> Visit me at www.cakemixdoctor.com,
> where you can pass along a favorite
> recipe, ask about one you've heard of
> but can't find, ask baking questions, or
> just share your latest baking adventure.
> You can also read back issues of the
> bimonthly newsletter "A Piece of Cake"
> on the Web site, where in each issue I
> share tested, but unpublished, recipes.

will rocket your fine-tuned taste buds into orbit.

I hope you get as much pleasure from these recipes as my family did. I'll share a quick story: My slim younger sister, Susan, sauntered through my kitchen the weekend after Thanksgiving. The counters were lined with chocolate cupcakes and stacked with sheet cakes. "I don't know if I could live in a house where there was this much chocolate cake baking going on," she said coyly, eyeing each dessert like a cat ready to pounce on a fat mouse. "It would be such a temptation." Then she spotted a still-warm Chocolate Cherry Chip Cupcake and popped it into her mouth. I smiled.

The aroma and appearance of a chocolate cake are tempting, but its *taste* is good for our soul.

Chocolate
Cake Mix 101

• • •

You may be anxious to get to the recipes, in the same way you're anxious to flip to the end of a mystery novel to find out "who done it." But if you skip this crash course in how to put together a chocolate cake, an unnecessary mystery might take place in your kitchen as you wonder how to tell if the cake is done, or what type of cocoa to use for the frosting.

These following pages should take the mystery out of cake baking for you. Take a look at the how-to section—my tips on turning that box of cake mix into a masterpiece. Note the types of chocolate that work best in cake baking plus review my suggested list of essential ingredients to keep on hand in the pantry, freezer, refrigerator, and cupboard. I also share my favorite tools for the job and answer some frequently asked questions.

One thing I know to be true—mysteries may be fun to read, but they are no fun to experience in the kitchen. Read on, then enjoy the recipes.

The ABCs of Cake Mix Baking

Imagine you're about to take a school exam. And on the first page of the exam the teacher neatly and concisely lays out the answers. That's how I'd like you to look at this section—the answers to your questions. In this crash course I have culled the most important information from *The Cake Mix Doctor,* have added what I have learned this year, and have focused just on chocolate.

1. CHOOSE A CHOCOLATE CAKE MIX

• *Size:* Unlike brownie mixes, which range in size from slightly over a pound to nearly a pound and a half, chocolate cake mixes come in one size. You can occasionally find the smaller one-layer chocolate mixes, but most mixes are 18.25 ounces. That makes for easy substituting between brands.

• *Plain vs. pudding:* That said, there is a crucial difference among those mixes: Duncan Hines and the generics are plain cake mix; Betty Crocker and Pillsbury mixes contain pudding. In *The Cake Mix Doctor* I said you should not use them interchangeably, but I have relaxed my rule a bit. You should *not* use a pudding cake mix when the recipe calls for a package of instant pudding. You should *not* use a pudding cake mix if the recipe calls for plain mix and contains a lot of heavy ingredients like sour cream, nuts, and chocolate chips, because the pudding mix will make the cake even heavier. But you *can* use a pudding cake mix in many layer recipes that call for plain mix. Just be forewarned that pudding mixes do not rise as much as plain; they don't dome but bake flat; and they will shrink back from the sides of the pan on cooling. However, they do make an incredibly moist cake and they are widely available, and for those two rea-

sons I have included more of them in this book.

You can also save a step by using a pudding cake mix in a recipe that calls for plain mix plus a package of pudding, although for some reason these cakes don't rise as well as the plain-plus-pudding-mix combination.

• *Flavor:* When making chocolate cakes, devil's food and chocolate can be used interchangeably. Dark chocolate mix is just that—very dark in color. Save it for those recipes where you want a bold color contrast. The German chocolate is an excellent mix and better suited to combinations of flavors, such as when adding zucchini or making orange or strawberry cheesecakes. White mixes can be turned into chocolate by adding a square of melted chocolate or 1/4 cup of cocoa. There are also fudge marble mixes and pound cake mixes, but I call for them only a few times. Both yellow and spice mixes can be used along with chocolate.

Brownie mixes, on the other hand, are a confusing lot. Your best bet is to buy as big a box as possible, with few frills (no fudge packets or add-ins); you'll be doing the doctoring yourself. I have tried to be as consistent as possible in brownie testing so that my recipes will work with a range of package sizes. As far as various brands go, the flavors differ. To decide which brand you prefer, bake

What's in a Cake Mix?

The manufacturers might like you to believe that cake mixes are some great mystery and that their recipes are closely guarded corporate secrets, but they're not that complicated.

They are like any other baking mix in that they contain flour, sugar, and the leavening needed to make the cake rise. In addition, they contain shortening, emulsifiers, flavorings such as chocolate, and colorings. The shortening makes the cake tender, the chocolate is for flavor and color, and the emulsifiers make the cake moist. Emulsifiers bind the fat and the liquid together; soy lecithin is the most common emulsifier.

Mixes also contain flavorings like vanillin, which is an artificial vanilla flavoring, thought by many to be the source of "cake mix taste," an aftertaste you get from cake mix. Yellow cake mixes suffer the most from "cake mix taste," I think, and they contain a heavy hand of artificial colorings, too. Chocolate mixes, on the other hand, are less cluttered.

Undoctored, they deliver the least "cake mix taste" of all, no matter what brand.

All you need to add to a cake mix is liquid (water or buttermilk, for example), vegetable oil (this varies from 2 table-spoons to ½ cup or more), and eggs. The number of eggs affects the texture and appearance of the cake. One-egg batters will yield a dry and tender cake, perfect for pressing into the bottom of a spring-form pan as the base for a cheesecake. Two-egg batters make dense sheet cakes, three-egg batters are just right for spongy layer cakes, and four-egg batters turn into those sturdy and well-formed Bundt and pound cakes.

You will, of course, want to add more to a cake mix, and that is why you're reading this book! On these pages I will show you how to incorporate mashed ripe bananas and other fruit, sour cream, chopped nuts, brewed coffee, and a pantry of other ready ingredients into chocolate cake mix batters to turn them into your signature desserts.

the brownies according to the package directions (no doctoring) and sample them. Then choose the brand you like best, and use that one in the recipes featured here.

2. READY THE OVEN

• *Temperature:* Oven temperature is the variable that I just cannot help you with, although I wish I could. No matter how carefully you follow my recipes, if your oven is not baking true, your cakes will not turn out right. If in doubt, buy an inexpensive oven thermometer at the hardware store, place it in the oven, and set the temperature to 350°F. The oven should cycle up and down and reach 350°F in about 15 minutes. If not, you should have your oven checked and possibly calibrated by an appliance expert. Always preheat the oven for 15 minutes before you bake. Most cakes bake at 350°F, but you'll find some recipes, such as the cheesecakes, call for a 325°F oven. If you are using pans with a dark finish or glass baking pans, reduce the temperature by 25 degrees. Do the same if the layers are larger than 9 inches in diameter.

• *Rack position:* Place the oven rack in the center position for most cakes, slightly lower for angel foods. For three-layer cakes, stagger the pans so two are on the middle rack, set slightly apart, and one is in the center on the next-higher rack. Take care that there is plenty of air circulation around the three pans, and be aware that the top layer will bake more quickly.

3. PREPARE THE PAN

• *Use the right pan:* Many cake disasters can be averted right here. Read through the recipe to see if you have the correct pan. To check a pan, turn it over and see if the measurements are inscribed on the bottom. If not, measure across the bottom of the pan with a ruler or measuring tape. If yours is not the right size, you may want to borrow a pan, buy a new one, or decide on another recipe.

If you decide to purchase pans, buy good ones. Good doesn't necessarily mean the most expensive. I don't like the heavy, dark (and expensive) type of bakeware because they overbrown cakes. I prefer shiny, heavy-weight, moderately priced aluminum pans for layers, sheet cakes, and roulades. (Stainless steel doesn't conduct heat as well as aluminum.) You can find these pans at cooking stores and in housewares departments, and if they are washed and dried well before being stored in a cool, dark place, they will last for a very long time.

• *Grease the pan:* Prepare cake pans according to the recipe instructions. Layers will release best if the pans are lightly misted with vegetable oil spray and dusted with flour. Tap out the excess flour over the sink or trash can. They will release even better if the pans are lightly spread with vegetable shortening and dusted with flour. Wilton makes a wonderful shortcut called Cake Release, a blend of vegetable oil and flour that you can brush on the pan with a pastry brush. For choco-

Substituting Pans

Can you use a different size pan than called for in the recipe? The pan called for is always the best, but in a pinch, you can substitute:

Recipe pan	Your pan	What to do
Layers	Bundt or tube	Choose sturdy cakes containing 3 to 4 eggs. Will bake in 50 to 60 minutes at 350°F.
Cupcake/muffin	Bundt or tube	Look for moist recipes with plenty of oil or liquid, containing 3 to 4 eggs.
Sheet cake	Bundt or tube	Look for moist recipes with plenty of oil or liquid, containing 3 to 4 eggs. Will bake in 50 to 60 minutes at 350°F.
Bundt or tube	Layers	Choose a lighter-weight cake with 3 eggs and few added ingredients. Bake 28 to 32 minutes at 350°F.
Cupcake/muffin	Layers	Choose a lighter-weight cake with 3 eggs and few added ingredients. Bake 28 to 32 minutes at 350°F. Omit the toppings.
Sheet cake	Layers	Make sure these lighter cakes don't have a lot of add-ins like chocolate chips, which will weigh down a layer cake and cause it to sink.

late cakes, you can dust the pans with unsweetened cocoa instead of flour. Do *not* use the aerosol cooking sprays to mist pans. They have an odd flavor, and they contain propellants (alcohol), which will cause your cake to bake quickly at the edges and over-brown. Instead, invest in a mister that you fill with your own vegetable oil. You'll find them in housewares departments.

Bundt pans are best prepared with a misting of oil and a dusting of flour. For some reason, lighter-weight Bundts release a cake better than the heavier types. Tube pans are sold shiny or non-stick. Nonstick is fine for pound cakes, but you will need a shiny pan for angel food cakes and chiffons, which are poured into an ungreased pan and must

Recipe pan	Your pan	What to do
Bundt or tube	Cupcake/muffin	A good conversion. Bake for 20 to 25 minutes at 350°F.
Layer	Cupcake/muffin	If the cake is lighter, the baking time will be less—only 20 minutes.
Sheet cake	Cupcake/muffin	Also a good conversion. Bake for 20 to 25 minutes at 350°F.
Bundt or tube	Sheet cake	Look for cakes that aren't heavy with sour cream, oil, or chocolate chips—they tend to sink in the center. Bake about 40 minutes at 350°F.
Layers	Sheet cake	Use the 3-egg cakes for sheet cakes; even 2 eggs work well.
Cupcake/muffin	Sheet cake	Use the less heavy recipes, and scatter the add-ins or toppings over the top before baking, or on the bottom of the pan before pouring in the batter to create an upside-down cake.

cool upside down over the neck of a bottle before slicing. Brownie pans need just a misting of oil or a light spreading of butter on the bottom of the pan. Roulades are poured onto buttered parchment paper lining the bottom of a jelly-roll pan. A washable and reusable parchment paper called Super Parchment is now available and works great.

4. Mix the Batter

• *Measure:* Bless the resilient cake mix. It has been formulated to work in spite of our foibles, in spite of our cold or hot ovens, our wrong pan sizes. But your cake will taste better and look better if you carefully follow the recipe. And measuring is critical. Pour liquids into liquid measuring cups (typically Pyrex) and check the measurement at eye level. Spoon dry ingredients like chocolate chips, raisins, or nuts into dry measuring cups and level off the top with the flat side of a dinner knife. Brown sugar should be packed lightly into a dry measuring cup and leveled off with a knife. For butter and margarine, use the tablespoon indicators on the wrapper.

• *The dump method:* Unless a recipe specifies folding in whipped egg whites, chips, or nuts at the end of the recipe, you can pretty much dump all the ingredients in the bowl at one time and turn on the mixer. The ingredients can be right out of the refrigerator unless stated "at room temperature"—important when working with cream cheese because it tends to lump when combined with cold ingredients. Turn the mixer on low speed to moisten the ingredients; the recipe will tell you how long to blend—from 30 seconds to 1 minute. Then, in the case of most layer, pound, and sheet cakes, mix for 2 minutes at medium speed. Angel food cakes need just 1 minute of mixing. Brownies need only 1 minute at low, or they can be stirred by hand.

• *Don't overbeat:* One of the greatest injustices you can do your chocolate cake mix cakes is to overbeat the batter until it has those grand tunnels going through. Use a hand mixer so you are less likely to overbeat, and save the big turbo mixer for scratch cakes and breads. Just be sure to stir once or twice along the bottom of the bowl with a rubber spatula, because cake mix can cling to the bottom.

5. TEST FOR DONENESS

• *The spring test:* If you bake enough cakes, you will be able to look at a cake and smell a cake and know that it is done. Until this epiphany, there are plenty of other cues for determining doneness. The most reliable is the spring test: When you think the cake might be done, open the oven door and lightly press the top of the cake with your finger. The cake should spring back. If your finger leaves an indentation, it's not done.

• *Other signs:* Other cues of doneness might be the cake pulling away from the sides of the pan; this is helpful in the larger cakes like Bundts and tubes. If in doubt with these big cakes, gently stick a toothpick or wooden skewer into the center of the cake. It should come out clean. (The toothpick test isn't the right one for layers because the hole it creates is just enough to deflate the layer if the cake is not yet done.) Brownies are tough to call. Always check at the first time indicated, and if in doubt, pull them out sooner rather than later. Angel foods are done when darkened and crusty on top. Take care not to underbake an angel food cake or it will fall while it cools. Cheesecakes look glossy in the center when they have cooked through, and they will still be a little jiggly when you gently shake the pan; the center will firm up as the cake cools.

6. OUT OF THE OVEN

• *Cool the cake:* Carefully place the cake pan on a wire rack or the stovetop grate to cool. Allow 10 minutes for cake layers, 20 minutes for tubes, Bundts, and sheet cakes. Angels and chiffons cool for a full hour, upside down over a bottle or resting on the feet built into the pan. Always allow a cake to cool before you try to move it or frost it; otherwise, it might tear.

• *Loosen the cake:* Before you invert the cake to remove it from the pan, run a sharp knife around the edges to loosen them. Then give the pan—layer, Bundt, tube, or sheet—a good shake. Rotate it a quarter turn and give it another shake. Continue to do this until you can see that the cake has left the pan sides all the way around.

• *Turn the cake out of the pan:* Place the rack or serving platter upside down on top of the cake pan, and then invert the two together. Layer cakes need to be inverted again so they are top side up. This will prevent lines from forming on the top of the cake as it cools and the cake sticking to the rack. Invert cakes baked in tube pans again, too, for they are served large side up, or the way they baked in the oven.

7. FROST THE CAKE

• *To level or not to level:* Don't! When I see a leveled cake, I think it came from a bakery. It appears dry and hard to me and doesn't evoke any of those warm and comforting feelings you get when you see a slightly domed cake, what I call the grandmother look. Plus, if you slice the top off the cake to level it, you will be spreading the frosting on cake crumbs, and this is very difficult unless you freeze the cake layer first. I understand that some bakers insist on leveled cakes because they are easier to transport and display. If the cake does dome and you really want it to be flat, while it is cooling in the pan, place a clean kitchen towel over the layer and press down firmly with your hand to flatten the cake in the center.

• *Icings:* In this book I make a distinction between fluffy uncooked frostings and what I like to call cooked icings. The icings need to go on warm; they set up hard as they cool on the cake. Mix and match them, or use my suggestions for which icings go with which cakes. Cakes with icings are easily stored at room temperature, and they tote well in warm

High-Altitude Baking: What You Need to Know

If you are living in a place that is 3,500 feet or more above sea level, you are living at high altitude. Because there is less air pressure at these altitudes, cakes may rise higher than they would at sea level. And if cakes do not have the structural strength to support the additional height, they fall. So, if you are baking at high altitudes, what you need to do is to strengthen the structure of your cake, or at least choose a cake recipe wisely. According to Bonnie West, a home economist and consultant in sky-high Denver, Colorado, some cakes are just more risky to bake at high altitudes.

If cakes were made up of just flour, eggs, and water, they would perform well at high altitudes. But we all know that is not the case. Sugar, oil, butter, even cocoa, tenderizes a cake, making it taste better, but they also make the cake's structure more delicate. More sugar in the form of gelatin and pudding creates an even more delicate structure, as do peanut butter, melted chocolate, and melted butter.

So what can you do? Learn to spot the high-risk cakes and avoid them. Learn to boost the structure of the cake you are baking. Here are some steps for high-altitude success from Bonnie West:

1. Choose the right pan. Bundt pans have lots of sides for the cake to cling to as it rises and bakes, so Bundt cakes tend to bake up dense and fall less. On the other hand, 13- by 9-inch sheet pans provide the least support. If additional sugar or fat is added to the cake mix, you will notice that the center of a sheet cake dips. High-altitude bakers say that if a cake works in a sheet pan, it will work in any pan.

weather because the icing doesn't run.

- *Frostings:* Most buttercreams—made with just butter, confectioners' sugar, and a liquid—work well on any cake. The heavier buttercreams—the cream cheese frostings—need a denser cake to support the weight, or the frosting can tear the top of the cake as you spread it. Look at the chocolate cake flavor and pick a frosting that is compatible in flavor—peppermint, orange, white chocolate—and compatible in texture.

- *Glazes:* Glazes are easy last-minute additions to a cake. I love all of the

2. Follow the high-altitude directions on the cake mix box; they are there to boost the structure of the cake. Often they call for adding a little extra flour (2 tablespoons to ⅓ cup), using slightly less oil (if I call for ½ cup of oil in a recipe, reduce that amount to ⅓ cup, for example), and/or baking at a higher temperature.

3. Higher oven temperatures are helpful in setting the structure of the high-altitude cake, but take care not to overbake it. "An overdone cake that is dry," says Bonnie, "is much worse than one that falls slightly."

4. Use plain cake mixes rather than ones with pudding included.

5. Make sure you beat the cake for the maximum time recommended. Beating develops the gluten in the flour, which is what provides structure. Bonnie recommends at least 3 minutes of beating time. Overbeating makes a tougher cake, says Bonnie, but usually the maximum time called for in a recipe is acceptable.

6. If your baked cakes have large air holes or pockets, the next time, before baking, hold the batter-filled pan 1 inch above the counter and drop it onto the counter. This will break up those bubbles.

7. And don't fret if your cakes crack on top. "I don't really consider this a problem. It comes from the air here being extra-dry," says Bonnie. "Adding a little more liquid may help, or try baking on a humid day—but I wouldn't worry about it."

Keep in mind that adjusting a cake for high altitudes is for visual purposes, not flavor. "Most family members will be so glad you've baked a cake," says Bonnie, "they won't care if it dips a little in the middle. For those of us who grew up at high altitude, we believe frosting was invented to fill the dip!"

chocolate glazes in this book, from the thin Shiny Chocolate Glaze to the seductive White Chocolate Glaze. Glazes will differ in thickness a bit. Unless the recipe says so, let the cake cool before glazing. Some cakes, however, need to be glazed while warm to allow the glaze to seep in. And some cakes need to be poked with a chopstick or skewer before pouring the glaze over.

• *Cake stands:* Cakes are easier to frost if they are raised a bit. Frost the cake on a cake stand, and turn it a quarter turn as you go. Or place the cake on a

How Much Frosting Is Enough?

One 13- by 9-inch layer, top only .1¼ to 2¼ cups

One 13- by 9-inch layer, top and sides . . . . .2½ cups

Two 8-inch layers, top and sides . . . . .1¼ to 2¼ cups

Three 8-inch layers, top and sides . . . . .2½ cups

Two 9-inch layers, top and sides . . . . .2½ cups

Three 9-inch layers, top and sides . . . . .3 to 4 cups

10-inch tube pan, top and sides . . . . .3 to 4 cups

12-cup Bundt pan, top and sides . . . . .3 to 4 cups

12 cupcakes, tops only . . . . .1 cup

cardboard round on top of an upside-down cake pan. This elevates the cake a couple of inches, and you can turn the cardboard as you work.

• *No frosting:* In a hurry? Nothing is as pretty on a chocolate cake as a dusting of confectioners' sugar. Spoon some into a small sifter or strainer and gently tap it over the top of the cake. For a corresponding look, sift on a little sweetened cocoa. See Fast Decorations (page 163).

8. STORING THE CAKE

• *Leftovers:* Understandably, people don't need to research storage too much with chocolate cake because leftovers are seldom an issue! But should you have leftover cake, be reassured that it will last at room temperature or in the refrigerator (check the recipe suggestions) for a week. Longer than that, and you will need to freeze the cake. Cakes can be covered with a cake dome or bell, be placed in a cake saver, or be lightly covered with waxed paper, plastic wrap, or aluminum foil.

• *Freezing cake:* If wrapped properly, cake will freeze well for up to 6 months. Some cakes are better freezers than others. The denser the cake, the better it will freeze. Thawed unfrosted cakes taste better than thawed frosted cakes. Heavy frostings like cream cheese frostings will freeze better than the cooked icings, but whipped cream frostings don't freeze well at all. Any cake must be thoroughly cooked before it heads for the freezer. You must wrap cakes in the right material or the freezer will rob them of moisture and flavor. Since it's easier to wrap a cake if the frosting is hard, chill cakes with buttercream and cream cheese frostings, uncovered, for at least 20 minutes before covering them; then the wrap won't pull the frosting off the cake. Place the cake on a cake round and cover it with heavy-duty aluminum foil (never plastic wrap). Or, if your freezer is large enough, place it in a plastic cake saver. Cakes stored in deep chest freezers that are not opened routinely will freeze better than cakes frozen in refrigerator/freezer combinations, which are opened many times during the day.

• *Thawing frozen cakes:* Most cakes—the Bundts, tubes, sheet cakes, and unfrosted layers—thaw just fine overnight on the kitchen counter. Depending on the temperature of your kitchen, some cakes with cream cheese frostings thaw better in the refrigerator than on the counter. And if the frozen cake has a creamy frosting or filling containing eggs, it absolutely must be thawed in the refrigerator for 8 hours to overnight. By the way, if you plan on frosting those unfrosted layers, thaw them three quarters of the way covered in aluminum foil, then uncover and complete the thawing. This allows the layers to dry out so the frosting will stick to them.

Chocolate Primer: What You Need to Know About Working with Chocolate

Chocolate is one of our most pleasurable foods. It lifts our spirits, signals celebration, looks elegant, and brings to mind all sorts of pleasant taste memories. But chocolate, for all its good, is a temperamental ingredient. Fortunately, when we stir it into cake batter or prepare a basic frosting using it, we don't have to take it through a lot of fancy processes. All we need to do is buy the right kind of chocolate, store it under optimum conditions so that it stays fresh, and melt it properly. If we do these three things, rarely will we experience a bump along the way.

TYPES OF CHOCOLATE
Read my lips: no fancy chocolate. First and foremost, don't use hoity-toity, expensive chocolate for baking. Save it for eating out of the box with your sweetheart on Valentine's Day. Chocolate is a delicate and delicious foodstuff, and its flavor is

volatile. The strong, irresistible smell that chocolate gives off while baking is your clue that flavors are being baked away. Any subtle nuances in that precious European chocolate that you paid so dearly for will be but history when it is blasted in a 350°F oven. Shop at your local supermarket for all the chocolate you'll need in this book.

Buy real chocolate. There is chocolate, and there is the imitation stuff that doesn't contain cocoa butter. Look for real chocolate, which isn't hard to find on your supermarket shelf.

The basics

• *Unsweetened chocolate:* Also known as bitter or baking chocolate. It contains cocoa particles, ground very fine and smooth, an emulsifier, pure or artificial vanilla, but no sugar. It is sold most often in 1-ounce squares in an 8-ounce box, but you can also buy it melted in a convenient plastic pouch.

• *Semisweet or bittersweet chocolate:* Sugar is added to unsweetened chocolate, and the amount of sugar varies with the manufacturer. The names of this chocolate will vary, too; it's often called extra-bittersweet. Taste it first to find your preference. This is especially important when making ganache, a frosting that relies solely on the flavor of the semisweet chocolate. Look for shiny chocolate that snaps, smells chocolaty, and melts smoothly in your mouth. It can be eaten out of hand, chopped and melted into frostings, or grated into cake batter for extra chocolate flavor.

• *Couverture chocolate:* Contains more cocoa butter than semisweet, so it melts better. It is used primarily in candy making and is not called for in this book.

• *Milk chocolate:* Contains more sugar than semisweet, and of course milk is added. It is delicious eaten out of hand, and will melt and fold into frostings. Milk chocolate chips can be added to cake and cookie batters. Be careful when melting milk chocolate; it doesn't take as long as semisweet. Because of the extra sugar added, you cannot substitute milk chocolate for semisweet chocolate.

• *White chocolate:* For something so simple in flavor, this is a mighty complicated confection. It is made from the cocoa butter pressed from the cacao bean, with sugar, milk solids, vanilla, and lecithin added. Because it contains no chocolate liquor, its flavor comes from the cocoa butter. And that is why the Food and Drug Administration (FDA) considers it "an infringement on the standard of identity for chocolate," according to the Chocolate Manufacturers Association (CMA). Some white chocolates are labeled "white confectionary coating." Others are called "white chocolate" on the package, which means the manufacturers have received special permission from the FDA to do so. The FDA is being petitioned by the CMA to relax the standard because the same product can be called "white chocolate" in Europe. (It is fine to use the term "white chocolate" in a recipe title because the FDA does not regulate food made at home or foods in cookbooks.) To make matters even more complicated, some brands are made with vegetable oils, like palm kernel oil, instead of cocoa butter. Look for the words "cocoa butter" on the label, and if you have a chance, look at the product itself. If it is made with a vegetable oil, it will be bright white, whereas with cocoa butter it is a more yellowish ivory color.

White chocolate is delicate and very sensitive to heat, and it won't substitute for dark chocolate in recipes. But it can be carefully melted and added to cake mix recipes in order to give the cake flavor and a rich, crumblike texture.

Other types of chocolate

• *German sweet chocolate:* A sweeter chocolate than semisweet, and the basis for the famous German chocolate cake. It is sold in a 4-ounce bar, and can be grated or melted and added to cake batters, or melted and turned into frostings.

• *Chocolate chips:* An invaluable cake-doctoring tool for folding into muffins, cupcakes, Bundt cakes, layers, sheet cakes, brownies, and cookies. But be careful when you melt chips: They may be melted before your realize, because they tend to hold their shape. Chips are most often semisweet chocolate, but they come in all sorts of flavors, such as cinnamon, white chocolate, milk chocolate, and peanut butter.

• *Chocolate syrup:* Swirl this through a Bundt cake or cheesecake. Drizzle it into cream as you are whipping it.

• *Chocolate ice cream sauce:* Thicker than the syrup, this can be used between layers of cake and ice cream in making frozen desserts. And it is turned into the batter of the Banana Split Fudge Cake (page 199) to create just that—a banana split taste and texture.

In addition to chocolate, cocoa is a popular addition to cake mix recipes and frostings. Look for two types:

• *Regular unsweetened cocoa:* Pressed chocolate with most of the cocoa butter removed is finely ground and then put through a sieve to make this basic cocoa powder. This is what your grandmother baked with: It is slightly acidic and therefore gives cakes a reddish-brown color. It was the ingredient behind the first devil's food cake (see Chocolate Cake Glossary, page 463).

• *Dutch-process unsweetened cocoa:* This cocoa is treated with an alkaline solution that darkens the color and mellows the flavor. Dutch-process cocoa is easier to dissolve in liquids. Use this type of cocoa, which can be found in many supermarkets, in cakes and frostings where you want a deep, dark color.

Breakfast cocoa, which is richer and contains more cocoa butter, is used in chocolate milk powders. It and other sweetened cocoas can be sifted on top of cakes for a pretty effect.

STORING CHOCOLATE

Chocolate is not the sort of friend you'd want to take on a beach vacation. While you were preparing for the outdoors, for some fresh air and sunshine, chocolate would be wrapping itself up in foil, finding the nearest cold, dark pantry, and sequestering itself in a corner so as not to mix and mingle with the other ingredients.

• *A cool, dark place:* Choose a cool (65°F) room temperature and a dark place with good air circulation. Chocolate shouldn't be stored in the refrigerator unless you happen to live in a hot and humid climate and have no other choice.

• *Wrap it well:* Wrap the chocolate first in foil, then in plastic wrap or a plastic bag. Chocolate needs to be on its own, away from foods with strong odors, as it will pick up those odors like a sponge.

• *Bloom:* I was dismayed to find that the chocolate I had been storing in a cupboard for less than a month had grayish-white blotches and streaks all over it. This was fat bloom, a sign that the chocolate had been stored in too warm a place. Then I figured out why. The fluorescent lights that lit my counters so well were mounted at the base of the overhead cabinets. If I left them on a great deal, which I was doing as a nightlight, the bottom cabinet shelf, where my chocolate was stored, became warm to the touch. I quickly remedied this by switching the chocolate to another cabinet. Rest assured, fat bloom will disappear when the chocolate is melted. It just doesn't look nice. There is another bloom, called sugar bloom, which occurs when chocolate is stored in too damp conditions. This leaves the chocolate feeling rough, and if it forms, the chocolate should be discarded.

• *Shelf life:* Under good conditions at home, semisweet chocolate and unsweetened chocolate will last up to a year, and milk and white chocolate will last 7 to 8 months.

MELTING CHOCOLATE

My mother still melts chocolate on the stovetop. She is untrusting of the microwave oven, and I'll admit I used to be. But there is no reason not to microwave chocolate. Both unsweetened and semisweet bar chocolates melt beautifully this way. The chips are a little trickier, and you have to stir them well. White chocolate chips are the trickiest. They contain the least amount of cocoa butter, and they don't ever seem to completely melt in appearance.

Here are a few tips, whether you use the microwave or stovetop:

- *Chop* chocolate into 1-inch or smaller pieces for more even melting.
- *Stir* during the melting process to keep the temperature even.
- *Chocolate* is finicky about liquid. Avoid contact with droplets of water or steam during the melting process, or the chocolate can seize up or harden. If you must add liquid, use at least 1 tablespoon liquid for every 2 ounces of chocolate for it to combine smoothly.
- *Melted* chocolate does not mind large amounts of liquid as long as when you combine the ingredients, the liquid is warm.

Microwaving

Melt chocolate in a microwave-safe container placed in the center of the oven. Use high (100 percent) power, but take care not to microwave too long. Check the container a few times, stir, and restart the microwave as needed. Even if the chocolate still keeps its shape, it may just need a stir to be melted.

- *Microwave* 4 ounces of chopped unsweetened or sweetened chocolate on high for 1 minute. If not melted, stir and microwave another 30 seconds.
- *Microwave* 6 ounces of chopped white chocolate on high for 1 minute. If not melted, stir and microwave another 15 seconds.
- *Microwave* 2 cups of semisweet chocolate chips on high for 1½ minutes. Stir and microwave another 15 seconds if not melted. For 1 cup of chips, microwave for 1 minute to 1 minute, 15 seconds.
- *Microwave* 2 cups of milk chocolate chips or other chips on high for 1 minute. For 1 cup of chips, microwave for 45 seconds. If additional time is needed, stir and heat again for 5 seconds.

Stovetop

Use very low heat and a heavy saucepan, and stir constantly with a wooden spoon so the chocolate does not stick and burn. (If it does, it must be thrown out, as there is no resurrecting it.) When the chocolate looks melted, remove the pan from the heat and stir until it is completely melted. White chocolate burns very easily on the stovetop; stay with it.

The Dump Method and Ingredient Temperature

I don't think you'll find the term "the dump method" outlined in any culinary reference book, and I wasn't trying to be irreverent when I used it in *The Cake Mix Doctor.* How best to describe the ease with which these cakes are prepared? Dump the ingredients into the bowl, rev up the mixer, and you're baking!

But, as is often the case when I oversimplify, questions do arise. If one dumps ingredients in the bowl, should the ingredients be at room temperature or straight out of the fridge? In most recipes, those ingredients can be right out of your refrigerator.

The exceptions are recipes that specifically call for butter to be softened or melted, and recipes that call for beaten egg whites. Room-temperature egg whites will whip to a greater volume than cold egg whites.

But take the most care when you are working with cream cheese. Not only should cream cheese be at room temperature (or softened in the microwave oven if your kitchen is cold), but the ingredients added to it should be around the same temperature, or they might cause the cream cheese to lump up. And you can beat the batter blue with an electric mixer—those lumps will never disappear.

I find, too, that when assembling buttercream frostings with softened butter, the frosting will pull together more easily if the liquid you are adding is at room temperature. Cold liquids, and even a cold mixing bowl, can cause that butter to firm up and make the frosting more difficult to spread.

Chocolate Cake Mix Pantry

Whether you're assembling a layer cake, pudding cake, chiffon cake, cheesecake, cookies, or biscotti, certain ingredients are essential to the process. Cake mix baking is easy, but just because the cake goes together simply doesn't mean the ingredients don't have to be just right. Keep these on hand and you'll be all set for spur-of-the-moment baking.

THE ESSENTIALS

• *Cake mixes:* Devil's food, chocolate fudge, butter recipe chocolate fudge, German chocolate, fudge marble, brownie mix, as well as angel food, white, yellow, butter recipe golden, and spice cake mixes went into this book. I found the devil's food and German chocolate the most versatile.

• *Chocolate:* Grate or melt German chocolate bars or semisweet chocolate bars into cake batter. Add chocolate chips (semisweet and milk, or miniature semisweet) to cakes, cookies, muffins, and bars. They also can be sprinkled on top just before baking. And other chips—peanut butter, toffee, white chocolate, cinnamon—can be folded into or sprinkled on top of batters. Chocolate chips can also be melted as the start for a quick frosting. Use either regular unsweetened cocoa powder or the Dutch-process cocoa, which is darker in color and milder in flavor, in frostings and to intensify a cake batter. White chocolate bars can be melted and folded into white cake mix for rich and memorable cakes with a pound cake texture. For more on chocolate, see the Chocolate Primer (page 13).

• *Milk:* Unless it is noted in the recipe that the cake or frosting requires whole milk, use whatever milk is in your refrigerator. Skim, 1 percent, and 2 percent are all fine. Some frostings and glazes need the extra fat of whole milk to make them taste rich, and some puddings and fillings need whole milk to firm them up. The higher-fat the milk, the better-tasting the outcome. When I was testing the first book, I had an infant in the house and we had a ready stash of whole milk. Now that little John has moved to 2 percent milk, I miss that whole milk for baking and try to buy a quart every now and then to have for frostings. Milk may be added cold to cake batter.

• *Eggs:* Always large. They don't have to be at room temperature. The whites, however, will whip to higher peaks if they are left at room temperature to warm up a bit.

Don't Forget Fresh Fruit

• **Bananas:** Select ripe ones, mash, and add to cakes and muffins.

• **Peaches:** The riper the better in frostings and batters.

• **Pears:** Slice, sauté, and layer in a chocolate terrine.

- *Butter:* Unless the recipe states "unsalted," use lightly salted butter. Lightly salted, I found, can offset the sweetness of many cake recipes. However, unsalted is needed when baking with brownie mixes, for they taste saltier than cake mix. Don't substitute margarine for butter unless it is called for in the recipe.

- *Vegetable oil:* Use light, unflavored vegetable oils such as canola, corn, safflower, soybean, and sunflower. Don't use olive oil.

- *Sugar:* The recipe will specify types of sugar if more than one kind is called for in that recipe. If the recipe simply lists sugar, it means granulated sugar. Besides granulated, you'll need confectioners' (powdered) sugar and light and dark brown sugars.

- *Extracts and spices:* Always use "pure" vanilla, almond, orange, and lemon extracts. For other flavorings that are not available in pure form, such as coconut flavoring, use what you can find. The most used spices are ground cinnamon, allspice, and ginger.

THE EXTENDED PANTRY

Refrigerator

- *Buttermilk:* If you can't find the liquid form, then use powdered buttermilk mixed with water as directed on the label.

- *Heavy (whipping) cream:* For sweetened cream frosting, fillings, and chocolate ganache.

- *Sour cream:* Makes cakes moister. You can substitute the lower-fat version, but don't use the fat-free.

- *Cream cheese:* Critical to cheesecakes, and it adds interest to brownies. You can get by with lower-fat, but not fat-free. Full-fat is best.

- *Yogurt:* Use plain yogurt as a substitute for sour cream. Experiment with vanilla, coffee, and chocolate flavors, too. Low-fat and nonfat yogurt work as well as full-fat.

- *Ricotta cheese:* Fold into pound cakes.

- *Citrus fruit:* Oranges, limes, and lemons provide juice and grated zest to flavor cakes, frostings, and glazes.

Freezer

- *Unsweetened grated coconut:* Available regionally, mostly in the South. Use to make the Chocolate Coconut Icebox Cake and in bars and cookies.

- *Pecans, walnuts, sliced almonds, and other nuts:* Keep a supply in the freezer (it extends their shelf life, too).

- *Whipped topping:* Certain recipes, like the Watergate Cake (page 186), call for this. Thaw before using.

Cool It!

*I*f you are in a real hurry to finish up a layer cake, here's how to cool it down pronto: Transfer the warm layers onto cardboard rounds and place them in the freezer for just under 5 minutes before frosting it. (When it's warm in the kitchen and the frosting is soft, professional pastry chefs run those layers in and out of the freezer to help set the frosting.)

When I was in St. Paul, Minnesota, baking in the kitchen of food writer Allison Campbell, we found something cooler than her freezer. It was bitterly cold outside and had been snowing. I had a plane to catch and needed to frost a warm cake in a hurry for a photo shoot. Allison and I remembered the one place guaranteed to cool down most anything—her back porch! Those yellow layers cooled down in no time, the chocolate frosting went on like a dream, the photographer snapped her photo, and I made my plane.

• *Frozen sweetened raspberries:* Thaw and purée; strain to remove seeds, if desired; then add to cake batter.

Cupboard

• *Instant pudding mixes:* Vanilla, chocolate, pistachio, and banana puddings marry well with chocolate.

• *Canned fruits:* Crushed pineapple and apricot halves add moisture to the batter.

• *Sweetened condensed milk:* Adds sweetness and consistency to cheesecakes.

• *Dried fruit:* Raisins, sweetened cranberries, sweetened cherries, and pitted prunes are delicious folded into batters or fillings.

• *Instant coffee powder:* Add to angel food cakes, syrups, frostings, and dark chocolate cake.

• *Red food coloring:* For Red Velvet Cake, of course.

• *Dried coconut:* Found at natural foods stores; sprinkle atop cookies and bars before baking.

• *Sweetened flaked coconut:* Sweeter than frozen coconut, but fine for frostings and fillings.

• *Marshmallow creme:* Use in fillings and frostings.

• *Chocolate sandwich cookies:* Crush and fold into whipped cream for sandwiching between layer cakes.

• *Chocolate mint candies:* Fold into pound cake batter or brownies.

• *Amaretto, rum, Kahlúa, sherry,*

brandy: These and other liquors, liqueurs, and fortified wines add flavor, moisture, and spirit to cakes and frostings.

• *Peppermint candy:* Crush and stir into buttercream frosting.

Cool Cake-Baking Tools

Here are the dozen kitchen gizmos, gadgets, and basics I could not bake a cake without. You might call these my dirty dozen! To find them, shop in housewares departments, at cookware shops, or in restaurant supply stores.

1. *Wooden spoon:* Not just one—I have a crock full of spoons of all widths and lengths. They feel good in your hand when you mix up brownie and cake batters, and they allow you to stir an icing over the heat.

2. *A seven-speed hand mixer:* I love this little machine. On low speed it is silent and gentle, combining dry ingredients without leaving me in the dust. On high it beats the heck out of heavy cream, and somewhere in between it knowingly blends a cake batter. And the beaters go right into the dishwasher.

3. *Stainless-steel nesting mixing bowls:* These lightweight but durable bowls fit nicely inside each other for convenient storage. The large bowl is perfect for mix-ing the cake batter, the medium is right for making frostings, and the baby bowl holds glazes or chopped nuts and other add-ins.

4. *Rubber spatulas:* Whether scraping the last bit of batter out of the bowl or smoothing the top of the batter before it goes into the oven, rubber spatulas are so useful. If you want to use them over the heat when making a frosting or stirring melted butter or chocolate, you will need to buy heat-tolerant spatulas. Especially handy are the spoon spatulas; their cupped edges make stirring brownies or getting the last bit of frosting out of the bowl a breeze.

5. *Palette knife:* Also known as an icing spreader, this 6- to 10-inch-long narrow metal spatula not only spreads frostings and icings effortlessly onto baked cakes, but it is also great for wedging under bars to lift them out of a 13- by 9-inch pan.

6. *Microplane:* This handy grater is found at cookware shops and gets the most zest from an orange, lemon, or lime without any of the bitter pith underneath. It also is a fine tool for grating chocolate to garnish the top of a cake.

7. *Tiny hand sifter/strainer:* For dusting just a tablespoon of confectioners' sugar atop a cake, for removing the seeds from fresh lemon juice, or for straining tiny seeds from raspberries, a small fine-mesh strainer comes in handy.

8. *Carbon steel chopping knife:* You want the sharpness of carbon steel to chop pecans and dried fruit quickly, to slice into the top of a cake mix pouch, or to chop chocolate into pieces for melting.

9. *Ruler or small tape measure:* When in doubt, measure the size of your pans. For perfect splitting, measure to find the midpoint of a cake layer.

10. *Quart-size glass measuring cup:*

Not only do these cups hold liquids (oil, milk, juices) for measuring, they are just the right size for melting butter and chocolate in the microwave.

11. *Vegetable oil mister:* You put your own oil in these misters, found in house-wares departments. They mist the hills and valleys of the Bundt pan easily and without the propellants found in aerosol sprays.

12. *Reusable parchment paper:* It is called Super Parchment, and it is a super and nominal investment if you bake a lot

A Quick Note on Pans

My favorite baking pans—whether layer, sheet cake, springform, or cookie—are heavy, shiny aluminum. Bundt pans come in a variety of materials, but I find the lighter-weight pans the easiest to unmold. Tube pans can be either shiny for angel foods or coated with a nonstick surface for most pound cakes. Most of the recipes in this book were tested with shiny aluminum pans.

Dark pans and glass pans will cause your cakes to bake more quickly and to darken on the bottom and the edges. However, when you are baking the pudding cakes that taste best warm and might need to be reheated, it just makes sense to bake them in glass so you can reheat them in the microwave. If you use glass or dark pans, don't spray them with an aerosol baking spray that contains propellants, for this will make that cake bake darker. And lower the oven temperature 25 degrees for these dark and glass pans.

Many people like to bake with insulated pans. They are fine for sheet cakes, but I find they don't brown cookies well, and for that reason I don't use them. If you must bake with insulated pans, be aware that the cakes and cookies might need 5 minutes more baking time.

of cookies or roulades. It can be wiped clean and used time and time again.

OTHER COOL TOOLS

Here is other equipment you should have on hand:

• *Pans:* You will need two or three 9-inch pans, a 13- by 9-inch pan, a 10-inch tube pan, a 12-cup Bundt pan, and some other pans—such as a 10-inch spring-form pan and 2½-inch cupcake pans—for preparing the recipes in this book. Choose heavy, shiny aluminum pans or aluminized steel pans for even heat distribution. The best bakeware has a folded construction to prevent warping.

• *Pastry brush:* To brush melted butter onto parchment paper, or liqueurs onto just-baked cake layers to moisten and flavor them.

• *Cooling racks:* The heavy wire racks are best because the flimsy lightweight racks will bend with constant use. Buy one long rack that will hold two cake layers and at least one smaller rack for inverting a layer at a time onto this larger rack.

• *Cake stands:* Beautiful pedestals on which to showcase your cakes. Choose from stainless steel, pottery, wood, or glass. See Standing Tall (page 288).

• *Cardboard cake rounds:* Useful rounds of many sizes that fit underneath cake layers. They make for easy transporting, should you need to travel with a cake. And many are decorative, should you want to serve the cake right from the cake round. They also make for easy storage if you want to freeze unbaked layers—just cover the layers with heavy-duty aluminum foil and pop in the freezer.

• *Shakers:* These small stainless-steel canisters fit neatly into your hand, and they have holes at the top for shaking out flour for dusting pans or confectioners' sugar for garnishing a roulade.

• *Sharp serrated knife:* So useful for splitting cake layers or for cutting angel food cake with a sawing motion.

• *Ice cream scoop:* Not only will the scoop make serving up ice cream a breeze, but the hinge attachment makes ladling muffin/cupcake batter into tins much easier.

• *Cake savers and carriers:* Plastic trays with snap-on plastic lids that will hold a cake for toting and traveling as well as storing and freezing right at home.

• *Waxed paper:* This is just the right wrap to lay across the top of a cream cheese frosting while it firms up in the refrigerator. Waxed paper keeps moisture in, but it won't stick to the frosting. Unfortunately, waxed paper doesn't stick to the sides of a plate, so you'll need to tape it to the plate for a secure fit. And waxed paper doesn't provide an effective moisture barrier, so it's useless for freezing cakes. But it's just right for lining a shirt box so that you can lay bars, brownies, and cupcakes inside for toting to a bake sale.

• *Aluminum foil:* The best protector in the freezer, especially when you use heavy-duty foil. Foil will neatly cover a 13- by 9-inch cake pan for keeping the cake fresh.

• *Plastic wrap:* This wrap is fine for cakes with no glaze or frosting. But it is best used at room temperature or in the refrigerator. In the freezer it offers the cake no protection from drying out.

• *White aprons:* I like plain white aprons for cake baking, the kind chefs use in a restaurant kitchen. I buy a pack of them at a restaurant supply store and keep them in a bottom kitchen drawer. Their bib will cover my nicest blouse, and they are long enough to nearly touch my knees, covering my slacks. And with white, you know when the apron needs to be laundered, which keeps the cake-baking process a hygienic one.

Chocolate Cake Mix Doctor Q&A

These questions and answers have appeared in issues of my newsletter, *A Piece of Cake.* My thanks to the readers who posed the questions.

Q. What is the best way to store cake mixes? And how long do they last? I'd like to take advantage of the sales and stock up.

A. *Believe it or not, cake mixes have a shelf life of up to 2 years if they're kept in a cool, dry place. Some climates are just naturally suited to keeping cake mixes fresh longer—where there is cooler, drier weather. But if you live in Houston, or Tampa, or even in Memphis, don't stock up on cake mixes for the long haul.*

"The important thing is not to stop questioning. Curiosity has its own reason for existing."
—ALBERT EINSTEIN

Q. I am watching the amount of sugar in recipes. Can I omit sugar, since cake mix already contains sugar?

A. *Yes, you can omit the sugar in most recipes. Cake mixes do contain sugar on their own, and whereas added sugar does help to make the cake more tender in texture, it is not mandatory.*

Q. Several of your cake recipes call for buttermilk. Can buttermilk powder be substituted?

A. *Absolutely. Following the directions on the package, add enough dry powder and liquid to equal the amount of buttermilk in the recipe.*

Q. May I substitute Egg Beaters for eggs in your recipes? How much should I use?

10 Things to Remember About Baking Chocolate Cakes

1. Don't buy expensive chocolate for doctoring up a cake mix. It loses its flavor when baked. The bar chocolate, cocoa, and chips from the supermarket work just fine.

2. Chocolate likes acidic flavors. It marries well with sour cream, yogurt, and buttermilk.

3. Don't worry about the temperature of the ingredients you add to the mix. Unlike scratch cakes, cake mix cakes turn out well when all the ingredients—room temperature or cold—are put in the bowl at one time. Unlike scratch cakes that call for cocoa, the water does not have to be boiling before it is added. The only exception is when you are working with cream cheese: It will lump up if cold ingredients are added, so when making a cheesecake, it's best to have all the ingredients at room temperature.

4. Stock up on vanilla extract. (At the wholesale clubs you can buy it in 16-ounce bottles for a huge savings.) It is a marvelous chocolate flavor enhancer.

5. The devil's food cake mix is both easy and difficult to doctor. The problem is that it is a good mix and doesn't need a lot of doctoring—perhaps just some coffee, cinnamon, or bananas. But it can be powerful in flavor, too. If you want to showcase more subtle flavors, such as zucchini, you're better off using a milder-flavored mix like the German chocolate.

A. *Yes, you can use Egg Beaters as an egg substitute. Use ¼ cup per egg in the recipe.*

Q. I can't find chocolate sweetened condensed milk in the local supermarket. Are there any substitutions?

A. *Yes. Melt 6 ounces (1 cup) semisweet chocolate chips with a 14½-ounce can of sweetened condensed milk over low heat. Allow to cool, and proceed with the recipe.*

Q. I am a little confused about the Duncan Hines cake mix label. It says "moist

6. Plain chocolate mixes and pudding mixes bake differently. The plain mix bakes up more beautifully. The chocolate pudding mix bakes flatter. The plain mix is softer in texture, the pudding mix denser and wetter.

7. Use shiny pans. If your pans are dark, the edges of your chocolate cakes will darken and harden as they bake.

8. Don't overbake. Cocoa has a drying effect on cake batters, causing them to bake more quickly. Be cautious. Get to know your oven, whether it underbakes or overbakes. Use a kitchen timer or write down the exact time the cake went in the oven. A dry chocolate cake will not taste as delicious as a moist chocolate cake.

9. You can't rely on visual doneness as easily with chocolate cakes. They don't turn golden brown, and by the time the layers pull away from the sides of the pan, they might be overdone. The fingertip press test is most reliable for layers, Bundts, tubes, and sheet cakes: Press lightly with your finger, and the cake should spring back. With brownies, you must rely on timing. If in doubt, pull them out a few minutes before you think they are done.

10. Use your nose. When chocolate cake is done, it smells done. You can train your nose to pick up on that strong aroma of chocolate and cooked eggs. It is an intoxicating smell, and you will remember it all your life. In fact, researchers have found that students exposed to the smell of chocolate while studying for exams can then recall the material better if they are exposed to the smell of chocolate while taking the exam. SATs in pastry kitchens, perhaps?

deluxe." Does this mean it contains pudding in the mix?

A. *Duncan Hines cake mixes do* not *contain pudding, even though the label says "moist."*

Q. What is the best way to get a crumb that closely resembles a homemade cake?

The doctoring improves the flavor, but a lot of times the crumb is too smooth and the cake is almost too moist.

A. *Substitute butter for vegetable oil. Increase the amount of fat in the recipe. The cake will be a bit flatter, but the crumb should be heavier. Also, omit the sugar in the recipes, as sugar acts as a tenderizer.*

Q. Cakes seem to stick to the bottom of my tube pan. This doesn't happen with my Bundt pan. Can I substitute the Bundt when the recipe calls for the tube pan?

A. *Yes, but watch the Bundt edges so they don't overbrown. I find that Bundts cook a little faster than tubes. As for keeping the cake from sticking to a tube pan, try greasing with vegetable shortening, dusting with flour, and when it's baked, letting the cake rest in the pan for about 20 minutes before unmolding. Run a long, sharp knife around the exterior and interior edges of the cake, shake the pan firmly with both hands to loosen the cake from the pan, then invert it onto a rack to cool.*

Q. I often burn the bottom of a cake, or at least it is drier than the rest of the cake. Any suggestions?

A. *First, check the oven rack position. Make sure it is as close to the center as possible and not at the bottom of the oven. Check your oven temperature with an oven thermometer from the hardware store. Let the oven fully preheat before adding the cake. And don't bake light-battered cakes in dark pans. Also, don't spray dark pans with vegetable oil sprays that contain propellants (alcohol). These will cause the edges of the cake to bake more quickly than the center.*

Q. I made a cake in a 13- by 9-inch glass pan. The cake tasted really great, but I just didn't like the way it looked. The bottom looked too well done. Would a metal pan give me better results?

A. *Glass bakes hotter than metal and causes cakes to burn on the bottom and darken in the corners. I like shiny metal pans. The cake will bake more evenly in metal, and it will rise better, too.*

Q. I am ready to bake a cake in a tube pan. When the cake is inverted over the neck of a bottle, what happens to the cake during the hour-long cooling process? Won't it fall out of the pan?

A. *First of all, not all cakes baked in a tube pan need to be inverted over the neck of a glass bottle to cool. Regular pound cakes can be baked in a greased and floured tube pan, left to cool in the pan for 20 minutes, and then turned out and cooled completely on a rack. But angel food and chiffon batters need to be poured into an ungreased shiny tube or angel food cake pan before baking. The angel and chiffon cakes cling to the sides of the ungreased pan as they bake. Their volume relies on egg whites, which expand in the hot oven and cause the cake to rise tall. You want to invert these cakes in midair over a bottle neck because letting them cool on a rack would deflate much of that hard-earned volume. And no, they won't fall out of the pan. Because you* *didn't grease the pan, the cake sticks to the sides until it's cool and you run a sharp knife around the edges to release it. The only exception is when you bake an angel or chiffon cake in a pan with a slippery non-stick surface. I have done this and my cakes still held fast, but some readers have told me they have inverted cakes in non-stick pans and the cakes have slid out. To be on the safe side, let the cake cool in the*

pan for 20 minutes, then turn it out and let it cool completely on a rack.

Q. How can I store cakes that are frosted with buttercream frosting? Do they need to be refrigerated, or are they safe to leave at room temperature?

A. *Buttercream frosting made with butter, confectioners' sugar, flavorings, and liquid can be stored in a cool place outside of the*

Chocolate Statistics

- Americans eat more than 12 pounds of chocolate per person per year.

- More than half of Americans prefer chocolate-flavored desserts. The next favorite flavor is a tie between strawberry and other berries and vanilla.

- More women than men choose chocolate desserts.

- Twice as many people prefer milk chocolate to dark.

- The older we get, the more we like dark chocolate.

- The first Valentine's box of chocolates was developed in England in 1868 by Richard Cadbury.

- More than 35 million heart-shaped boxes of chocolates are sold for Valentine's Day. But ironically, Valentine's is only the fourth top candy holiday, preceded by Halloween, the winter holidays, then Easter, according to the Chocolate Manufacturers Association.

- Older but wiser? Men over age fifty are more likely to request chocolate than flowers for Valentine's Day.

- Chocolate manufacturers use 40 percent of the world's almond supply, 20 percent of the world's peanut crop, and 8 percent of the world's sugar.

How Chocolate Is Made

Chocolate comes from the fruit of the cacao tree, which grows in rain forests primarily in West Africa—in Ghana, the Ivory Coast, and Nigeria. Since the tree will thrive only in hot and rainy climates, it is cultivated within 20 degrees north or south of the Equator. Here is the journey the cream-colored cocoa beans take after they are removed from the large pods of the cacao tree and before they wind up in your chocolate layer cake:

1. *Fermentation.* The creamy beans are put into boxes or thrown on heaps and covered. They ferment for up to a week. The raw, bitter flavor disappears and the new flavor develops as the beans turn a rich brown color.

2. *Drying.* So they won't spoil during shipping, the beans are dried in the sun or in a heated indoor area. Then they are bagged for shipping.

3. *Cleaning.* A machine removes dried pulp and other materials before the beans are roasted.

4. *Roasting.* This develops the beans' flavor, aroma, and color. The cocoa beans are roasted in large rotary cylinders, the amount of time depending on the variety of bean and the recipe of the manufacturer.

5. *Cooling.* The beans are cooled down and the thin shells removed.

6. *Nibs crushed into chocolate liquor.* The very essence of the bean is crushed to form a chocolate liquid, which can then be poured into molds and solidified to make unsweetened or bitter chocolate.

7. *Separating cocoa particles and cocoa butter.* If the chocolate liquor is placed in a giant press, the cocoa butter drains away, leaving a pressed cake that is cooled, pulverized, and sifted to form cocoa powder.

8. *Making semisweet, milk, and other eating chocolate.* Sugar, cream or milk, spices or other flavorings, an emulsifier, and more cocoa butter are combined with the chocolate liquor and kneaded (called conching) to make sweet and creamy chocolate.

9. *Tempering and molding.* The chocolate is heated, cooled, and reheated—or tempered—and then poured into molds, from small candy bars to large 10-pound blocks.

10. The chocolate is cooled, wrapped, and shipped.

refrigerator for 2 or 3 days. After that, you will want to wrap and refrigerate the cake. Cakes frosted with a French buttercream frosting containing eggs, however, must be refrigerated at once. Use your head when making food safety decisions. If it's summertime and the kitchen is hot, go ahead and refrigerate leftover cake with any buttercream frosting.

Q. When I make chocolate frostings using cocoa, they turn out darker than yours. Is this because I use a Dutch-process cocoa? **A.** Precisely. Dutch-process cocoas produce beautiful but darker frostings compared with those made with regular cocoa. Suit yourself. And did you know that the longer you beat a chocolate frosting, the lighter in color it gets?

Q. When you make a glaze with confectioners' sugar and a liquid, such as orange juice, is there a way of getting rid of the confectioners' sugar taste and intensifying the orange flavor? **A.** Be sure to add some of the grated orange zest to the glaze. The oil in the zest has an intense flavor and will mask that sugary taste. No fresh oranges? Try orange oil. It's available in specialty shops and through food catalogs, but it is quite expensive. Or you can heat the glaze in a double boiler over simmering water for 10 to 15 minutes and then cool it slightly before using.

Luscious Layers

• • •

When we think of birthday cake, we see layers stacked one on top of the other, with a wonderfully creamy frosting sandwiched between and spread around the sides and over the top. It seems inconceivable that cake has ever been anything but soft and spongy layers.

But layer cakes weren't always the norm. The 1860s wedding cake recipe Henrietta Dull includes in her book *Southern Cooking* contains a pound of flour, a pound of sugar, whites of sixteen eggs, and twelve ounces of butter, and is baked in a loaf in a slow oven. Her Twentieth Century Pound Cake, on the other hand, is lighter and is baked in layers in a hotter oven. With the new, easier-to-control ovens, cakes in the last century were transformed from hefty loaves into heavenly layers.

Resembling the famed sponge cakes of Europe, these lighter, airier cakes were baked in white, yellow, chocolate, and shades in between. They were filled with custards and creams, and they were spread with fluffy buttercream frostings or cooked icings. Some of the most famous American cakes— the devil's food cake, the carrot cake, the coconut cake, the German chocolate cake— have sprung from layer pans. Today they celebrate holidays, weddings, anniversaries, and christenings as well as birthdays.

Much of the allure of the layer cake is the surprise that lies within. When you cut into a layer cake, you have an inkling of what may be inside, but you're never quite sure. Thus, the appeal of marbled cakes, checkerboard cakes, contrasting cakes, and those eye-popping Red Velvets.

....

"As for chocolate and strawberries, we could all survive without them and they don't form the backbone of any cuisine, but now that we have them, they brighten our lives, add whole dimensions of delight to the ends of meals all over the planet. . . ."

—RAYMOND SOKOLOV

....

The possibility of surprise is also what makes it fun for the cook, who can experiment and be creative: Try lemon curd, jam, or a whipped-cream filling, for example, and sandwich it between four instead of two layers.

There isn't a layer cake here that wouldn't be appreciated at a special celebration. Some of the cakes are more suited to a particular season, such as the peach cake in the summertime and the German Chocolate Spice Cake in the depths of winter. You'll have a hard time deciding which devil's food cake to try first. Don't pass by the old standbys, such as Yellow Pound Cake with Chocolate Pan Frosting, which I'd be happy to fork into any day. And don't forget that some layer cakes can be made ahead and frozen or refrigerated (Martha's Chocolate Cherry Ice Cream Cake, the Cookies and Cream Cake, the Chocolate Coconut Icebox Cake, Natalie's fabulous Chocolate Café au Lait Cake) for easier entertaining.

Layer cakes are a diverse and delicious lot. They are fun and festive, but not fussy. Oh sure, they take a bit longer to prepare than pouring a hot glaze over a Bundt. But aren't they worth it?

THE PERFECT CHOCOLATE CAKE

This is our family's Christmas cake, and it is truly perfect for the special birthdays and holidays in your home, too. It seems that by the time our Christmas dinner rolls around, everyone is so exhausted from the festivities that unless a cake is already made or in progress, it might not be served! Well, this cake is a snap to prepare the day before Christmas, and you can make the filling a day ahead as well, so all that's left on Christmas afternoon is to make  the satiny chocolate frosting and assemble the cake. We serve it alongside ambrosia, that wonderful orange compote that Southerners love. It's delicious with vanilla or peppermint ice cream, too. Make sure you place this cake on a special platter or cake stand, perhaps one that belonged to your grandmother.

....

SERVES: 16

PREPARATION TIME: 10 MINUTES

BAKING TIME: 20 TO 25 MINUTES

ASSEMBLY TIME: 15 MINUTES

....

CAKE:

Solid vegetable shortening for greasing the pans
Flour for dusting the pans
1 package (18.25 ounces) devil's food cake mix with pudding
1 cup sour cream
¾ cup water
½ cup vegetable oil
4 large eggs
1 teaspoon pure vanilla extract

How to Cut the First Slice of Cake Like a Pro

*A*ll eyes are on you. Can you lift that first piece of birthday cake from the platter to the plate without it collapsing in midair? Well, you can if you slice it with the right knife.

Choose a long, thin, sharp blade for slicing layer cakes with soft buttercream or cream cheese frostings. Cut into the cake, and as it reaches the platter, wiggle the knife and slide it out at the bottom. Don't run the knife back up through the slice or it will drag frosting onto the sides of the cake and the second slice won't look as pretty.

For layer cakes with hard frostings, use a long, sharp knife. Or use one of the specially designed wedge-shaped cake cutters. Both sides of the slicer cut into the cake at one time, then you pinch the handle together like a tweezer and pull out the slice. Release the handle and the slice drops onto the serving plate. This gizmo is not suited for ganache-topped cakes because it just presses the cake down and can't cut through the sticky ganache.

For angel food and chiffon cakes, use a long, sharp serrated knife. Cheesecakes need a long, sharp knife or unflavored dental floss.

Remember that cake slices easiest when it has cooled. If frosting builds up on the knife as you cut your way around the cake, dip the knife into a tall glass of hot water, wipe it dry, and resume slicing.

FILLING:

Sweetened Cream (page 445)

FROSTING:

Perfect Chocolate Frosting (page 436)

1. Place a rack in the center of the oven and preheat the oven to 350°F. Lightly grease three 9-inch round cake pans with solid vegetable shortening, then dust with flour. Shake out the excess flour. Set the pans aside.

2. Place the cake mix, sour cream, water, oil, eggs, and vanilla in a large mixing bowl. Blend with an electric mixer on low speed for 1 minute. Stop the machine and scrape down the sides of the bowl with a rubber spatula. Increase the mixer speed to medium and beat 2 minutes more, scraping down the sides again if needed. The batter should look well combined. Divide the batter among the prepared pans, smoothing it out with the rubber spatula, and place them in

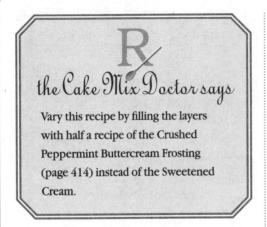

the Cake Mix Doctor says

Vary this recipe by filling the layers
with half a recipe of the Crushed
Peppermint Buttercream Frosting
(page 414) instead of the Sweetened
Cream.

the oven. If your oven is not large enough
to hold them on one rack, place two pans
on the center rack and the third in the
center of the highest rack.

3. Bake the cakes until they spring back
when lightly pressed with your finger, 20
to 25 minutes. Be careful not to overcook
the layer on the highest oven rack.
Remove the pans from the oven and
place them on wire racks to cool for 10
minutes. Run a sharp knife around the
edge of each layer and invert each onto a
rack, then invert again onto another rack
so that the cakes are right side up. Allow
to cool completely, 30 minutes.

4. Meanwhile, prepare the Sweetened
Cream.

5. To assemble, place one cake layer,
right side up, on a serving platter.
Spread the top with half of the whipped
cream, spreading it to within ½ inch of
the sides. Place the second layer, right
side up, on top of the first layer and
spread with the remaining whipped
cream, spreading it to within ½ inch of
the sides. Place the third layer on top,
and cover the cake lightly with waxed
paper. Place it in the refrigerator to chill.

6. Prepare the Perfect Chocolate Frosting.

7. To finish the assembly, spread the
top and the sides of the cake with the
frosting, using clean, smooth strokes.
Slice and serve.

✱ *Store this cake, in a cake saver or
under a glass dome, in the refrigerator for
up to 1 week.*

EVER-SO-MOIST CHOCOLATE CAKE

WITH CHOCOLATE SOUR CREAM FROSTING

My daughters had a wonderful teacher named Sandy Stringfellow, who mentioned to me one day that she loves her chocolate cakes really moist. I told her to try the Chocolate-Covered Cherry Cake—the wettest, moistest cake I could think of in *The Cake Mix Doctor.* When it came time to develop recipes for this book, I still had Sandy in the back of my mind, so I combined a devil's food mix that contains pudding with sour cream and a few other ingredients to make this incredibly moist cake. And I carried over that sour cream theme into a dandy of a frosting—something I am sure Sandy will agree deserves an A+.

SERVES: 16
PREPARATION TIME: 10 MINUTES
BAKING TIME: 28 TO 32 MINUTES
ASSEMBLY TIME: 10 MINUTES

*Solid vegetable shortening for greasing
    the pans*
Flour for dusting the pans
*1 package (18.25 ounces) devil's food cake
    mix with pudding*
1 cup sour cream
¾ cup water
½ cup vegetable oil
3 large eggs
1 teaspoon pure vanilla extract
*Chocolate Sour Cream Frosting
    (page 410)*

1. Place a rack in the center of the oven and preheat the oven to 350°F. Generously grease two 9-inch round cake pans with solid vegetable shortening, then dust with flour. Shake out the excess flour. Set the pans aside.

2. Place the cake mix, sour cream, water, oil, eggs, and vanilla in a large mixing bowl. Blend with an electric mixer on low speed for 1 minute. Stop the machine and scrape down the sides of the bowl with a rubber spatula. Increase the mixer speed to medium and beat 2 minutes more, scraping down the sides again if needed. The batter should look well combined. Divide the batter between the prepared pans, smoothing it out with the rubber spatula. Place the pans in the oven side by side.

3. Bake the cakes until they spring back when lightly pressed with your finger, 28 to 32 minutes. Remove the pans from the oven and place them on wire racks to cool for 10 minutes. Run a dinner knife around the edge of each layer and invert each onto a rack, then invert again onto another rack so that the cakes are right side up. Allow to cool completely, 30 minutes more.

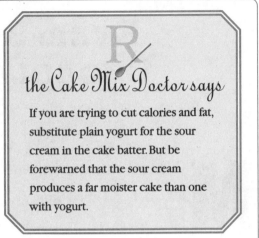

the Cake Mix Doctor says

If you are trying to cut calories and fat, substitute plain yogurt for the sour cream in the cake batter. But be forewarned that the sour cream produces a far moister cake than one with yogurt.

4. Meanwhile, prepare the Chocolate Sour Cream Frosting.

5. Place one cake layer, right side up, on a serving platter. Spread the top with frosting. Place the second layer, right side up, on top of the first layer and frost the top and sides of the cake with clean, smooth strokes.

✳ *Store this cake in a cake saver or under a glass dome, in the refrigerator for up to 1 week. Or freeze it, in a cake saver, for up to 6 months. Thaw the cake overnight in the refrigerator before serving.*

MY FAVORITE BIRTHDAY CAKE

YELLOW POUND CAKE WITH CHOCOLATE PAN FROSTING

Many readers asked what cake I was holding in the cover photo of *The Cake Mix Doctor*. It was the Yellow Pound Cake baked into layers and then frosted with Fluffy Chocolate Frosting. I don't know why I didn't put the instructions for how to turn that pound cake into layers in the first book, but I'm making up for it by including them now. This is not only a pretty cake to slice into (or photograph!), it is moist and all ages love it. My frosting of choice for birthdays, however, would be a Chocolate Pan Frosting, an easy cooked frosting my mother always spread on our childhood birthday cakes. A little nostalgia in every bite.

R the Cake Mix Doctor says

The beauty of this cake is that it is a keeper, should there be any leftovers. It will stay moist for a week stored at room temperature (the hard frosting seals in the moisture).

If you want to add some chopped nuts, such as chopped toasted pecans or slivered toasted almonds, on top of the cake, do so while the frosting is still warm.

SERVES: 16

PREPARATION TIME: 8 MINUTES

BAKING TIME: 30 TO 35 MINUTES

ASSEMBLY TIME: 10 MINUTES

Easy Ways to Decorate a Birthday Cake

You have never taken a cake-decorating class in your life, but you want to dress up the birthday cake with more than supermarket candles? Here are some ideas:

- **Choose a fluffy frosting.** Fluffy looks more festive than the sleek ganache or silky glaze. Apply it first with a metal icing spatula, then create a decorative effect on top by spreading more frosting on in circles with the spatula, as though you were waxing a car. Or, for a different effect, spread on more frosting and with the back of a teaspoon make small indentations or grooves in the frosting.

- **Fresh flowers.** Surround the base of the cake with a necklace of blossoms, or poke a small hole in the top of the cake and stick a cluster of sweetheart roses, or one large beautiful peach rose snipped off its stem, in the hole. Be sure to choose nonpoisonous flowers like hibiscus, honeysuckle, daylilies, pansies, lilacs, nasturtiums, roses, tulips, and violets.

- **Chopped candies.** Scatter the birthday boy's or girl's favorite candies on top of the cake, be they M&Ms, crushed peppermints, or crushed toffee bars.

- **Make a letter cake.** Bake the cake in a 13- by 9-inch pan. When the cake is cool, invert it onto a cutting board and cut the cake to form the honoree's first

---

Solid vegetable shortening for greasing
    the pans
Flour for dusting the pans
1 package (18.25 ounces) plain yellow
    cake mix
1 package (3.4 ounces) vanilla instant
    pudding mix
1¼ cups whole milk
½ cup vegetable oil

3 large eggs
1 teaspoon pure vanilla extract
Chocolate Pan Frosting (page 434)

1. Place a rack in the center of the oven and preheat the oven to 350°F. Generously grease two 9-inch round cake pans with solid vegetable shortening, then dust with

initial. Then frost the cake and cover it with grated chocolate or candy sprinkles.

- **Spell it out.** Pipe on a happy birthday greeting using the supermarket squeeze tubes of icing or a thick cream cheese frosting that has been well chilled. Don't own a pastry bag? Place icing in a clean zipper-lock food bag. Seal, snip off a tiny corner, and squeeze out the frosting. Practice writing first on a piece of waxed paper.

- **Ribbon.** Waterproof ribbon is best. Run it along the bottom of the cake, pressing it into the frosting. Remove the ribbon before slicing the cake.

- **Candle holders.** Pretty holders raise the candles off the cake and add a decorative effect. They can be found at gift stores and where silver and crystal are sold. They make a nice birthday gift to a child.

Other Fun, Fast Decorations

- Mint leaves
- Fruit leathers cut into shapes
- Coconut, plain or toasted
- Sliced toasted almonds pressed onto the sides of the cake
- Rose petals on the platter
- Fruit slices and spirals when fruit is used in the recipe
- Grated chocolate
- Chocolate curls

flour. Shake out the excess flour. Set the pans aside.

2. Place the cake mix, pudding mix, milk, oil, eggs, and vanilla in a large mixing bowl. Blend with an electric mixer on low speed for 1 minute. Stop the machine and scrape down the sides of the bowl with a rubber spatula. Increase the mixer speed to medium and beat 2 minutes more, scraping down the sides again if needed. The batter should look well combined. Divide the batter between the prepared pans, smoothing it out with the rubber spatula. Place the pans in the oven side by side.

3. Bake the cakes until they turn golden brown and spring back when lightly pressed with your finger, 30 to 35 minutes. Remove the pans from the oven and place them on wire racks to cool for 10 minutes. Run a dinner knife around the edge of each layer and invert each onto a rack, then invert again onto another rack so that the cakes are right side up. Allow to cool completely, 30 minutes more.

4. Meanwhile, prepare the Chocolate Pan Frosting.

5. Place one cake layer, right side up, on a serving platter. Spread the top with frosting. Place the second layer, right side up, on top of the first layer and frost the top and sides of the cake with clean, smooth strokes.

✳ *Store this cake, in a cake saver or under a glass dome, at room temperature for up to 1 week. Or freeze it, wrapped in aluminum foil or in a cake saver, for up to 6 months. Thaw the cake overnight in the refrigerator before serving.*

EASY AND ELEGANT DEVIL'S FOOD CAKE

WITH WHIPPED CHOCOLATE GANACHE

There's nothing fancy in this cake, and yet the results are memorable. It's moist but understated, just the right partner for an elegant frosting made by whipping up a chocolate ganache. And, it's a real eye-catcher. The dark flecks of chocolate suspended in the frosting match the deep chocolate cake. It's birthday and dinner party material, without a doubt.

SERVES: 16
PREPARATION TIME: 8 MINUTES
BAKING TIME: 28 TO 32 MINUTES
ASSEMBLY TIME: 10 MINUTES

Whipped Chocolate Ganache (page 442)
Solid vegetable shortening for greasing
    the pans
Flour for dusting the pans
1 package (18.25 ounces) plain devil's food
    cake mix
¾ cup milk (see "The Cake Mix Doctor says")
¾ cup vegetable oil
3 large eggs
2 teaspoons pure vanilla extract

1. Prepare the Whipped Chocolate Ganache as described in Step 1 of the recipe, and chill it uncovered in the refrigerator while you prepare the cake.

2. Place a rack in the center of the oven and preheat the oven to 350°F. Generously grease two 9-inch round cake pans with solid vegetable shortening, then dust with flour. Shake out the excess flour. Set the pans aside.

3. Place the cake mix, milk, oil, eggs, and vanilla in a large mixing bowl. Blend with an electric mixer on low speed for 1

It's My Party

It should come as no surprise to learn that the wealthy were the first to celebrate their birthdays in ancient times. On their birthdays, the pharaohs fed their servants lavish meals. Cleopatra is said to have given Antony such an extravagant birthday party that many guests arrived penniless but left wealthy. Persian nobility marked their birthdays by cooking an ox and serving small cakes. And in Rome, the emperor would host a party on his birthday, complete with food, parade, gladiators, and circus. The usual stuff!

The birthday party as Americans know it is said to have come from German traditions, where the birthday child was presented with gifts, selected his or her favorite foods to eat for the day, and was given a butter or jam cake ringed with candles. It is thought that the lighted candles symbolized the birthday of the Greek moon goddess Artemis, who was honored with moon-shaped honey cakes surrounded by lighted tapers. Some say that because people were once fearful that evil spirits might prey on the birthday child, friends and family members would congregate with the honoree and bring only good thoughts and wishes to protect the child. Presents and happy foods reinforced the cheerful mood and shielded the child from harm. Many people still believe that the candles on a birthday cake carry good wishes up to God.

Different cultures have their own ways of celebrating a birthday—flying a flag outside the birthday house in Denmark, blindfolding and cracking open a piñata in Mexico, passing out chocolates to friends in India. Some cultures place special importance on certain birthdays: the thirteenth birthday of a Jewish child, the fifteenth birthday of a Mexican girl, and the sixtieth birthday of a Chinese man or woman are celebrated with ritual and fanfare.

And what naturally goes along with candles, cake, and ice cream? The "Happy Birthday to You" song, composed by two sisters, Mildred and Patty Hill, in 1893. It has changed slightly from their original words: "Good Morning to You." If this is your special day, then by all means "Happy Birthday to You"!

minute. Stop the machine and scrape down the sides of the bowl with a rubber spatula. Increase the mixer speed to medium and beat 2 minutes more, scraping down the sides again if needed. The batter should look well combined. Divide the batter evenly between the prepared pans, smoothing it out with the rubber spatula. Place the pans in the oven side by side.

4. Wash the electric mixer beaters and place them in the refrigerator to chill.

5. Bake the cakes until they spring back when lightly pressed with your finger, 28 to 32 minutes. Remove the pans from the oven and place them on wire racks to cool for 10 minutes. Run a dinner knife around the edge of each layer and invert each onto a rack, then invert again onto another rack so that the cakes are right side up. Allow to cool completely, 30 minutes more.

6. Meanwhile, remove the chilled beaters and the bowl of chilled Whipped Chocolate Ganache from the refrigerator. Whip the ganache on high speed for 2 to 3 minutes, or until it lightens in color and triples in volume.

7. Place one cake layer, right side up, on a serving platter. Spread the top with frosting. Place the second layer, right side up, on top of the first layer and frost the top and sides of the cake with clean, smooth strokes.

✳ *Store this cake, in a cake saver or under a glass dome, in the refrigerator for up to 1 week.*

R

the Cake Mix Doctor says

This cake contains a little more vegetable oil than other chocolate cakes. It is also better when made with whole milk, although you can use low-fat milk. The added oil and whole milk make the cake moister, but the added fat causes the cake to bake flatter. Many cooks consider this a blessing because they prefer a level cake to stack and frost. If you want a domed look, try the Old-Fashioned Devil's Food Cake (page 48)—or just pile extra frosting on top of this cake to give it added height.

CHOCOLATE SOUR CREAM MARBLE CAKE

WITH CHOCOLATE SOUR CREAM FROSTING

As a teenager I loved to experiment with cake recipes by marbling them. I'd spoon out a cupful of batter and stir in melted chocolate to color it brown and give it a chocolate flavor. Then I'd swirl that chocolate batter through the vanilla batter and create a truly beautiful birthday cake.

Nowadays I can buy a "marble" cake mix, but I don't stop there! And I encourage you not to as well. This recipe takes that box mix a step further, adding sour cream to enrich it. If you're feeling fancy, add a teaspoon of grated orange zest to the yellow batter, or add a tablespoon of espresso powder to the chocolate.

And whatever you do, don't forget the sour cream frosting.

SERVES: 16
PREPARATION TIME: 10 MINUTES
BAKING TIME: 26 TO 30 MINUTES
ASSEMBLY TIME: 10 MINUTES

Solid vegetable shortening for greasing
*   the pans*
Flour for dusting the pans
1 package (18.25 ounces) plain fudge marble
*   cake mix*
1 cup water
1 cup sour cream
3 large eggs
1 teaspoon pure vanilla extract
Chocolate Sour Cream Frosting (page 410)

1. Place a rack in the center of the oven and preheat the oven to 350°F. Generously grease two 9-inch round cake pans with solid vegetable shortening, then dust with flour. Shake out the excess flour. Set the pans aside.

2. Place the cake mix, water, sour cream, eggs, and vanilla in a large mixing bowl. Blend with an electric mixer on low speed for 1 minute. Stop the machine and scrape down the sides of the bowl with a rubber spatula. Increase the mixer speed to medium and beat 2 minutes more, scraping down the sides again if needed. The batter should look well combined.

3. Spoon a cup of batter into a small mixing bowl. Stir in the packet of cocoa that came with the cake mix until well combined. Divide the plain batter evenly between the prepared pans, smoothing it out with the rubber spatula. Drop the chocolate batter by tablespoonfuls over the plain batter in both pans, and using the blunt end of a wooden skewer or a dinner knife, swirl the chocolate batter through the plain batter to marble it. Take care not to scrape the bottom of the pans. Place the pans in the oven side by side.

4. Bake the cakes until they spring back when lightly pressed with your finger, 26 to 30 minutes. Remove the pans from the oven and place them on wire racks to cool for 10 minutes. Run a dinner knife around the edge of each layer and invert each onto a rack, then invert again onto another rack so that the cakes are right side up. Allow to cool completely, 30 minutes more.

5. Meanwhile, prepare the Chocolate Sour Cream Frosting.

6. Place one cake layer, right side up, on a serving platter. Spread the top with frosting. Place the second layer, right side up, on top of the first layer and frost the top and sides of the cake with clean, smooth strokes.

✻ *Store this cake, in a cake saver or under a glass dome, in the refrigerator for up to 1 week. Or freeze it, in a cake saver, for up to 6 months. Thaw the cake overnight in the refrigerator before serving.*

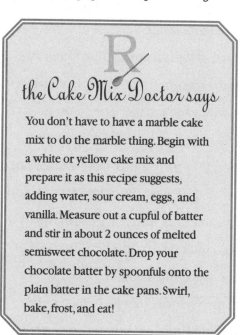

the Cake Mix Doctor says

You don't have to have a marble cake mix to do the marble thing. Begin with a white or yellow cake mix and prepare it as this recipe suggests, adding water, sour cream, eggs, and vanilla. Measure out a cupful of batter and stir in about 2 ounces of melted semisweet chocolate. Drop your chocolate batter by spoonfuls onto the plain batter in the cake pans. Swirl, bake, frost, and eat!

OLD-FASHIONED DEVIL'S FOOD CAKE

WITH FLUFFY CHOCOLATE FROSTING

I wish there were only one type of cake mix on the market; things would be much simpler. But there are both plain mixes and pudding-in-the-mix mixes, and they bake up differently. In the following recipe you may use either type of devil's food cake mix, and when it's frosted with a dandy of a chocolate buttercream frosting, you will have a winner of a cake. The plain mix will bake up domed, whereas the pudding-in-the-mix cake will be flatter and heavier. I learned this lesson in front of seventy-five students in a St. Louis pastry kitchen. Instead of the plain mix I'd asked for, the pudding type was placed before me. I had no time to dash to the store, so I went ahead with my recipe, using the wrong mix. The students raved about the cake! It is, in fact, the beautiful cake featured on the cover of this book.

....

SERVES: 16

PREPARATION TIME: 8 MINUTES

BAKING TIME: 28 TO 30 MINUTES

ASSEMBLY TIME: 10 MINUTES

....

Solid vegetable shortening for greasing
*   the pans*
Flour for dusting the pans
1 package (18.25 ounces) plain devil's food
*   cake mix or devil's food cake mix*
*   with pudding*
2 tablespoons unsweetened cocoa powder
1⅓ cups buttermilk
½ cup vegetable oil

3 large eggs

1 teaspoon pure vanilla extract

Fluffy Chocolate Frosting (page 408)

1. Place a rack in the center of the oven and preheat the oven to 350°F. Generously grease two 9-inch round cake pans with solid vegetable shortening, then dust with flour. Shake out the excess flour. Set the pans aside.

2. Place the cake mix, cocoa, buttermilk, oil, eggs, and vanilla in a large mixing bowl. Blend with an electric mixer on low speed for 1 minute. Stop the machine and scrape down the sides of the bowl with a rubber spatula. Increase the mixer speed to medium and beat 2 minutes more, scraping down the sides again if needed. The batter should look well combined. Divide the batter evenly between the prepared pans, smoothing it out with the rubber spatula. Place the pans in the oven side by side.

3. Bake the cakes until they spring back when lightly pressed with your finger, 28 to 30 minutes. Remove the pans from the oven and place them on wire racks to cool for 10 minutes. Run a dinner knife around the edge of each layer and invert each onto a rack, then invert again onto another rack so that the cakes are right side up. Allow to cool completely, 30 minutes more.

R

the Cake Mix Doctor says

Adding extra cocoa to a devil's food cake recipe can crank up the flavor immensely, but I must play the devil's advocate, so to speak, here. Cocoa has a drying effect on cake batter. Adding 1 to 2 tablespoons of cocoa to this batter improves the flavor. A full 3 tablespoons of cocoa provides a real punch, but also a drier cake.

4. Meanwhile, prepare the Fluffy Chocolate Frosting.

5. Place one cake layer, right side up, on a serving platter. Spread the top with frosting. Place the second layer, right side up, on top of the first layer and frost the top and sides of the cake with clean, smooth strokes.

✳ *Store this cake, in a cake saver or under a glass dome, at room temperature for up to 3 days, or in the refrigerator for up to 1 week. Or freeze it, wrapped in aluminum foil or in a cake saver, for up to 6 months. Thaw the cake overnight in the refrigerator before serving.*

EBONY AND IVORY CAKE

This cake is like that perfect little black dress: simple but stunning. The ganache drapes over the cake much the way a pearl necklace slides over silk. Depending on the season, garnish the cake with a necklace of edible flower buds around the base, a string of red raspberries, sprigs of fresh mint from the garden, rosy peach slices, or crisp Bosc pear wedges.

SERVES: 16

PREPARATION TIME: 10 MINUTES

BAKING TIME: 28 TO 32 MINUTES

ASSEMBLY TIME: 10 MINUTES

Solid vegetable shortening for greasing
*   the pans*
Flour for dusting the pans
6 ounces white chocolate, coarsely chopped
1 package (18.25 ounces) plain white
*   cake mix*
⅔ cup water
⅓ cup vegetable oil
3 large eggs
2 large egg whites
Chocolate Ganache (page 441)

the Cake Mix Doctor says

A fast and memorable way to decorate this cake is to toast sliced almonds for 1 to 2 minutes in a 350°F oven, just until they develop some color. Let them cool, and then carefully scatter them over the top and along the sides of the cake. It gives the cake a more rustic look and another flavor dimension. Or, if you want to keep in the black-and-white theme, shower the cake with white and dark chocolate curls or arrange chocolate leaves on top (see How to Make Chocolate Curls, page 250).

White-on-White Cake

When I was a child, family birthday celebrations were a big deal. My mother always asked us kids what kind of birthday cake we'd like. After deliberating as to whether it should be double chocolate or chocolate marbled or chocolate baked in the shape of the letter of our first name (yes, we did that), we'd announce our decision, greeted by oohs and aahs from the others at the dinner table. So you can imagine my disappointment when I asked my younger daughter, Litton, what flavor cake she would like for her birthday party and she just deadpanned "White cake with white frosting." "Do you mean white chocolate or vanilla?" I asked. "No, just white," she proclaimed confidently. For the yummy white chocolate cake with white chocolate frosting that I baked for Litton—and for all those folks who just like white cake—prepare the white chocolate chiffon cake in the Ebony and Ivory recipe, and instead of frosting it with Chocolate Ganache, make up the White Chocolate Cream Cheese Frosting (page 425)!

1. Place a rack in the center of the oven and preheat the oven to 350°F. Generously grease two 9-inch round cake pans with solid vegetable shortening, then dust with flour. Shake out the excess flour. Set the pans aside.

2. Melt the white chocolate in a small saucepan over low heat, stirring constantly, 3 to 4 minutes. Or microwave the white chocolate in a small glass bowl on high power for 1 minute, then stir with a small rubber spatula until smooth. (See Melting White Chocolate, page 92.)

3. Place the cake mix, water, oil, whole eggs, and egg whites in a large mixing bowl. Pour in the slightly cooled white chocolate. Blend with an electric mixer on low speed for 1 minute. Stop the machine and scrape down the sides of the bowl with a rubber spatula. Increase the mixer speed to medium and beat 2 minutes more, scraping down the sides again if needed. The batter should look well blended. Divide the batter evenly between the prepared pans, smoothing it out with the rubber spatula. Place the pans in the oven side by side.

4. Bake the cakes until they are golden brown and spring back when lightly pressed with your finger, 28 to 32 minutes. Remove the pans from the oven and place them on wire racks to cool for 10 minutes. Run a dinner knife around the edge of each layer and invert each onto a rack, then invert again onto another rack so that the cakes are right side up. Allow to cool completely, 30 minutes more.

5. Meanwhile, prepare the Chocolate Ganache.

6. Place one cake layer, right side up, on a serving platter. Spread the top with ganache frosting. Place the second layer, right side up, on top of the first layer and frost the top and sides of the cake with clean, smooth strokes.

✳ *Place this cake, uncovered or in a cake saver, in the refrigerator until the frosting sets, 20 minutes. Then cover the cake with waxed paper, or place in a cake saver or under a glass dome, and store in the refrigerator for up to 1 week. Or freeze it in a cake saver for up to 6 months. Thaw the cake overnight in the refrigerator before serving.*

CHOCOLATE SNICKERDOODLE CAKE

WITH CINNAMON-CHOCOLATE CREAM CHEESE FROSTING

Snickerdoodles are a crisp cinnamon cookie first baked in New England in the nineteenth century. Today the term is used to describe a variety of sweets starring cinnamon. Chocolate and cinnamon have been partners for hundreds of years, and the combination is deeply rooted in Mexican cuisine. However, this cake is purely American, and purely delicious.

SERVES: 16

PREPARATION TIME: 8 MINUTES

BAKING TIME: 28 TO 32 MINUTES

ASSEMBLY TIME: 10 MINUTES

Solid vegetable shortening for greasing the pans
Flour for dusting the pans
1 package (18.25 ounces) plain dark chocolate fudge cake mix
¾ cup milk
¾ cup vegetable oil
3 large eggs
2 teaspoons ground cinnamon
1 teaspoon pure vanilla extract
Cinnamon-Chocolate Cream Cheese Frosting (page 423)

1. Place a rack in the center of the oven and preheat the oven to 350°F. Generously grease two 9-inch round cake pans with solid vegetable shortening, then dust with flour. Shake out the excess flour. Set the pans aside.

2. Place the cake mix, milk, oil, eggs, cinnamon, and vanilla in a large mixing bowl. Blend with an electric mixer on low speed for 1 minute. Stop the machine and

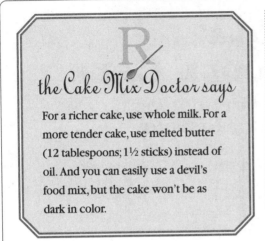

the Cake Mix Doctor says

For a richer cake, use whole milk. For a more tender cake, use melted butter (12 tablespoons; 1½ sticks) instead of oil. And you can easily use a devil's food mix, but the cake won't be as dark in color.

scrape down the sides of the bowl with a rubber spatula. Increase the mixer speed to medium and beat 2 minutes more, scraping down the sides again if needed. The batter should look well combined. Divide the batter evenly between the prepared pans, smoothing it out with the rubber spatula. Place the pans in the oven side by side.

3. Bake the cakes until they spring back when lightly pressed with your finger, 28 to 32 minutes. Remove the pans from the oven and place them on wire racks to cool for 10 minutes. Run a dinner knife around the edge of each layer and invert each onto a rack, then invert again onto another rack so that the cakes are right side up. Allow to cool completely, 30 minutes more.

4. Meanwhile, prepare the Cinnamon-Chocolate Cream Cheese Frosting.

5. Place one cake layer, right side up, on a serving platter. Spread the top with frosting. Place the second layer, right side up, on top of the first layer and frost the top and sides of the cake with clean, smooth strokes.

✹ *Place this cake, uncovered or in a cake saver, in the refrigerator until the frosting sets, 20 minutes. Then store it in a cake saver or under a glass dome at room temperature for up to 3 days, or in the refrigerator for up to 1 week. Or freeze it, wrapped in aluminum foil or in a cake saver, for up to 6 months. Thaw the cake overnight in the refrigerator before serving.*

CHOCOLATE MIDNIGHT CAKE

WITH VANILLA BUTTERCREAM FROSTING

The devil's food cake has developed a reputation as an incredibly dark chocolate cake. But its name comes from the reddish color that the cocoa powder in the recipe provides. If you want a cake that is not only intensely flavored but also amazingly moist, then this Chocolate Midnight Cake is for you. The secret ingredient is mayonnaise. Don't look so surprised! Mayonnaise has long been used to moisten chocolate layer cakes. Be sure to use a real mayo— such as Hellmann's—here. I chose a bright white, slightly sweet frosting to offset the richness of the cake and to contrast with its lights-out hue.

SERVES: 16

PREPARATION TIME: 8 MINUTES

BAKING TIME: 28 TO 32 MINUTES

ASSEMBLY TIME: 10 MINUTES

*Solid vegetable shortening for greasing
    the pans*
Flour for dusting the pans
*1 package (18.25 ounces) plain dark
    chocolate fudge cake mix*
1 cup water
1 cup mayonnaise
3 large eggs
2 teaspoons pure vanilla extract
*Vanilla Buttercream Frosting
    (page 412)*

1. Place a rack in the center of the oven and preheat the oven to 350°F. Gener-

Mayonnaise, the Secret Ingredient

In 1937 the makers of Hellmann's mayonnaise were searching for more ways to incorporate mayonnaise into American recipes, when they learned that the wife of one of their sales distributors was baking *cakes* with mayonnaise! Her cake was chocolate, filled with walnuts and dates, and oh so moist. A blend of vegetable oil, eggs, and seasonings, mayonnaise can replace oil in many cake recipes. Hellmann's says that mayonnaise can be added to scratch or cake mix cakes.

Here is a very basic way to add mayonnaise to a chocolate cake batter:

Chocolate Mayonnaise Cake: Combine 1 package (18.25 ounces) of chocolate cake mix with pudding, 1 cup mayonnaise, 1 cup water, and 3 eggs. Proceed with the package directions for a layer cake. Bake at 350°F for about 30 minutes. Sprinkle individual layers with confectioners' sugar, and cut into wedges, or stack the layers, with the frosting of your choice in between them.

ously grease two 9-inch round cake pans with solid vegetable shortening, then dust with flour. Shake out the excess flour. Set the pans aside.

2. Place the cake mix, water, mayonnaise, eggs, and vanilla in a large mixing bowl. Blend with an electric mixer on low speed for 1 minute. Stop the machine and scrape down the sides of the bowl with a rubber spatula. Increase the mixer speed to medium and beat 2 minutes more, scraping down the sides again if needed. The batter should look well combined. Divide the batter evenly between the prepared pans, smoothing

it out with the rubber spatula. Place the pans in the oven side by side.

3. Bake the cakes until they spring back when lightly pressed with your finger, 28 to 32 minutes. Remove the pans from the oven and place them on wire racks to cool for 10 minutes. Run a dinner knife around the edge of each layer and invert each onto a rack, then invert again onto another rack so that the cakes are right side up. Allow to cool completely, 30 minutes more.

4. Meanwhile, prepare the Vanilla Buttercream Frosting.

R

the Cake Mix Doctor says

It's tough to frost a dark chocolate cake with a white frosting without getting some of the dark cake crumbs in the frosting. Personally, I like the attractive speckled look that the frosting then takes on. But if it bothers you, here are two possible solutions: The first is to carefully frost the cake sides and top with a thin, or skim, coat of frosting to seal those crumbs so they don't move. Then go back over the cake with a thicker and more decorative coat. The second way to avert cake crumbs in the frosting is to partially freeze the cake layers before frosting them. Let them cool about 15 minutes on the counter, then pop them, uncovered, into the freezer for about 30 minutes; they will firm up and become a cinch to frost. Remove them from the freezer and frost as directed.

5. Place one cake layer, right side up, on a serving platter. Spread the top carefully with frosting, making sure you don't drag any of the chocolate crumbs into the frosting (see "the Cake Mix Doctor says"). Place the second layer, right side up, on top of the first layer and carefully frost the top and sides of the cake with clean, smooth strokes.

✳ *Store this cake, in a cake saver or under a glass dome, at room temperature for up to 4 days, or in the refrigerator for up to 1 week. Or freeze it, wrapped in aluminum foil or in a cake saver, for up to 6 months. Thaw the cake overnight in the refrigerator before serving.*

CHOCOLATE CINNAMON BANANA CAKE

WITH A QUICK CARAMEL FROSTING

Fruit is a terrific way of adding moisture and flavor to a cake, so when you've got a couple of overripe bananas on the kitchen counter, don't toss them out! Combine them with some cinnamon and whip up a luscious chocolate cake. The flavor of this cake improves each day, but don't expect leftovers to last past day one.

SERVES: 16

PREPARATION TIME: 10 MINUTES

BAKING TIME: 28 TO 32 MINUTES

ASSEMBLY TIME: 10 MINUTES

R℞ the Cake Mix Doctor says

When I was testing this recipe, we had a family debate as to which frosting suited it best. I was in favor of the caramel, as were my mother and my cousin Joe. But my husband and children preferred a cream cheese frosting. It's a tough but delicious decision—an old-fashioned hard caramel frosting versus the likable soft cream cheese frosting. If you choose the latter, either spice it up with cinnamon or make it with crushed pineapple (see Pineapple Cream Cheese Frosting, page 431).

Solid vegetable shortening for greasing the pans

Flour for dusting the pans

2 ripe bananas, sliced (¾ cup)

Round Pans, Square Pans

I was once foolish enough to suggest to my readers that round and square pans hold the same amount of cake batter. My cousin Joe Brady, a mathematician, set me straight. He said the best way to calculate how much one pan holds versus another is to measure by volume. Fill the pans with water, measuring it as you go along. I found that a 9-inch round and an 8-inch square, both 2 inches deep, will hold about 7 cups of water. A 9-inch square pan, on the other hand, holds more. And round and square pans bake differently, too. Round pans bake more evenly. Cakes baked in square pans are more likely to dome up in the center because the batter in the corners cooks quickly. This doming in square pans, and in the large round pans used for wedding cakes, can be prevented if you wrap Teflon baking strips (found at stores where cake-decorating supplies are sold) around the outside of the pans before they go into the oven. If you can't find these strips, cut old bath towels into strips, wet them, and use them around the pans instead.

1 package (18.25 ounces) plain devil's food
    cake mix
1 cup buttermilk
½ cup vegetable oil
3 large eggs
1 teaspoon pure vanilla extract
1 teaspoon ground cinnamon
Quick Caramel Frosting (page 440)

1. Place a rack in the center of the oven and preheat the oven to 350°F. Generously grease two 9-inch round cake pans with solid vegetable shortening, then dust with flour. Shake out the excess flour. Set the pans aside.

2. Place the bananas in a large mixing bowl. Blend with an electric mixer on low speed for 45 seconds, or until smooth. Add the cake mix, buttermilk, oil, eggs, vanilla, and cinnamon. Blend with the electric mixer on low speed for 1 minute. Stop the machine and scrape down the sides of the bowl with a rubber spatula. Increase the mixer speed to medium and beat 2 minutes more, scraping down the sides again if needed. The batter should look well combined. Divide the batter evenly between the prepared pans, smoothing it out with the rubber spatula. Place the pans in the oven side by side.

3. Bake the cakes until they spring back when lightly pressed with your finger, 28 to 32 minutes. Remove the pans from the oven and place them on wire racks to cool for 10 minutes. Run a dinner knife around the edge of each layer and invert each onto a rack, then invert again onto another rack so that the cakes are right side up. Allow to cool completely, 30 minutes more.

4. Meanwhile, prepare the Quick Caramel Frosting.

5. Place one cake layer, right side up, on a serving platter. While the frosting is still warm, spread the top with frosting.

Place the second layer, right side up, on top of the first layer and frost the top and then the sides of the cake with clean, smooth strokes.

✴ *Store this cake, in a cake saver or under a glass dome, at room temperature for up to 1 week. Or freeze it, wrapped in aluminum foil or in a cake saver, for up to 6 months. Thaw the cake overnight in the refrigerator before serving.*

COOKIES AND CREAM CAKE

This is hands down the most kid-friendly cake recipe I know. Then again, adults smile when they eat it, too. Who wouldn't like crushed chocolate sandwich cookies folded into cake layers that are sandwiched together with whipped cream containing more crushed cookies? Leigh Anne McInerney, of Libertyville, Illinois, gets the credit for this recipe. She makes hers in two layers, while I slice the layers in half to create a four-layer cake. Either way—delicious.

SERVES: 16

PREPARATION TIME: 15 MINUTES

BAKING TIME: 28 TO 32 MINUTES

ASSEMBLY TIME: 10 MINUTES

18 chocolate sandwich cookies, plus additional if needed
Solid vegetable shortening for greasing the pans
Flour for dusting the pans
1 package (18.25 ounces) white cake mix with pudding
1 cup water
½ cup vegetable oil
3 large eggs
2 cups heavy (whipping) cream

1. Place the chocolate sandwich cookies, in batches, in a food processor and process until you have crumbs. You should have 2¼ cups crumbs. If not, process more cookies until you have the correct amount. Set aside.

2. Place a rack in the center of the oven and preheat the oven to 350°F. Generously grease two 9-inch round cake pans with solid vegetable shortening, then dust with flour. Shake out the excess flour. Set the pans aside.

3. Place the cake mix, water, oil, and eggs in a large mixing bowl. Blend with an elec-

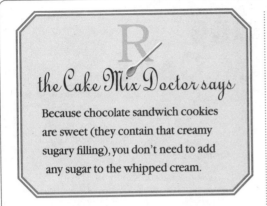

the Cake Mix Doctor says

Because chocolate sandwich cookies are sweet (they contain that creamy sugary filling), you don't need to add any sugar to the whipped cream.

tric mixer on low speed for 1 minute. Stop the machine and scrape down the sides of the bowl with a rubber spatula. Increase the mixer speed to medium and beat 2 minutes more, scraping down the sides again if needed. The batter should look well combined. Fold in 1 cup of the cookie crumbs until well distributed. Divide the batter evenly between the prepared pans, smoothing it out with the rubber spatula. Place the pans in the oven side by side.

4. Place a clean, large mixing bowl and clean electric mixer beaters in the refrigerator while the cake bakes. You will use these to prepare the whipped cream.

5. Bake the cakes until they spring back when lightly pressed with your finger, 28 to 32 minutes. Remove the pans from the oven and place them on wire racks to cool for 10 minutes. Run a dinner knife around the edge of each layer and invert each onto a rack, then invert again onto another rack so that the cakes are right side up. Allow to cool completely, 30 minutes more.

6. Prepare the whipped cream: Remove the chilled bowl and beaters from the refrigerator. Pour the cream into the bowl and beat with the electric mixer on high speed until it forms stiff peaks, 2½ to 3½ minutes. Gently fold in 1 cup of the remaining cookie crumbs, distributing them well (see How to Fold, page 445). Chill the whipped cream until the cake has cooled completely.

7. Carefully slice the cake layers in half horizontally, using a large, sharp serrated bread knife or a long piece of unflavored dental floss. You will have four layers. Place the bottom half of a cake layer on a serving platter, cut side up. Spread with some of the whipped cream. Top with the matching top half of the layer, cut side down. Spread with whipped cream. Next, add the bottom half of the second layer, cut side up, and spread with whipped cream. Top with the matching top half of the layer, cut side down. Spread the top and sides of the entire cake with the remaining whipped cream using clean, smooth strokes.

8. Sprinkle the remaining ¼ cup cookie crumbs on top of the cake. Place the cake in a cake saver or under a glass dome and chill until time to serve.

✳ *Store this cake, in a cake saver, under a glass dome, or lightly covered with waxed paper, in the refrigerator for up to 5 days.*

PEANUT BUTTER CAKE

WITH FLUFFY CHOCOLATE FROSTING

Confession time. One morning when *Chocolate from the Cake Mix Doctor* was nearly completed, I was testing recipes for my newsletter. One was a peanut butter sheet cake with a wonderful crunchy topping that bubbled up under the broiler. I took a single bite and knew I had to make this cake in layers and frost it with a creamy chocolate buttercream frosting. Since I had no peanut butter layer cake on my recipe list, I suppose this cake was meant to be!

SERVES: 16
PREPARATION TIME: 5 MINUTES
BAKING TIME: 23 TO 28 MINUTES
ASSEMBLY TIME: 10 MINUTES

*Solid vegetable shortening for
    greasing the pans*
Flour for dusting the pans
*1 package (18.25 ounces) plain yellow
    cake mix*
1⅓ cups water
⅓ cup smooth peanut butter
⅓ cup vegetable oil
3 large eggs
1 teaspoon pure vanilla extract
*Fluffy Chocolate Frosting
    (page 408)*
*½ cup chopped dry-roasted peanuts,
    for garnish*

1. Place a rack in the center of the oven and preheat the oven to 350°F. Lightly grease two 9-inch round cake pans with solid vegetable shortening, then dust with

15 Great Chocolate Birthday Cakes

1. The Perfect Chocolate Cake

2. Ever-So-Moist Chocolate Cake with Chocolate Sour Cream Frosting

3. My Favorite Birthday Cake

4. Old-Fashioned Devil's Food Cake with Fluffy Chocolate Frosting

5. Chocolate Snickerdoodle Cake with Cinnamon-Chocolate Cream Cheese Frosting

6. Cookies and Cream Cake

7. Peanut Butter Cake with Fluffy Chocolate Frosting

8. German Chocolate Cake with Pecan-Coconut Frosting

9. Triple-Decker Raspberry Chocolate Cake with Chocolate Ganache

10. Martha's Chocolate Cherry Ice Cream Cake with Hot Fudge Sauce

11. Dark Chocolate Roulade with Chocolate Cream Filling

12. White Chocolate Angel Food Mousse Cake

13. Chocolate Chiffon Cake with Crushed Peppermint Buttercream Frosting

14. Debbie's Dazzling Red Velvet Cake

15. White-on-White Cake

flour. Shake out the excess flour. Set the pans aside.

2. Place the cake mix, water, peanut butter, oil, eggs, and vanilla in a large mixing bowl. Blend with an electric mixer on low speed for 30 seconds. Stop the machine and scrape down the sides of the bowl with a rubber spatula. Increase the mixer speed to medium and beat 2 minutes more, scraping the sides down again if needed. The batter should look well com-

bined. Divide the batter evenly between the prepared pans, smoothing it out with the rubber spatula. Place the pans in the oven side by side.

3. Bake the cakes until they spring back when lightly pressed with your finger, 23 to 28 minutes. Remove the pans from the oven and place them on wire racks to cool for 10 minutes. Run a dinner knife around the edge of each layer and invert each onto a rack, then invert again onto another rack

R

the Cake Mix Doctor says

If you like a crunchy texture, use crunchy peanut butter instead of smooth in this cake.

so that the cakes are right side up. Allow to cool completely, 30 minutes more.

4. Meanwhile, prepare the Fluffy Chocolate Frosting.

5. Place one cake layer, right side up, on a serving platter. Spread the top with frosting. Place the second layer, right side up, on top of the first layer and frost the top and sides of the cake with clean, smooth strokes. Scatter the chopped peanuts on top of the cake, then slice and serve.

✳ *Store this cake, in a cake saver or under a glass dome, at room temperature for up to 3 days, or in the refrigerator for up to 1 week. Or freeze it, wrapped in aluminum foil or in a cake saver, for up to 6 months. Thaw the cake overnight in the refrigerator before serving.*

GERMAN CHOCOLATE CAKE

WITH PECAN-COCONUT FROSTING

This is the beloved classic cake that many of us remember from sometime in our past. But who makes German Chocolate Cake from scratch anymore? Here is a fast and delicious way to put the cake back into your repertoire. And just wait until you taste the real star—the frosting. It's a humdinger, with pecans and coconut folded into it once it's been cooked and thickened. With a frosting like this, the cake stays moist for days, and no one will ever know it started with a box!

SERVES: 16

PREPARATION TIME: 30 MINUTES

BAKING TIME: 32 TO 34 MINUTES

ASSEMBLY TIME: 5 MINUTES

PECAN-COCONUT FROSTING:

1½ cups chopped pecans

1 package (7 ounces; 2⅓ cups) sweetened flaked coconut

1 can (12 ounces) evaporated milk

1½ cups sugar

12 tablespoons (1½ sticks) unsalted butter

4 large egg yolks, slightly beaten

1½ teaspoons pure vanilla extract

CAKE:

Solid vegetable shortening for greasing the pans

Flour for dusting the pans

1 package (18.25 ounces) plain German chocolate cake mix

1 cup buttermilk

½ cup vegetable oil

3 large eggs

1 teaspoon pure vanilla extract

R the Cake Mix Doctor says

The pecans and coconut need to be toasted, and the cooked frosting needs to cool down for 30 minutes before you are able to spread it on the cake. If you need to speed the cooling process, place the pan of frosting in a bowl of ice water. Stir constantly, and the frosting will cool in 15 minutes. Or pour the frosting out into a shallow pan and stir until cool. The increased surface area will speed cooling. And since it is easier to frost cooled cake layers, place the layers in the refrigerator to chill if they are not completely cool.

1. Place a rack in the center of the oven and preheat the oven to 350°F.

2. For the frosting, spread the pecans and coconut on a baking sheet, and toast in the oven for 7 minutes, or until the pecans deepen in color and the coconut turns golden brown. Remove the baking sheet from the oven and set aside.

3. Place the evaporated milk, sugar, butter, egg yolks, and vanilla in a large saucepan over medium heat. Cook, stirring constantly, until thickened and golden brown in color, 10 to 12 minutes. Remove from the heat. Stir in the toasted pecans and coconut. Cool to room temperature and spreading consistency, 30 minutes (see "the Cake Mix Doctor says" on this page).

4. Meanwhile, generously grease two 9-inch round cake pans with solid vegetable shortening, then dust with flour. Shake out the excess flour. Set the pans aside.

5. Place the cake mix, buttermilk, oil, eggs, and vanilla in a large mixing bowl. Blend with an electric mixer on low speed for 1 minute. Stop the machine and scrape down the sides of the bowl with a rubber spatula. Increase the mixer speed to medium and beat 2 minutes more, scraping down the sides again if needed. The batter should look well combined. Divide the batter between the prepared pans, smoothing it out with the rubber spatula. Place the pans in the oven side by side.

6. Bake the cakes until they spring back when lightly pressed with your finger, 32 to 34 minutes. Remove the pans from the oven and place them on wire racks to cool for 10 minutes. Run a dinner knife around the edge of each layer and invert each onto a rack, then invert again onto another rack so that the cakes are right side up. Allow to cool completely, 30 minutes more.

German Chocolate Cake

In the 1950s a spectacular layer cake was making the rounds at Texas and Oklahoma parties and picnics. It was based on Baker's German sweet chocolate and was frosted with a gooey coconut and pecan–filled frosting.

According to the *Dallas Morning News*, the first recipe for this German Chocolate Cake was printed in that newspaper in 1957. It came from a Texas homemaker. Amazingly, that recipe drove Texas sales of German chocolate through the roof. So Baker company executives, realizing they were in the midst of a public relations dream, sent the recipe to more than one hundred newspaper food editors. U.S. sales of German chocolate shot up 73 percent that year. The cake was on course to become an American classic.

There is nothing German about this cake, although this has confused some people because of Texas's German immigrant heritage. The cake was named for the German chocolate that went into it, and the chocolate was named for Samuel German—an Englishman who emigrated to Boston and worked at the Walter Baker Chocolate Company in the mid-1800s. German was intrigued by the sweet smell of chocolate, and he developed his own particular style in 1852. It would be named for him but manufactured by Baker, which is now owned by Kraft Foods.

I have found that the classic recipe adapts well to a cake mix as long as you use buttermilk in the cake batter and as long as you make the original homemade frosting. To intensify the frosting flavor, I toast the pecans and coconut first.

7. Place one cake layer, right side up, on a serving platter. Spread the top with frosting. Place the second layer, right side up, on top of the first layer and frost the top with the remaining frosting, leaving the sides unfrosted.

❋ Store this cake, in a cake saver or under a glass dome, at room temperature for up to 3 days, or in the refrigerator for up to 1 week. Or freeze it, wrapped in aluminum foil or in a cake saver, for up to 6 months. Thaw the cake overnight in the refrigerator before serving.

GERMAN CHOCOLATE SPICE CAKE

WITH FRUIT AND NUT FILLING

This wonderful cake has an Old World charm about it. The earthy flavors of prunes, raisins, and nuts marry beautifully with the spiced batter and the sweet richness of German chocolate. For a decorative look, sift confectioners' sugar over a cake stencil, then carefully lift the stencil from the cake. Or add a dollop of Sweetened Cream.

SERVES: 16
PREPARATION TIME: 30 MINUTES
BAKING TIME: 28 TO 30 MINUTES
ASSEMBLY TIME: 5 MINUTES

CAKE:

Solid vegetable shortening for greasing the pans
Flour for dusting the pans
1 bar (4 ounces) German chocolate

3 large eggs, separated
1 package (18.25 ounces) plain German chocolate cake mix
1 cup buttermilk
½ cup vegetable oil
1 teaspoon ground cinnamon
½ teaspoon ground allspice
1 teaspoon pure vanilla extract

FRUIT AND NUT FILLING:

2 large eggs
½ cup granulated sugar
1 cup chopped pitted prunes
½ cup raisins
4 tablespoons (½ stick) butter, chopped
½ cup chopped pecans, walnuts, or almonds
¼ cup heavy (whipping) cream

1 tablespoon confectioners' sugar, sifted, for garnish
Sweetened Cream, optional (page 445)

1. Place a rack in the center of the oven and preheat the oven to 350°F. Gener-

ously grease three 9-inch round cake pans with solid vegetable shortening, then dust with flour. Shake out the excess flour. Set the pans aside.

2. Break the German chocolate bar into small pieces. Turn on a food processor and drop the pieces, a few at a time, into the processor through the feed tube. Process until the chocolate is finely grated. Set aside.

3. Turn the egg whites into a medium-size mixing bowl and beat with an electric mixer on high speed until stiff peaks form, 2 to 3 minutes. Set the bowl aside.

4. Place the egg yolks, cake mix, buttermilk, oil, cinnamon, allspice, and vanilla in a large mixing bowl. Blend with an electric mixer on low speed for 30 seconds. Stop the machine and scrape down the sides of the bowl with a rubber spatula. Increase the mixer speed to medium and beat 2 minutes more, scraping down the sides again if needed. The batter should look well combined. Fold the beaten egg whites and grated German chocolate into the batter with the rubber spatula. Divide the batter among the prepared pans, smoothing it out with the rubber spatula. Place the pans in the oven side by side; if your oven is not large enough to accommodate them, place two pans on the center rack and the third pan in the center of the highest rack.

R/
the Cake Mix Doctor says

By separating the eggs and folding stiffly beaten whites into the batter, you will get a taller and lighter cake. There's no need to add a pinch of cream of tartar to stabilize the whites, but if you are in the habit of doing so, go ahead. The baked layers are able to stand up to the rich and heavy cooked filling, and they look beautiful when presented unfrosted, with just a sprinkling of confectioners' sugar on the top and sides.

5. Bake the cakes until they spring back when lightly pressed with your finger, 28 to 30 minutes. Check the pan on the highest rack first, as it will bake the quickest.

6. Meanwhile, prepare the filling: Place the eggs and sugar in a medium-size saucepan off the heat. Whisk until the mixture is lemon-colored and slightly thickened. Add the prunes and raisins. Place the saucepan over medium-low heat and cook, stirring constantly with a wooden spoon, until the mixture thickens, 6 to 8 minutes. Remove the pan from the heat and add the butter and nuts. Stir until the butter has melted. Let the filling cool in the pan for 5 minutes; then add the cream and stir until smooth. Let the filling cool to room temperature.

7. Remove the cake pans from the oven and place them on wire racks to cool for 10 minutes. Run a dinner knife around the edge of each layer and invert each onto a rack, then invert again onto another rack so that the cakes are right side up. Allow to cool completely, 30 minutes more.

8. Place one cake layer on a serving platter. Spread with half of the filling. Top with a second layer, and spread with the remaining filling. Finally, top with the third cake layer. Sprinkle the confectioners' sugar over the top.

9. Slice the cake, and serve with Sweetened Cream if desired.

✳ *Store this cake, in a cake saver, under a glass dome, or lightly covered with waxed paper, for 3 days at room temperature or up to 1 week in the refrigerator. Or freeze it, wrapped in aluminum foil or in a cake saver, for up to 6 months. Thaw the cake overnight in the refrigerator before serving.*

CHOCOLATE COCONUT ICEBOX CAKE

This coconut refrigerator cake is a mainstay down South, where we have easy access to frozen unsweetened coconut, an ingredient I sometimes wish I had never mentioned in my first book! Finding the fragrant and powerfully flavorful shredded unsweetened coconut in other areas of the country is like searching for a wool sweater in the tropics. Some people have found it at health food stores, Asian markets, even Wal-Mart. A couple of supermarket chains in the Northeast carry it. And you do need it if you want to make the Coconut Icebox Cake in *The Cake Mix Doctor* or its chocolate cousin, this Chocolate Coconut Ice-box Cake. You can't substitute the sweetened stuff from the baking aisle because the frosting contains all the sugar the cake needs.

For those lucky enough to find the right coconut, you're in for a treat. For those who can't, I say it's worth petitioning your local market to carry it.

Note that you need to let this cake rest for 3 days before you serve it. It takes willpower, I know, not to slice into it ahead of time, but it certainly builds character.

....

SERVES: 20

PREPARATION TIME: 5 TO 7 MINUTES

BAKING TIME: 28 TO 32 MINUTES

ASSEMBLY TIME: 15 MINUTES

....

CAKE:

Solid vegetable shortening for greasing
*   the pans*
Flour for dusting the pans
1 package (18.25 ounces) plain German
*   chocolate cake mix*
1¼ cups water
¼ cup vegetable oil
3 large eggs

COCONUT FROSTING:

2 cups granulated sugar
2 cups (16 ounces) sour cream
1 package (12 ounces; 3½ cups) frozen
*   unsweetened grated coconut, thawed*

1. Place a rack in the center of the oven and preheat the oven to 350°F. Generously grease two 9-inch round cake pans with solid vegetable shortening, then dust with flour. Shake out the excess flour. Set the pans aside.

2. Place the cake mix, water, oil, and eggs in a large mixing bowl. Blend with an electric mixer on low speed for 1 minute. Stop the machine and scrape down the sides of the bowl with a rubber spatula. Increase the mixer speed to medium and beat 2 minutes more, scraping down the sides again if needed. The batter should look well combined. Divide the batter between the prepared pans, smoothing it out with the rubber spatula. Place the pans in the oven side by side.

3. Bake the cakes until they spring back when lightly pressed with your finger, 28 to 32 minutes.

4. Meanwhile, prepare the frosting: Combine the sugar, sour cream, and thawed coconut in a medium-size bowl. Let the mixture rest in the refrigerator, stirring it occasionally, until the sugar dissolves, 30 minutes.

5. Remove the cake pans from the oven and place them on wire racks to cool for 10 minutes. Run a dinner knife around the edge of each layer and invert each onto a rack, then invert again onto another rack so that the cakes are right side up. Allow to cool completely, 30 minutes more.

6. When the frosting is ready, assemble the cake: Carefully slice the cake layers in half horizontally, using a large, sharp serrated bread knife or a long piece of unflavored dental floss. You will have 4 layers. Place the bottom half of a cake layer on the base of a cake saver or on a serving platter, cut side up. Spread with some of the coconut frosting. Top with the matching top half of the layer, cut side down. Spread with frosting. Next, add the bottom half of the second layer, cut side up, and spread with frosting. Top with the

R the Cake Mix Doctor says

For an even more spectacular presentation, pat on sweetened flaked coconut just before serving. You can also garnish the top with some German chocolate shavings. Make these shavings ever so carefully by running a bar of German chocolate along the side of a cheese grater.

matching top half of the layer, cut side down. Spread the top and sides of the entire cake with the remaining coconut frosting using clean, smooth strokes. The frosting will be loose.

7. Place the top of the cake saver over the cake, or cover the platter with a glass dome. Chill the cake until the frosting sets up, about 4 hours. Pull the frosting back up the sides of the cake with a metal spatula. (If you do not have a cake saver or a glass cake dome, chill the cake uncovered until the frosting is firm. Pull the frosting back up the sides of the cake, if needed. Then lightly cover the cake with waxed paper, taped down along the underside of the platter to keep it snug.)

8. Chill the cake for 3 days before serving.

✳ *Store this cake, in a cake saver, under a glass dome, or lightly covered with waxed paper, in the refrigerator for up to 1 week.*

TRIPLE-DECKER RASPBERRY CHOCOLATE CAKE

WITH CHOCOLATE GANACHE

When strawberry season has waned, when fresh blackberries are but a distant memory, when the regal red raspberries look shriveled, head to the freezer case. Oh, you might wish for a handful of fresh raspberries to garnish this cake, but for the intense flavor and moist texture, all you need is a package of frozen raspberries in juice. Folded into an intense chocolate and sour cream batter, the berries add a mysterious flavor and a delightful texture. This showstopper cake bakes up tall and impressive for a dinner party, that significant birthday, or even Valentine's Day.

SERVES: 16
PREPARATION TIME: 10 MINUTES
BAKING TIME: 25 TO 28 MINUTES
ASSEMBLY TIME: 10 MINUTES

Solid vegetable shortening for greasing the pans
Flour for dusting the pans
1 package (10 ounces) frozen raspberries packed with sugar, thawed
1 package (18.25 ounces) devil's food cake mix with pudding
1 cup sour cream
½ cup vegetable oil
3 large eggs
Chocolate Ganache (page 441)
1 tablespoon Chambord (raspberry liqueur; optional)
½ cup fresh raspberries, for garnish (optional)

1. Place a rack in the center of the oven and preheat the oven to 350°F. Generously grease three 9-inch round cake pans with solid vegetable shortening, then dust with flour. Shake out the excess flour. Set the pans aside.

2. Strain the raspberries through a fine-mesh sieve if you don't want the seeds in your cake. (I like the bit of crunch they add.) Place the cake mix, raspberries and their juice, sour cream, oil, and eggs in a large mixing bowl. Blend with an electric mixer on low speed for 1 minute. Stop the machine and scrape down the sides of the bowl with a rubber spatula. Increase the mixer speed to medium and beat 2 minutes more, scraping down the sides again if needed. The batter should look well blended. Divide the batter evenly among the prepared pans, smoothing it out with the rubber spatula. Place the pans in the oven side by side, or if your oven is not large enough, place two pans on the center rack and the third pan in the center of the highest rack.

3. Bake the cakes until they spring back when lightly pressed with your finger, 25 to 28 minutes. Check the pan on the highest rack first, as it will bake the quickest. Remove the pans from the oven and place them on wire racks to cool for 10 minutes. Run a dinner knife around the edge of each layer and invert each onto a rack, then invert again onto another rack so that the cakes are right side up. Allow to cool completely, 30 minutes more.

4. Meanwhile, prepare the Chocolate Ganache, adding the Chambord, if desired, after all the chocolate has melted.

R the Cake Mix Doctor says

If you have only two cake pans, you can still make this cake. Divide the batter between the two pans (it won't overflow), and bake for 32 to 35 minutes.

I adore this cake enrobed in Chocolate Ganache flavored with Chambord, but you could substitute rum for the Chambord or you could omit the liqueur altogether.

If you're in the market for a softer or sweeter frosting, here are some ideas: Add about ¼ cup sifted confectioners' sugar to the ganache to make it more child-friendly. Or use the Chocolate Sour Cream Frosting (page 410), which is rich and creamy. The Chocolate Pan Frosting (page 434) is another alternative. It hardens on the cake, making it less messy for toting.

15 Cakes for Your Valentine's Sweetheart

1. Triple-Decker Raspberry Chocolate Cake with Chocolate Ganache

2. Debbie's Dazzling Red Velvet Cake

3. Easy and Elegant Devil's Food Cake with Whipped Chocolate Ganache

4. Chocolate Love Cake

5. Lemon Lovers' White Chocolate Cake

6. The Perfect Chocolate Cake

7. Strawberry Brownie Torte

8. Pear and Chocolate Terrine

9. Chocolate Strawberry Cheesecake

10. White Chocolate Angel Food Mousse Cake

11. Chocolate Shortbread Hearts

12. Guatemalan Wedding Cake

13. Raspberry Brownies with Creamy Chocolate Frosting

14. Good-for-You Chocolate Pound Cake with Shiny Chocolate Glaze

15. Red Velvet Cupcakes with White Chocolate Cream Cheese Frosting

5. Place one cake layer, right side up, on a serving platter. Spread the top with ganache frosting. Place the second layer, right side up, on top of the first layer. Spread the top with ganache. Place the third layer, right side up, on top of the second layer and frost the top and sides of the cake. Work with clean, smooth strokes.

6. Decorate the top attractively with the fresh raspberries, if desired.

✳ *Place this cake, uncovered or in a cake saver, in the refrigerator until the frosting sets, 20 minutes. Then cover the cake with waxed paper, or place it in a cake saver or under a glass dome, and store in the refrigerator for up to 1 week. Or freeze it in a cake saver for up to 6 months. Thaw the cake overnight in the refrigerator before serving.*

MARTHA'S CHOCOLATE CHERRY ICE CREAM CAKE

WITH HOT FUDGE SAUCE

My friend and diligent recipe tester Martha Bowden remembers her sister Elizabeth requesting a chocolate ice cream cake whenever her birthday rolled around. So Martha had a good time testing this recipe, which is based on a small chocolate cake mix—the perfect size for assembling into this loaf-shaped layer cake. When it's sliced, the cake reveals stripes of chocolate brown, creamy white, and cherry red. For birthdays it looks festive sealed in whipped cream and showered with chocolate curls. Or for other occasions year-round, omit the cream coating and just pour the easy Hot Fudge Sauce over the slices.

SERVES: 12

PREPARATION TIME: 15 MINUTES

BAKING TIME: 35 TO 37 MINUTES

ASSEMBLY/FREEZING TIME: 2 HOURS AND 20 MINUTES

CAKE:

Solid vegetable shortening for greasing
    the pan
Flour for dusting the pan
1 small package (9 ounces) devil's food
    cake mix
½ cup buttermilk or plain milk
1 egg
½ teaspoon pure vanilla
    extract or pure
    almond extract

FILLING:

1 can (12 ounces) cherry filling, or 1½ cups
    cherry preserves
1 gallon vanilla ice cream, in rectangular
    block

Sweetened Cream (page 445)

Chocolate Curls, for garnish (optional; see
    How to Make Chocolate Curls, page 250)

Hot Fudge Sauce (page 456)

Maraschino cherries, for garnish (optional)

1. Place a rack in the center of the oven and preheat the oven to 350°F. Generously grease a 9- by 5-inch loaf pan with solid vegetable shortening, then dust with flour. Shake out the excess flour. Set the pan aside.

2. Place the cake mix, ¼ cup of the buttermilk, the egg, and the vanilla in a large mixing bowl. Blend with an electric mixer on low speed for 1 minute. Stop the machine and scrape down the sides of the bowl with a rubber spatula. Add the remaining ¼ cup buttermilk. Increase the mixer speed to medium and beat 2 minutes more, scraping down the sides again if needed. The batter should look well combined. Pour the batter into the prepared pan, smoothing it out with the rubber spatula. Place the pan in the oven.

3. Bake the cake until it springs back when lightly pressed with your finger, 35 to 37 minutes.

4. Remove the pan from the oven and place it on a wire rack to cool for 10 minutes. Run a dinner knife around the edge of the cake and shake the pan to release

it. Invert it over one hand and then invert again onto a rack so that the cake is right side up. Allow to cool completely, 30 minutes more.

5. Slice the cake lengthwise into 3 equal layers. Place a sheet of waxed paper between the layers, and cover the cake with plastic wrap. Place it in the freezer for 1 hour, or until firm. At the same time, place the can of cherry filling, a large mixing bowl, and the electric mixer beaters in the refrigerator to chill.

6. Remove the cherry filling from the refrigerator and divide it in half. Remove the cake from the freezer. Lift off the top 2 layers and the waxed paper. Place the bottom layer on a piece of cardboard covered with aluminum foil or on a serving platter that will fit in the freezer.

7. Place a clean sheet of waxed paper on the counter, or work on a clean cutting board. Remove the ice cream from the freezer. Working carefully and quickly, unfold the cardboard from around the top and sides of the ice cream. Using a sharp serrated knife, cut off a ½-inch-thick slice of ice cream. Place the ice cream slice on the cake layer. Trim off any ice cream that extends beyond the edges of the layer. Cover the cake layer completely with slices of ice cream. Spread one half of the cherry filling over the ice cream, just to the

the Cake Mix Doctor says

Save pieces of sturdy cardboard that you can cover with foil to make an impromptu platter for freezing desserts like this one.

To make the assembly of this cake as effortless as possible, make sure all the ingredients are cold. Cut the ice cream when it is cold, and lay the slices onto cold cake. This helps the cake hold its shape and shortens the freezing time.

edges. Cut more slices of ice cream, and arrange them in a layer over the cherry filling, just to the edges of the cake.

8. Gently place the middle layer of the cake on top of the ice cream and repeat the layers of ice cream, the remaining cherry filling, and more ice cream. (Place the unused ice cream in an airtight container back in the freezer for future use.) Gently place the top cake layer on top of

the last layer of ice cream. Cover the assembled cake with plastic wrap, and immediately return it to the freezer for 1 hour.

9. Meanwhile, prepare the Sweetened Cream.

10. Remove the frozen cake from the freezer. Spread a thin layer of Sweetened Cream on the top and sides of the cake. Sprinkle with the Chocolate Curls, if desired. Return the cake to the freezer, uncovered, for a few hours, or preferably overnight.

11. When you are ready to serve the cake, prepare the Hot Fudge Sauce.

12. To serve, slice the cake crosswise and drizzle each slice with Hot Fudge Sauce. Garnish with a maraschino cherry, if desired. Lightly wrap any leftover cake in aluminum foil and return it to the freezer.

✴ *Store this cake, wrapped in aluminum foil or in a cake saver, in the freezer for 2 weeks.*

CHOCOLATE ORANGE CAKE

WITH ORANGE-COCOA CREAM CHEESE FROSTING

This is one of the easiest and most effective ways to doctor up a cake mix: Simply substitute good-quality orange juice for the water in the batter, add a little orange zest, and *voilà*—a spectacular cake in both taste and appearance. The dark, deep, moist orange-flavored cake reminds me of those orange-shaped chocolates from England—the ones that open into wedges. Delicious anytime, but especially in the depths of winter.

....

SERVES: 16

PREPARATION TIME: 8 MINUTES

BAKING TIME: 30 TO 32 MINUTES

ASSEMBLY TIME: 10 MINUTES

....

Solid vegetable shortening for greasing
the pans
Flour for dusting the pans
1 package (18.25 ounces) plain devil's food
cake mix
1⅓ cups orange juice
½ cup vegetable oil
3 large eggs
1 teaspoon grated orange zest
Orange-Cocoa Cream Cheese Frosting
(page 429)

1. Place a rack in the center of the oven and preheat the oven to 350°F. Generously grease two 9-inch round cake pans with solid vegetable shortening, then dust with flour. Shake out the excess flour. Set the pans aside.

2. Place the cake mix, orange juice, oil, eggs, and orange zest in a large mixing bowl. Blend with an electric mixer on low speed for 1 minute. Stop the machine and scrape down the sides of the bowl with a rubber spatula. Increase the mixer speed to medium and beat 2 minutes more, scraping down the sides again if needed.

The batter should look well combined. Divide the batter evenly between the prepared pans, smoothing it out with the rubber spatula. Place the pans in the oven side by side.

3. Bake the cakes until they spring back when lightly pressed with your finger, 30 to 32 minutes. Remove the pans from the oven and place them on wire racks to cool for 10 minutes. Run a dinner knife around the edge of each layer and invert each onto a rack, then invert again onto another rack so that the cakes are right side up. Allow to cool completely, 30 minutes more.

4. Meanwhile, prepare the Orange-Cocoa Cream Cheese Frosting.

5. Place one cake layer, right side up, on a serving platter. Spread the top with frosting. Place the second layer, right side up, on top of the first layer and frost the top and sides of the cake with clean, smooth strokes.

✳ *Store this cake, in a cake saver or under a glass dome, at room temperature for up to 3 days, or in the refrigerator for up to 1 week. Or freeze it, wrapped in aluminum foil or in a cake saver, for up to 6 months. Thaw the cake overnight in the refrigerator before serving.*

the Cake Mix Doctor says

About that orange zest: Did you know you can grate the zest from oranges ahead of time and freeze it in little plastic bags? That's what my clever friend Martha Bowden does. I have found the best tool for zesting is the Microplane (see Cool Cake-Baking Tools, page 22). It grates only the zest, leaving the bitter white part behind, and the bald orange is smooth and ready for eating or juicing.

NATALIE'S CHOCOLATE CAFÉ AU LAIT CAKE

Natalie Haughton is a Los Angeles food writer and cookbook author who knows how to put together a great recipe, and this cake is no exception. The recipe first appeared in Natalie's book *365 Great Chocolate Desserts*. She recommended that I try it when she was interviewing me for a story in the *Los Angeles Daily News*. What I love about this cake is that it has such complex flavors—coffee, chocolate, and walnuts—and yet it's a breeze to assemble. For parties it can be prepared a day in advance and refrigerated. Just before serving, dust the top with powdered sweetened cocoa, if desired.

SERVES: 16
PREPARATION TIME: 20 MINUTES
BAKING TIME: 32 TO 35 MINUTES
ASSEMBLY TIME: 5 MINUTES

CAKE:

*Solid vegetable shortening for greasing
    the pans*
Flour for dusting the pans
8 tablespoons (1 stick) margarine
1½ cups graham cracker crumbs
1 cup semisweet chocolate chips
½ cup chopped walnuts
*1 package (18.25 ounces) plain dark
    chocolate fudge or devil's
    food cake mix*
1⅓ cups water
½ cup vegetable oil
3 large eggs

WHIPPED CREAM FROSTING:

1½ cups heavy (whipping) cream
1 tablespoon instant coffee powder
*⅓ cup sifted confectioners' sugar,
    or to taste*

1. Place a rack in the center of the oven and preheat the oven to 350°F. Generously grease two 9-inch round cake pans with solid vegetable shortening, then dust with flour. Shake out the excess flour. Set the pans aside.

2. Place a large mixing bowl and electric mixer beaters in the refrigerator to chill.

3. Place the margarine in a medium-size saucepan over low heat and melt it, or place it in a medium-size glass bowl and melt it in the microwave on high power for 1 minute. Fold in the graham cracker crumbs and let cool, about 15 minutes. When the mixture is cool, fold in the chocolate chips and walnuts. Set aside.

4. Place the cake mix, water, oil, and eggs in a large mixing bowl. Blend with an electric mixer on low speed for 1 minute. Stop the machine and scrape down the sides of the bowl with a rubber spatula. Increase the mixer speed to medium and beat 2 minutes more, scraping down the sides again if needed. The batter should look well combined. Divide the batter evenly between the prepared pans, smoothing it out with the rubber spatula. Sprinkle the chocolate chip–walnut mixture evenly over the cake batter in both pans. Using your fingertips or the back of a spoon, lightly

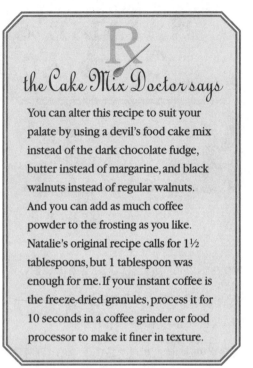

the Cake Mix Doctor says

You can alter this recipe to suit your palate by using a devil's food cake mix instead of the dark chocolate fudge, butter instead of margarine, and black walnuts instead of regular walnuts. And you can add as much coffee powder to the frosting as you like. Natalie's original recipe calls for 1½ tablespoons, but 1 tablespoon was enough for me. If your instant coffee is the freeze-dried granules, process it for 10 seconds in a coffee grinder or food processor to make it finer in texture.

press the mixture into the batter so it sticks, but not so hard as to let it sink into the batter. Place the pans in the oven side by side.

5. Bake the cakes until they spring back when lightly pressed with your finger, 32 to 35 minutes. Remove the pans from the oven and place them on wire racks to cool for 30 minutes. Run a dinner knife around the edge of each layer and invert each onto a rack, then invert again onto another rack so that the cooled cakes are right (topping) side up.

6. For the frosting, remove the chilled bowl and beaters from the refrigerator. Pour the cream into the chilled bowl and beat with the electric mixer on high speed until it begins to thicken, 1 minute. Add the coffee powder and confectioners' sugar. Continue beating on high speed until the cream forms stiff peaks, 1½ to 2 minutes longer.

7. Place one cake layer, right side up, on a serving platter. Spread the top with half of the frosting. Place the second layer, right side up, on top of the first layer. Frost the sides of the cake with the remaining frosting. Do not frost the top of the cake.

8. Place the cake in a cake saver or under a glass dome, and chill until time to serve.

✻ *Store this cake, in a cake saver, under a glass dome, or lightly covered with waxed paper, in the refrigerator for up to 5 days.*

BUTTERMILK CHOCOLATE SPICE CAKE

WITH CHOCOLATE PAN FROSTING

Spice cake mix is one of the easiest varieties to doctor up. With the flavorings built in, you just need to add oil, eggs, and some kind of liquid. I tend to favor buttermilk with spice cake mix. And I have come to like the combination of chocolate and spice cake, especially when the chocolate is swirled into the batter so that the cake bakes up into a beautiful tan and brown marble pattern. All you need is a simple topper—the Chocolate Pan Frosting—and you have a remarkable cake with little effort!

SERVES: 16

PREPARATION TIME: 10 MINUTES

BAKING TIME: 26 TO 28 MINUTES

ASSEMBLY TIME: 10 MINUTES

Solid vegetable shortening for greasing the pans
Flour for dusting the pans
1 package (18.25 ounces) plain spice cake mix
1⅓ cups buttermilk
⅓ cup vegetable oil
3 large eggs
1 ounce semisweet chocolate, coarsely chopped
Chocolate Pan Frosting (page 434)

1. Place a rack in the center of the oven and preheat the oven to 350°F. Generously grease two 9-inch round cake pans with solid vegetable shortening, then dust with flour. Shake out the excess flour. Set the pans aside.

2. Place the cake mix, buttermilk, oil, and eggs in a large mixing bowl. Blend with an electric mixer on low speed for 1 minute. Stop the machine and scrape down the sides of the bowl with a rubber spatula. Increase the mixer speed to medium and beat 2 minutes more, scraping down the sides again if needed. The batter should look well combined. Divide the batter between the prepared pans, smoothing it out with the rubber spatula.

3. Melt the chocolate in a small saucepan over low heat for 2 minutes, stirring constantly, or in a small glass bowl in the microwave at high power for 45 seconds. Stir with a small rubber spatula until the chocolate is smooth and thoroughly melted.

4. Drizzle the melted chocolate over the batter in both pans. With the blunt end of a wooden skewer or with a dinner knife, swirl the chocolate through the batter to marble it. Take care not to scrape the bottom of the pan. Place the pans in the oven side by side.

5. Bake the cakes until they spring back when lightly pressed with your finger, 26 to 28 minutes. Remove the pans from the oven and place them on wire racks to cool for 10 minutes. Run a dinner knife around the edge of each layer and invert each onto a rack, then invert again onto another rack so that the cakes are right side up. Allow to cool completely, 30 minutes more.

6. Meanwhile, prepare the Chocolate Pan Frosting.

7. Place one cake layer, right side up, on a serving platter. Spread the top with frosting. Place the second layer, right side up, on top of the first layer and frost the top and sides of the cake with clean, smooth strokes.

✳ *Store this cake, in a cake saver or under a glass dome, at room temperature for up to 1 week. Or freeze it, wrapped in aluminum foil or in a cake saver, for up to 6 months. Thaw the cake overnight in the refrigerator before serving.*

R̶

the Cake Mix Doctor says

This is a dark and elegant cake. When cut open, it looks like marble. If you want to lighten its appearance, omit the chocolate frosting and opt for a creamy White Chocolate Cream Cheese Frosting (page 425) or the Quick Caramel Frosting (page 440).

DEBBIE'S DAZZLING RED VELVET CAKE

I met Debbie Mays at a Birmingham book signing. A caterer and cake baker, she raved about her Red Velvet Cake, telling me that people order one from her as much as a year in advance for Christmas. Well, she had me so curious that I tracked her down as I prepared to write this book. Variations abound on the legendary Red Velvet Cake, and let's face it, you either love (as most people do) or hate this scarlet confection. Debbie gets the vivid red color in her cake

by beginning with a white cake mix and adding cocoa plus *two* bottles of red food coloring. It is delicious—and if you top it with a Cream Cheese Frosting and bright red raspberries, you have the most camera-ready cake I know.

SERVES: 16
PREPARATION TIME: 8 MINUTES
BAKING TIME: 28 TO 30 MINUTES
ASSEMBLY TIME: 10 MINUTES

Solid vegetable shortening for greasing
*   the pans*
Flour for dusting the pans
1 package (18.25 ounces) white cake mix
*   with pudding*
1 cup buttermilk
8 tablespoons (1 stick) margarine, melted
3 tablespoons unsweetened cocoa powder
3 large eggs
2 bottles (1 ounce each) red food coloring
1 teaspoon pure vanilla extract
Cream Cheese Frosting (page 420)

1. Place a rack in the center of the oven and preheat the oven to 350°F. Gener-

R

the Cake Mix Doctor says

Don't be alarmed by the two bottles of red food coloring. Yes, each is a 1-ounce bottle, but this is a really red cake! Want it less red? Use just one bottle.

ously grease two 9-inch round cake pans with solid vegetable shortening, then dust with flour. Shake out the excess flour. Set the pans aside.

2. Place the cake mix, buttermilk, melted margarine, cocoa powder, eggs, red food coloring, and vanilla in a large mixing bowl. Blend with an electric mixer on low speed for 1 minute. Stop the machine and scrape down the sides of the bowl with a rubber spatula. Increase the mixer speed to medium and beat 2 minutes more, scraping down the sides again if needed. The batter should look well combined. Divide the batter evenly between the prepared pans, smoothing it out with the rubber spatula. Place the pans in the oven side by side.

3. Bake the cakes until they spring back when lightly pressed with your finger, 28 to 30 minutes. Remove the pans from the oven and place them on wire racks to cool for 10 minutes. Run a dinner knife around the edge of each layer and invert each onto a rack, then invert again onto another rack so that the cakes are right side up. Allow to cool completely, 30 minutes more.

4. Meanwhile, prepare the Cream Cheese Frosting.

5. Place one cake layer, right side up, on a serving platter. Spread the top with frosting. Place the second layer, right side up, on top of the first layer and frost the top and sides of the cake with clean, smooth strokes.

✳ *Store this cake, in a cake saver or under a glass dome, at room temperature for up to 3 days, or in the refrigerator for up to 1 week. Or freeze it, wrapped in aluminum foil or in a cake saver, for up to 6 months. Thaw the cake overnight in the refrigerator before serving.*

WHITE CHOCOLATE PEACH CAKE

WITH FRESH PEACH BUTTERCREAM FROSTING AND SLICED SUMMER PEACHES

Make this white chocolate cake with ripe summer peaches and it will taste extraordinarily peachy. But it's also delicious made with ordinary, not-so-sweet, out-of-season peaches. They'll contribute moisture and tenderness to the cake, if not that memorable flavor. Be careful to measure out just 1 cup of peach purée for the cake. Ripe peaches have more juice and may produce more purée than is needed.

....

SERVES: 16

PREPARATION TIME: 15 MINUTES

BAKING TIME: 30 TO 33 MINUTES

ASSEMBLY TIME: 10 MINUTES

....

Solid vegetable shortening for greasing
*   the pans*
Flour for dusting the pans
8 large fresh peaches
¼ cup sugar
6 ounces white chocolate, coarsely chopped
1 package (18.25 ounces) plain white
*   cake mix*
⅓ cup vegetable oil
3 large eggs
2 large egg whites
Fresh Peach Buttercream Frosting (page 418)

1. Place a rack in the center of the oven and preheat the oven to 350°F. Generously grease two 9-inch round cake pans with solid vegetable shortening, then dust with flour. Shake out the excess flour. Set the pans aside.

2. Peel, pit, and slice 4 of the peaches. Place the peach slices in a small glass bowl, add the sugar, and toss to coat the slices well. Cover the bowl with plastic wrap and chill.

3. Peel, pit, and quarter the remaining 4 peaches. Place the peach quarters in a food processor and process until puréed. You should have about 1¼ cups. Pour ¼ cup of the purée into a small glass bowl, cover with plastic wrap, and reserve in the refrigerator. Pour 1 cup of the purée into a large mixing bowl. Set aside.

4. Melt the white chocolate in a small saucepan over low heat, stirring constantly, 3 to 4 minutes. Or microwave the white chocolate in a small glass bowl on high power for 1 minute, then stir with a small rubber spatula until smooth. (See Melting White Chocolate, page 92.)

5. Place the cake mix, oil, whole eggs, and egg whites in the mixing bowl with the peach purée. Pour in the slightly cooled white chocolate. Blend with an electric mixer on low speed for 1 minute. Stop the machine and scrape down the sides of the bowl with a rubber spatula. Increase the mixer speed to medium and beat 2 minutes more, scraping down the sides again if needed. The batter should look well combined. Divide the batter evenly between the prepared pans, smoothing it out with the rubber spatula. Place the pans in the oven side by side.

> ℞
> ### the Cake Mix Doctor says
>
> Adding white chocolate to cake batter is tricky. It is so rich that it can weigh down batter and make a cake much too oily. But if you add extra egg whites, they seem to lighten the load and add loft, producing a tall and gorgeous cake. You don't even need to beat them to peaks as you might in a chiffon cake batter. If you need to prepare those sweetened peach slices early in the day, add 1 tablespoon of lemon juice to keep them looking pretty.

6. Bake the cakes until they are golden brown and spring back when lightly pressed with your finger, 30 to 33 minutes. Remove the pans from the oven and place them on wire racks to cool for 10 minutes. Run a dinner knife around the edge of each layer and invert each onto a rack, then invert again onto another rack so that the cakes are right side up. Allow to cool completely, 30 minutes more.

7. Meanwhile, prepare the Fresh Peach Buttercream Frosting.

Melting White Chocolate

When it comes to melting chocolate, white or dark, there is no safer place than the microwave. Keep the time short, the setting on high, and stir frequently, and you'll have a creamy mass of chocolate in no time. Chop the chocolate into pieces before melting and you'll have that mass in even less time. The tricky part about melting white chocolate is that it will still hold its shape when it has melted, so watch the time and then stir it for 30 to 40 seconds until smooth.

Should you want to forgo the microwave, place white chocolate pieces in a nonstick saucepan over low heat. Stir constantly for 3 to 4 minutes, and then remove the pan from the heat and continue stirring until it is thoroughly melted and smooth.

8. Place one cake layer, right side up, on a serving platter. Spread the top with frosting. Place the second layer, right side up, on top of the first layer and frost the top and sides of the cake with clean, smooth strokes.

9. Slice and serve the cake, topped with the sweetened sliced peaches.

✳ *Store this cake, in a cake saver or under a glass dome, at room temperature for up to 4 days, or in the refrigerator for up to 1 week. Or freeze it, wrapped in aluminum foil or in a cake saver, for up to 6 months. Thaw the cake overnight in the refrigerator before serving.*

LEMON LOVERS'
WHITE CHOCOLATE CAKE

When I offered my husband, John, a piece of this lemon cake after dinner one night, he said with a grin, "This is incredible, but too bad you can't use it in the chocolate book." Well, of course I can. Here it is—lemon, white chocolate (the unexpected secret ingredient), and all. This is just the delicious sort of cake to serve on birthdays and special occasions like christenings and showers. Lemon curd is sandwiched between white chocolate layers and all is covered with a lemon-flavored white chocolate frosting.

....

SERVES: 16

PREPARATION TIME: 10 MINUTES

BAKING TIME: 28 TO 32 MINUTES

ASSEMBLY TIME: 12 MINUTES

....

Solid vegetable shortening for greasing
   the pans
Flour for dusting the pans
6 ounces white chocolate, coarsely chopped
1 package (18.25 ounces) plain white
   cake mix
2/3 cup water
1/3 cup vegetable oil
3 large eggs
2 large egg whites
2 tablespoons fresh lemon juice
1 teaspoon grated lemon zest
Lemony White Chocolate Cream Cheese
   Frosting (page 427)
1/2 cup store-bought lemon curd (half of a
   10-ounce jar)

1. Place a rack in the center of the oven and preheat the oven to 350°F. Generously grease two 9-inch round cake pans with solid vegetable shortening, then dust with flour. Shake out the excess flour. Set the pans aside.

2. Melt the white chocolate in a small glass bowl in the microwave oven on high power for 1 minute. Remove the bowl

Toting a Cake

*I*t's the journey that matters, as the saying goes. So to give your gorgeous triple-decker chocolate cake or perfectly mounded coffee cake a suitable ride, you may need a proper carrying case. Now, this might range from the basic shirt box lined with waxed paper for a sheet cake, to a cardboard cake box from a cake decorating store, to a hat box lined with waxed or tissue paper. Rubbermaid makes a simple and inexpensive cake carrier with a snap-on lid, but it has no handle. If you want a sturdier carrier—with both a handle and a lid lock—look at the pricier Tupperware carriers; they come in layer cake and sheet cake sizes.

The latter even flips over to hold cupcakes. (Tupperware products are available online at www.Tupperware.com.) Another option is the fun Piatto Bakery Box, which is collapsible, has a handle, and has the bonus of a slide-in shelf that divides the compartment into two sections so you can carry two layers, two pies, or thirty-six cupcakes. Piatto boxes are less expensive than Tupperware, come in various colors, and are sold through the Home Shopping Network (Website www.hsn.com).

from the oven and stir with a small rubber spatula until it is smooth, (see Melting White Chocolate, page 92).

3. Place the cake mix, water, oil, whole eggs, egg whites, lemon juice, and lemon zest in a large mixing bowl. Pour in the slightly cooled white chocolate. Blend with an electric mixer on low speed for 1 minute. Stop the machine and scrape down the sides of the bowl with a rubber spatula. Increase the mixer speed to medium and beat 2 minutes more, scraping down the sides again if needed.

The batter should look well combined. Divide the batter evenly between the prepared pans, smoothing it out with the rubber spatula. Place the pans in the oven side by side.

4. Bake the cakes until they are golden brown and spring back when lightly pressed with your finger, 28 to 32 minutes. Remove the pans from the oven and place them on wire racks to cool for 10 minutes. Run a dinner knife around the edge of each layer and invert each onto a rack, then invert again onto another rack so that the cakes are right side up. Allow to cool completely, 30 minutes more.

5. Meanwhile, prepare the Lemony White Chocolate Cream Cheese Frosting.

6. Place one cake layer, right side up, on a serving platter. Spread the top with the lemon curd. Place the second layer, right side up, on top of the first layer and frost the top and sides of the cake with frosting.

✳ *Place this cake, uncovered or in a cake saver, in the refrigerator until the frosting sets, 20 minutes. Then store it, in a cake saver or under a glass dome, at room temperature for up to 3 days, or in the refrigerator for up to 1 week. Or freeze it, wrapped in aluminum foil or in a cake saver, for up to 6 months. Thaw the cake overnight in the refrigerator before serving.*

R℞ the Cake Mix Doctor says

You've got lots of room to improvise with this recipe. Use a lemon cake mix instead of white. Or try it with a yellow mix if that's what you have on hand. Add more lemon zest. Or use lime curd, lime juice, and lime zest. Experiment with lemon oil, lime oil, or orange oil in the frosting. How about filling the center of the cake with the White Chocolate Cream Cheese Frosting swirled with the lemon curd for effect? Save a little lemon curd to swirl on the top of the cake, too. And for garnish, surround the cake with lemon slices or, better yet, candied lemon peel (see How to Make Candied Orange Zest, page 228).

Chocolate Pound Cakes

• • •

Meet the big boys: sturdy, moist, sensible pound cakes, traditionally baked in tube and Bundt pans, needing little fuss and feeding many. They're at home in the morning, at midday, for dessert, or even just before bedtime. In both the straight-sided tube pan and the fluted Bundt pan, the thick and dense cake bakes evenly because of the hollow center tube. It allows heat to come up through the middle of the cake, which shortens the baking time of these thick batters and allows them to rise more dramatically.

Tube pans have been around forever, but it was the Bundt that made cake-baking history. Based on the design of the German *kugelhopf* pan, the Bundt hadn't knocked anyone's socks off when it first appeared in the 1950s. Then in 1966, Ella Rita Helfrich, of Texas, entered her Bundt-baked Tunnel of Fudge Cake in the Pillsbury Bake-Off and won $5,000. The Bundt rose to stardom and Bundt-mania spread in the United States. Cakes baked in Bundts became symbols of domesticity. No suburban coffee klatch or office potluck lunch was complete without one. And today these Bundts have branched out into miniature sizes and even star-shaped pans.

As you can see from the scope of this chapter, I could have written an entire book on the versatile pound cake. Although there are pound cake mixes on the market, you can use almost any mix to get started—yellow, white, devil's food, or German chocolate cake. Stud it with chocolate chips or chopped candy bars, or fill it with rings of pudding or chewy coconut macaroon. Create a dark, dense, intense beauty like the Chocolate Cream Cheese Pound Cake, or something a little less heavy like A Lighter Chocolate Pound Cake, made with yogurt.

The pound cake needs no topping to finish it off, but that shouldn't stop you from coating it with a thin shiny glaze or a sturdier frosting made from cocoa and marshmallow. Seal it in a chocolate ganache, or cover it with a spoonful of warm lemon curd sauce. And it is delicious soaked in amaretto, rum, or Kahlúa.

"Research tells us fourteen out of any ten individuals like chocolate."

—SANDRA BOYNTON

Chocolate pound cakes are versatile, and they're good keepers. You can freeze them for up to 6 months if you like to bake ahead. And they ship well—just in case the lucky recipients aren't living close to home.

QUICK TUNNEL OF FUDGE CAKE

When Ella Rita Helfrich won $5,000 in the 1966 Pillsbury Bake-Off for her chocolate and walnut Tunnel of Fudge Cake, the fluted Bundt pan immediately rose to stardom. The Texan's catchy title aptly described the gooey center of fudge that lay buried in the middle of the cake.

Many people asked me to come up with a cake mix version of this legend. The cake was the easy part. The difficult task lay within. How to develop a fudgy interior when the Pillsbury chocolate frosting mix called for in that early recipe was no longer available? I tried it with another brand of dry frosting mix, but it kept sinking to the bottom of the pan. Pillsbury suggested pudding mix, and that's what I settled on. The results aren't as gloriously gooey as in the original, but the "tunnel" is definitely fudgy and satisfying. If you serve the cake warm, the filling will be runny, but when cool, it firms up.

....

SERVES: 16
PREPARATION TIME: 10 MINUTES
BAKING TIME: 45 TO 50 MINUTES
ASSEMBLY TIME: 2 MINUTES

....

FILLING:

1½ cups milk

1 package (3.4 ounces) chocolate fudge pudding and pie filling mix (not instant)

1 cup semisweet chocolate chips

1 tablespoon butter

CAKE:

Vegetable oil spray for misting the pan

Flour for dusting the pan

1 package (18.25 ounces) devil's food
   cake mix with pudding

½ cup vegetable oil

½ cup sour cream

½ cup water

4 large eggs

1 teaspoon pure vanilla extract

2 cups finely chopped walnuts

Martha's Chocolate Icing (page 433)

1. Place the milk in a medium-size saucepan and whisk in the pudding mix. Cook, stirring, over medium heat until the mixture comes to a boil, 4 to 5 minutes. Remove the pan from the heat and stir in the chocolate chips and butter. Stir until the pudding is smooth and thickened and the chocolate has melted. Set the pan aside.

2. Place a rack in the center of the oven and preheat the oven to 350°F. Lightly mist a 12-cup Bundt pan with vegetable oil spray, then dust with flour. Shake out the excess flour. Set the pan aside.

3. Place the cake mix, oil, sour cream, water, eggs, and vanilla in a large mixing bowl. Blend with an electric mixer on low speed for 1 minute. Stop the machine and scrape down the sides of the bowl with a

the Cake Mix Doctor says

This cake contains a lot of walnuts simply because that's how Ella Rita Helfrich created it. If you want to cut back to 1½ cups, that's fine. Just make sure the nuts are finely chopped so they don't interfere with the crumb of the cake. You can do this easily in a food processor, or with a good sharp knife and a cutting board.

   Pour your favorite chocolate glaze over the cake, or Martha's Chocolate Icing as I recommend here. Or just dust it with some confectioners' sugar and leave it as is. With the pudding inside, this cake needs little adornment. Note that I call for regular pudding mix here, not the instant kind.

rubber spatula. Increase the mixer speed to medium and beat 2 minutes more, scraping the sides down again if needed. The batter should look thick and well combined. Fold in the walnuts, making sure they are well distributed throughout the batter.

4. Reserve 2 cups of the batter. Pour the remaining batter into the prepared pan. Spoon the pudding filling in a ring on top of the batter, making sure it does not touch the sides of the pan. Spoon the reserved batter over the filling, smoothing it out with the rubber spatula. Place the pan in the oven.

5. Bake the cake until it springs back when lightly pressed with your finger and is just starting to pull away from the sides of the pan, 45 to 50 minutes. Remove the pan from the oven and place it on a wire rack to cool for 20 minutes. Run a long, sharp knife around the edge of the cake and invert it onto a rack to cool completely, 20 minutes more.

6. Meanwhile, prepare Martha's Chocolate Icing.

7. Place the cake on a serving platter and pour the warm icing over it. Let the cake rest for 10 minutes before slicing.

8. Slice and serve.

✹ *Store this cake, wrapped in aluminum foil or plastic wrap, or in a cake saver, at room temperature for up to 1 week. Or freeze it, wrapped in foil, for up to 6 months. Thaw the cake overnight in the refrigerator before serving.*

CHOCOLATE CHIP PECAN COFFEE CAKE

The older I get, the more I'm willing to allow myself a little chocolate at breakfast. Don't tell my children! Seriously, chocolate is superb woven into coffee cakes (or folded into waffles or pancakes or muffins). If you are of a similar bent, then bake on with this friendly recipe. It is suitable for most crowds and can be toted to breakfasts, coffees, luncheons, even served for dessert.

SERVES: 16

PREPARATION TIME: 10 MINUTES

BAKING TIME: 55 TO 60 MINUTES

Vegetable oil spray for misting the pan
Flour for dusting the pan
½ cup finely chopped pecans
1 package (18.25 ounces) plain yellow
cake mix
1 package (3.4 ounces) vanilla
instant pudding mix
1 cup whole milk
¾ cup vegetable oil
4 large eggs
1 cup semisweet chocolate chips
1 tablespoon confectioners' sugar, for
garnish (optional)

1. Place a rack in the center of the oven and preheat the oven to 350°F. Lightly mist a 12-cup Bundt pan with vegetable oil spray, then dust with flour. Shake out the excess flour. Sprinkle the pecans evenly over the bottom of the pan. Set the pan aside.

2. Place the cake mix, pudding mix, milk, oil, and eggs in a large mixing bowl. Blend with an electric mixer on low speed for 1 minute. Stop the machine and scrape down the sides of the bowl with a rubber spatula. Increase the mixer speed to

R

the Cake Mix Doctor says

To me, nuts taste better when they are toasted and when they have some crunch to them. The only problem with adding nuts to a cake batter is that they get lost and soggy and have no chance to toast. And they just interfere with the crumb of the cake. But when the nuts are tossed onto the bottom of the pan before you pour in the cake batter, they form the most delicious crust on top of the cake. This way they take on flavor and crunch and make a real contribution.

medium and beat 2 to 3 minutes more, scraping the sides down again if needed. The batter should look thick and well combined. Fold in the chocolate chips, making sure they are well distributed throughout the batter. Pour the batter into the prepared pan, smoothing it out with the rubber spatula. Place the pan in the oven.

3. Bake the cake until it is golden brown and springs back when lightly pressed with your finger, 55 to 60 minutes. Remove the pan from the oven and place it on a wire rack to cool for 20 minutes. Run a long, sharp knife around the edge of the cake and invert it onto a rack to cool completely, 20 minutes more.

4. Slide the cake onto a serving platter, dust with confectioners' sugar if desired, and slice.

✳ *Store this cake, wrapped in aluminum foil or plastic wrap, or in a cake saver, at room temperature for up to 1 week. Or freeze it, wrapped in foil, for up to 6 months. Thaw the cake overnight in the refrigerator before serving.*

CHOCOLATE CREAM CHEESE POUND CAKE

Maybe I should call this the "Chocolate Mailbox Masterpiece." When my friend Kathy Sellers was testing recipes for me, she would drive by early in the morning and place slices of the ones that she gave thumbs-up to in my mailbox. What a treat it was to hurry down to the mailbox those July mornings to see if a sample had arrived. Oh yes, I know it's against the law to place anything but mail in the box, but I am sure that if the mail carrier had come earlier than his usual time, he might have forgiven the plate of warm, moist, cream-cheese-laden chocolate pound cake. Or more likely, he might have helped himself to a slice and rescheduled his route for the future! Should I add that this cake is best served warm, or at summer-morning mailbox temperature?

SERVES: 16

PREPARATION TIME: 8 MINUTES

BAKING TIME: 58 TO 62 MINUTES

Vegetable oil spray for misting the pan
Flour for dusting the pan
1 package (18.25 ounces) plain butter
*   recipe fudge cake mix*
1 package (8 ounces) cream cheese,
*   at room temperature*
½ cup water
½ cup vegetable oil
¼ cup sugar
4 large eggs
2 teaspoons pure vanilla extract

1. Place a rack in the center of the oven and preheat the oven to 325°F. Lightly mist a 10-inch tube pan with vegetable oil spray, then dust with flour. Shake out the excess flour. Set the pan aside.

2. Place the cake mix, cream cheese, water, oil, sugar, eggs, and vanilla in a large mixing bowl. Blend with an electric mixer on low speed for 1 minute. Stop the machine and scrape down the sides of the bowl with a rubber spatula. Increase the mixer speed to medium and beat 2 minutes more, scraping the sides down again if needed. The batter should look well combined. Pour the batter into the prepared pan, smoothing it out with the rubber spatula. Place the pan in the oven.

3. Bake the cake until it springs back when lightly pressed with your finger and is just starting to pull away from the sides of the pan, 58 to 62 minutes. Remove the pan from the oven and place it on a wire rack to cool for 20 minutes. Run a long, sharp knife around the edge of the cake and invert it onto a rack, then invert it onto another rack so that it is large side up. Allow to cool for 20 minutes more.

4. Slide the cake onto a serving platter. Slice and serve.

R the Cake Mix Doctor says

Notice the lower oven temperature for baking this cake. That's because it is in a tube pan and needs to be baked slowly to cook through. Also, if you cook a cake this big at 350°F, it will darken and get crusty on the top and sides.

You must use room-temperature, or soft, cream cheese in this batter or it will lump up. To quickly soften cold cream cheese, unwrap it, place it on a microwave-safe plate, and microwave on high power for 30 seconds.

If you can't find the butter recipe fudge cake mix in your supermarket, use a plain devil's food cake mix, but increase the water to ¾ cup.

✳ *Store this cake, wrapped in aluminum foil or plastic wrap, or in a cake saver, at room temperature for up to 1 week. Or freeze it, wrapped in foil, for up to 6 months. Thaw the cake overnight in the refrigerator before serving.*

CHOCOLATE-ORANGE CREAM CHEESE POUND CAKE

WITH FRESH ORANGE DRIZZLE

My family was obsessed with cakes from scratch, pies from scratch, custards, puddings, cookies, and meringues—whether or not there was a special occasion! But while I vividly recall my grandmother's fresh orange cake at one end of the Christmas table and a triple-decker chocolate cake at the other end, I cannot think of a single family dessert that combined chocolate with orange. That was a taste combination I would be introduced to later in Paris while at cooking school. And merging those two was a taste revelation! This cake is a superb example. It calls for fresh orange juice because you need the oranges anyway for the zest.

SERVES: 16
PREPARATION TIME: 10 MINUTES
BAKING TIME: 60 TO 65 MINUTES
ASSEMBLY TIME: 5 MINUTES

Vegetable oil spray for misting the pan
Flour for dusting the pan
1 package (18.25 ounces) plain butter recipe fudge cake mix
1 package (8 ounces) cream cheese, at room temperature
½ cup fresh orange juice
½ cup vegetable oil
¼ cup sugar
4 large eggs
2 teaspoons pure vanilla extract
1 teaspoon grated orange zest
Fresh Orange Drizzle (page 453)

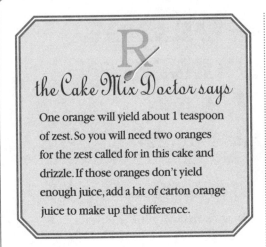

the Cake Mix Doctor says

One orange will yield about 1 teaspoon of zest. So you will need two oranges for the zest called for in this cake and drizzle. If those oranges don't yield enough juice, add a bit of carton orange juice to make up the difference.

1. Place a rack in the center of the oven and preheat the oven to 325°F. Lightly mist a 10-inch tube pan with vegetable oil spray, then dust with flour. Shake out the excess flour. Set the pan aside.

2. Place the cake mix, cream cheese, orange juice, oil, sugar, eggs, vanilla, and orange zest in a large mixing bowl. Blend with an electric mixer on low speed for 1 minute. Stop the machine and scrape down the sides of the bowl with a rubber spatula. Increase the mixer speed to medium and beat 2 minutes more, scraping the sides down again if needed. The batter should look well combined. Pour the batter into the prepared pan, smooth-

ing it out with the rubber spatula. Place the pan in the oven.

3. Bake the cake until it springs back when lightly pressed with your finger and is just starting to pull away from the sides of the pan, 60 to 65 minutes. Remove the pan from the oven and place it on a wire rack to cool for 25 minutes. Run a long, sharp knife around the edge of the cake and invert it onto a rack, then invert it onto another rack so the cake is large side up. Allow to cool for 25 minutes more.

4. Meanwhile, prepare the Fresh Orange Drizzle.

5. Spoon the glaze over the cooled cake, letting it drizzle down the sides and center of the cake. Let the cake rest for 10 minutes before slicing.

6. Slide the cake onto a serving platter. Slice and serve.

✱ *Store this cake, wrapped in aluminum foil or plastic wrap, or in a cake saver, at room temperature for up to 1 week. Or freeze it, wrapped in foil, for up to 6 months. Thaw the cake overnight in the refrigerator before serving.*

MINT CHOCOLATE CREAM CHEESE POUND CAKE

Mint and chocolate are one of the best flavor duos in the world. This cake combines both and is extremely easy, but the results are subtle because the Andes mints almost disappear in the baking. "What did you put in here? Mint extract? Fresh mint? Mint ice cream?" You don't have to reveal your secret. Rustle up some fresh mint from the garden or at the market for garnish, and leave them wondering.

SERVES: 16

PREPARATION TIME: 15 MINUTES

BAKING TIME: 58 TO 62 MINUTES

ASSEMBLY TIME: 2 MINUTES

Vegetable oil spray for misting the pan

Flour for dusting the pan

1 package (18.25 ounces) plain butter-recipe fudge cake mix

1 package (8 ounces) cream cheese, at room temperature

½ cup water

½ cup vegetable oil

¼ cup sugar

4 large eggs

1 teaspoon pure vanilla extract

1¼ cups (about 28) Andes chocolate mint candies, broken in half

1 tablespoon confectioners' sugar, for garnish

½ cup fresh mint sprigs, for garnish

1. Place a rack in the center of the oven and preheat the oven to 325°F. Lightly mist a 10-inch tube pan with vegetable oil spray, then dust with flour. Shake out the excess flour. Set the pan aside.

2. Place the cake mix, cream cheese,

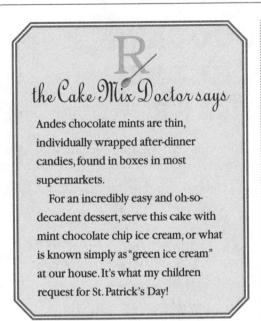

the Cake Mix Doctor says

Andes chocolate mints are thin, individually wrapped after-dinner candies, found in boxes in most supermarkets.

For an incredibly easy and oh-so-decadent dessert, serve this cake with mint chocolate chip ice cream, or what is known simply as "green ice cream" at our house. It's what my children request for St. Patrick's Day!

water, oil, sugar, eggs, and vanilla in a large mixing bowl. Blend with an electric mixer on low speed for 1 minute. Stop the machine and scrape down the sides of the bowl with a rubber spatula. Increase the mixer speed to medium and beat 2 minutes more, scraping the sides down again if needed. The batter should look well combined. Fold in the candy pieces

until they are well incorporated. Pour the batter into the prepared pan, smoothing it out with the rubber spatula. Place the pan in the oven.

3. Bake the cake until it springs back when lightly pressed with your finger and is just starting to pull away from the sides of the pan, 58 to 62 minutes. Remove the pan from the oven and place it on a wire rack to cool for 20 minutes. Run a long, sharp knife around the edge of the cake and invert it onto a rack, then invert it onto another rack so the cake is large side up. Allow to cool for 20 minutes more.

4. Slide the cake onto a serving platter, dust it with the confectioners' sugar, and garnish with the mint sprigs. Slice and serve.

✻ *Store this cake, wrapped in aluminum foil or plastic wrap, or in a cake saver, at room temperature for up to 1 week. Or freeze it, wrapped in foil, for up to 6 months. Thaw the cake overnight in the refrigerator before serving.*

A LIGHTER CHOCOLATE POUND CAKE

When it's summertime and the living isn't easy in the sweltering heat, I still have cake on the brain. And this is the one that often comes to mind. It has all the richness of the best pound cakes, but it is lighter on the palate. The secret is the vanilla yogurt, which adds body and depth but less fat than if you prepared the cake with sour cream. Serve it with vanilla frozen yogurt and sliced fresh peaches and you'll have a refreshing, comforting dessert that all ages will enjoy.

SERVES: 16

PREPARATION TIME: 10 MINUTES

BAKING TIME: 48 TO 52 MINUTES

R the Cake Mix Doctor says

The lower baking temperature keeps the edges from getting too dark and crusty. If you want to enrich it, go ahead and add a cup of semisweet chocolate chips. Or if you want to add an exotic touch, use almond extract instead of vanilla and scatter sliced toasted almonds on top of the cake and over the frozen yogurt you serve alongside. Yum.

Vegetable oil spray for misting the pan
Flour for dusting the pan
1 package (18.25 ounces) plain devil's food
    cake mix
1 package (3.9 ounces) chocolate instant
    pudding mix
1 cup vanilla low-fat yogurt
½ cup water
½ cup vegetable oil
4 large eggs
1 teaspoon pure vanilla extract

Special Diets

Dairy-free: For dietary and religious reasons many people forgo dairy products. It can be difficult finding a substitute for sour cream and buttermilk, but here are some suggestions from readers:

- Add white vinegar to a nondairy creamer to make buttermilk.

- Tofutti makes a dairy-free sour cream and cream cheese.

Sugar-free: Sugar-free cake mixes are available in most supermarkets. Frost them with sugar-free puddings. Or to cut back on sugar, omit any sugar that is added to cake mix recipes in this book. Instead of frosting the cake, dust it with cocoa powder before serving.

Low-cholesterol: Egg substitutes can be used instead of eggs. Consult the package directions for making this substitution. When melted butter is called for, substitute canola oil. And if desired, omit half the oil and use applesauce, pumpkin, or mashed banana instead.

1. Place a rack in the center of the oven and preheat the oven to 325°F. Lightly mist a 12-cup Bundt pan with vegetable oil spray, then dust with flour. Shake out the excess flour. Set the pan aside.

2. Place the cake mix, pudding mix, yogurt, water, oil, eggs, and vanilla in a large mixing bowl. Blend with an electric mixer on low speed for 1 minute. Stop the machine and scrape down the sides of the bowl with a rubber spatula. Increase the mixer speed to medium and beat 2 minutes more, scraping the sides down again if needed. The batter should look thick and well combined. Pour the batter into the prepared pan, smoothing it out with the rubber spatula. Place the pan in the oven.

3. Bake the cake until it springs back when lightly pressed with your finger, 48 to 52 minutes. Remove the pan from the oven and place it on a wire rack to cool for 20 minutes. Run a long, sharp knife around the edge of the cake and invert it onto a rack to cool completely, 20 minutes more.

4. Slide the cake onto a serving platter and slice.

✳ *Store this cake, wrapped in plastic wrap or aluminum foil, or in a cake saver or under a glass dome, at room temperature for up to 1 week. Or freeze it, wrapped in foil, for up to 6 months. Thaw the cake overnight in the refrigerator before serving.*

GOOD-FOR-YOU CHOCOLATE POUND CAKE

WITH SHINY CHOCOLATE GLAZE

Everyone should be able to enjoy chocolate cake. This unbeliev- ably moist pound cake is perfect for the cholesterol-conscious who can't eat eggs. It calls for egg substitute and for unsweetened applesauce, which keeps it so moist that you don't need to add oil.

....

SERVES: 16

PREPARATION TIME: 8 MINUTES

BAKING TIME: 37 TO 40 MINUTES

ASSEMBLY TIME: 5 MINUTES

....

Vegetable oil spray for misting the pan

Flour for dusting the pan

1 package (18.25 ounces) plain devil's food cake mix

1 cup water

the Cake Mix Doctor says

When substituting Egg Beaters for whole eggs, figure on ¼ cup per egg. If you are using another brand of egg substitute, check the label to see how much you need to use for each egg. (This is a three-egg cake, should you want to bake it with real eggs.)

The chocolate glaze is shiny, sticky, and low-fat. It is delicious, but it will not set up hard like some glazes. So you can glaze and slice without waiting!

½ cup unsweetened applesauce

¾ cup Egg Beaters (or other egg substitute; see "the Cake Mix Doctor says")

Shiny Chocolate Glaze (page 450)

1. Place a rack in the center of the oven and preheat the oven to 325°F. Lightly

If the Cake Sticks to the Pan

Help! What a horrible situation. You've baked this magnificent cake, and when you go to invert the cake onto a rack to cool, nothing happens. The cake will not budge. So you shake a little harder, getting aggravated by this point, and only a portion of the cake lets go. The rest hangs onto the pan. Believe me, I've been there.

If half the cake is on the rack and the other half remains glued to the pan, run a metal spatula underneath the remaining cake to help it give way, then piece the cake back together on the platter. If you pour enough glaze over the top of a patched Bundt or tube cake, you can hide the damage. (I have even done this right before appearing on television!) Layer cakes are even easier to patch back together, since you're covering them with frosting—if necessary, a lot of frosting!

The next time you're about to invert a cake, run a knife around the edge of the pan first and give the cake quarter-turn shakes to loosen it. Place the rack or serving platter upside down on top of the cake pan, then invert both with one final shake so the cake lands right side up.

You can reduce the chances of sticking if you prepare the pan the right way first. For layers, grease the pan with solid vegetable shortening and dust them with flour. For Bundts and tubes, mist well with a vegetable oil spray, making sure the spray gets between all the grooves, and dust well with flour. The same applies

---

mist a 12-cup Bundt pan with vegetable oil spray, then dust with flour. Shake out the excess flour. Set the pan aside.

2. Place the cake mix, water, applesauce, and Egg Beaters in a large mixing bowl. Blend with an electric mixer on low speed for 1 minute. Stop the machine and scrape down the sides of the bowl with a rubber spatula. Increase the mixer speed to medium and beat 2 minutes more, scraping the sides down again if needed. The batter should look thick and well combined. Pour the batter into the prepared pan, smoothing it out with the rubber spatula. Place the pan in the oven.

3. Bake the cake until it springs back when lightly pressed with your finger, 37 to 40 minutes. Remove the pan from the oven and place it on a wire rack to cool for

to miniature Bundts and tubes, which can be frustrating to unmold because the surfaces are so much smaller. If you will be unmolding a sheet cake, mist the pan with vegetable oil spray, then dust with flour. Angel foods and chiffon cakes are different creatures: Their batters should be poured into ungreased, unfloured pans so they rise up tall. Just run a long sharp knife around the inside and outside edges of the pan and give that cake a good shake. It will come out.

And if not? Here are some ways to create an incredible layered dessert out of those pieces, hunks, or strips of cake.

• **Trifles.** As in the Brownie Chocolate Mousse Trifle (page 251), layer 1-inch pieces of brownies, chocolate mousse, thawed whipped topping, and toffee chips in a large glass bowl or trifle dish. You can also use chocolate cake, brushing it with an orange- or coffee-flavored liqueur first.

• **Terrines.** Following the instructions for the Pear and Chocolate Terrine (page 241), layer strips of cake with sautéed fruit and a cream cheese filling in a loaf pan. Place heavy canned goods on top of the terrine for 24 hours to weight it down. Slice the compressed terrine, and serve it with whipped cream or a chocolate sauce.

• **Icebox cakes.** See the Deep Chocolate Almond Angel Icebox Cake (page 280). Tear off chunks of angel food or chiffon cake, and layer them with ice cream and whipped cream in a pretty dish. Cover and freeze until firm. Let soften a bit before spooning into bowls.

20 minutes. Run a long, sharp knife around the edge of the cake and invert it onto a rack to cool completely, 20 minutes more.

4. Meanwhile, prepare the Shiny Chocolate Glaze.

5. Pour the glaze over the cake on the rack, then slide the cake onto a serving platter and slice.

✳ *Store this cake, in a cake saver or under a glass dome, at room temperature for up to 1 week. Or freeze it, wrapped in foil, for up to 6 months. Thaw the cake overnight in the refrigerator before serving.*

INCREDIBLE MOCHA MELTED ICE CREAM CAKE

WITH CHOCOLATE MARSHMALLOW FROSTING

Nothing pleases me more than for someone to adapt one of my recipes, adding their own choice of ingredients, and turning out a fun and different cake. That's precisely what happened with this talked-about recipe, which usually is made with Ben & Jerry's Cherry Garcia Ice Cream. A meeting was scheduled at my publisher's office in New York, and those clever people at Workman folded coffee ice cream into my ice cream cake, added a dash of espresso powder, and enrobed it in Chocolate Marsh-mallow Frosting. That cake had us all sitting up and paying attention!

SERVES: 16

PREPARATION TIME: 7 MINUTES

BAKING TIME: 40 TO 45 MINUTES

ASSEMBLY TIME: 5 MINUTES

Vegetable oil spray for misting the pan
Flour for dusting the pan
1 package (18.25 ounces) plain white
   cake mix
2 cups best-quality coffee ice cream, melted
3 large eggs
1 tablespoon instant coffee powder or
   espresso powder
Chocolate Marshmallow Frosting (page 439)

1. Place a rack in the center of the oven and preheat the oven to 350°F. Lightly mist a 12-cup Bundt pan with vegetable oil spray, then dust with flour. Shake out the excess flour. Set the pan aside.

2. Place the cake mix, melted ice cream, eggs, and coffee powder in a large mixing bowl. Blend with an electric mixer on low speed for

1 minute. Stop the machine and scrape down the sides of the bowl with a rubber spatula. Increase the mixer speed to medium and beat 2 to 3 minutes more, scraping the sides down again if needed. The batter should look thick and well combined. Pour the batter into the prepared pan, smoothing it out with the rubber spatula. Place the pan in the oven.

3. Bake the cake until it springs back when lightly pressed with your finger and is just starting to pull away from the sides of the pan, 40 to 45 minutes. Remove the pan from the oven and place it on a wire rack to cool for 20 minutes. Run a long, sharp knife around the edge of the cake and invert it onto a rack to cool completely, 20 minutes more.

4. Meanwhile, prepare the Chocolate Marshmallow Frosting.

5. Slide the cake onto a serving platter, and pour the warm frosting over the cake. Let the cake rest for 10 minutes before slicing.

6. Slice and serve.

✳ *Store this cake, in a cake saver or under a glass dome, at room temperature for up to 1 week. Or freeze it, wrapped in aluminum foil, for up to 6 months. Thaw the cake overnight in the refrigerator before serving.*

R℔

the Cake Mix Doctor says

You will find espresso powder at most supermarkets and in specialty markets. If not, just grind instant coffee granules in a coffee grinder or food processor until smooth.

Make sure you use super-premium ice cream in this recipe. Not only do you want the pure and simple ingredients that it offers, but you will find that it melts true. That is, 2 cups of ice cream will melt into 2 cups liquid ice cream. (And you know, it doesn't matter if it isn't completely melted. I've mixed up plenty of these cakes on television when the ice cream was semi-melted, and they turned out beautifully!)

I have tested this recipe with other flavors of cake mix, but I don't find the consistency as good as it is with a white cake mix. Above all, make sure the mix doesn't contain pudding. This is a heavy cake on its own and has been known to sink around the center as it is removed from the oven. You don't want pudding in this recipe!

DARN GOOD CHOCOLATE CAKE

WITH MARTHA'S CHOCOLATE ICING

Great recipes need repeating. When this book was in the planning stages, I was thinking of the handful of recipes I wanted to carry over from book one to book two. Surely some of the frostings, and most definitely the Darn Good Chocolate Cake, I thought. It's a classic in our family. While in college, a cousin of mine used to call her Aunt Louise a week or so before she planned a visit home just to make sure there would be a Darn Good Chocolate Cake ready and waiting on the kitchen counter. And from the looks of the letters and e-mail messages that have poured in, this cake gets a warm reception no matter where you call home. So why in the world would I bother to gild the lily and suggest you frost this perfection of a chocolate cake? Well, just in case you want to dress it up for a dinner party or a birthday—instead of sprinkling it with a tablespoon of confectioners' sugar, pour Martha Bowden's terrific cooked icing over the cake. Chocolate on chocolate, and chocolate inside chocolate. Serious stuff, indeed!

....

SERVES: 16

PREPARATION TIME: 10 MINUTES

BAKING TIME: 58 TO 62 MINUTES

ASSEMBLY TIME: 5 MINUTES

....

Vegetable oil spray for misting the pan

Flour for dusting the pan

1 package (18.25 ounces) plain devil's food
or dark chocolate fudge cake mix

1 package (3.9 ounces) chocolate instant
pudding mix

1 cup sour cream

½ cup water

½ cup vegetable oil

4 large eggs

1½ cups semisweet chocolate chips

Martha's Chocolate Icing (page 433)

1. Place a rack in the center of the oven and preheat the oven to 350°F. Lightly mist a 12-cup Bundt pan with vegetable oil spray, then dust with flour. Shake out the excess flour. Set the pan aside.

2. Place the cake mix, pudding mix, sour cream, water, oil, and eggs in a large mixing bowl. Blend with an electric mixer on low speed for 1 minute. Stop the machine and scrape down the sides of the bowl with a rubber spatula. Increase the mixer speed to medium and beat 2 to 3 minutes more, scraping the sides down again if needed. The batter should look thick and well combined. Fold in the chocolate chips, making sure they are well distributed throughout the batter. Pour the batter into the prepared pan, smoothing it out with the rubber spatula. Place the pan in the oven.

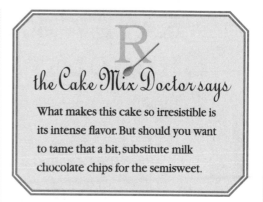

the Cake Mix Doctor says

What makes this cake so irresistible is its intense flavor. But should you want to tame that a bit, substitute milk chocolate chips for the semisweet.

3. Bake the cake until it springs back when lightly pressed with your finger and is just starting to pull away from the sides of the pan, 58 to 62 minutes. Remove the pan from the oven and place it on a wire rack to cool for 20 minutes. Run a long, sharp knife around the edge of the cake and invert it onto a rack to cool completely, 20 minutes more.

4. Meanwhile, prepare Martha's Chocolate Icing.

5. Place the cake on a serving platter and pour the warm icing over it. Let the cake rest for 10 minutes before slicing, then slice and serve.

✳ *Store this cake, wrapped in aluminum foil or plastic wrap, or in a cake saver, at room temperature for up to 1 week. Or freeze it, wrapped in foil, for up to 6 months. Thaw the cake overnight in the refrigerator before serving.*

KATHY'S CHOCOLATE CHOCOLATE CHIP CAKE

Here's another lip-smacking chocolate pound cake and a slightly different way of arriving at it. This recipe is a bit lighter than the Darn Good Chocolate Cake. It uses milk instead of sour cream, and it incorporates miniature chocolate chips, which suspend better in this batter. There's no need to frost the cake—it's that rich and good. If you want to dress it up, however, dust it with a bit of confectioners' sugar or pour the Simple Sugar Glaze (page 455) over it. My friend Kathy Sellers, who created this recipe, suggests serving it with peppermint ice cream and hot fudge sauce. Go ahead—I dare you!

SERVES: 16
PREPARATION TIME: 10 MINUTES
BAKING TIME: 50 TO 55 MINUTES
ASSEMBLY TIME: 5 M FINUTES

Vegetable oil spray for misting the pan
Flour for dusting the pan
1 package (18.25 ounces) plain devil's food
    or dark chocolate fudge cake mix
1 package (3.9 ounces) chocolate instant
    pudding mix
1 cup whole milk
1 cup vegetable oil
4 large eggs
1½ cups miniature semisweet chocolate chips

1. Place a rack in the center of the oven and preheat the oven to 350°F. Lightly mist a 10-inch tube pan with vegetable oil spray, then dust with flour. Shake out the excess flour. Set the pan aside.

2. Place the cake mix, pudding mix, milk, oil, and eggs in a large mixing bowl. Blend with an electric mixer on low speed for

the Cake Mix Doctor says

Many experienced bakers believe that Bundt and tube cakes bake up more moist and tender when they cook at 325° instead of 350°F. This recipe was tested at both temperatures and with different amounts of chocolate chips. The lower temperature did produce a moist cake, but it was not enough of a difference to warrant the longer cooking time. So I settled for 350°F. To make sure your chocolate cakes that bake at 350°F for nearly an hour don't overbrown, place the rack near the center of the oven and not higher. If your oven tends to bake hot, bake at 325°F. (See "The Ideal Temperature," page 149.)

1 minute. Stop the machine and scrape down the sides of the bowl with a rubber spatula. Increase the mixer speed to medium and beat 2 to 3 minutes more,

scraping the sides down again if needed. The batter should look thick and well combined. Fold in the chocolate chips, making sure they are well distributed throughout the batter. Pour the batter into the prepared pan, smoothing it out with the rubber spatula. Place the pan in the oven.

3. Bake the cake until it springs back when lightly pressed with your finger and is just starting to pull away from the sides of the pan, 50 to 55 minutes. Remove the pan from the oven and place it on a wire rack to cool for 20 minutes. Run a long, sharp knife around the edge of the cake and invert it onto a rack, then invert it onto another rack so the cake is large side up. Allow to cool for 20 minutes more.

4. Slide the cake onto a serving platter and slice.

✳ *Store this cake, wrapped in aluminum foil or plastic wrap, or in a cake saver, at room temperature for up to 1 week. Or freeze it, wrapped in foil, for up to 6 months. Thaw the cake overnight in the refrigerator before serving.*

CHOCOLATE MACAROON RING CAKE

Jeanne Taylor, who lives in Florida, sent in this wonderful recipe for a chocolate cake filled with a chewy almond and coconut macaroon. I added a simple almond glaze to give a crowning touch to this special cake.

·················

SERVES: 16
PREPARATION TIME: 20 MINUTES
BAKING TIME: 53 TO 57 MINUTES
ASSEMBLY TIME: 5 MINUTES

·················

MACAROON FILLING:

2 large eggs
½ teaspoon pure almond extract
½ cup granulated sugar
⅔ cup sweetened flaked coconut
¼ cup all-purpose flour

CAKE:

Vegetable oil spray for misting the pan
Flour for dusting the pan
1 package (18.25 ounces) devil's food cake mix with pudding
1 large egg
1 cup water
⅓ cup vegetable oil

ALMOND GLAZE:

1¼ cups confectioners' sugar, sifted
1 to 2 tablespoons milk
½ teaspoon pure almond extract

1. Prepare the filling: Separate the eggs, placing the whites in a medium-size mixing bowl and the yolks in a large mixing bowl. Set the yolks aside. Add the almond extract to the egg whites and beat with an electric mixer on high speed until frothy, 30 seconds. Gradually add the sugar while beating at high speed until soft peaks form, 1 to 1½ minutes. Fold in the coconut and flour until just incorporated. Set the bowl aside while you prepare the cake.

2. Place a rack in the center of the oven and preheat the oven to 350°F. Lightly mist a 12-cup Bundt pan with vegetable oil spray, then dust with flour. Shake out the excess flour. Set the pan aside.

3. Place the cake mix in the bowl with the reserved egg yolks. Add the whole egg, water, and oil. Blend with an electric mixer on low speed for 30 seconds. Stop the machine and scrape down the sides of the bowl with a rubber spatula. Increase the mixer speed to medium and beat 2 minutes more, scraping the sides down again if needed. The batter should look thick and well combined.

4. Pour half of the batter into the prepared pan. Spoon the macaroon filling in a ring on top of the batter, making sure it does not touch the sides of the pan. Spoon the remaining batter over the filling, smoothing it out with the rubber spatula. Place the pan in the oven.

5. Bake the cake until it springs back when lightly pressed with your finger and is just starting to pull away from the sides of the pan, 53 to 57 minutes. Remove the pan from the oven and place it on a wire rack to cool for 20 minutes. Run a long, sharp knife around the edge of the cake and invert it onto a rack to cool completely, 20 minutes more.

6. For the glaze, place the confectioners' sugar in a small bowl and whisk in enough milk to make a spoonable mixture. Whisk in the almond extract.

7. Place the cake on a serving platter and spoon the glaze over it. Let the cake rest for 10 minutes before slicing.

8. Slice and serve.

✳ *Store this cake, in a cake saver or under a glass dome, at room temperature for up to 1 week. Or freeze it, wrapped in foil, for up to 6 months. Thaw the cake overnight in the refrigerator before serving.*

R
the Cake Mix Doctor says

If you want to pull out all the stops, toast a handful of sliced almonds and flaked coconut and sprinkle the mixture on the cake while the glaze is still sticky.

Remember that egg whites will whip to a greater volume if they are at room temperature. So if you have a chance to remove the eggs from the refrigerator an hour before baking, do so.

MILK CHOCOLATE CHERRY POUND CAKE

WITH MILK CHOCOLATE GLAZE

When I first prepared this cake with chocolate chips in the batter, and a yummy milk chocolate glaze, I kept tasting the flavor of cherry. And I liked it. And I wanted more of that taste. So the next version of the recipe contained just what the cake needed: chopped maraschino cherries. If you are not a cherry fan, you can omit them. But you still may taste them—the Swiss chocolate mix plus the milk chocolate chips equals a faint cherry flavor.

SERVES: 16
PREPARATION TIME: 10 MINUTES
BAKING TIME: 55 TO 60 MINUTES
ASSEMBLY TIME: 5 MINUTES

Vegetable oil spray for misting the pan
Flour for dusting the pan
1 package (18.25 ounces) plain Swiss
 chocolate or devil's food cake mix
1 package (3.9 ounces) chocolate instant
 pudding mix
¾ cup water
⅔ cup vegetable oil
4 large eggs
1½ cups milk chocolate chips
½ cup chopped maraschino cherries
Milk Chocolate Glaze (page 448)

1. Place a rack in the center of the oven and preheat the oven to 325°F. Lightly mist a 10-inch tube pan with vegetable oil spray, then dust with flour. Shake out the excess flour. Set the pan aside.

All About Pudding Mix

I am often asked which type of pudding mix to add to cake batters—instant or cook-and-serve? (The instant pudding is assembled with cold milk; the cook-and-serve is made with hot milk, and then the mixture is chilled.) When adding dry pudding mix to a cake mix batter, I find little difference between the two types (although what I have read suggests the instant should dissolve better in cold batters). The real difference here is selection: There are more flavors of instant pudding mix (banana, pistachio, white chocolate, as well as the usual vanilla and chocolate) than there are of cook-and-serve.

Why add pudding mix? It makes a cake more moist, makes the crumb more dense, and gives the cake more structure. That's why pudding mix cakes are especially suited to Bundt and tube pans—they hold their shape, withstand the longer baking time required, and give the support needed to suspend chocolate chips, nuts, and dried fruit in the batter.

Why add pudding mix to a plain cake mix when you can buy a cake mix with the pudding already inside? The plain cake mix will bake up taller and is less likely to shrink back from the edges as it cools. You can use the mix with pudding inside, but the cake will not rise as much.

And what about preparing the pudding mix with milk as the package directs and then folding the pudding into the cake batter? I have tried this, but I find the cakes too heavy. What does work is the pudding cake method, in which prepared pudding is poured over the batter before the cake goes into the oven and the cake bakes up with a moist and gooey center (see the Molten Chocolate Pudding Cake, page 230, and the Chocolate-Cinnamon Banana Pudding Cake, page 233).

2. Place the cake mix, pudding mix, water, oil, and eggs in a large mixing bowl. Blend with an electric mixer on low speed for 1 minute. Stop the machine and scrape down the sides of the bowl with a rubber spatula. Increase the mixer speed to medium and beat 2 minutes more, scraping the sides down again if needed. The batter will be very thick. Fold in the chocolate chips and cherries, making sure they are well distributed throughout the batter. Pour the batter into the prepared pan, smoothing it out with the rubber spatula. Place the pan in the oven.

R

the Cake Mix Doctor says

It's funny how one brand or flavor of cake mix will be available in your market but may never appear in the stores in a neighboring state. It has to do with which mixes sell best in your area. If you cannot find the Swiss chocolate cake mix in your store, just use devil's food. And if you want a more upscale cake, substitute dried cherries that you have soaked in a little kirsch or cherry liqueur.

3. Bake the cake until it springs back when lightly pressed with your finger and is just starting to pull away from the sides of the pan, 55 to 60 minutes. Remove the pan from the oven and place it on a wire rack to cool for 20 minutes. Run a long, sharp knife around the edge of the cake and invert it onto a rack, then invert it onto another rack so the cake is large side up. Allow to cool for 20 minutes more.

4. Meanwhile, prepare the Milk Chocolate Glaze.

5. Place the cake on a serving platter and pour the warm glaze over it. Let the cake rest for 10 minutes before slicing.

6. Slice and serve.

✸ *Store this cake, wrapped in aluminum foil or plastic wrap, or in a cake saver, at room temperature for up to 1 week. Or freeze it, wrapped in foil, for up to 6 months. Thaw the cake overnight in the refrigerator before serving.*

EASY HERSHEY® BAR SWIRL CAKE

According to the folks at Hershey's, the Hershey® Bar Swirl Cake has been a most-requested recipe for a long time. To simplify the recipe, Hershey's came up with a cake mix version not too long ago. This is one fun cake, and I have tweaked Hershey's recipe only slightly, reducing the number of pecans in the swirl and adding vanilla to the cake and the glaze. Two gargantuan Hershey bars, as well as half a cup of chocolate syrup, went into this cake and glaze. Do I need to say that this is a very sweet cake?

SERVES: 16
PREPARATION TIME: 15 MINUTES
BAKING TIME: 43 TO 47 MINUTES
ASSEMBLY TIME: 5 MINUTES

CAKE:

Vegetable oil spray for misting the pan
Flour for dusting the pan
1 package (18.25 ounces) yellow cake mix
    with pudding
1⅓ cups water
½ cup vegetable oil
3 large eggs
1 teaspoon pure vanilla extract
¼ cup light corn syrup
½ cup finely chopped pecans
1 large Hershey's milk chocolate bar
    (7 ounces)
½ cup chocolate syrup

EASY MILK CHOCOLATE GLAZE:

1 large Hershey's milk chocolate bar
    (7 ounces)
2 tablespoons solid vegetable shortening
1 teaspoon pure vanilla extract

1. Place a rack in the center of the oven and preheat the oven to 350°F. Lightly mist a 12-cup Bundt pan with vegetable oil spray, then dust with flour. Shake out the excess flour. Set the pan aside.

2. Place the cake mix, water, oil, eggs, and vanilla in a large mixing bowl. Blend with an electric mixer on low speed for 1 minute. Stop the machine and scrape down the sides of the bowl with a rubber spatula. Increase the mixer speed to medium and beat 2 minutes more, scraping the sides down again if needed. The batter should look thick and well combined.

3. Measure out 2 cups of the batter and place it in a medium-size mixing bowl. Stir in the corn syrup and pecans. Set the bowl aside.

R

the Cake Mix Doctor says

This glaze is incredibly easy, but you must use vegetable shortening, not butter, margarine, oil, or any of the blends or spreads.

The light corn syrup in the batter allows the pecan batter to swirl perfectly throughout the cake.

4. Break the chocolate bar into pieces, and place those pieces in a small microwave-safe bowl along with the chocolate syrup. Microwave the chocolate at high power for 1 minute and then stir until smooth; return the bowl to the microwave for a few seconds if needed. Fold the melted chocolate into the remaining plain batter until well incorporated.

5. Pour the chocolate batter into the prepared pan, smoothing it out with the rubber spatula. Spoon the pecan batter evenly over the top. Place the pan in the oven.

6. Bake the cake until it springs back when lightly pressed with your finger and is just starting to pull away from the sides of the pan, 43 to 47 minutes. Remove the pan from the oven and place it on a wire rack to cool for 20 minutes. Run a long, sharp knife around the edge of the cake and invert it onto a rack to cool completely, 20 minutes more.

7. To prepare the glaze, break the chocolate bar into pieces, and place those pieces and the shortening in a small microwave-safe bowl. Microwave at high power for 1 minute, and then stir until the chocolate has melted; return the bowl to the microwave for a few more seconds if needed. Stir in the vanilla. Spoon the glaze over the cooled cake,

Chocolate Whipped Cream

$\mathcal{T}$here are several ways to add the flavor of chocolate to whipped cream. Remember that it is better to slightly underwhip cream than to overwhip it.

• Whip 1 cup heavy cream until soft peaks just begin to form. Drizzle 1 tablespoon chocolate syrup over it. Continue whipping until soft peaks have formed.

• For every 1 cup heavy cream, add ¼ cup confectioners' sugar and 1 tablespoon Dutch-process cocoa powder. Beat on highest speed until thickened but not stiff, 3 to 4 minutes.

• Fold whipped cream into cooled melted semisweet chocolate. Use about 2 ounces of chocolate for every 2 cups whipped cream.

• And for a chocolate chip appearance, drizzle just-melted semisweet chocolate into very cold whipped cream, then fold to combine. The chocolate cap cools and breaks into small pieces when folded in. Use 1 ounce of chocolate for every 2 cups whipped cream.

allowing it to drip down the sides of the cake. Let the cake rest for 10 minutes before slicing.

8. Slide the cake onto a serving platter. Slice and serve.

✳ *Store this cake, in a cake saver or under a glass dome, at room temperature for up to 1 week. Or freeze it, wrapped in foil, for up to 6 months. Thaw the cake overnight in the refrigerator before serving.*

AMAZING GERMAN CHOCOLATE CAKE

I have a special affinity for Raleigh, North Carolina, and it all has to do with this recipe. Before I was to make a scheduled book publicity visit to Raleigh, I was the guest on a local radio program. A woman called and asked if I had ever heard of a German chocolate cake recipe in which you dump a container of store-bought frosting into the bowl with the rest of the ingredients. At first, I was aghast! After all, I'm a believer in from-scratch frosting *on* my cake mix cakes. Why would I want store-bought frosting *in* my cake? And then people called in and chatted about this cake and desperately wanted the recipe. When I finally arrived in Raleigh, people were still talking about that cake at my book signing. And this was a cake I had never laid eyes on. Well, I realized I had to get back in my kitchen and try to come up with that recipe. And I must tell you it's worth all the commotion. It's a dandy of a Bundt cake, containing just five ingredients. And no one would ever believe the amazing "secret" ingredient!

....

SERVES: 16
PREPARATION TIME: 8 MINUTES
BAKING TIME: 48 TO 52 MINUTES

....

Vegetable oil spray for misting the pan
Flour for dusting the pan
1 package (18.25 ounces) plain German
*   chocolate cake mix*
1 container (15 ounces) coconut pecan frosting
1 cup water
⅓ cup vegetable oil
3 large eggs

R

the Cake Mix Doctor says

This is a super-moist cake, obviously, with all the fat in the frosting! So you really don't want a glaze on it at all. If anything, dust it with confectioners' sugar just before serving.

If you have a little extra grated German chocolate on hand, add up to ½ cup to the batter. German chocolate is easily grated in a food processor, and it keeps in a cool dry place in a zipper-lock bag. Add it to German chocolate cake batters to intensify the flavor.

1. Place a rack in the center of the oven and preheat the oven to 350°F. Lightly mist a 12-cup Bundt pan with vegetable oil spray, then dust with flour. Shake out the excess flour. Set the pan aside.

2. Place the cake mix, frosting, water, oil, and eggs in a large mixing bowl. Blend with an electric mixer on low speed for 1 minute. Stop the machine and scrape down the sides of the bowl with a rubber spatula. Increase the mixer speed to medium and beat 2 minutes more, scraping the sides down again if needed. The batter should look thick and well combined. Pour the batter into the prepared pan, smoothing it out with the rubber spatula. Place the pan in the oven.

3. Bake the cake until it springs back when lightly pressed with your finger, 48 to 52 minutes. Remove the pan from the oven and place it on a wire rack to cool for 20 minutes. Run a long, sharp knife around the edge of the cake and invert it onto a rack to cool completely, 20 minutes more.

4. Slide the cake onto a serving platter and slice.

✽ *Store this cake, wrapped in plastic wrap or aluminum foil, or in a cake saver or under a glass dome, at room temperature for up to 1 week. Or freeze it, wrapped in foil, for up to 6 months. Thaw the cake overnight in the refrigerator before serving.*

CHOCOLATE BANANA POUND CAKE

WITH CHOCOLATE CINNAMON GLAZE

Now you see them, now you don't. That applies to the cinnamon chips, which disappear as they bake into this cake, and it also describes how slices of this moist banana-fragrant cake will disappear as soon as they are served. But that's hardly surprising. Begin with a German chocolate cake mix, add buttermilk, ripe bananas, and cinnamon chips, and top the cake with a cocoa and cinnamon chip glaze, and, well, you have magic flavors in the mouth!

SERVES: 16
PREPARATION TIME: 8 MINUTES
BAKING TIME: 38 TO 40 MINUTES
ASSEMBLY TIME: 5 MINUTES

Vegetable oil spray for misting the pan
Flour for dusting the pan
2 ripe bananas
1 package (18.25 ounces) plain German chocolate cake mix
¾ cup buttermilk
½ cup vegetable oil
3 large eggs
1 teaspoon pure vanilla extract
1 cup cinnamon chips
Chocolate Cinnamon Glaze (page 451)

1. Place a rack in the center of the oven and preheat the oven to 350°F. Lightly mist a 12-cup Bundt pan with vegetable oil spray, then dust with flour. Shake out the excess flour. Set the pan aside.

2. Peel the bananas and place them in a large mixing bowl. With the electric mixer on low speed, blend them until mashed. Add the cake mix, buttermilk, oil, eggs, and vanilla to the bananas. Blend with an electric mixer on low speed for 1 minute. Stop the machine and scrape down the sides of the bowl with a rubber spatula. Increase the mixer speed to medium and beat 2 minutes more, scraping the sides down again if needed. The batter should look thick and well combined. Fold in the cinnamon chips, making sure they are well distributed throughout the batter. Pour the batter into the prepared pan, smoothing it out with the rubber spatula. Place the pan in the oven.

3. Bake the cake until it springs back when lightly pressed with your finger and is just starting to pull away from the sides of the pan, 38 to 40 minutes. Remove the pan from the oven and place it on a wire rack to cool for 20 minutes. Run a long, sharp knife around the edge of the cake and invert it onto a rack to cool completely, 20 minutes more.

4. Meanwhile, prepare the Chocolate Cinnamon Glaze. Spoon the glaze over the cooled cake. Let the cake rest for 10 minutes before slicing.

5. Place the cake on a serving platter, slice, and serve.

❋ *Store this cake, wrapped in aluminum foil or plastic wrap, or in a cake saver, at room temperature for up to 1 week. Or freeze it, wrapped in foil, for up to 6 months. Thaw the cake overnight in the refrigerator before serving.*

the Cake Mix Doctor says

Cinnamon chips, made by Hershey's, are wonderful folded into chocolate cookies and cakes, but when combined with bananas, their intensity is near magical. A 10-ounce bag of these chips will yield about 1⅔ cups, enough for both the cake and the glaze.

Cinnamon chips melt more quickly than chocolate chips, so they dissolve into the cake batter instead of firming up on cooling.

GERMAN CHOCOLATE CHIP POUND CAKE

This cake had barely a moment to cool on my kitchen counter when it was sliced into by my cousin Joe. The Brady boys are notorious for diving into hot bread right from the oven, so how could I have expected Joe to resist hot chocolate cake? And I will admit the combination of German chocolate batter and semisweet chips is intoxicating. Especially when chased by a glass of cold milk.

SERVES: 16

PREPARATION TIME: 10 MINUTES

BAKING TIME: 58 TO 62 MINUTES

ASSEMBLY TIME: 3 MINUTES

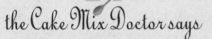

the Cake Mix Doctor says

This recipe conveniently uses up a large bag of miniature chocolate chips: 1½ cups in the cake batter and the remaining ½ cup in the glaze.

In a rush? Forgo the glaze, and use a German chocolate cake mix with pudding instead of adding pudding mix. In the mood for almond? Add 1 teaspoon pure almond extract to the batter.

CAKE:

Vegetable oil spray for misting the pan

Flour for dusting the pan

1 package (18.25 ounces) plain German chocolate cake mix

1 package (3.9 ounces) chocolate fudge instant pudding mix

1 cup sour cream

½ cup water

½ cup vegetable oil

4 large eggs

1½ cups miniature semisweet chocolate chips

Sour Cream

Sour cream could be called the silent hero of this book. Why is it so delicious added to a chocolate cake batter? Like buttermilk, sour cream works well with chocolate because it is acidic, as is chocolate. Sour cream is made from light cream (18 to 20 percent fat) that is pasteurized and treated with lactic acid–producing bacteria that give it that distinctive tang. It is delicious atop baked potatoes or tortilla soup because it is a foil to hot and spicy foods, being cool and wet and quenching. And in baked goods it adds moisture to the batter and makes the result more dense and rich and palatable. Light or reduced-fat sour cream, made from half-and-half, contains 40 percent less fat than regular sour cream. Reduced-fat sour cream will work in recipes that call for sour cream— the outcome just won't be as rich. Fat-free sour cream, on the other hand, should not be substituted for regular sour cream.

GLAZE:

½ cup miniature semisweet
    chocolate chips

2 tablespoons milk

1. Place a rack in the center of the oven and preheat the oven to 350°F. Lightly mist a 12-cup Bundt pan with vegetable oil spray, then dust with flour. Shake out the excess flour. Set the pan aside.

2. Place the cake mix, pudding mix, sour cream, water, oil, and eggs in a large mixing bowl. Blend with an electric mixer on low speed for 1 minute. Stop the machine and scrape down the sides of the bowl with a rubber spatula. Increase the mixer speed to medium and beat 2 to 3 minutes more, scraping the sides down again if needed. The batter should look thick and well combined. Fold in the chocolate chips, making sure they are well distributed throughout the batter. Pour the batter into the prepared pan, smoothing it out with the rubber spatula. Place the pan in the oven.

3. Bake the cake until it springs back when lightly pressed with your finger and is just starting to pull away from the sides of the pan, 58 to 62 minutes. Remove the pan from the oven and place it on a wire rack to cool for 20 minutes. Run a long, sharp knife around the edge of the cake and invert it onto a rack to cool completely, 20 minutes more.

4. For the glaze, combine the chocolate chips and milk in a small saucepan over low heat. Stir until the chocolate has melted and the mixture has thickened slightly, 1 to 2 minutes.

5. Place the cake on a serving platter and spoon the warm glaze over it. Let the cake rest for 10 minutes before slicing.

6. Slice and serve.

✻ *Store this cake, wrapped in aluminum foil or plastic wrap, or in a cake saver, at room temperature for up to 1 week. Or freeze it, wrapped in foil, for up to 6 months. Thaw the cake overnight in the refrigerator before serving.*

BOSTON CREAM PIE CAKE

ohn Mariani writes in *The Dictionary of American Food and Drink* that if a Boston Cream Pie is topped with a chocolate glaze, it should not be called a Boston Cream Pie, but rather a Parker House Chocolate Pie, after the Boston hotel where it was first bedecked with chocolate. Since I have seldom seen a Boston Cream Pie that hasn't been topped with chocolate, I've decided to call the following chocolate-glazed and pudding-filled cake a Boston Cream Pie Cake. It may be a misnomer, but it's easier this way.

SERVES: 16
PREPARATION TIME: 15 MINUTES
BAKING TIME: 33 TO 35 MINUTES
ASSEMBLY TIME: 15 MINUTES

FILLING:

2 cups milk
1 package (3.4 ounces) vanilla instant
    pudding mix
1 tablespoon butter, melted
1 teaspoon pure vanilla
    extract

CAKE:

Vegetable oil spray for
    misting the pan
Flour for dusting the pan
1 package (18.25 ounces) plain butter recipe
    golden cake mix
⅔ cup water
8 tablespoons (1 stick) butter, at room
    temperature
3 large eggs
Rich Chocolate Glaze (page 449)

1. Prepare the filling: Pour the milk into a large mixing bowl. Add the pudding mix. Blend with an electric mixer on medium-low speed for 2 minutes, or until well combined. Stir in the melted butter and the vanilla until incorporated. Cover the bowl with plastic wrap and place in the refrigerator to chill for 1 hour.

2. Place a rack in the center of the oven and preheat the oven to 350°F. Lightly mist a 12-cup Bundt pan with vegetable oil spray, then dust with flour. Shake out the excess flour. Set the pan aside.

3. Place the cake mix, water, butter, and eggs in a large mixing bowl. Blend with an electric mixer on low speed for 30 seconds. Stop the machine and scrape down the sides of the bowl with a rubber spatula. Increase the mixer speed to medium and beat 3 to 4 minutes more, scraping the sides down again if needed. The batter should look thick and well combined. Pour the batter into the prepared pan, smoothing it out with the rubber spatula. Place the pan in the oven.

4. Bake the cake until it is golden brown and springs back when lightly pressed with your finger, 33 to 35 minutes. Remove the pan from the oven and place it on a wire rack to cool for 20 minutes. Run a long, sharp knife around the edge of the cake and invert it onto a rack to cool completely, 20 minutes more.

5. Meanwhile, prepare the Rich Chocolate Glaze.

6. Slice the cooled cake into three hori-

R the Cake Mix Doctor says

I first tested this cake with a harder, more candy-like topping, Martha's Chocolate Icing (page 433). While the flavor was superb, Boston Cream Pie devotees yearned for a softer, thinner chocolate glaze, and thus this rendition. To make this an authentic Boston Cream Pie, however, you should forgo the glaze completely and dust confectioners' sugar on top. But then the cake wouldn't be as luscious—and it wouldn't be in this book!

zontal layers. Place the bottom layer on a serving platter and spread half of the chilled pudding over it. Place the middle layer on top, and spread it with the remaining pudding. Place the top layer of cake on top. Spoon the glaze over the cake so that it falls down the sides and the middle of the cake. Place the cake in the refrigerator to chill for at least 20 minutes before serving.

7. Remove the cake from the refrigerator, slice, and serve.

✳ *Store this cake, in a cake saver or under a glass dome, in the refrigerator for up to 1 week.*

ALMOND MARBLED CHOCOLATE POUND CAKE

break with my own tradition here and begin this recipe with a pound cake mix. Make that two pound cake mixes. You get incredible volume with this cake. It bakes up beautifully and is easily marbled with store-bought chocolate syrup. The almond extract adds a flavor punch. To glaze or not to glaze? I think this one can stand alone.

....
SERVES: 16

PREPARATION TIME: 20 MINUTES

BAKING TIME: 65 TO 70 MINUTES
....

Vegetable oil spray for misting the pan

Flour for dusting the pan

2 packages (16 ounces each) pound cake mix

1 cup sour cream

½ cup water

8 tablespoons (1 stick) butter, melted

4 large eggs

R

the Cake Mix Doctor says

No chocolate syrup? You could just as easily melt 1 cup of semisweet chocolate chips and fold that into the batter.

2 teaspoons pure almond extract

⅔ cup chocolate syrup

1. Place a rack in the center of the oven and preheat the oven to 325°F. Lightly mist a 10-inch tube pan with vegetable oil spray, then dust with flour. Shake out the excess flour. Set the pan aside.

2. Place the cake mixes, sour cream, water, melted butter, eggs, and almond extract in a large mixing bowl. Blend with an electric mixer on low speed for 1 minute. Stop the machine and scrape down the sides of the bowl with a rubber spatula. Increase the mixer speed to medium and beat 2 minutes more, scraping the sides down again if needed. The batter should look thick and well combined.

3. Divide the batter in half. Add the chocolate syrup to one half of the batter, and stir until well combined. Pour the batters, alternating plain and chocolate, into the prepared pan. With a dinner knife, swirl through the batter to create a marbled effect. Be careful not to scrape the bottom of the pan. Smooth out the top with the rubber spatula. Place the pan in the oven.

4. Bake the cake until it springs back when lightly pressed with your finger and is just starting to pull away from the sides of the pan, 65 to 70 minutes. Remove the pan from the oven and place it on a wire rack to cool for 20 minutes. Run a long, sharp knife around the edge of the cake and invert it onto a rack, then invert it onto another rack so that the cake is large side up. Allow to cool for 20 minutes more.

5. Slide the cake onto a serving platter. Slice and serve.

✳ *Store this cake, wrapped in plastic wrap or aluminum foil, or in a cake saver or under a glass dome, at room temperature for up to 1 week. Or freeze it, wrapped in foil, for up to 6 months. Thaw the cake overnight in the refrigerator before serving.*

MILKY WAY® SWIRL CAKE

I have looked for this recipe for years and finally found a version of it in an issue of *Vogue* magazine, of all places. The cake is a sinful combination of Milky Way bars and your usual cake ingredients, topped with a creamy glaze made with more Milky Way bars. The only problem is that candy bars are like many other products on the grocery store shelf—they are forever shrinking in size. The original recipe called for four 2.23-ounce bars, but by the time I adapted the cake, they were down to 2.05 ounces each, and by the time this recipe reaches you, they may very well weigh slightly less. So do a little math, and if you need to buy an extra candy bar to make up the difference, eat what's left over!

SERVES: 16
PREPARATION TIME: 15 MINUTES
BAKING TIME: 45 TO 50 MINUTES
ASSEMBLY TIME: 5 MINUTES

CAKE:

Vegetable oil spray for misting the pan
Flour for dusting the pan
2½ Milky Way bars (2.05 ounces each), sliced
2 tablespoons plus 1 cup water
1 package (18.25 ounces) yellow cake mix
*   with pudding*
8 tablespoons (1 stick) butter, melted
3 large eggs
1 tablespoon all-purpose flour

GLAZE:

2½ Milky Way bars (2.05 ounces each),
*   sliced*
2 tablespoons butter
2 teaspoons water

1. Place a rack in the center of the oven and preheat the oven to 325°F. Lightly mist a 12-cup Bundt pan with vegetable oil spray, then dust with flour. Shake out the excess flour. Set the pan aside.

2. Place the Milky Way bars and 2 tablespoons water in a medium-size saucepan over medium-low heat. Heat, stirring, until the candy bars melt and the mixture is smooth, 3 to 4 minutes. Remove the pan from the heat and set it aside.

3. Place the cake mix, 1 cup water, melted butter, and eggs in a large mixing bowl. Blend with an electric mixer on low speed for 1 minute. Stop the machine and scrape down the sides of the bowl with a rubber spatula. Increase the mixer speed to medium and beat 2 minutes more, scraping the sides down again if needed. The batter should look thick and well combined.

4. Measure out ⅔ cup of the batter and pour it into the cooled candy bar mixture. Add the flour and stir until the mixture is smooth. Pour the plain cake batter into the prepared pan. Spoon the Milky Way mixture in a ring on top of the batter, making sure not to touch the sides of the pan. With a dinner knife, swirl through the batter to create a marbled effect. Do not scrape the bottom of the pan. Smooth out the top with the rubber spatula. Place the pan in the oven.

5. Bake the cake until it springs back when lightly pressed with your finger and is just starting to pull away from the sides of the pan, 45 to 50 minutes. Remove the pan from the oven and place it on a wire rack to cool for 20 minutes. Run a long, sharp knife around the edge of the cake and invert it onto a rack to cool completely, 20 minutes more.

6. For the glaze, rinse out the saucepan and wipe it dry. Place the Milky Way bars in the saucepan over medium-low heat. Add the butter and water. Cook, stirring, until smooth, 3 to 4 minutes. Let the glaze cool for 10 minutes.

7. Slide the cake onto a serving platter. Spoon the glaze over the cake so that it drips down the sides. Let the cake rest for 10 minutes, then slice and serve.

✳ *Store this cake, in a cake saver or under a glass dome, at room temperature for up to 1 week. Or freeze it, wrapped in foil, for up to 6 months. Thaw the cake overnight in the refrigerator before serving.*

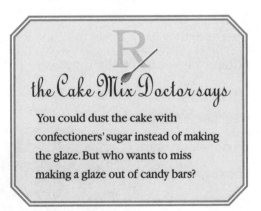

the Cake Mix Doctor says

You could dust the cake with confectioners' sugar instead of making the glaze. But who wants to miss making a glaze out of candy bars?

WHITE CHOCOLATE POUND CAKE

WITH STRAWBERRIES AND WARM LEMON SAUCE

hy is it that when you're asked to bring dessert to a picnic, your mind freezes and the only thing you can think of is brownies? Never again. *This* is the dessert to bring to the next movable feast. The cake can be made ahead of time and wrapped in foil, the sauce can be stored in a jar to be poured on-site, and those strawberries or raspberries can be prepared and tucked inside a sturdy plastic container until it's dessert time. Then, when everyone thinks that you're reaching into the basket for brownies, you pull out the components and assemble this little number. Music for the mouth.

SERVES: 16
PREPARATION TIME: 10 MINUTES
BAKING TIME: 45 TO 50 MINUTES
ASSEMBLY TIME: 5 MINUTES

Vegetable oil spray for misting the pan
Flour for dusting the pan
6 ounces white chocolate, coarsely chopped
1 package (18.25 ounces) plain white cake mix
¾ cup whole milk
8 tablespoons (1 stick) butter, melted
4 large eggs
2 teaspoons pure vanilla extract
Warm Lemon Curd Sauce (page 457)
2 cups rinsed, sliced or whole, and lightly sweetened strawberries, for garnish (see "the Cake Mix Doctor says")

the Cake Mix Doctor says

To sweeten the strawberries, sprinkle 2 tablespoons sugar over them, stir, and let sit for 15 to 20 minutes before serving.

Substitute almond extract for vanilla and you have an entirely different cake. This cake is also delicious cut into thirds, sandwiched with softened ice cream, and frozen.

1. Place a rack in the center of the oven and preheat the oven to 350°F. Lightly mist a 10-inch tube pan with vegetable oil spray, then dust with flour. Shake out the excess flour. Set the pan aside.

2. Melt the white chocolate in a small saucepan over low heat, stirring constantly, 3 to 4 minutes. Or microwave the white chocolate in a small glass bowl on high power for 1 minute, then stir with a small rubber spatula until smooth. (See Melting White Chocolate, page 92.) Let it cool slightly.

3. Place the cake mix, milk, melted butter, eggs, vanilla, and white chocolate in a large mixing bowl. Blend with an electric mixer on low speed for 1 minute. Stop the machine and scrape down the sides of the bowl with a rubber spatula. Increase the mixer speed to medium and beat 2 minutes more, scraping the sides down again if needed. The batter should look thick and well combined. Pour the batter into the prepared pan, smoothing it out with the rubber spatula. Place the pan in the oven.

4. Bake the cake until it springs back when lightly pressed with your finger and is just starting to pull away from the sides of the pan, 45 to 50 minutes. Remove the pan from the oven and place it on a wire rack to cool for 20 minutes. Run a long, sharp knife around the edge of the cake and invert it onto a rack, then invert it onto another rack so the cake is large side up. Allow to cool for 20 minutes more.

5. Meanwhile, prepare the Warm Lemon Curd Sauce.

6. Slice the cake, and serve it with the sweetened strawberries and lemon sauce.

✳ *Store this cake, wrapped in aluminum foil or plastic wrap, or in a cake saver, at room temperature for up to 1 week. Or freeze it, wrapped in foil, for up to 6 months. Thaw the cake overnight in the refrigerator before serving.*

PUMPKIN CHOCOLATE CHIP CAKE

Here is a delicious example of how a puréed vegetable—canned pumpkin—creates a cake so moist that it needs no oil. The recipe comes from Rebecca Robb, of Fremont, California, and it is a favorite that her mother, Lillah, likes to make in the fall—it's perfect for Halloween. If you want to top this cake with a glaze, the Chocolate Cinnamon Glaze (page 451), Chocolate Dream Glaze (page 447), or Chocolate Marshmallow Frosting (page 439) would carry on that good chocolate flavor. Or just dust it with some confectioners' sugar as I do here. This cake is scrumptious warm, when the chocolate chips are still melted, gooey, and wonderful.

SERVES: 16
PREPARATION TIME: 10 MINUTES
BAKING TIME: 42 TO 46 MINUTES

Vegetable oil spray for misting the pan
Flour for dusting the pan
1 package (18.25 ounces) plain yellow cake mix
1 can (15 ounces; 1¾ cups) pumpkin
¼ cup water
2 large eggs
2 teaspoons pumpkin pie spice
2 teaspoons baking soda
1 cup semisweet chocolate chips
1 cup finely chopped pecans
1 tablespoon confectioners' sugar, for garnish

1. Place a rack in the center of the oven and preheat the oven to 350°F. Lightly mist a 12-cup Bundt pan with vegetable oil spray, then dust with flour. Shake out the excess flour. Set the pan aside.

2. Place the cake mix, pumpkin, water, eggs, pumpkin pie spice, and baking soda in a large mixing bowl. Blend with an electric mixer on low speed for 1 minute. Stop the machine and scrape down the sides of the bowl with a rubber spatula. Increase the mixer speed to medium and beat 2 minutes more, scraping the sides down again if needed. The batter should look thick and well combined. Fold in the chocolate chips and pecans, making sure they are well distributed throughout the batter. Spoon the batter into the prepared pan, smoothing it out with the rubber spatula. Place the pan in the oven.

3. Bake the cake until it is lightly browned and springs back when lightly pressed with your finger, 42 to 46 minutes. Remove the pan from the oven and place it on a wire rack to cool for 20 minutes. Run a long, sharp knife around the edge of the cake and invert it onto a rack to cool completely, 20 minutes more.

4. Slide the cake onto a serving platter, dust with confectioners' sugar, and slice.

R

the Cake Mix Doctor says

The chocolate chips suspend beautifully in this cake because the batter is thick enough to support them. Yet the final result isn't overly dense—the baking soda helps lighten it. Make sure to chop the pecans fine so that they blend into the texture of the cake. If you don't have pumpkin pie spice, add 1 teaspoon ground cinnamon, ½ teaspoon ground nutmeg, and ½ teaspoon ground allspice.

✳ *Store this cake, wrapped in aluminum foil or plastic wrap, or in a cake saver, at room temperature for up to 1 week. Or freeze it, wrapped in foil, for up to 6 months. Thaw the cake overnight in the refrigerator before serving.*

WHITE CHOCOLATE POUND CAKE

WITH RICOTTA AND ORANGE

If you think cake mixes can only produce soft, spongy cakes, try this recipe. The texture is akin to from-scratch pound cake, with the dense crumb coming from the combination of white chocolate, oil, and ricotta. But don't think for a moment that this cake tastes greasy. The fresh orange juice and zest make it pleasing and light.

....

SERVES: 16

PREPARATION TIME: 12 MINUTES

BAKING TIME: 38 TO 42 MINUTES

ASSEMBLY TIME: 5 MINUTES

....

Vegetable oil spray for misting the pan

Flour for dusting the pan

2 large oranges

Carton orange juice as needed

6 ounces white chocolate, coarsely chopped

1 package (18.25 ounces) plain white cake mix

⅔ cup ricotta cheese

⅓ cup vegetable oil

3 large eggs

2 large egg whites

½ teaspoon pure almond extract

Fresh Orange Drizzle (page 453)

1. Place a rack in the center of the oven and preheat the oven to 350°F. Lightly mist a 10-inch tube pan with vegetable oil spray, then dust with flour. Shake out the excess flour. Set the pan aside.

2. Zest the oranges, and measure out 2 teaspoons grated zest for the cake batter. (If you have extra, save it for making the Fresh Orange Drizzle.) Juice the oranges. You will need ½ cup juice; add carton orange juice as needed to make up the ½ cup. Set the juice aside. (If you have more than ½ cup juice, save it for making the Fresh Orange Drizzle.)

3. Melt the white chocolate in a small saucepan over low heat, stirring constantly, 3 to 4 minutes. Or microwave the white chocolate in a small glass bowl on high power for 1 minute, then stir with a small rubber spatula until smooth. (See Melting White Chocolate, page 92.) Let it cool slightly.

4. Place the cake mix, ricotta, oil, eggs, egg whites, almond extract, reserved ½ cup orange juice, reserved 2 teaspoons orange zest, and the white chocolate in a large mixing bowl. Blend with an electric mixer on low speed for 1 minute. Stop the machine and scrape down the sides of the bowl with a rubber spatula. Increase the mixer speed to medium and beat 2 minutes more, scraping the sides down again if needed. The batter should look thick and well combined. Pour the batter into the prepared pan, smoothing it out with the rubber spatula. Place the pan in the oven.

5. Bake the cake until it springs back when lightly pressed with your finger and is just starting to pull away from the sides of the pan, 38 to 42 minutes. Remove the pan from the oven and place

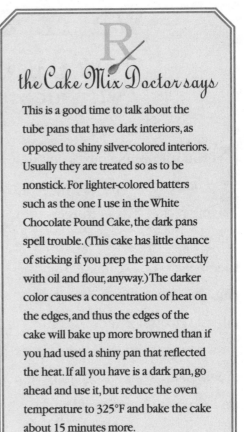

the Cake Mix Doctor says

This is a good time to talk about the tube pans that have dark interiors, as opposed to shiny silver-colored interiors. Usually they are treated so as to be nonstick. For lighter-colored batters such as the one I use in the White Chocolate Pound Cake, the dark pans spell trouble. (This cake has little chance of sticking if you prep the pan correctly with oil and flour, anyway.) The darker color causes a concentration of heat on the edges, and thus the edges of the cake will bake up more browned than if you had used a shiny pan that reflected the heat. If all you have is a dark pan, go ahead and use it, but reduce the oven temperature to 325°F and bake the cake about 15 minutes more.

it on a wire rack to cool for 20 minutes. Run a long, sharp knife around the edge of the cake and invert it onto a rack, then invert it onto another rack so the cake is large side up. Allow to cool for 20 minutes more.

6. Meanwhile, prepare the Fresh Orange Drizzle.

7. Spoon the drizzle over the cake so that it runs down the sides of the cake. Let the cake rest for 10 minutes.

8. Slide the cake onto a serving platter. Slice and serve.

✻ *Store this cake, wrapped in aluminum foil or plastic wrap, or in a cake saver, at room temperature for up to 1 week. Or freeze it, wrapped in foil, for up to 6 months. Thaw the cake overnight in the refrigerator before serving.*

LIBBIE'S CHOCOLATE AMARETTO CAKE

L ibbie Jae was my book tour escort on a particularly humid Florida morning. As we whizzed along the highways between Tampa and St. Petersburg, keeping an eye on the sliding fresh strawberry cakes baked for a television appearance, we talked about children, traffic, and invariably cakes. Libbie promised to send me her favorite chocolate cake mix creation. Well, the recipe was well worth the wait. Libbie begins with a devil's food cake mix, to which she adds pudding mix and a little mayonnaise to keep things moist. Then she pours in both amaretto and almond extract, plus a handful of chocolate chips. It is a powerful cake, but not too boozy—you can tote it to that church supper without a worry.

....

SERVES: 16
PREPARATION TIME: 12 MINUTES
BAKING TIME: 53 TO 56 MINUTES

....

Vegetable oil spray for misting the pan
Flour for dusting the pan
1 package (18.25 ounces) plain devil's food cake mix
1 package (3.9 ounces) chocolate instant pudding mix
¾ cup whole milk
½ cup vegetable oil
½ cup water
¼ cup mayonnaise
4 large eggs
¼ cup amaretto (almond liqueur)
1 teaspoon pure almond extract
1 cup semisweet chocolate chips
1 tablespoon confectioners' sugar, for garnish

The Ideal Temperature

I had heard from a couple of veteran bakers that you get moister cakes if you bake at 325°F rather than 350°F. So when I was testing these recipes, I gave the lower temperature a try on some of my basic cakes—devil's food, for example. Two 9-inch round layers took 32 minutes to bake at 325°F and 28 minutes at 350°F. If there was any structural difference in the cakes, I could not see or taste it. So, I chose to stick with 350°F for layer cakes and most other cakes, for the time saved.

A few exceptions do call for 325°F, however. The lower temperature is better for cheesecakes because it produces a more tender and uniform cake. It is also recommended for cake layer pans that are larger than 10 inches because the layer will rise more evenly at the lower temperature. And when a tube or Bundt cake takes a long time to bake through and you don't want to overbrown the top, baking at 325°F is preferable. On the other hand, for pudding cakes, such as the Chocolate Soufflé Pudding Cake on page 235, where you want the edges crisp and the center moist and gooey, sometimes 375°F is the right temperature.

1. Place a rack in the center of the oven and preheat the oven to 350°F. Lightly mist a 12-cup Bundt pan with vegetable oil spray, then dust with flour. Shake out the excess flour. Set the pan aside.

2. Place the cake mix, pudding mix, milk, oil, water, mayonnaise, eggs, amaretto, and almond extract in a large mixing bowl. Blend with an electric mixer on low speed for 1 minute. Stop the machine and scrape down the sides of the bowl with a rubber spatula. Increase the mixer speed to medium and beat 2 minutes more, scraping the sides down again if needed.

The batter should look thick and well combined. Fold in the chocolate chips, making sure they are well distributed throughout the batter. Pour the batter into the prepared pan, smoothing it out with the rubber spatula. Place the pan in the oven.

3. Bake the cake until it springs back when lightly pressed with your finger and is just starting to pull away from the sides of the pan, 53 to 56 minutes. Remove the pan from the oven and place it on a wire rack to cool for 20 minutes. Run a long, sharp knife around the edge of the cake and invert it onto a rack to cool completely, 20 minutes more.

4. Place the cake on a serving platter. Sprinkle with confectioners' sugar, slice, and serve.

✳ *Store this cake, wrapped in aluminum foil or plastic wrap, or in a cake saver, at room temperature for up to 1 week. Or freeze it, wrapped in foil, for up to 6 months. Thaw the cake overnight in the refrigerator before serving.*

R

the Cake Mix Doctor says

I liked this cake plain and simple, with just a sprinkling of confectioners' sugar on top. And that is how Libbie Jae serves it. If you want more of an amaretto flavor, stir together ½ cup confectioners' sugar and ¼ cup amaretto, and pour this over the cake.

RICK'S CHOCOLATE RUM BUNDT CAKE

Rick Delaney, of Warner Robbins, Georgia, has been making this cake for more than fifteen years, adjusting it a tad every so often. He says he has it where he wants it now and has passed it along to share. The cake is delicious, but of course I like to tinker and have added a bit more rum than in Rick's version. And I included chocolate chips because they work so well with the rum. Try it and see for yourself, then make your own adjustments. But don't change one thing: Rick says to serve the cake with cold milk!

SERVES: 16
PREPARATION TIME: 8 MINUTES
BAKING TIME: 43 TO 47 MINUTES
ASSEMBLY TIME: 5 MINUTES

Vegetable oil spray for misting the pan
Flour for dusting the pan
1 package (18.25 ounces) plain yellow cake mix
1 package (3.9 ounces) chocolate instant pudding mix
1 cup sour cream
½ cup vegetable oil
⅓ cup light rum
4 large eggs
1 teaspoon pure vanilla extract
1 cup semisweet chocolate chips
Rich Chocolate Glaze (page 449)

1. Place a rack in the center of the oven and preheat the oven to 350°F. Lightly mist a 12-cup Bundt pan with vegetable oil spray, then dust with flour. Shake out the excess flour. Set the pan aside.

2. Place the cake mix, pudding mix, sour cream, oil, rum, eggs, and vanilla in a large mixing bowl. Blend with an electric mixer on low speed for 1 minute. Stop the machine and scrape down the sides of the bowl with a rubber spatula. Increase the mixer speed to medium and beat 2 minutes more, scraping the sides down again if needed. The batter should look thick and well combined. Fold in the chocolate chips, making sure they are well distributed throughout the batter. Pour the batter into the prepared pan, smoothing it out with the rubber spatula. Place the pan in the oven.

3. Bake the cake until it springs back when lightly pressed with your finger and is just starting to pull away from the sides of the pan, 43 to 47 minutes. Remove the pan from the oven and place it on a wire rack to cool for 20 minutes. Run a long, sharp knife around the edge of the cake and invert it onto a rack to cool completely, 20 minutes more.

4. Meanwhile, prepare the Rich Chocolate Glaze.

5. Place the cake on a serving platter and pour the warm icing over it. Let the cake rest for 10 minutes.

6. Slice and serve.

✳ *Store this cake, in a cake saver or under a glass dome, at room temperature for up to 1 week. Or freeze it, wrapped in foil, for up to 6 months. Thaw the cake overnight in the refrigerator before serving.*

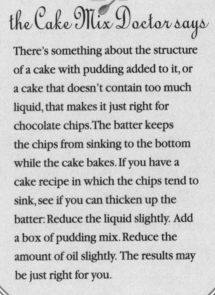

the Cake Mix Doctor says

There's something about the structure of a cake with pudding added to it, or a cake that doesn't contain too much liquid, that makes it just right for chocolate chips. The batter keeps the chips from sinking to the bottom while the cake bakes. If you have a cake recipe in which the chips tend to sink, see if you can thicken up the batter. Reduce the liquid slightly. Add a box of pudding mix. Reduce the amount of oil slightly. The results may be just right for you.

CHOCOLATE KAHLÚA CAKE

Lois Anne Holley, of Morehead, Kentucky, jokingly says that her hometown is known for its natural beauty and for its good cooks with short memories. Well, she is surely joking, because Lois Anne quickly recalled and shared with me the chocolate cake recipe she loves best. It begins with a butter-recipe fudge cake mix, to which you add all kinds of goodies, particularly Kahlúa. I liked the coffee liqueur taste so much that I drizzled a little over the cake while it was cooling. This is one rich cake worth remembering!

SERVES: 16
PREPARATION TIME: 10 MINUTES
BAKING TIME: 55 TO 60 MINUTES
ASSEMBLY TIME: 2 MINUTES

Vegetable oil spray for misting the pan
Flour for dusting the pan
1 package (18.25 ounces) plain butter-recipe
*   fudge cake mix*
1 package (3.9 ounces) chocolate instant
*   pudding mix*
1 cup sour cream
8 tablespoons (1 stick) butter, melted
½ cup vegetable oil
4 large eggs
7 tablespoons Kahlúa or other coffee liqueur
1 teaspoon pure vanilla extract
1 cup semisweet chocolate chips
1 tablespoon confectioners' sugar, sifted,
*   for garnish*

1. Place a rack in the center of the oven and preheat the oven to 350°F. Lightly mist a 12-cup Bundt pan with vegetable oil spray, then dust with flour. Shake out the excess flour. Set the pan aside.

2. Place the cake mix, pudding mix, sour cream, melted butter, oil, eggs, 4 tablespoons of the Kahlúa, and the vanilla in a large mixing bowl. Blend with an electric mixer on low speed for 1 minute. Stop the machine and scrape down the sides of the bowl with a rubber spatula. Increase the mixer speed to medium and beat 2 minutes more, scraping the sides down again if needed. The batter should look thick and well combined. Fold in the chocolate chips, making sure they are well distributed throughout the batter. Pour the batter into the prepared pan, smoothing it out with the rubber spatula. Place the pan in the oven.

3. Bake the cake until it springs back when lightly pressed with your finger and is just starting to pull away from the sides of the pan, 55 to 60 minutes. Remove the pan from the oven and place it on a wire rack to cool for 20 minutes. Run a long, sharp knife around the edge of the cake and invert it onto a rack.

4. With a wooden skewer, poke holes in the top of the cake. Spoon the remaining 3 tablespoons Kahlúa over the cake, letting it seep down into the holes. Let the cake cool completely, 20 minutes more.

5. Place the cake on a serving platter and dust with confectioners' sugar. Slice and serve.

✱ *Store this cake, wrapped in aluminum foil or plastic wrap, or in a cake saver, at room temperature for up to 1 week. Or freeze it, wrapped in foil, for up to 6 months. Thaw the cake overnight in the refrigerator before serving.*

R
the Cake Mix Doctor says

The best way to let a liqueur seep down into a warm cake is to poke holes in the top and then spoon the liqueur over the cake. A wooden skewer makes nice thin holes, chopsticks larger holes. As for topping this cake, just a dusting of confectioners' sugar is all you need.

BLACK RUSSIAN CAKE

While I was on my book tour with *The Cake Mix Doctor*, conversations understandably centered on cake. Did I have this recipe or that one? It was fun because it gave me a chance to find out what people in different regions of the country are baking and what they'd like to be baking. The topic of Black Russian Cake came up more than once. (A Black Russian is a cocktail consisting of two parts vodka and one part coffee liqueur—dangerously delicious.) Did I have a recipe? Could I find a recipe? Well, to be honest, I had never given any thought to a Black Russian Cake. Fortunately, Carolyn Kent, of Danville, Virginia, had. She e-mailed me her recipe. No more guessing—this is one awesome cake.

SERVES: 16
PREPARATION TIME: 10 MINUTES
BAKING TIME: 60 TO 65 MINUTES
ASSEMBLY TIME: 5 MINUTES

CAKE:

Vegetable oil spray for misting the pan
Flour for dusting the pan
1 package (18.25 ounces) plain yellow cake mix
1 large package (5.9 ounces) chocolate instant pudding mix
1 cup vegetable oil
¾ cup water
½ cup granulated sugar
4 large eggs
¼ cup Kahlúa or other coffee liqueur
¼ cup vodka

GLAZE:

½ cup confectioners' sugar, sifted
¼ cup Kahlúa or other coffee liqueur

the Cake Mix Doctor says

Want to make a White Russian Cake? Heat 2 tablespoons Kahlúa and 2 tablespoons heavy cream until warm. Stir in ½ cup confectioners' sugar, and spoon this glaze over the cooled cake.

1. Place a rack in the center of the oven and preheat the oven to 350°F. Lightly mist a 12-cup Bundt pan with vegetable oil spray, then dust with flour. Shake out the excess flour. Set the pan aside.

2. Place the cake mix, pudding mix, oil, water, sugar, eggs, Kahlúa, and vodka in a large mixing bowl. Blend with an electric mixer on low speed for 1 minute. Stop the machine and scrape down the sides of the bowl with a rubber spatula. Increase the mixer speed to medium and beat 2 minutes more, scraping the sides down again if needed. The batter should look thick and well combined. Pour the batter into the prepared pan, smoothing it out with the rubber spatula. Place the pan in the oven.

3. Bake the cake until it springs back when lightly pressed with your finger and is just starting to pull away from the sides of the pan, 60 to 65 minutes. Remove the pan from the oven and place it on a wire rack to cool for 20 minutes. Run a long, sharp knife around the edge of the cake and invert it onto a rack to cool completely, 20 minutes more.

4. For the glaze, place the confectioners' sugar in a small bowl and stir in the Kahlúa. Spoon this over the cooled cake so that it drips down the sides and is absorbed into the cake. Let the cake rest for 10 minutes.

5. Slide the cake onto a serving platter. Slice and serve.

✳ *Store this cake, wrapped in aluminum foil or plastic wrap, or in a cake saver, at room temperature for up to 1 week. Or freeze it, wrapped in foil, for up to 6 months. Thaw the cake overnight in the refrigerator before serving.*

CHOCOLATE FOUR-SEASONS WINE CAKE

Nashville cook Stacey Romo makes this sherry-soaked cake during the winter holidays. It is an adaptation of one made with a white cake mix by her aunt in New Orleans. Stacey switched to chocolate! As if the duo of sweet cream sherry and chocolate weren't enough, this cake is enhanced by a topping of pecans and marinated maraschino cherries. It's one impressive and easy cake, perfect for serving or giving during the winter holidays or for surprising someone on a birthday.

SERVES: 16

PREPARATION TIME:
20 TO 25 MINUTES

BAKING TIME: 50 TO 55 MINUTES

ASSEMBLY TIME: 2 MINUTES

CAKE:

Softened butter for greasing the pan

1 jar (6 ounces) maraschino cherries

½ cup cream sherry

*1 package (18.25 ounces) plain
     devil's food cake mix*

*1 package (3.4 ounces) vanilla instant
     pudding mix*

½ cup water

½ cup vegetable oil

4 large eggs

*½ cup chopped
     pecans*

GLAZE:

4 tablespoons (½ stick) butter

½ cup sugar

¼ cup cream sherry

2 tablespoons water

1. Place a rack in the center of the oven and preheat the oven to 325°F. Generously grease a 12-cup Bundt pan with butter. Set the pan aside.

2. Drain the cherries and cut them in

15 Cakes to Tote to a Potluck

1. Chocolate Four-Seasons Wine Cake

2. Amazing German Chocolate Cake

3. Mint Chocolate Cream Cheese Pound Cake

4. Deep Chocolate Almond Angel Icebox Cake

5. Chocolate-Cinnamon Banana Cake with a Quick Caramel Frosting

6. Peanut Butter Cake with Fluffy Chocolate Frosting

7. Chocolate Cherry Chip Cupcakes with Martha's Chocolate Icing

8. Chocolate Zucchini Raisin Cake

9. The Watergate Cake

10. White Chocolate Banana-Macadamia Cheesecake

11. Mocha Brownie Cheesecake

12. Dark Chocolate Roulade with Chocolate Cream Filling

13. Chocolate Potluck Cake

14. White Chocolate Pineapple Upside-Down Cake

15. Cream Cheese Brownie Pie

half. Place the cherries and the sherry in a small bowl. Let the cherries soak for 10 minutes.

3. Place the cake mix, pudding mix, water, oil, and eggs in a large mixing bowl. Drain the sherry from the cherries and add it to the mixing bowl. Blend with an electric mixer on low speed for 30 seconds. Stop the machine and scrape down the sides of the bowl with a rubber spatula. Increase the mixer speed to medium and beat 2 minutes more, scraping the sides down again if

needed. The batter should look thick and well combined.

4. Arrange 3 or 4 cherry halves, round side down, in the large indentations at the bottom of the Bundt pan. Place 1 or 2 cherries in the small indentations. Sprinkle the chopped pecans over the bottom of the pan, including the cherries. Pour the batter into the prepared pan, smoothing it out with the rubber spatula. Place the pan in the oven.

5. Bake the cake until it springs back

when lightly pressed with your finger and is just starting to pull away from the sides of the pan, 50 to 55 minutes. Remove the pan from the oven and place it on a wire rack to cool for 10 minutes.

6. While the cake is cooling, prepare the glaze: Place the butter, sugar, sherry, and water in a small saucepan over medium heat. Bring to a boil, then reduce the heat and simmer the mixture until it reduces by a third and thickens slightly, stirring often, 6 to 8 minutes. Remove the pan from the heat. Run a long, sharp knife around the edge of the cake and invert it onto a serving platter. Spoon the warm glaze over the warm cake. Let the cake rest for 10 minutes.

7. Slice and serve.

❋ *Store this cake, wrapped in aluminum foil or plastic wrap, or in a cake saver,*

R/
the Cake Mix Doctor says

You are going to love how the pecans toast in the butter on the bottom of the pan and then, when the cake is unmolded, create a crunchy topping. Add ¼ cup more pecans for an even more delicious crust. And, for added holiday color, alternate red and green maraschino cherry halves in the bottom of the pan.

at room temperature for up to 1 week. Or freeze it, wrapped in foil, for up to 6 months. Thaw the cake overnight in the refrigerator before serving.

Sheet Cakes

• • •

The chocolate layer cake may be America's most beloved cake, aglow with candles and surrounded by birthday nostalgia, but the flatter, larger chocolate sheet cake is certainly the most versatile.

Baked in pans that range from 13 to 16 inches long and from 9 to 12 inches wide, this is the cake that America bakes most often. The cake mix companies know that from consumer research. And no doubt just a quick look in anyone's pantry will most likely turn up that rectangular pan.

It was our brownie passion that placed that pan in so many cupboards, as well as the clever marketing efforts of housewares folks who made it affordable and totable to gatherings with a snap-on cover. Its presence in every kitchen led to its presence at every bake sale, church supper, and neighborhood picnic—but seldom at a yard sale because these pans don't wear out!

Before going further, I want to say for the record that the name "sheet cake" may not be technically correct. The first sheet cakes were wafer-thin cakes baked in what resembled a jelly-roll pan. They were frosted and sliced. But through the years "sheet cake" has come to describe any large flat cake, served as is or frosted. And although pan sizes may vary, you'll be able to fill up to a 15¼- by 10½-inch pan with any of these recipes. Go any larger and you'll need a recipe and a half. If in doubt, check the side panel of white cake mix boxes for information on how much batter fits into wedding and larger pan sizes. But remember that the larger the pan, the shorter the baking time because of more surface area and less height.

Those of you who live at higher altitudes (over 3,500 feet) should be forewarned that sheet cake cooking in your territory is risky business. There is less structural support for the cake batter, and because cakes at higher altitudes tend to bake higher than they might at sea level, sheet cakes rise and then sink in the middle. Consult the cake mix box for advice or see my High-Altitude Baking tips (pages 10 to 11). The good news is, you can always fill the dip with extra frosting!

"Chocolate: It flatters you for a while, it warms you for an instant; then all of a sudden, it kindles a mortal fever in you."

—MARIE, MARQUISE DE SÉVIGNÉ

With your sheet pan lightly misted with vegetable oil spray, you're ready to bake any of the cakes in this chapter. The German Chocolate Velvet Crumb Cake, the Chocolate Zucchini Raisin Cake, the Watergate Cake, and the Banana Split Fudge Cake are sliced and served right from the pan. Dust the pan with a little flour if you want to invert the cake and frost it—like the Chocolate Coconut Cream Cake with German Chocolate Frosting or the Chocolate Eggnog Cake with Eggnog Buttercream Frosting. (If you'll want to unmold the cake, don't bake it in a glass pan. Glass pans cook more quickly and the cake will stick to the corners.) Some cakes are inverted because there are goodies on the bottom—for example, the German Chocolate Upside-Down Cake and the White Chocolate Pineapple Upside-Down Cake.

You don't have to be a math whiz to figure out that the sheet cake is the cake that feeds the crowd. These cakes will generously feed sixteen, amply feed twenty, easily feed twenty-four, and I know my frugal grandmother could stretch one to feed an entire school! And I know she'd approve of every one of these versatile and crowd-pleasing recipes!

GERMAN CHOCOLATE UPSIDE-DOWN CAKE

Upside-down cakes are often made in skillets: Pineapple upside-down cake and the classic French apple *tarte tatin* are great examples. But if you're thinking bottoms up, don't rule out the 13- by 9-inch pan! In this rich and memorable chocolate cake, coconut and pecans form the bottom layer, followed by German chocolate batter and then a sweet creamy topping—then the cake is turned upside down, and on top you have those toasted pecans and sweet coconut flakes with cream cheese–filled cake below! My friend Kathy Sellers passed along this recipe from her friend Jana Capello, and now I pass it along to you.

SERVES: 20

PREPARATION TIME: 12 MINUTES

BAKING TIME: 43 TO 48 MINUTES

Softened butter for greasing
    the pan
Flour for dusting the pan
1 cup sweetened flaked coconut
1 cup finely chopped pecans
3½ cups confectioners' sugar
1 cup (2 sticks) margarine, melted
1 package (8 ounces) cream cheese, at room
    temperature
1 package (18.25 ounces) German chocolate
    cake mix with pudding
1¼ cups water
⅓ cup vegetable oil
3 large eggs

1. Place a rack in the center of the oven and preheat the oven to 375°F. Generously grease a 13- by 9-inch pan with butter, then dust with flour. Shake out the excess flour. Sprinkle the coconut and pecans evenly over the bottom of the pan, and set the pan aside.

Fast Decorations

*D*ress up that simple cake with these goodies:

- **Chocolate shavings.** Run a sharp knife down the side of a bar of chocolate (white or semisweet) and scatter the shavings evenly across the top of the cake, or pile them in the center.

- **Candied almonds.** Buy these in the candy store; they come in bright colors. Scatter them around a simple white chocolate cake.

- **Candied violets.** Buy these at a gourmet shop or where cake-decorating supplies are sold.

- **Cocoa powder.** Sift it over a white chocolate frosting.

- **Confectioners' sugar.** Dust dark chocolate cakes at the last minute, or the sugar will be absorbed into the cake. Buy stencils in cookware shops and sift on polka dot and other patterns. Or to create a filigree pattern, sift the sugar over a paper doily placed on top of the cake.

- **Melon ball chocolate curls.** Warm a semisweet block of chocolate and run a melon baller against it. The colder the chocolate, the smaller and flakier the curls.

2. Place the confectioners' sugar, melted margarine, and cream cheese in a large mixing bowl. Blend with an electric mixer on low speed for 30 seconds, then increase the mixer speed to medium and beat 30 seconds more, or until smooth. Set the bowl aside.

3. Place the cake mix, water, oil, and eggs in a large mixing bowl. Blend with an electric mixer (using the same beaters—no need to wash them) on low speed for 1 minute. Stop the machine and scrape down the sides of the bowl with a rubber spatula. Increase the mixer speed to medium and beat 2 minutes more, scraping the sides down again if needed. The batter should look well combined. Pour the batter over the coconut and pecans in the prepared pan, smoothing it out with the rubber spatula. Spoon the cream cheese mixture on top of the batter, leaving a 1-inch border of cake mix on all sides. Spread out the cream cheese mixture with the rubber spatula until smooth. Place the pan in the oven.

the Cake Mix Doctor says

If you want to bake this cake ahead and tote it to a party or gathering, leave it in the pan. Cut the cooled cake into squares on-site, then flip them upside down onto serving plates.

4. Bake the cake until it springs back when lightly pressed with your finger and the cream cheese mixture has turned golden brown, 43 to 48 minutes. Remove the pan from the oven and place it on a wire rack to cool for 20 minutes. Run a sharp knife around the edge of the cake and invert it onto a serving platter. Let the cake rest 20 minutes more. Slice into squares and serve.

✳ *Store this cake, wrapped in aluminum foil or plastic wrap, at room temperature for up to 1 week. Or freeze it, wrapped in foil, for up to 6 months. Thaw the cake overnight in the refrigerator before serving.*

WHITE CHOCOLATE PINEAPPLE UPSIDE-DOWN CAKE

Martha Bowden, my friend and recipe tester, comes from serious upside-down cake people. Her family raises this modest type of cake to an art form— blending crushed pineapple into melted butter and brown sugar, arranging maraschino cherries just so, and then pouring a rich batter over all. So when Martha and I talked about a white chocolate version of the old standby, I knew I could count on her to create it. And boy, did she ever, assembling this modest but sinful chocolate version of the American classic. Her response? "Yummy."

SERVES: 20
PREPARATION TIME: 25 MINUTES
BAKING TIME: 43 TO 48 MINUTES

Softened butter for greasing the pan
12 tablespoons (1½ sticks) butter
¾ cup (packed) light brown sugar
1 can (20 ounces) crushed pineapple
1 jar (6 ounces) maraschino cherries,
*   drained*
6 ounces white chocolate, finely chopped
1 package (18.25 ounces) plain white
*   cake mix*
3 large eggs
2 teaspoons pure vanilla extract

1. Place a rack in the center of the oven and preheat the oven to 350°F. Lightly grease a 13- by 9-inch pan with butter. Set the pan aside.

2. Place 6 tablespoons of the butter in a small microwave-safe bowl and microwave at high power until melted, 45 seconds. Or melt the butter in a small saucepan over low heat. Stir the brown sugar into the melted butter. Turn this mixture into the prepared baking pan, and spread it with the back of a wooden spoon until it completely covers the bottom. Allow the mixture to cool for 2 to 3 minutes.

3. Drain the pineapple in a fine-mesh strainer, reserving the liquid. Press on the pineapple with a rubber spatula to extract as much liquid as possible. Measure out 1 cup of the liquid and set it aside.

4. Pour the drained pineapple onto the brown sugar mixture, and spread it out evenly with the rubber spatula. Pat the cherries dry and arrange them randomly on top of the pineapple. Set the pan aside.

5. Cut the remaining 6 tablespoons butter into pieces. Place the butter and the white chocolate in a small microwave-safe bowl and microwave on high power until the butter has melted, 1 minute. Stir until the white chocolate is thoroughly melted and the mixture is smooth.

6. Place the cake mix, reserved 1 cup pineapple juice, eggs, vanilla, and melted white chocolate mixture in a large mixing bowl. Blend with an electric mixer on low speed for 1 minute. Stop the machine and scrape down the sides of the bowl with a rubber spatula. Increase the mixer speed to medium and beat 2 minutes more, scraping the sides down again if needed. The batter should look well combined and thick. Pour the batter over the pineapple and cherries, smoothing it out with the rubber spatula. Place the pan in the oven.

7. Bake the cake until it springs back when lightly pressed with your finger, 43 to 48 minutes. Remove the pan from the oven and place it on a wire rack to cool for 10 minutes. Run a sharp knife around the edge of the cake and invert it onto a serving platter so the cherries and pineapple are on top. Slice, and serve warm.

✳ *Store this cake, wrapped in aluminum foil or plastic wrap, at room temperature for 3 days or in the refrigerator for up to 1 week. Or freeze it, wrapped in foil, for up to 6 months. Thaw the cake overnight in the refrigerator before serving.*

R

the Cake Mix Doctor says

Allowing the brown sugar mixture to cool and harden a bit on the bottom of the pan makes it easier to spread the crushed pineapple over it.

Instead of using 1 cup reserved pineapple juice, use ½ cup pineapple juice and ½ cup milk. It makes a richer batter.

CHOCOLATE COCONUT CREAM CAKE

WITH GERMAN CHOCOLATE CREAM CHEESE FROSTING

oconut is a natural partner to German chocolate—you don't have to look any further than the classic German chocolate layer cake to figure that out. But in this cake those flavors combine in a different way. If you serve this incredibly moist cake at a gathering, people will plead with you for the recipe. Or they may insist you bake the cake again!

SERVES: 20

PREPARATION TIME: 8 MINUTES

BAKING TIME: 40 TO 45 MINUTES

ASSEMBLY TIME: 3 MINUTES

Vegetable oil spray for misting the pan

Flour for dusting the pan

1 package (18.25 ounces) German chocolate cake mix with pudding

1 can (8.5 ounces; about 1 cup) cream of coconut

1 cup sour cream

¼ cup vegetable oil

3 large eggs

German Chocolate Cream Cheese Frosting (page 421)

1 cup sweetened flaked coconut, for garnish

1. Place a rack in the center of the oven and preheat the oven to 350°F. Lightly mist a 13- by 9-inch pan with vegetable oil spray, then dust with flour. Shake out the excess flour. Set the pan aside.

2. Place the cake mix, cream of coconut, sour cream, oil, and eggs in a large mixing bowl. Blend with an electric mixer on low speed for 1 minute. Stop the machine and scrape down the sides of the bowl with a rubber spatula. Increase the mixer speed to medium and beat 2 minutes more, scraping the sides down again if needed. The batter should look well combined. Pour the batter into the prepared pan, smoothing it out with the rubber spatula. Place the pan in the oven.

3. Bake the cake until it springs back when lightly pressed with your finger, 40 to 45 minutes. Remove the pan from the oven and place it on a wire rack to cool for 20 minutes. Run a sharp knife around the edge of the cake and invert it onto a serving platter. Let the cake rest 20 minutes before frosting.

4. Meanwhile, prepare the German Chocolate Cream Cheese Frosting.

5. Frost the top and sides of the cake with smooth, clean strokes. Sprinkle the coconut on top.

the Cake Mix Doctor says

Suit yourself: Frost this cake in the pan, or turn it out as I suggest and then frost the top and sides. You will not need as much frosting if you leave it in the pan and just frost the top.

✻ *To make slicing easier, store this cake, lightly covered with waxed paper, in the refrigerator until the frosting sets, 1 hour. Then wrap it in aluminum foil and store it in the refrigerator for up to 1 week. Or freeze it, wrapped in foil, for up to 6 months. Thaw the cake overnight in the refrigerator before serving.*

GERMAN CHOCOLATE CHIP ZUCCHINI CAKE

What's not to like about this sheet cake? It begins with a German chocolate cake mix, but it doesn't stop there. Buttermilk, cinnamon, grated zucchini, pecans, and semi-sweet chocolate chips are folded into the batter. The zucchini adds moisture and texture to the cake, and it complements the German chocolate mix nicely. What you wind up with is a rich, moist cake that doesn't need frosting and stays right in its pan—perfect for traveling or for weekend guests.

SERVES: 20
PREPARATION TIME: 20 MINUTES
BAKING TIME: 38 TO 42 MINUTES

Vegetable oil spray for misting the pan
1 large zucchini
1 package (18.25 ounces) plain German
    chocolate cake mix
½ cup buttermilk
½ cup vegetable oil
3 large eggs
1 teaspoon pure vanilla extract
1 teaspoon ground cinnamon
1 cup semisweet chocolate chips
1 cup chopped pecans or walnuts

1. Place a rack in the center of the oven and preheat the oven to 350°F. Lightly mist a 13- by 9-inch pan with vegetable oil spray. Set the pan aside.

2. Rinse and pat dry the zucchini. Grate the zucchini and measure out 2 cups, lightly packed. Set it aside.

3. Place the cake mix, buttermilk, oil, eggs, vanilla, and cinnamon in a large mixing

R

the Cake Mix Doctor says

This is a very chocolaty cake. For a less intense cake, and one in which the zucchini shines through, try the Chocolate Zucchini Raisin Cake (facing page), which begins with a white cake mix. To dress this up, dust the cake with confectioners' sugar before slicing.

bowl. Blend with an electric mixer on low speed for 1 minute. Stop the machine and scrape down the sides of the bowl with a rubber spatula. Increase the mixer speed to medium and beat 2 minutes more,

scraping the sides down again if needed. The batter will be thick. Fold in the zucchini until well distributed. Pour the batter into the prepared pan, smoothing it out with the rubber spatula. Sprinkle the chocolate chips and nuts evenly over the top. Place the pan in the oven.

4. Bake the cake until it springs back when lightly pressed with your finger, 38 to 42 minutes. Remove the pan from the oven and place it on a wire rack to cool for 20 minutes, then serve.

✳ *Store this cake, covered with aluminum foil, at room temperature for 3 days, or in the refrigerator for up to 1 week. Or freeze it, wrapped in foil, for up to 6 months. Thaw the cake overnight in the refrigerator before serving.*

CHOCOLATE ZUCCHINI RAISIN CAKE

A lighter version of a chocolate zucchini cake, here the flavors of the cinnamon and zucchini are more pronounced than in the cake on page 169. In fact, this is more like zucchini bread than chocolate cake. The raisins marry well with the zucchini and chocolate. This is one moist, memorable cake for picnics and casual suppers.

SERVES: 20
PREPARATION TIME: 20 MINUTES
BAKING TIME: 38 TO 42 MINUTES

Vegetable oil spray for misting the pan
1 large zucchini
1 bar (4 ounces) German chocolate
1 package (18.25 ounces) plain white cake mix

½ cup buttermilk
½ cup vegetable oil
3 large eggs
1 teaspoon pure vanilla extract
1 teaspoon ground cinnamon
½ cup raisins
½ cup semisweet chocolate chips
½ cup chopped pecans or walnuts

1. Place a rack in the center of the oven and preheat the oven to 350°F. Lightly mist a 13- by 9-inch pan with vegetable oil spray. Set the pan aside.

R
the Cake Mix Doctor says

Remember that glass pans cook more quickly than metal pans. To use a glass pan with this recipe, reduce the oven temperature to 325°F.

For variations, try golden raisins or chopped dried sweetened cherries instead of the dark raisins.

Hot Tips
(from "A Piece of Cake," My Newsletter)

"To make cakes bake with more level tops, I wrap a water-soaked strip of heavy fabric around the pan and secure it with a pin before I pop the pan in the oven. These work because the sides of the cake do not bake before the center of the cake. I bought strips at a cake-decorating store, but they are just worn out with years of use, and I'm going to make replacements by cutting up an old bath towel in strips about 1½ inches wide and sewing about three layers together."
—Sue Buchanan, Jefferson City, Missouri

"I mash a ripe banana in the bowl before I start mixing a cake. This is especially good with chocolate mixes, but I have tried it with other flavors. Then I add chocolate chips and ground walnuts. I get rave reviews. People can't believe I use mixes."
—Lois Takach, Cottonwood, Arizona

"When baking a cake that doesn't need frosting, I grease the cake pan with vegetable shortening and then dust it with granulated sugar instead of flour. It comes out of the pan just as easily."
—Sandra Swan, Andover, New York

"Years ago a friend told me she made petits fours by freezing the pieces of cake on a cookie sheet first and then frosting them while still frozen."
—Anita Nelson, Georgetown, Texas

"If I am preparing a recipe that calls for sour cream and I do not have any, I have substituted yogurt and it works just fine."
—Ingrid Hall, Kettering, Ohio

"I have found that the recent humid days in Florida have given my chocolate frostings a fit unless I set them first. I put the frosted cake in my cake carrier in the freezer for 15 minutes. That is enough time to set the frosting but not harden the cake. Then I take it out and remove the cover so I can wipe out the excess moisture from inside the carrier. I replace the cover and tote it to the party, where it sits at room temperature."
—Margo Pope, St. Augustine, Florida

2. Rinse and pat dry the zucchini. Grate the zucchini and measure out 2 cups, lightly packed. Set it aside.

3. Chop the German chocolate, place it in a glass measuring cup, and melt it in a microwave oven on high power for 1 minute; stir until the chocolate is thoroughly melted and smooth.

4. Place the cake mix, buttermilk, oil, eggs, vanilla, cinnamon, and melted chocolate in a large mixing bowl. Blend with an electric mixer on low speed for 1 minute. Stop the machine and scrape down the sides of the bowl with a rubber spatula. Increase the mixer speed to medium and beat 2 minutes more, scraping the sides down again if needed. The batter will be thick.

Fold in the zucchini and raisins until well distributed. Pour the batter into the prepared pan, smoothing it out with the rubber spatula. Sprinkle the chocolate chips and nuts evenly over the top. Place the pan in the oven.

5. Bake the cake until it springs back when lightly pressed with your finger, 38 to 42 minutes. Remove the pan from the oven and place it on a wire rack to cool for 20 minutes, then serve.

✳ *Store this cake, covered with aluminum foil, at room temperature for 3 days, or in the refrigerator for up to 1 week. Or freeze it, wrapped in foil, for up to 6 months. Thaw the cake overnight in the refrigerator before serving.*

GERMAN CHOCOLATE VELVET CRUMB CAKE

One of the best things about traveling as a cookbook author is venturing into new territory and finding out about new cakes. I had heard of Velvet Crumb Cakes (cakes with a buttery, crunchy topping that are broiled before serving) when I was in St. Louis on my book tour, and I heard about them again as a guest on WHO radio in Des Moines with host Stephen Winzenburg.

Stephen told me that his mother makes a brown sugar, butter, and coconut topping, spreads it over a freshly baked cake, and then places the cake under the broiler until the topping bubbles and turns golden. I took that idea and came up with my own version for a German chocolate sheet cake. This is one fabulous cake that I will share in Des Moines anytime!

R℞
the Cake Mix Doctor says

Feel free to experiment with the topping combinations. Stephen's family recipe calls for more butter, a little heavy cream, and vanilla in addition to the coconut and brown sugar. It does not include pecans. If you cannot find the frozen unsweetened coconut in your market, substitute sweetened flaked coconut. This type of topping works well on just about any sheet cake. I think the combination is perfect with the mildness of German chocolate, but you could just as easily use it on a white or yellow cake as well as a devil's food cake.

My 10 Top Chocolate Cake Add-Ins (in no particular order)

1. Sour cream

2. Ripe bananas

3. Ground cinnamon

4. Semisweet chocolate chips

5. Coffee

6. Pecans and walnuts

7. Vanilla

8. Cherries (pie filling, sweetened dried, or maraschino)

9. Peanut butter

10. Peppermint

SERVES: 20

PREPARATION TIME: 10 MINUTES

BAKING TIME: 35 TO 38 MINUTES

ASSEMBLY TIME: 10 MINUTES

CAKE:

Vegetable oil spray for misting the pan

2 ounces German chocolate

1 package (18.25 ounces) plain German chocolate cake mix

1 cup sour cream

1 cup water

½ cup vegetable oil

3 large eggs

1 teaspoon pure vanilla extract

TOPPING:

½ cup pecans

½ cup (packed) light brown sugar

¼ cup frozen unsweetened grated coconut (see "the Cake Mix Doctor says")

2 tablespoons cold butter, cut into 4 pieces

1. Place a rack in the center of the oven and preheat the oven to 350°F. Lightly mist a 13- by 9-inch pan with vegetable oil spray. Set the pan aside.

2. Break the chocolate in half. Turn on a food processor and drop the chocolate through the feed tube, one piece at a time. Process until finely grated.

3. Place the cake mix, sour cream, water, oil, eggs, vanilla, and grated chocolate in a large mixing bowl. Blend with an electric mixer on low speed for 1 minute. Stop the machine and scrape down the sides of the bowl with a rubber spatula. Increase the mixer speed to medium and beat 2 minutes more, scraping the sides down again if needed. The batter should look well combined. Pour the batter into the prepared pan, smoothing it out with the rubber spatula. Place the pan in the oven.

4. Bake the cake until it springs back when lightly pressed with your finger, 35 to 38 minutes. Remove the pan from the oven and place it on a wire rack to cool while you assemble the topping.

5. Place the pecans, brown sugar, coconut, and cold butter in the food processor (no need to wash the processor after grating the chocolate). Pulse 20 times, or until the mixture is coarse and crumbly.

6. Preheat the broiler to medium-high.

7. Scatter the topping over the cake and broil 4 inches from the heat until the topping is bubbly and the pecans have browned, 1 to 2 minutes. Remove the cake from under the broiler and let it rest for 10 minutes. Then slice and serve.

✹ *Store this cake, covered with aluminum foil, at room temperature for 3 days or in the refrigerator for up to 1 week. Or freeze it, wrapped in foil, for up to 6 months. Thaw the cake overnight in the refrigerator before serving.*

CHOCOLATE CARROT CAKE

WITH PINEAPPLE CREAM CHEESE FROSTING

This cake is so much more than just a carrot cake. In fact, it's a carrot, pineapple, raisin, walnut, and chocolate cake, and it's topped with one of the most delicious cream cheese frostings around. And it's just the earthy, substantial sort of dessert you hope someone's brought to a potluck supper. Why take chances? Next time you be the one to bring it!

....

SERVES: 20
PREPARATION TIME: 15 MINUTES
BAKING TIME: 40 TO 45 MINUTES
ASSEMBLY TIME: 5 MINUTES

....

Vegetable oil spray for misting the pan
1 can (15¼ ounces) crushed pineapple in its own juice

5 to 6 carrots
1 package (18.25 ounces) German chocolate cake mix with pudding
½ cup vegetable oil
3 large eggs
2 teaspoons ground cinnamon
½ cup raisins
½ cup finely chopped walnuts
Pineapple Cream Cheese Frosting (page 431)

1. Place a rack in the center of the oven and preheat the oven to 350°F. Lightly mist a 13- by 9-inch pan with vegetable oil spray. Set the pan aside.

2. Drain the pineapple, reserving ⅔ cup of the juice. Set the juice aside, and reserve the drained crushed pineapple for the frosting. Grate the carrots to measure 3 cups. Set the carrots aside.

3. Place the cake mix, oil, eggs, cinnamon, and reserved pineapple juice in a large mixing bowl. Blend with an electric mixer on low speed for 1 minute. Stop the machine and scrape down the sides of the bowl with a rubber spatula.

15 Patriotic Cakes for the Fourth of July

Free up your imagination and you'll find that many cakes in this book can star on the July 4 buffet table. Yes, I'm taking creative license, but humor and patriotism go hand in hand.

1. (Oh, Beautiful!) White Chocolate Pound Cake with Blueberries and Strawberries and Warm Lemon Curd Sauce

2. Boston (Tea Party) Cream Pie Cake

3. (Red), White (and Blue) Chocolate Banana-Macadamia Cheesecake

4. (Francis Scott) Key Lime Chocolate Cheesecake

5. Chocolate (All-American) Carrot Cake with Pineapple Cream Cheese Frosting

6. (Betsy Ross) Chocolate Biscotti with Dried Sweet Cherries (on a blue plate)

7. (Old Glory) Kentucky Bourbon Pecan Fudge Pie

8. (I Pledge Allegiance) Pear and Chocolate Terrine

9. Lemon Lovers' (Very Washingtonian) White Chocolate Cake

10. (Patriotic) White Chocolate Peach Cake

11. Red (White and Blue) Velvet Cupcakes with White Chocolate Cream Cheese Frosting

12. (Colonial) Chocolate Pineapple Angel Food Cake

13. (Fourth of July) Frozen Chocolate Neapolitan Cake (made with blueberry and strawberry ice creams)

14. (South Carolina) Strawberry Brownie Torte

15. (Star-Spangled) Fudge Snowtops

Increase the mixer speed to medium and beat 2 minutes more, scraping the sides down again if needed. The batter should look well combined. Fold in the grated carrots, raisins, and walnuts until well distributed. Pour the batter into the pre-pared pan, smoothing it out with the rubber spatula. Place the pan in the oven.

4. Bake the cake until it springs back when lightly pressed with your finger, 40 to 45 minutes. Remove the pan from the oven and place it on a wire rack to cool completely, 20 minutes.

5. Meanwhile, prepare the Pineapple Cream Cheese Frosting.

6. Frost the top of the cake with smooth, clean strokes. Slice and serve.

✳ *To make slicing easier, store this cake, lightly covered with waxed paper, in the refrigerator until the frosting sets, 1 hour. Then wrap it in aluminum foil and store in the refrigerator for up to 1 week. Or freeze it, wrapped in foil, for up to 6 months. Thaw the cake overnight in the refrigerator before serving.*

R/

the Cake Mix Doctor says

You will need only ⅓ cup of the drained crushed pineapple in the frosting; reserve the remainder to add to fruit salad. Want a less substantial cake? Just omit the walnuts and raisins. Should you want to forgo the pineapple flavor, substitute orange or apple juice in the cake batter, and make a simple cream cheese frosting without the pineapple.

This cake also bakes well in layers. Allow about 30 minutes for 9-inch layers to bake at 350°F.

GERMAN CHOCOLATE SHEET CAKE

WITH ROCKY ROAD FROSTING

Maybe I'm sticking my neck out, but I do believe that this recipe alone is worth the price of the book! It's the cake that had my finicky family lining up for seconds. Yes, the frosting is incredible. But so is the cake: flecks of German chocolate baked into a sour cream–enriched German chocolate batter. This is the cake you tote to the office for a potluck lunch, and it's the one you make for the Fourth of July picnic, too. After all, what could be more American than peanuts and marshmallows?

SERVES: 20

PREPARATION TIME: 10 MINUTES

BAKING TIME: 35 TO 38 MINUTES

ASSEMBLY TIME: 5 MINUTES

Vegetable oil spray for misting the pan
2 ounces German chocolate
*1 package (18.25 ounces) plain German
    chocolate cake mix*
1 cup sour cream
1 cup water
½ cup vegetable oil
3 large eggs
1 teaspoon pure vanilla extract
Rocky Road Frosting (page 438)

1. Place a rack in the center of the oven and preheat the oven to 350°F. Lightly mist a 13- by 9-inch pan with vegetable oil spray. Set the pan aside.

2. Break the chocolate in half. Turn on a food processor and drop the chocolate through the feed tube, one piece at a time. Process until finely grated.

R/
the Cake Mix Doctor says

Change the roasted peanuts in the
frosting to toasted pecans, and this
cake becomes Mississippi Mud Cake!

3. Place the cake mix, sour cream,
water, oil, eggs, vanilla, and grated
chocolate in a large mixing bowl. Blend
with an electric mixer on low speed for 1
minute. Stop the machine and scrape
down the sides of the bowl with a rubber
spatula. Increase the mixer speed to
medium and beat 2 minutes more,
scraping the sides down again if needed.
The batter should look well combined.
Pour the batter into the prepared pan,
smoothing it out with the rubber spatula. Place the pan in the oven.

4. Bake the cake until it springs back
when lightly pressed with your finger, 35
to 38 minutes. Remove the pan from the
oven and place it on a wire rack to cool
for 20 minutes.

5. Meanwhile, prepare the Rocky Road
Frosting.

6. While the frosting is still warm,
spread it over the cake in the pan. Let
the cake rest another 20 minutes before
slicing.

✳ *Store this cake, covered with aluminum foil, at room temperature for 3
days or in the refrigerator for up to 1
week. Or freeze it, wrapped in foil, for up
to 6 months. Thaw the cake overnight in
the refrigerator before serving.*

EASY CHOCOLATE POKE CAKE

My daughters, Litton and Kathleen, loved helping to make this cake. And I'll admit it was fun to jab the handle of a wooden spoon into a freshly baked cake and then pour warm pudding into the holes. You've got to work quickly here, because the instant pudding will set up and thicken too much if you start discussing the weather or the state of the economy. My husband, John, who likes desserts that have to be scooped onto plates, declared the result was pure and delicious comfort food.

SERVES: 20

PREPARATION TIME: 15 MINUTES

BAKING TIME: 33 TO 38 MINUTES

CHILLING TIME: 1 HOUR

CAKE:

Vegetable oil spray for misting the pan

1 package (18.25 ounces) plain devil's food cake mix

1⅓ cups buttermilk

¼ cup vegetable oil

3 large eggs

1 teaspoon pure vanilla extract

1 tablespoon unsweetened cocoa powder

TOPPING:

1 large package (5.1 ounces) vanilla instant pudding mix

½ cup confectioners' sugar

3 cups cold milk

1 tablespoon pure vanilla extract

1. Place a rack in the center of the oven and preheat the oven to 350°F. Lightly mist a 13- by 9-inch pan with vegetable oil spray. Set the pan aside.

2. Place the cake mix, buttermilk, oil, eggs, vanilla, and cocoa powder in a large mixing bowl. Blend with an electric mixer on low speed for 1 minute. Stop the machine and scrape down the sides of the bowl with a rubber spatula. Increase the mixer speed to medium and beat 2 minutes more, scraping the sides down again if needed. The batter should look well combined. Pour the batter into the prepared pan, smoothing it out with the rubber spatula. Place the pan in the oven.

3. Bake the cake until it springs back when lightly pressed with your finger, 33 to 38 minutes. Remove the pan from the oven and place it on a wire rack. Immediately poke holes, 1 inch apart, in the cake with the handle of a wooden spoon.

4. Quickly prepare the topping by combining the pudding mix, confectioners' sugar, cold milk, and vanilla in a large mixing bowl. Whisk for 1 minute, or until the mixture just begins to thicken. Spoon half of the mixture (1¾ cups) down into the holes of the cake. While you are doing this, the remaining pudding will thicken. Spread the thickened pudding evenly over the top of the cake. Cover the pan with

waxed paper or plastic wrap and chill for 1 hour. Then spoon onto plates and serve.

✻ *Store this cake, covered with plastic wrap, in the refrigerator for up to 1 week.*

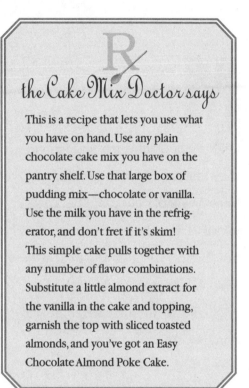

the Cake Mix Doctor says

This is a recipe that lets you use what you have on hand. Use any plain chocolate cake mix you have on the pantry shelf. Use that large box of pudding mix—chocolate or vanilla. Use the milk you have in the refrigerator, and don't fret if it's skim! This simple cake pulls together with any number of flavor combinations. Substitute a little almond extract for the vanilla in the cake and topping, garnish the top with sliced toasted almonds, and you've got an Easy Chocolate Almond Poke Cake.

MARCIA'S EASY CHOCOLATE TOFFEE CRUNCH POKE CAKE

Marcia LeVake, of West Allis, Wisconsin, told me that she always has to give people a copy of this recipe once they taste a bite. So I tasted, and knew immediately that she wasn't joking. The cake is easy to prepare, but the flavors of chocolate, caramel, whipped topping, and crushed toffee create quite an intricate combination. My children adore this cake, and they request it over and over again. As Marcia says, it's a crowd-pleaser, and no need to worry about storage suggestions: There probably won't be any left.

SERVES: 20
PREPARATION TIME: 15 MINUTES
BAKING TIME: 32 TO 37 MINUTES

Vegetable oil spray for misting the pan
1 package (18.25 ounces) plain devil's food cake mix
1⅓ cups water
½ cup vegetable oil
3 large eggs
1 cup caramel or butterscotch ice cream topping
1 small container (8 ounces) frozen whipped topping, thawed
1 cup toffee-flavored chips (see "the Cake Mix Doctor says")

1. Place a rack in the center of the oven and preheat the oven to 350°F. Lightly mist a 13- by 9-inch pan with vegetable oil spray. Set the pan aside.

2. Place the cake mix, water, oil, and eggs in a large mixing bowl. Blend with an electric mixer on low speed for 1

3. Bake the cake until it springs back when lightly pressed with your finger, 32 to 37 minutes. Remove the pan from the oven and place it on a wire rack to cool completely, 30 minutes.

4. Poke holes, 1 inch apart, in the cake with the handle of a wooden spoon. Fill each hole with caramel ice cream topping. Let the topping settle into the holes, then go back and fill them once again. Using a rubber spatula, spread the whipped topping smoothly over the top of the cake. Sprinkle the toffee-flavored chips evenly over the top. Cover the pan lightly with waxed paper and place it in the refrigerator to chill until it's time to serve.

✳ *Store this cake, covered with waxed paper or plastic wrap, in the refrigerator for up to 1 week.*

the Cake Mix Doctor says

There are several types of toffee-flavored chips in the baking aisle. Heath is one brand name; Skorr is another. One is chocolate-coated, one contains almonds. It's your choice!

minute. Stop the machine and scrape down the sides of the bowl with a rubber spatula. Increase the mixer speed to medium and beat 2 minutes more, scraping the sides down again if needed. The batter should look well combined. Pour the batter into the prepared pan, smoothing it out with the rubber spatula. Place the pan in the oven.

Lumps in the Cake Mix

Cake mix manufacturers say not to worry about some lumps in the cake mix. The lumps are normal—they form when the cake mix settles during shipping and will bake out. But if lumps in the cake mix do worry you, go ahead and work them out with a whisk, the back of a wooden spoon, or a pastry blender before you add the rest of the ingredients. Should lumps still be present after mixing the batter, don't fret. They will bake out, and it's better to have a few lumps than to overbeat the batter. Overbeating causes big holes—tunneling—to form while the cake bakes.

THE WATERGATE CAKE

Although this cake was born in the 1970s—about the time of the real Watergate intrigue, when pistachio pudding mix was all the rage—it didn't come my way until recently. Someone had mentioned that *The Cake Mix Doctor* didn't include a recipe for the famed Watergate Cake. Having never heard of it, I asked my newsletter readers whether they had, and if so, would they share the recipe. Well, they shared it all right— by the hundreds! I chose a handful to test and this one, from Ruth Duncan, of Whitehall, Michigan, was my favorite. I added the topping, which gives it some chocolate and some crunch and justifies including this yummy cake in this book!

SERVES: 20
PREPARATION TIME: 10 MINUTES
BAKING TIME: 35 TO 40 MINUTES
ASSEMBLY TIME: 5 MINUTES

CAKE:

Vegetable oil spray for
    misting the pan
1 package (18.25 ounces) plain
    white cake mix
1 package (3.4 ounces) pistachio instant
    pudding mix
1 cup vegetable oil
1 cup ginger ale
3 large eggs

COVER-UP FROSTING:

1 package (3.4 ounces) pistachio instant
    pudding mix
1½ cups milk
1 small container (8 ounces) frozen whipped
    topping, thawed

TOPPING:

½ cup crushed chocolate wafers
⅓ cup slivered almonds, toasted (see
    Toasting Nuts, page 196)

1. Place a rack in the center of the oven and preheat the oven to 350°F. Lightly mist a 13- by 9-inch pan with vegetable oil spray. Set the pan aside.

2. Place the cake mix, pudding mix, oil, ginger ale, and eggs in a large mixing bowl. Blend with an electric mixer on low speed for 1 minute. Stop the machine and scrape down the sides of the bowl with a rubber spatula. Increase the mixer speed to medium and beat 2 minutes more, scraping down the sides again if needed. The batter should look well combined. Pour the batter into the prepared pan, smoothing the top with the rubber spatula. Place the pan in the oven.

3. Bake the cake until it springs back when lightly pressed with your finger, 35 to 40 minutes. Remove the pan from the oven and place it on a wire rack to cool completely, 30 minutes.

4. Meanwhile, prepare the frosting: Whisk together the pudding mix and milk in a large mixing bowl. It should thicken up (but not set) in 2 to 3 minutes. Then gently fold in the whipped topping. Spread the frosting over the top of the cake.

the Cake Mix Doctor says

Yes, this cake contains a lot of oil, which means it doesn't rise a lot, but it does create a nicely browned top.

You can vary the cake by folding miniature chocolate chips into the batter, and you could use a lemon-lime type of soda instead of ginger ale—it's a nice complement to the pistachio flavor. And here is a fun twist: Bake the cake in a tube pan at 350°F for 50 to 55 minutes. Cool, unmold, and slice the cake in half horizontally. Fill the center and frost the sides and top with the Cover-up Frosting. Cover the cake with grated coconut.

5. Sprinkle the crushed chocolate wafers and toasted almonds over the top of the cake. Slice and serve.

✳ *Store this cake, lightly covered with waxed paper, in the refrigerator for up to 1 week.*

CHOCOLATE RUM RAISIN CAKE

People frequently ask me, "How do you come up with so many new recipes?" And I say, "It's easy when you think about cake as much as I do!" But I guess I should rephrase that answer: It gets easier when you learn which flavors belong together. And two of those flavor-mates are in this cake: rum and raisins. Pair them with chocolate and you've got a winner—no, make that a triple crown! To quickly infuse the raisins with rum flavor, heat them together in a microwave oven. To top this cake? What else—a Fluffy Chocolate Rum Frosting.

SERVES: 20

PREPARATION TIME: 20 MINUTES

BAKING TIME: 38 TO 42 MINUTES

ASSEMBLY TIME: 3 MINUTES

CAKE:

¼ cup dark rum

½ cup golden raisins

Vegetable oil spray for misting the pan

1 package (18.25 ounces) devil's food cake mix with pudding

1 cup sour cream

½ cup water

½ cup vegetable oil

3 large eggs

FLUFFY CHOCOLATE RUM FROSTING:

8 tablespoons (1 stick) butter, at room temperature

⅔ cup unsweetened cocoa powder

1 tablespoon dark rum

3 cups confectioners' sugar, sifted

¼ cup milk

1. Combine the rum and raisins in a small glass bowl and place in the microwave. Heat on high power for 45 seconds. Set the bowl aside so the raisins can soak in the rum for 10 minutes.

2. Place a rack in the center of the oven and preheat the oven to 350°F. Lightly mist a 13- by 9-inch pan with vegetable oil spray. Set the pan aside.

3. Place the cake mix, sour cream, water, oil, and eggs in a large mixing bowl. Blend with an electric mixer on low speed for 1 minute. Stop the machine and scrape down the sides of the bowl with a rubber spatula. Increase the mixer speed to medium and beat 2 minutes more, scraping the sides down again if needed. The batter should look well combined. Fold in the raisins and rum until well distributed. Pour the batter into the prepared pan, smoothing it out with the rubber spatula. Place the pan in the oven.

4. Bake the cake until it springs back when lightly pressed with your finger, 38 to 42 minutes. Remove the pan from the oven and place it on a wire rack to cool for 20 minutes.

5. Meanwhile, prepare the frosting: Place the butter and cocoa powder in a large mixing bowl. Blend with an electric mixer on low speed until the mixture is soft and well combined, 30 seconds. Stop the machine. Place the rum, confectioners' sugar, and milk in the bowl, and beat with the mixer on low speed until the frosting lightens and becomes fluffy, 2 to 3 minutes. Add more milk or rum if the frosting is too thick, or confectioners' sugar, 1 tablespoon at a time, if it is too thin.

6. When the cake has cooled, spread the top with the frosting, using clean, smooth strokes. Let the cake rest for 20 minutes before slicing.

✳ *Store this cake, covered with aluminum foil or plastic wrap, at room temperature for 3 days or in the refrigerator for up to 1 week. Or freeze it, wrapped in foil, for up to 6 months. Thaw the cake overnight in the refrigerator before serving.*

R̶x

the Cake Mix Doctor says

You can frost this cake in the pan or out of the pan. If you want to turn the cake out, make sure it has cooled completely before inverting it onto a long serving platter. There will be plenty of frosting to coat the top and sides.

CHOCOLATE APRICOT CAKE

Years ago one of my favorite desserts was a nearly flourless chocolate cake that contained slivers of dried apricots. The combination of semisweet chocolate and apricots was irresistible! Here the chocolate and apricots are in a cake that is much, much easier to assemble. The chocolate is in the cake mix, and the apricots are simply the canned variety, puréed in your food processor or blender. The apricots add flavor, negate the need for oil in the batter, and add a lot of moisture—so this cake stays fresh for days.

SERVES: 20

PREPARATION TIME: 8 MINUTES

BAKING TIME: 38 TO 42 MINUTES

ASSEMBLY TIME: 3 MINUTES

Vegetable oil spray for misting the pan

1 can (15 ounces) apricot halves, packed in their own juice

1 package (18.25 ounces) devil's food cake mix with pudding

3 large eggs

1 teaspoon pure almond extract

Martha's Chocolate Icing (page 433)

1. Place a rack in the center of the oven and preheat the oven to 350°F. Lightly mist a 13- by 9-inch pan with vegetable oil spray. Set the pan aside.

2. Drain the apricot halves, reserving the juice. Purée the apricots in a food processor or blender until smooth. Place the apricot purée, reserved juice (¾ to 1 cup), cake mix, eggs, and almond extract in a large mixing bowl. Blend with an electric mixer on low speed for 30 seconds. Stop the machine and scrape down the sides of the bowl with a rubber spatula. Increase the mixer speed to medium and beat 2 minutes more, scraping the sides down again if needed. The batter should look thick and well combined. Pour the batter into the prepared pan, smoothing it out with the rubber spatula. Place the pan in the oven.

3. Bake the cake until it springs back when lightly pressed with your finger, 38 to 42 minutes. Remove the pan from the oven and place it on a wire rack to cool for 20 minutes.

4. Meanwhile, prepare Martha's Chocolate Icing.

5. While the frosting is still warm, spread it over the cake in the pan. Let the cake rest for 20 minutes before slicing.

❋ *Store this cake, covered with aluminum foil, at room temperature for 3 days or in the refrigerator for up to 1 week. Or freeze it, wrapped in foil, for up to 6 months. Thaw the cake overnight in the refrigerator before serving.*

R/

the Cake Mix Doctor says

This cake is pretty low in fat, but if you want to make it even lower, use egg substitute for the eggs and dust the top with confectioners' sugar instead of cloaking it in frosting. On the other hand, if you want to crank it up a notch, sprinkle it with toasted sliced almonds after frosting it with the warm icing. Be sure to sprinkle those almonds on while the frosting is warm so they will stick.

CHOCOLATE EGGNOG CAKE

WITH EGGNOG BUTTERCREAM FROSTING

My children anticipate eggnog season with the same eagerness they have for peaches in the summertime. And you know the cartons of eggnog will be displayed in the supermarket dairy case about the same time that candied cherries, nuts, raisins, and foil pans are placed at the front of the store. Definite signals of fruitcake season. When you can get your hands on prepared eggnog, it is time to make this great cake. I can't think of a better choice for toting to parties during the winter holidays.

SERVES: 20

PREPARATION TIME: 15 MINUTES

BAKING TIME: 38 TO 42 MINUTES

ASSEMBLY TIME: 5 MINUTES

CAKE:

Vegetable oil spray for misting the pan

Flour for dusting the pan

2 ounces semisweet chocolate

1 package (18.25 ounces) plain German chocolate cake mix

1 cup eggnog

⅓ cup brandy or water

¼ cup vegetable oil

3 large eggs

1 teaspoon pure vanilla extract

½ teaspoon ground nutmeg

EGGNOG BUTTERCREAM FROSTING:

8 tablespoons (1 stick) butter, at room temperature

3½ to 4 cups confectioners' sugar, sifted

3 to 4 tablespoons eggnog

2 teaspoons brandy or pure vanilla extract

⅛ teaspoon ground nutmeg, for garnish (optional)

1. Place a rack in the center of the oven and preheat the oven to 350°F. Lightly mist a 13- by 9-inch pan with vegetable oil spray, then dust with flour. Shake out the excess flour. Set the pan aside.

2. Carefully rub the chocolate along the largest holes of a cheese grater to make 1 tablespoon grated chocolate; set it aside. Break the remaining chocolate into 5 or 6 pieces and place them in a small glass bowl. Microwave for 1 minute at high power. Stir to melt any remaining lumps.

3. Place the cake mix, eggnog, brandy, oil, eggs, vanilla, nutmeg, and melted chocolate in a large mixing bowl. Blend with an electric mixer on low speed for 30 seconds. Stop the machine and scrape down the sides of the bowl with a rubber spatula. Increase the mixer speed to medium and beat 2 minutes more, scraping the sides down again if needed. The batter should look well combined. Pour the batter into the prepared pan, smoothing it out with the rubber spatula. Place the pan in the oven.

4. Bake the cake until it springs back when lightly pressed with your finger, 38 to 42 minutes. Remove the pan from the oven and place it on a wire rack to cool for 10 minutes. Run a sharp knife

R the Cake Mix Doctor says

You can just as well fold grated chocolate instead of melted chocolate into the cake batter. But rather than grate that much chocolate on a grater (and chance scraped knuckles), use a food processor. With the motor running, drop pieces of the chocolate through the feed tube, one at a time; process until ground. Reserve 1 tablespoon for the garnish, and fold the remainder into the batter instead of the melted chocolate. When grating the chocolate with a cheese grater, be sure it is a little soft to make the job easier on your knuckles!

Feel free to substitute bourbon or rum for the brandy in this recipe.

around the edge of the cake, and invert it onto a serving platter to cool completely, 20 minutes.

5. Meanwhile, prepare the frosting: Place the butter and 1 cup of the confectioners' sugar in a large mixing bowl. Blend with an electric mixer on low speed for 30 seconds to incorporate. Stop the machine and add the remaining confectioners' sugar, eggnog, and brandy. Increase the speed to medium and beat until light and fluffy, 1 minute. Add more confectioners' sugar if the frosting is too runny to spread. Add a touch more eggnog if it is too stiff.

6. Spread the frosting over the top and sides of the cake, using smooth, clean strokes. Sprinkle the top lightly with the reserved grated chocolate, and with a little nutmeg if desired. Slice and serve.

✳ *Store this cake, covered with aluminum foil or plastic wrap, at room temperature for 3 days or in the refrigerator for up to 1 week. Or freeze it, wrapped in foil, for up to 6 months. Thaw the cake overnight in the refrigerator before serving.*

CHOCOLATE PUMPKIN SPICE CAKE

WITH CINNAMON-CHOCOLATE CREAM CHEESE FROSTING

I toted this sheet cake to a family Halloween party, and it was the perfect dessert for the occasion! Not only was it festive, containing pumpkin and spices, but it was moist and mess-free, brought right in its pan. Pumpkin is a yummy cake addition, and you don't need to use vegetable oil when you include it.

As for the cinnamon taste in the frosting, it comes from cinnamon chips. The perfect last touch? Chopped toasted pecans scattered over the top.

SERVES: 20
PREPARATION TIME: 8 MINUTES
BAKING TIME: 35 TO 40 MINUTES
ASSEMBLY TIME: 3 MINUTES

Vegetable oil spray for misting the pan
1 package (18.25 ounces) plain German
    chocolate cake mix
1 can (15 ounces; 1¾ cups) pumpkin
3 large eggs
1 teaspoon ground cinnamon
½ teaspoon ground nutmeg
½ cup cinnamon chips
Cinnamon-Chocolate Cream Cheese Frosting
    (page 423)
½ cup chopped toasted pecans

R the Cake Mix Doctor says

In a hurry? Make a plain cream cheese frosting. Want to turn this into a fun summertime cake? Frost it with the Pineapple Cream Cheese Frosting (page 431).

Toasting Nuts

*I*f you have a few extra minutes, toasting nuts really brings out their flavor. Begin with a 350°F oven. Spread the nuts out in one layer in a baking pan and place in the oven. Stir once or twice with a metal spatula or long wooden spoon while they are toasting. Remove the nuts just when you smell the sweet toasty aroma and before their color deepens too much. Take care not to overcook chopped nuts; they take less time to toast than whole nuts.

Almonds: Whole, about 10 minutes; slivered, 2 to 3 minutes, until light brown.

Hazelnuts (filberts): 20 minutes; rub off the skins with a clean kitchen towel while the nuts are warm.

Macadamia nuts: 8 minutes, or until golden brown.

Pecans: 4 to 5 minutes, or until deep brown.

Walnuts: 10 minutes, or until golden brown.

1. Place a rack in the center of the oven and preheat the oven to 350°F. Lightly mist a 13- by 9-inch pan with vegetable oil spray. Set the pan aside.

2. Place the cake mix, pumpkin, eggs, cinnamon, and nutmeg in a large mixing bowl. Blend with an electric mixer on low speed for 1 minute. Stop the machine and scrape down the sides of the bowl with a rubber spatula. Increase the mixer speed to medium and beat 2 minutes more, scraping the sides down again if needed. The batter will be thick and should look well combined. Fold in the cinnamon chips until well distributed. Pour the batter into the prepared pan, smoothing it out with the rubber spatula. Place the pan in the oven.

3. Bake the cake until it springs back when lightly pressed with your finger, 35 to 40 minutes. Remove the pan from the oven and cool it on a wire rack for 20 minutes.

4. Meanwhile, prepare the Cinnamon-Chocolate Cream Cheese Frosting.

5. Spread the frosting over the cake in the pan with smooth, clean strokes. Sprinkle the pecans over the top.

✳ *To make slicing easier, store this cake, lightly covered with waxed paper, in the refrigerator until the frosting sets, 1 hour. Then wrap it in aluminum foil and store in the refrigerator for up to 1 week. Or freeze it, wrapped in foil, for up to 6 months. Thaw the cake overnight in the refrigerator before serving.*

DARK CHOCOLATE SHEET CAKE

WITH FRESH ORANGE CREAM CHEESE FROSTING

I almost named this cake "Versatile Chocolate Sheet Cake," but that doesn't make you hungry or paint a mouthwatering picture. Let me just say that when spread with the orange frosting, it's perfect for Halloween. When topped with Crushed Peppermint Buttercream Frosting (page 414), it's ready for Christmas. If you like cakes plain and simple, crown it with White Chocolate Cream Cheese Frosting (page 425) or Martha's Chocolate Icing (page 433)—but do throw on a handful of chopped toasted pecans or walnuts for good measure. Like the little black dress or the dark suit, no matter what its name, this delicious cake can be taken anywhere.

SERVES: 20
PREPARATION TIME: 8 MINUTES
BAKING TIME: 38 TO 42 MINUTES
ASSEMBLY TIME: 3 MINUTES

Vegetable oil spray for misting the pan
1 package (18.25 ounces) devil's food cake mix with pudding
1 cup sour cream
1 cup water
½ cup vegetable oil
3 large eggs
1 teaspoon pure vanilla extract
Fresh Orange Cream Cheese Frosting (page 428)

1. Place a rack in the center of the oven and preheat the oven to 350°F. Lightly mist a 13- by 9-inch pan with vegetable oil spray. Set the pan aside.

2. Place the cake mix, sour cream, water, oil, eggs, and vanilla in a large mixing bowl. Blend with an electric mixer on low speed for 1 minute. Stop the machine and scrape down the sides of the bowl with a rubber spatula. Increase the mixer speed to medium and beat 2 minutes more, scraping the sides down again if needed. The batter should look well combined. Pour the batter into the prepared pan, smoothing it out with the rubber spatula. Place the pan in the oven.

3. Bake the cake until it springs back when lightly pressed with your finger, 38 to 42 minutes. Remove the pan from the oven and place it on a wire rack to cool for 20 minutes.

4. Meanwhile, prepare the Fresh Orange Cream Cheese Frosting.

5. Frost the top of the cake with smooth, clean strokes.

✳ *To make slicing easier, store this cake, lightly covered with waxed paper, in the refrigerator until the frosting sets, 1 hour. Then wrap it in aluminum foil and store in the refrigerator for up to 1 week. Or freeze it, wrapped in foil, for up to 6 months. Thaw the cake overnight in the refrigerator before serving.*

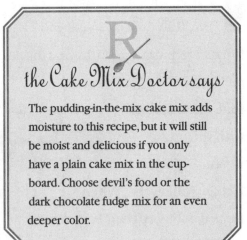

the Cake Mix Doctor says

The pudding-in-the-mix cake mix adds moisture to this recipe, but it will still be moist and delicious if you only have a plain cake mix in the cupboard. Choose devil's food or the dark chocolate fudge mix for an even deeper color.

BANANA SPLIT FUDGE CAKE

Assemble the same ingredients you might use for a banana split, and you have the makings of a stellar sheet cake! This recipe is adapted from one devised by Natalie Haughton for her cookbook *365 Great Chocolate Desserts*. The bananas are mashed and added to the cake batter, then the nuts and chocolate sauce are sprinkled in the middle and on top before baking. To complete the banana split theme, serve this with vanilla ice cream, more chocolate topping, whipped cream, and maraschino cherries.

....

SERVES: 20
PREPARATION TIME: 12 MINUTES
BAKING TIME: 42 TO 47 MINUTES

....

Vegetable oil spray for misting the pan

1 package (18.25 ounces) yellow cake mix with pudding

1 cup mashed ripe bananas (3 medium or 2 large bananas)

1 cup buttermilk

4 tablespoons (½ stick) butter, melted

3 large eggs

1 cup chopped walnuts

1 cup chocolate topping for ice cream (see "the Cake Mix Doctor says")

1. Place a rack in the center of the oven and preheat the oven to 325°F. Lightly mist a 13- by 9-inch pan with vegetable oil spray. Set the pan aside.

2. Place the cake mix, mashed bananas, buttermilk, melted butter, and eggs in a large mixing bowl. Blend with an electric mixer on low speed for 1 minute. Stop the machine and scrape down the sides of the bowl with a rubber spatula. Increase the mixer speed to medium and beat 2 minutes more, scraping the sides down again if needed. The batter should look well

the Cake Mix Doctor says

Chocolate ice cream topping is the thick topping sold in glass jars in the ice cream aisle. It is thicker than chocolate syrup. Make sure that you microwave the topping for a minute so that it is slightly runny and you are able to spoon it over the batter.

combined. Pour two thirds of the batter into the prepared pan, smoothing it out with the rubber spatula. Sprinkle half of the nuts over the batter.

3. Melt the chocolate ice cream topping in a glass bowl in the microwave oven on high power for 1 minute, or until slightly runny. Spoon the chocolate topping evenly over the nuts.

4. Pour the remaining batter over the topping, and spread it out evenly with the rubber spatula to cover the chocolate topping. Sprinkle the remaining walnuts over the batter. Place the pan in the oven.

5. Bake the cake until it springs back when lightly pressed with your finger, 42 to 47 minutes. Remove the pan from the oven and place it on a wire rack to cool slightly, 10 minutes. Slice, and serve warm.

✳ *Store this cake, covered with waxed paper or plastic wrap, in the refrigerator for up to 1 week.*

CHOCOLATE SYRUP COFFEE CAKE

I love this dense, homey cake with its near-pound-cake consistency. And I love the versatility of this recipe— perfect for breakfast, afternoon tea, or dessert. Bake this cake to tote to new neighbors. They'll be glad they moved to *your* neighborhood!

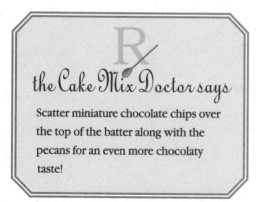

the Cake Mix Doctor says

Scatter miniature chocolate chips over the top of the batter along with the pecans for an even more chocolaty taste!

SERVES: 20
PREPARATION TIME: 15 MINUTES
BAKING TIME: 38 TO 42 MINUTES

Vegetable oil spray for misting the pan
1 package (18.25 ounces) plain yellow
  cake mix
1 package (3.4 ounces) vanilla instant
  pudding mix
1 cup sour cream
¾ cup water
½ cup vegetable oil
3 large eggs
1 teaspoon pure vanilla extract
½ teaspoon ground cinnamon
½ cup chocolate syrup
½ cup chopped pecans or walnuts

1. Place a rack in the center of the oven and preheat the oven to 350°F. Lightly mist a 13- by 9-inch pan with vegetable oil spray. Set the pan aside.

2. Place the cake mix, pudding mix, sour cream, water, oil, eggs, vanilla, and cinnamon in a large mixing bowl. Blend with an electric mixer on low speed for 1 minute. Stop the machine and scrape down the sides of the bowl with a rubber spatula. Increase the mixer speed to medium and beat 2 minutes more, scraping the sides down again if needed. The batter should look well combined. Pour the batter into the prepared pan, smoothing it out with the rubber spatula.

3. Drizzle the chocolate syrup over the top of the cake, and swirl it through the batter with a dinner knife to create a marbled effect. (Be careful not to scrape the bottom of the pan.) Scatter the pecans over the top of the batter. Place the pan in the oven.

4. Bake the cake until it springs back when lightly pressed with your finger, 38 to 42 minutes. Remove the pan from the oven and place it on a wire rack to cool for 20 minutes. Slice and serve.

✳ *Store this cake, covered with aluminum foil, at room temperature for 3 days or in the refrigerator for up to 1 week. Or freeze it, wrapped in foil, for up to 6 months. Thaw the cake overnight in the refrigerator before serving.*

CHOCOLATE TIRAMISÙ

'll never forget a cooking class I attended 20 or more years ago when our teacher, Nathalie Dupree, told twelve of us to make chicken soup, all following the same recipe. In 2 hours, we uncovered our pots and tasted the results. Not one of the soups tasted or looked the same! Nathalie explained that this exercise was to illustrate that we all cook subjectively, without thinking—blending, seasoning, and chopping in our own way, so that in the end the recipe is all our own. That's how it goes with tiramisù. Here are the ingredients and the proportions I use. Now, go ahead and make it your own. Enjoy!

SERVES: 20
PREPARATION TIME: 15 MINUTES
BAKING TIME: 32 TO 35 MINUTES
ASSEMBLY TIME: 5 MINUTES

CAKE:

Vegetable oil spray for misting the pan
1 package (18.25 ounces) plain devil's food
    or German chocolate cake mix
1¼ cups water
⅓ cup vegetable oil
3 large eggs
1 teaspoon pure vanilla extract

SYRUP:

¾ cup hot water
2 tablespoons instant coffee powder
3 tablespoons granulated sugar
¼ cup Kahlúa or other coffee-flavored liqueur

TOPPING:

2 cups low-fat or nonfat vanilla yogurt
2 packages (8 ounces each) cream cheese, at
    room temperature
¼ cup confectioners' sugar
1 teaspoon unsweetened or sweetened cocoa
    powder (see "the Cake Mix Doctor says")

1. Place a rack in the center of the oven and preheat the oven to 350°F. Lightly mist a 13- by 9-inch pan with vegetable oil spray. Set the pan aside.

2. Place the cake mix, water, oil, eggs, and vanilla in a large mixing bowl. Blend with an electric mixer on low speed for 1 minute. Stop the machine and scrape down the sides of the bowl with a rubber spatula. Increase the mixer speed to medium and beat 2 minutes more, scraping the sides down again if needed. The batter should look thick and well com-

the Cake Mix Doctor says

In *The Cake Mix Doctor* I also offered up a creamy mixture of vanilla yogurt and cream cheese as a substitute for the traditional mascarpone cheese, which may be hard to find outside of an upscale grocery or Italian market. Suit yourself here, using the mock mascarpone or real mascarpone if you can locate it.

For those of you who do not like bitter chocolate, use sweetened cocoa powder instead of unsweetened for dusting on top.

bined. Pour the batter into the prepared pan, smoothing it out with the rubber spatula. Place the pan in the oven.

3. Bake the cake until it springs back when lightly pressed with your finger, 32 to 35 minutes. Remove the pan from the oven and place it on a wire rack to cool.

4. Meanwhile, prepare the syrup: Place the hot water, coffee powder, and sugar in a small bowl and stir until the coffee and sugar dissolve. Stir in the Kahlúa.

5. Using a chopstick or a drinking straw, poke holes in the cake. Spoon the syrup over the cake so that it seeps down into the holes. Set the cake aside.

6. Prepare the topping: Place the yogurt, cream cheese, and confectioners' sugar in a large mixing bowl and blend with an electric mixer on low speed until the mixture is well combined and thick, 1 to 2 minutes. Spread the topping over the syrup-soaked cake, using the rubber spatula to spread it out to the edges of the cake.

7. No more than an hour before serving, sift the cocoa powder over the topping so that it covers the top of the cake. Cut the cake into squares, and serve.

✱ *Store this cake, covered in plastic wrap, in the refrigerator for up to 3 days.*

CHOCOLATE POTLUCK CAKE

Theresa Hart and her daughter Madeline attended my book signing in Lexington, Kentucky, but I didn't know at the time that Theresa was a cake mix skeptic. She had bought *The Cake Mix Doctor* for Madeline, and many months later she e-mailed me a note saying she was now a cake mix convert and that both she and Madeline were cooking up a storm from the book. The Harts concocted this wonderful topping of pecans, chocolate chips, and brown sugar that they scatter on cake batter before it goes into the oven. They begin with yellow, white, or coffee-flavored cake, but I couldn't wait to try it with chocolate. No frosting is needed, and this cake is true to its name—as Theresa says, "It is easy to make, easy to carry, and easy to serve right out of the pan!" Vanilla ice cream makes a great addition.

....

SERVES: 20

PREPARATION TIME: 10 MINUTES

BAKING TIME: 30 TO 35 MINUTES

....

CAKE:

Vegetable oil spray for misting the pan

1 package (18.25 ounces) plain devil's food cake mix

1 cup vanilla low-fat or nonfat yogurt

½ cup water

½ cup vegetable oil

3 large eggs

TOPPING:

⅓ cup finely chopped pecans

⅓ cup (packed) light brown sugar

⅓ cup miniature semisweet chocolate chips

1. Place a rack in the center of the oven and preheat the oven to 350°F. Lightly mist a 13- by 9-inch pan with vegetable oil spray. Set the pan aside.

2. Place the cake mix, yogurt, water, oil, and eggs in a large mixing bowl. Blend with an electric mixer on low speed for 1 minute. Stop the machine and scrape down the sides of the bowl with a rubber spatula. Increase the mixer speed to medium and beat 2 minutes more, scraping the sides down again if needed. The batter should be stiff but smooth. Pour the batter into the prepared pan, smoothing it out with the rubber spatula. Set the pan aside.

3. Stir together the pecans, brown sugar, and chocolate chips in a small bowl. Sprinkle the mixture over the top of the cake batter. Place the pan in the oven.

4. Bake the cake until it springs back when lightly pressed with your finger, 30 to 35 minutes. Remove the pan from the oven and place it on a wire rack to cool for 20 minutes. Serve slightly warm.

✳ *Store this cake, covered with aluminum foil, at room temperature for 3 days or in the refrigerator for up to 1 week. Or freeze it, wrapped in foil, for up to 6 months. Thaw the cake overnight in the refrigerator before serving.*

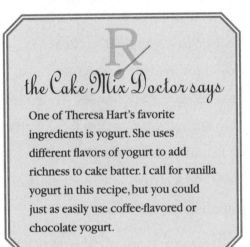

the Cake Mix Doctor says

One of Theresa Hart's favorite ingredients is yogurt. She uses different flavors of yogurt to add richness to cake batter. I call for vanilla yogurt in this recipe, but you could just as easily use coffee-flavored or chocolate yogurt.

WHITE CHOCOLATE WEDDING CAKE

SERVES: 20
PREPARATION TIME: 15 MINUTES
BAKING TIME: 28 TO 32 MINUTES
ASSEMBLY TIME: 5 MINUTES

Occasions do exist when you need that white cake—a wedding reception, a wedding shower, a spring birthday. But white doesn't have to mean chocolate-free. Here is a dandy, flavored with white chocolate. To top the white cake, I suggest a delicious white chocolate cream cheese frosting. Or if you aren't as set on white, try the Quick Caramel Frosting (page 440), sprinkled with toffee chips or finely chopped pecans while the frosting is still hot. Note the number of servings here: This cake will yield twenty ample pieces in a 13- by 9-inch pan; when baked in the larger-size pan, it will easily feed thirty.

Vegetable oil spray for misting the pan

Flour for dusting the pan

6 ounces white chocolate, finely chopped

5 tablespoons butter, cut into pieces

1 package (18.25 ounces) plain white cake mix or white cake mix with pudding

1¼ cups milk or water

3 large eggs

2 teaspoons pure vanilla extract

White Chocolate Cream Cheese Frosting (page 425)

1. Place a rack in the center of the oven and preheat the oven to 350°F. Lightly mist a 15¼- by 10½-inch pan with vegetable oil spray and dust with flour. Shake

Chocolate Groom's Cakes

Cake decorators are seeing a trend away from one big glorious white wedding cake to a number of smaller, more interesting cakes, often with some containing chocolate. A chocolate cake has frequently been used as a groom's cake, as a foil for the snowy white bride's cake.

Groom's cakes derive from English wedding cakes, spirited with whiskey and filled with fruits and nuts. Chocolate marries well, so to speak, with these flavors.

Here are half a dozen suggestions for groom's cakes. They are so delicious, they just might steal the show:

- Guatemalan Wedding Cake
- Debbie's Dazzling Red Velvet Cake
- Chocolate Love Cake
- German Chocolate Spice Cake with Fruit and Nut Filling
- Triple-Decker Raspberry Chocolate Cake with Chocolate Ganache
- Libbie's Chocolate Amaretto Cake

out the excess flour, and set the pan aside.

2. Place the white chocolate and the butter in a small microwave-safe bowl and microwave on high power until the butter has melted, 1 minute. Stir until the white chocolate is thoroughly melted and the mixture is smooth.

3. Place the cake mix, milk, eggs, vanilla, and melted white chocolate mixture in a large mixing bowl. Blend with an electric mixer on low speed for 1 minute. Stop the machine and scrape down the sides of the

bowl with a rubber spatula. Increase the mixer speed to medium and beat 2 minutes more, scraping the sides down again if needed. The batter should look thick and well combined. Pour the batter into the prepared pan, smoothing it out with the rubber spatula. Place the pan in the oven.

4. Bake the cake until it springs back when lightly pressed with your finger and is golden brown, 28 to 32 minutes. Remove the pan from the oven and place it on a wire rack to cool for 20 minutes.

5. Meanwhile, prepare the White Chocolate Cream Cheese Frosting.

6. When the cake has cooled, invert it onto a serving platter. Spread the frosting over the top and sides of the cake with smooth, clean strokes.

7. Slice and serve.

✻ *To make slicing easier, store this cake, lightly covered with waxed paper, in the refrigerator until the frosting sets, 1 hour. Then wrap it in aluminum foil and store in the refrigerator for up to 1 week. Or freeze it, wrapped in foil, for up to 6 months. Thaw the cake overnight in the refrigerator before serving.*

R

the Cake Mix Doctor says

You can bake this cake in a 13- by 9-inch pan, allowing 32 to 37 minutes' baking time.

Microwaving white chocolate and butter together is a good idea. But take care not to overcook the mixture; stir when the butter has melted, even if the white chocolate doesn't look melted. It will be after you stir! You can reduce the time it takes for these two to melt by cutting the butter into pieces and chopping the chocolate beforehand.

Chocolate Cheesecakes, Pudding Cakes, and So Much More

• • •

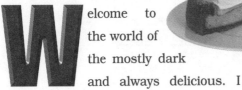

Welcome to the world of the mostly dark and always delicious. I could have called these cakes "What Ifs" because that is what I muttered more and more as my testing progressed: "What if I turned the Key Lime Cheesecake into a Double-Chocolate Lime Cheesecake by adding semisweet chocolate?" Or "What if I turned the Double-Chocolate Lime Cheesecake into Mocha Brownie Cheesecake by adding coffee-flavored yogurt and a little cinnamon?" This is the chapter that really got my creative juices flowing.

In my first book, all of the cheesecakes were baked in a 13- by 9-inch pan, but here I offer cheesecakes in both the 13- by 9-inch and the more classic 10-inch springform. The recipes can be baked in either size pan at 325°F; the springform cheesecake will simply take longer to cook, about an hour. I am sure that once you try some of my suggestions, you'll have many more good ideas of your own, using your local ingredients and your panache.

If you work your way past the cheesecakes (and you're still hungry!), don't pass up the pudding cakes. Two of these are made by covering cake batter with an instant pudding and then baking the mixture until the center is still soft. Another is made by covering cake batter with brown sugar, cocoa, and boiling water. The latter is a favorite, served warm with peppermint ice cream, at a ladies' club in Nashville, Tennessee (and shared with me by a club staff member), but don't be concerned that this is kid-glove stuff. It even tastes great as a weeknight dessert served up by the kids on paper plates!

....

"Life is like a box of chocolates. You never know what you're gonna get."

—ERIC ROTH
(from the screenplay for Forrest Gump)

....

The more challenging recipes in this chapter follow those wiggly, jiggly pudding cakes—the terrines. You may very well discover the architect hidden in you as you stack layers of baked cake and creamy fillings into a loaf pan, weight it down to compress both flavors and size, and then unmold it to produce one of the most elegant desserts around. Sliced and served with a little sweetened whipped cream, the intricate flavors will captivate your guests and your family.

Then, for the sweethearts on your list, bake up the Chocolate Love Cake or a fast brownie torte or trifle. The first is shaped into a heart, and the latter is a fast dessert the children will whole-heartedly assemble from a simple brownie mix.

But the surprises don't end there. I'm also offering two roulades based on chocolate cake batters, gooey fillings, and a foolproof dark chocolate frosting that spreads with ease. And to prove that cakes can turn into pies, there's the Pillsbury Bake-Off winner Cream Cheese Brownie Pie and a bourbon-spiked pecan and chocolate fudge pie to serve on Kentucky Derby day—or any day.

These recipes aptly illustrate the adaptability of the cake mix. And while you may need a few different pans—the 10-inch springform for the cheesecakes, a 9-inch loaf pan for the terrines, and a jelly-roll pan for the roulades— mostly all you need is a little time and a hankering for chocolate cake!

CHOCOLATE STRAWBERRY CHEESECAKE

Loving the combination of strawberries and dark chocolate, I wondered how to incorporate that strawberry flavor and yet arrive at a cheesecake with the right creamy consistency. It took a number of tries—from adding mashed fresh berries, to frozen, and finally to preserves, which proved to be the answer. You want to buy the preserves that are called "all fruit," made with the fruit juice. A portion of the preserves goes into the filling, and the remainder is warmed and spread on top of the cake once it has baked and cooled. For a Valentine's cake, garnish this with curls of semisweet chocolate.

SERVES: 16

PREPARATION TIME:
18 MINUTES

BAKING TIME:
60 TO 65 MINUTES

ASSEMBLY TIME:
2 MINUTES

the Cake Mix Doctor says

Briefly microwaving the strawberry preserves makes them easier to incorporate into the cheesecake filling and easier to spread onto the cooled cheesecake.

CRUST:

*1 package (18.25 ounces) plain devil's
    food cake mix*

6 tablespoons (¾ stick) butter, melted

1 large egg

Cheesecake Tips

- Use either a 10-inch springform pan (with removable side and bottom) or a 13- by 9-inch pan.

- Melt the butter for the crust in a small glass bowl in the microwave oven on high power for 45 seconds to 1 minute.

- Don't overbeat the filling. This will cause cracking on the surface while the cheesecake bakes.

- Make sure the cream cheese is soft before you begin.

- Bake the cheesecake until it looks glossy in the center, or as the recipe directs. It may still be a little jiggly in the center. You do not want to overbake cheesecake—it will set up as it cools.

- Baked cheesecake without topping freezes well. Cool it completely, then wrap it in heavy-duty foil and freeze for up to 2 months.

- Cool the cheesecake first on a wire rack at room temperature; then cover and chill it in the refrigerator for at least 1 hour, or preferably 24 hours.

FILLING AND TOPPING:

2 packages (8 ounces each) cream cheese, at room temperature

1 can (14 ounces) sweetened condensed milk

1 jar (10 ounces) strawberry preserves made with fruit juice

1 tablespoon fresh lemon juice

3 large eggs, at room temperature

1. Place a rack in the center of the oven and preheat the oven to 325°F. Set aside a 10-inch springform pan.

2. Prepare the crust: Place the cake mix, melted butter, and 1 egg in a large mixing bowl. Blend with an electric mixer on low speed for 2 minutes. Stop the machine and scrape down the sides of the bowl with a rubber spatula. The batter should come together into a ball. With your fingertips, pat the batter evenly over the bottom and up the sides of the springform pan, spreading it out with your fingers until smooth. Set the pan aside.

3. Place the cream cheese and sweetened condensed milk in the same mixing bowl that was used for the crust. With the same beaters (no need to clean them either), blend with an electric mixer on low speed until just combined, 30 seconds. Increase the mixer speed to medium and beat 1 minute more to thoroughly cream the mixture. Stop the machine.

4. Measure out ½ cup of the strawberry preserves and place it in a small glass bowl. Heat in the microwave oven on high power for 15 seconds. Stir in the lemon juice. Add the preserves mixture and the 3 eggs to the batter, and beat on medium speed for 1 minute. Stop the machine and scrape down the sides of the bowl with the rubber spatula. Pour the filling onto the crust and spread it out with the rubber spatula so that it is smooth. Place the pan in the oven.

5. Bake the cheesecake until it looks shiny and the center barely jiggles when you shake the pan, 60 to 65 minutes. Remove the pan from the oven and place it on a wire rack to cool for 30 minutes.

6. Place the remaining strawberry preserves in the same small glass bowl and heat them in the microwave on high power for 15 seconds. Stir with a small rubber spatula, and spread this mixture over the cooled cheesecake. Lightly cover the pan with plastic wrap and place it in the refrigerator to chill for at least 1 hour, and preferably 24 hours, for the flavors to meld.

7. Remove the outside rim from the springform pan. Either cut the cheesecake into slices and serve right from the base of the pan, or run a long sharp knife under the cheesecake crust to separate it from the base and carefully transfer the cheesecake to a serving platter, then slice and serve.

✳ *Store this cake, covered first in plastic wrap and then in aluminum foil, in the refrigerator for up to 1 week. Or freeze it, wrapped in foil, for up to 2 months. Thaw the cake overnight in the refrigerator before serving.*

WHITE CHOCOLATE BANANA-MACADAMIA CHEESECAKE

One bite of this white chocolate cheesecake and you would swear you were sitting in some trendy restaurant eating it. The macadamias add crunch to the crust, and the bananas meld beautifully with the white chocolate. Because of the crowd appeal, bake this in a 13- by 9-inch pan so you can get more servings and take it to potluck suppers and parties. But you can just as easily bake it in a 10-inch springform pan, allowing about an hour's baking time.

....
SERVES: 20

PREPARATION TIME: 15 MINUTES

BAKING TIME: 45 TO 50 MINUTES
....

Softened butter for greasing the pan

1 package (18.25 ounces) plain white cake mix

½ cup finely chopped macadamia nuts

4 tablespoons (½ stick) butter, melted

4 large eggs, at room temperature

6 ounces white chocolate, chopped

2 packages (8 ounces each) cream cheese, at room temperature

1 can (14 ounces) sweetened condensed milk

2 small ripe bananas, peeled and mashed (about ¾ cup)

½ teaspoon pure vanilla extract

1. Place a rack in the center of the oven and preheat the oven to 325°F. Lightly grease a 13- by 9-inch pan with softened butter. Set the pan aside.

2. Measure out ½ cup of the cake mix and set it aside for the filling.

℞

the Cake Mix Doctor says

Remember that when making cheesecakes, all your ingredients should be at room temperature. If they are not, they might cause the cream cheese to lump, and you won't be able to remove those lumps with a mixer.

3. Place the remaining cake mix, the macadamias, the melted butter, and 1 egg in a large mixing bowl. Blend with an electric mixer on low speed for 2 minutes. Stop the machine and scrape down the sides of the bowl with a rubber spatula. The batter should come together into a ball. With your fingertips, pat the batter evenly over the bottom and 1 inch up the sides of the prepared pan, spreading it out with your fingers until smooth. Set the pan aside.

4. Place the white chocolate in a small glass bowl and heat in the microwave oven on high power for 1 minute. Remove the bowl from the oven and stir with a small rubber spatula until it is melted. (See Melting White Chocolate, page 92.) Let it cool slightly.

5. Place the melted white chocolate, cream cheese, and sweetened condensed milk in the same mixing bowl that was used for the crust. With the same beaters (no need to clean them either), blend with an electric mixer on low speed until just combined, 30 seconds. Stop the machine and add the reserved cake mix, the remaining 3 eggs, the mashed bananas, and the vanilla. Beat on medium speed for 1 minute. Stop the machine and scrape down the sides of the bowl with the rubber spatula. Pour the filling onto the crust, and spread it out with the rubber spatula so that it covers the entire surface and reaches the sides of the pan. Place the pan in the oven.

6. Bake the cheesecake until it looks shiny and golden brown and the center no longer jiggles when you shake the pan, 45 to 50 minutes. Remove the pan from the oven and place it on a wire rack to cool for 30 minutes. Lightly cover the pan with plastic wrap and place it in the refrigerator to chill for at least 1 hour, or preferably 24 hours, for the flavors to meld. Cut into squares and serve.

✳ *Store this cake, covered first in plastic wrap and then in aluminum foil, in the refrigerator for up to 1 week. Or freeze it, wrapped in foil, for up to 2 months. Thaw the cake overnight in the refrigerator before serving.*

KEY LIME CHOCOLATE CHEESECAKE

I adore this cheesecake, and I've got three good reasons why: the pungent lime juice flavor has me dreaming of the beach, the dark contrast of the chocolate crust reminds me of a buttery chocolate wafer, and the velvety creaminess of the filling comes together and bakes so perfectly. Use the bottled Key lime juice in this recipe; you can find it at most supermarkets. Or if you actually *are* at the beach and find those marvelous tiny Key limes at a roadside market, buy a sackful, juice them, and bake cheesecake! Do make sure your ingredients are at room temperature, for cream cheese will lump up if it gets cold.

SERVES: 16
PREPARATION TIME: 15 MINUTES
BAKING TIME: 58 TO 62 MINUTES

CRUST:

*1 package (18.25 ounces) plain devil's food
    cake mix*
6 tablespoons (¾ stick) butter, melted
1 large egg

FILLING:

*2 packages (8 ounces each) cream cheese,
    at room temperature*
*1 can (14 ounces) sweetened condensed
    milk*
3 large eggs, at room temperature
½ cup Key lime juice, at room temperature

TOPPING:

*1 cup Sweetened Cream (page 445) or
    frozen whipped topping, thawed*

1. Place a rack in the center of the oven and preheat the oven to 325°F. Set aside a 10-inch springform pan.

Softening Cream Cheese

Nothing could be easier than assembling a cheesecake that begins with a cake mix. But you must remember to use soft, room-temperature cream cheese when blending the filling. Unless that cream cheese is soft, and the ingredients added to it are at room temperature, you will wind up with lumps of cream cheese in the batter, and they will never disappear. If you want to make cheesecake but your cream cheese has been in the refrigerator, warm it up in the microwave oven: Unwrap the block of cream cheese, place it on a microwave-safe plate, and microwave on high power for 20 to 30 seconds.

2. Place the cake mix, melted butter, and 1 egg in a large mixing bowl. Blend with an electric mixer on low speed for 2 minutes. Stop the machine and scrape down the sides of the bowl with a rubber spatula. The batter should come together into a ball. With your fingertips, pat the batter evenly over the bottom and up the sides of the springform pan, spreading it out with your fingers until smooth. Set the pan aside.

3. Place the cream cheese and sweetened condensed milk in the same mixing bowl that was used for the crust. With the same beaters (no need to clean them either), blend with an electric mixer on low speed until just combined, 30 seconds. Increase the mixer speed to medium and beat 1 minute more to thoroughly cream the mixture. Stop the machine and add the 3 eggs and the lime juice to the batter. Beat on medium speed for 1 minute. Stop the machine and scrape down the sides of the bowl with the rubber spatula. Pour the filling onto the crust and spread it out with the rubber spatula so that it is smooth. Place the pan in the oven.

4. Bake the cheesecake until it looks shiny and the center barely jiggles when you shake the pan, 58 to 62 minutes. Remove the pan from the oven and place it on a wire rack to cool for 30 minutes. Then lightly cover the pan with plastic wrap and place it in the refrigerator to chill for at least 1 hour, or preferably 24 hours, for the flavors to meld.

5. Meanwhile, prepare the Sweetened Cream.

6. Remove the outside rim from the springform pan. Either cut the cheesecake into slices and serve right from the base of the pan, or run a long sharp knife under the cheesecake crust to separate it from the base and carefully transfer the cheesecake to a serving platter, then slice. Serve with a dollop of Sweetened Cream.

✳ *Store this cake, covered first in plastic wrap and then in aluminum foil, in the refrigerator for up to 1 week. Or freeze it, wrapped in foil, for up to 2 months. Thaw the cake overnight in the refrigerator before serving.*

R

the Cake Mix Doctor says

Can't get enough of that great lime flavor? Add 1 teaspoon grated lime zest to the filling.

DOUBLE-CHOCOLATE LIME CHEESECAKE

Remember those fussy little desserts called *pots de crème,* where you got this eensy portion of ultra-rich chocolate in a demitasse cup? The hostess said it was "just enough," and you muttered under your breath, "Enough for whom?" Well, consider this dessert your great chocolate revenge.

SERVES: 16

PREPARATION TIME:
15 MINUTES

BAKING TIME:
58 TO 62 MINUTES

CRUST:

1 package (18.25 ounces) plain
*   devil's food cake mix*

6 tablespoons (¾ stick) butter, melted

1 large egg

FILLING:

2 cups semisweet chocolate
*   chips*

2 packages (8 ounces each) cream
*   cheese, at room temperature*

1 can (14 ounces) sweetened condensed milk

3 large eggs, at room temperature

½ cup Key lime juice, at room temperature

TOPPING:

1 cup Sweetened Cream (page 445) or
*   frozen whipped topping, thawed*

1 teaspoon grated lime zest

1. Place a rack in the center of the oven and preheat the oven to 325°F. Set aside a 10-inch springform pan.

2. Place the cake mix, melted butter, and 1 egg in a large mixing bowl. Blend with an electric mixer on low speed for 2 minutes. Stop the machine and scrape down the sides of the bowl with a rubber spatula. The batter should come together into a ball. With your fingertips, pat the batter evenly over the bottom and up the sides of the springform pan, spreading it out with your fingers until smooth. Set the pan aside.

3. Place the chocolate chips in a medium-size glass bowl and heat in the microwave oven on high power for 1½ minutes. Remove the bowl from the oven and stir with a small rubber spatula until they are melted. Let the chocolate cool slightly. Place the melted chocolate, cream cheese, and sweetened condensed milk in the same mixing bowl that was used for the crust. With the same beaters (no need to clean them either), blend with an electric mixer on low speed until just combined, 30 seconds. Increase the mixer speed to medium and beat 1 minute more to thoroughly cream the mixture. Stop the machine and add the 3 eggs and the lime juice to the batter. Beat on medium speed for 1 minute. Stop the machine and scrape down the sides of the bowl with the rubber spatula. Pour the filling onto the crust and spread it out with the rubber spatula so that it is smooth. Place the pan in the oven.

4. Bake the cheesecake until it looks shiny and the center barely jiggles when you shake the pan, 58 to 62 minutes. Remove the pan from the oven and place it on a wire rack to cool for 30 minutes. Then lightly cover the pan with plastic wrap and place it in the refrigerator to chill for at least 1 hour, or preferably 24 hours, for the flavors to meld.

5. Meanwhile, prepare the Sweetened Cream. Fold in the grated lime zest.

6. Remove the outside rim from the springform pan. Either cut the cheesecake into slices and serve right from the base of the pan, or run a long sharp knife under the cheesecake crust to separate it from the base and carefully transfer the cheesecake to a serving platter, then slice. Serve the cheesecake with a dollop of the whipped cream.

✱ *Store this cake, covered first in plastic wrap and then in aluminum foil, in the refrigerator for up to 1 week. Or freeze it, wrapped in foil, for up to 2 months. Thaw the cake overnight in the refrigerator before serving.*

the Cake Mix Doctor says

If you ever run into a recipe that calls for chocolate sweetened condensed milk and you can't find any, here's the solution: Melt 1 cup semisweet chocolate chips with a 14-ounce can of regular sweetened condensed milk and *voilà*. I took that substitution to heart in devising this recipe, but the outcome just wasn't chocolaty enough for me. So I took the plunge and tried using twice as much chocolate—perfect.

MOCHA BROWNIE CHEESECAKE

This dense and fudgy cake is a cross between a cheesecake and a brownie, and it is another crowd-pleaser. The intense chocolate flavor comes from 2 cups of semisweet chocolate chips, which are melted and added to the filling. The cake is also flavored with coffee yogurt, and thus its name. If the subtle coffee flavor isn't strong enough for you, sip a cup alongside or see "the Cake Mix Doctor says," page 224. Unlike some of the other cheesecakes, this one contains no cake mix in the filling, so it has a creamier consistency. You will need to remove it from the oven sooner than the others—it should look shiny but still be a little wobbly in the center. It will firm up as it cools.

....

SERVES: 20
PREPARATION TIME: 15 MINUTES
BAKING TIME: 45 TO 50 MINUTES

....

CRUST:

1 package (18.25 ounces) plain devil's food
    cake mix
6 tablespoons (¾ stick) butter, melted
1 large egg
½ teaspoon ground cinnamon

FILLING:

2 cups semisweet chocolate chips
2 packages (8 ounces each) cream cheese,
    at room temperature
1 can (14 ounces) sweetened
    condensed milk
3 large eggs, at room
    temperature
½ cup coffee or vanilla nonfat
    yogurt

TOPPING:

1 cup Sweetened Cream (page 445) or
frozen whipped topping, thawed
Ground cinnamon, instant coffee powder, or
grated chocolate, for garnish (optional)

1. Place a rack in the center of the oven and preheat the oven to 325°F. Set aside a 13- by 9-inch pan.

2. Place the cake mix, melted butter, 1 egg, and cinnamon in a large mixing bowl. Blend with an electric mixer on low speed for 2 minutes. Stop the machine and scrape down the sides of the bowl with a rubber spatula. The batter should come together into a ball. With your fingertips, pat the batter evenly over the bottom and 1 inch up the sides of the pan, spreading it out with your fingers until smooth. Set the pan aside.

3. Melt the chocolate chips in a medium-size glass bowl in the microwave oven on high power for 1½ minutes. Remove the bowl from the oven and stir with a small

15 Cakes to Bake for Your Dad

1. Old-Fashioned Devil's Food Cake with Fluffy Chocolate Frosting

2. German Chocolate Cake with Toasted Pecan-Coconut Frosting

3. Mocha Brownie Cheesecake

4. Chocolate Snickerdoodle Cake with Cinnamon-Chocolate Cream Cheese Frosting

5. Kathy's Chocolate Chocolate Chip Cake

6. Chocolate Macaroon Ring Cake

7. Boston Cream Pie Cake

8. Rick's Chocolate Rum Bundt Cake

9. Chocolate Banana Cupcakes with Pineapple Cream Cheese Frosting

10. German Chocolate Upside-Down Cake

11. German Chocolate Chip Zucchini Cake

12. Chocolate Eggnog Cake with Eggnog Buttercream Frosting

13. Molten Chocolate Pudding Cake

14. Joy of Almond Bars

15. Texas Sheet Cake

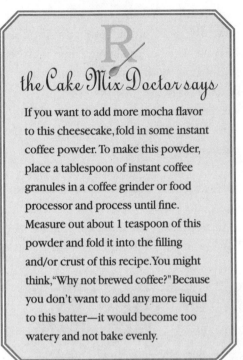

the Cake Mix Doctor says

If you want to add more mocha flavor to this cheesecake, fold in some instant coffee powder. To make this powder, place a tablespoon of instant coffee granules in a coffee grinder or food processor and process until fine. Measure out about 1 teaspoon of this powder and fold it into the filling and/or crust of this recipe. You might think, "Why not brewed coffee?" Because you don't want to add any more liquid to this batter—it would become too watery and not bake evenly.

rubber spatula until the chocolate is melted. Let it cool slightly.

4. Place the melted chocolate, cream cheese, and sweetened condensed milk in the same mixing bowl that was used for the crust. With the same beaters (no need to clean them either), blend with an electric mixer on low speed until just combined, 30 seconds. Stop the machine, add the 3 eggs and the yogurt, and beat on medium speed for 1 minute. Stop the machine and scrape down the sides of the bowl with the rubber spatula. Pour the filling onto the crust and spread it out with the rubber spatula so that it covers the entire surface and reaches the sides of the pan. Place the pan in the oven.

5. Bake the cheesecake until it looks shiny and the center jiggles only slightly when you shake the pan, 45 to 50 minutes (it will firm up after cooling). Remove the pan from the oven and place it on a wire rack to cool for 30 minutes. Then lightly cover the pan with plastic wrap and place it in the refrigerator to chill for at least 1 hour, or preferably 24 hours, for the flavors to meld.

6. Meanwhile, prepare the Sweetened Cream.

7. Cut into squares and serve with a dollop of Sweetened Cream and a sprinkling of cinnamon, instant coffee powder, or grated chocolate if desired.

✳ *Store this cake, covered first in plastic wrap and then in aluminum foil, in the refrigerator for up to 1 week. Or freeze it, wrapped in foil, for up to 2 months. Thaw the cake overnight in the refrigerator before serving.*

PUMPKIN SPICE GERMAN CHOCOLATE CHEESECAKE

Have 13- by 9-inch pan, will travel! For autumn potlucks and dinner parties, prepare this easy cheesecake ahead of time, happy in the knowledge that it will feed twenty people. The flavor of the German chocolate mix goes well with the canned pumpkin and spices, making the cake both homey and spectacular. The sour cream topping may add a little baking time, but it dresses the cake up ever so nicely.

....

SERVES: 20

PREPARATION TIME: 15 MINUTES

BAKING TIME: 52 TO 57 MINUTES

ASSEMBLY TIME: 2 MINUTES

....

CRUST AND FILLING:

Softened butter for greasing the pan

1 package (18.25 ounces) plain German chocolate cake mix

4 tablespoons (½ stick) butter, melted

4 large eggs, at room temperature

2 packages (8 ounces each) cream cheese, at room temperature

1 can (14 ounces) sweetened condensed milk

1 cup canned pumpkin

½ cup (packed) light brown sugar

1 teaspoon ground cinnamon

½ teaspoon ground ginger

TOPPING:

1 cup sour cream

¼ cup (packed) light brown sugar

1. Place a rack in the center of the oven and preheat the oven to 325°F. Lightly grease a 13- by 9-inch pan with softened butter. Set the pan aside.

2. Measure out ½ cup of the cake mix and set it aside for the filling.

3. Place the remaining cake mix, the melted butter, and 1 egg in a large mixing bowl. Blend with an electric mixer on low speed for 2 minutes. Stop the machine and scrape down the sides of the bowl with a rubber spatula. The batter should come together into a ball. With your fingertips, pat the batter evenly over the bottom and 1 inch up the sides of the prepared pan, spreading it out with your fingers until smooth. Set the pan aside.

4. Place the cream cheese and the sweetened condensed milk in the same mixing bowl that was used for the crust, and with the same beaters (no need to clean them either), blend with an electric mixer on low speed until just combined, 30 seconds. Stop the machine and add the reserved cake mix, the remaining 3 eggs, the pumpkin, brown sugar, cinnamon, and ginger. Beat on medium speed for 1 minute. Stop the machine and scrape down the sides of the bowl with the rubber spatula. Pour the filling onto the crust and spread it out with the rubber spatula so that it covers the entire surface and reaches the sides of the pan. Place the pan in the oven.

5. Bake the cheesecake until it looks shiny and the center no longer jiggles when you shake the pan, 45 to 49 minutes. Remove the pan from the oven while you prepare the topping. Leave the oven on.

6. For the topping, place the sour cream and brown sugar in a small mixing bowl and stir with a spoon until well combined. Spread the topping over the cheesecake, and return the pan to the oven.

7. Bake until the topping sets, 7 to 8 minutes. Remove the pan from the oven and place it on a wire rack to cool for 30 minutes. Then lightly cover the pan with plastic wrap and place it in the refrigerator to chill for at least 1 hour, or preferably 24 hours, for the flavors to meld.

8. Cut into squares and serve.

✳ *Store this cake, covered first in plastic wrap and then in aluminum foil, in the refrigerator for up to 1 week. Or freeze it, wrapped in foil, for up to 2 months. Thaw the cake overnight in the refrigerator before serving.*

R

the Cake Mix Doctor says

Yes, there's cream cheese *and* butter in this recipe, but the pumpkin is a high-fiber food and makes a healthy addition . . . right? For more chocolate flavor, fold 4 ounces grated German chocolate into the filling.

ORANGE-GINGER GERMAN CHOCOLATE CHEESECAKE

When ground ginger meets German chocolate cake mix and butter in this crust, it takes on the flavor of gingerbread. And envision for a moment how nice a creamy orange filling will be on top of this crisp gingery crust. Bake this cheesecake for cheesecake lovers of all ages. And if the occasion calls for fancy, garnish it with candied orange zest (see page 228).

SERVES: 16

PREPARATION TIME: 20 MINUTES

BAKING TIME: 75 TO 80 MINUTES

ASSEMBLY TIME: 2 MINUTES

CRUST:

Softened butter for greasing the pan

1 package (18.25 ounces) plain German chocolate cake mix

4 tablespoons (½ stick) butter, melted

1 large egg

1 teaspoon grated orange zest

½ teaspoon ground ginger

FILLING AND TOPPING:

2 packages (8 ounces each) cream cheese, at room temperature

1 can (14 ounces) sweetened condensed milk

3 large eggs, at room temperature

½ cup fresh orange juice, at room temperature

2 teaspoons grated orange zest

1 cup sour cream

½ cup (packed) light brown sugar

½ teaspoon ground ginger

1. Place a rack in the center of the oven and preheat the oven to 325°F. Lightly grease a 10-inch springform pan with softened butter. Set the pan aside.

2. Measure out ½ cup of the cake mix and set it aside for the filling.

3. Prepare the crust: Place the remaining cake mix, the melted butter, 1 egg, orange zest, and ginger in a large mixing bowl. Blend with an electric mixer on low speed for 2 minutes. Stop the machine and scrape down the sides of the bowl with a rubber spatula. The batter should come together into a ball. With your fingertips, pat the batter evenly over the bottom and up the sides of the prepared pan, spreading it out with your fingers until smooth. Set the pan aside.

How to Make Candied Orange Zest

One of the prettiest ways to dress up cake, whether it's a chocolate layer cake, a cheesecake, or a chocolate roulade, is to surround it with candied orange zest. Lucille Osborn, a Philadelphia food stylist, garnished my cakes on a Discovery Channel show not too long ago. The zest cascaded down the cake in magnificent sparkling spirals. And Lucille revealed her secrets for making candied zest.

First, scrub and dry the oranges. Then cut the zest in long strands, using a zester. (This gadget cuts long, narrow strands. You can also run a sharp vegetable peeler around the orange, creating long 1-inch-wide strips, and then slice those into ¼-inch-wide strands.) Two medium oranges will yield about 1 cup of loosely packed strands.

Place 2 cups sugar and 1¼ cups water in a medium-size saucepan over medium heat. Stir until the sugar dissolves and the syrup comes to a simmer. Drop the orange zest into the pan, and stir so that all the strands are covered in syrup. Let this barely simmer for 1 to 1½ hours, or until the zest is translucent. Simmering it the full amount of time will yield a crunchy zest; the shorter time, a softer zest. With metal tongs, transfer the zest to a wire rack, and leave to dry for several hours or overnight. While the zest is still pliable, curl it or twist it to your liking. If desired, coat the zest in additional sugar.

When the candied zest has dried, store it in a tightly covered plastic container. Use it as a garnish around or on top of cakes. Or dip it into melted semisweet chocolate for an extra-special treat!

4. For the filling, place the cream cheese and the sweetened condensed milk in the same mixing bowl that was used for the crust. With the same beaters (no need to clean them either), blend with an electric mixer on low speed until just combined, 30 seconds. Stop the machine and add the reserved cake mix, the 3 eggs, orange juice, and orange zest to the batter. Beat on medium speed for 1 minute. Stop the machine and scrape down the sides of the bowl with the rubber spatula. Pour the filling onto the crust and spread it out with the rubber spatula so that it is smooth. Place the pan in the oven.

5. Bake the cheesecake until it looks browned and shiny, and the center still jiggles slightly when you shake the pan, 68 to 72 minutes. Remove the pan from the oven while you prepare the topping. Leave the oven on.

6. For the topping, place the sour cream, brown sugar, and ginger in a small mixing bowl and stir with a spoon until well combined. Spread the topping over the cheesecake, and return the pan to the oven.

7. Bake until the topping sets, 7 to 8 minutes. Remove the pan from the oven and place it on a wire rack to cool for 30 minutes. Then lightly cover the pan with plastic wrap and place it in the refrigera-

R

the Cake Mix Doctor says

The orange juice in this cheesecake adds flavor, but it also increases the time it takes for the cake to bake. Even if a cheesccake jiggles slightly in the center of the springform pan when the baking time has been reached, remove it. The cheesecake will firm up as it cools.

tor to chill for at least 1 hour, or preferably 24 hours, for the flavors to meld.

8. Remove the outside rim from the springform pan. Either cut the cheesecake into slices and serve right from the base of the pan, or run a long sharp knife under the cheesecake crust to separate it from the base and carefully transfer the cheesecake to a serving platter, then slice and serve.

✳ *Store this cake, covered first in plastic wrap and then in aluminum foil, in the refrigerator for up to 1 week. Or freeze it, wrapped in foil, for up to 2 months. Thaw the cake overnight in the refrigerator before serving.*

MOLTEN CHOCOLATE PUDDING CAKE

Sensory experts tell us we need liquid to help transport flavors to the tongue so we can enjoy them. And so you can see the attraction of pudding cake. However, there is so much liquid here that you may say to yourself, "This is never going to work," but it does. Much of the liquid is absorbed and makes the cake moist; the remainder forms a wonderful chocolate sauce on the bottom of the pan. Eaten together, the cake takes on a pudding quality. My children and my nephews love this cake served warm with vanilla ice cream. We have even reheated it in the microwave the next day for round two! (Reheating keeps the sauce saucy.)

SERVES: 16

PREPARATION TIME: 10 MINUTES

BAKING TIME: 55 TO 60 MINUTES

R

the Cake Mix Doctor says

Use whatever milk you have on hand—whole, 2 percent, or skim. I used 2 percent milk in testing this recipe, and it was plenty rich. Bake this cake until it is firm around the edges but still jiggly in the middle. Don't bake it until firm! And one last word: You can bake this in a glass pan (which makes for easy reheating in the microwave), but you will need to reduce the oven temperature to 325°F and extend the baking time slightly.

Baking in Glass Pans

*A*s much as I don't like to bake in glass pans (they cook quickly and can overbrown the corners of a cake), it's the best choice if you'll need to reheat the cake.

Let's say you want to take a pudding cake to a party or a potluck supper, or simply want to bake the cake ahead of time. Preheat the oven to 325°F (25 degrees lower than if you bake it in metal).

Prepare the cake in a glass pan and bake it for about 70 minutes. When it comes time to reheat it, just pop it in the microwave on high power for 1½ to 2 minutes, checking every 15 seconds. Of course, if you bake the cake in a metal pan, you can still reheat it, but you'll need to do so in a regular oven. If you use a regular oven, just be sure to cover the cake first with aluminum foil.

Vegetable oil spray for misting the pan

1 package (18.25 ounces) plain devil's food cake mix

1⅓ cups water

½ cup vegetable oil

3 large eggs

1 large package (5.9 ounces) instant chocolate pudding mix

3 cups milk

1 teaspoon pure vanilla extract

1 cup semisweet chocolate chips

Vanilla or peppermint ice cream, for serving

1. Place a rack in the center of the oven and preheat the oven to 350°F. Lightly mist a 13- by 9-inch pan with vegetable oil spray. Set the pan aside.

2. Place the cake mix, water, oil, and eggs in a large mixing bowl. Blend with an electric mixer on low speed for 1 minute. Stop the machine and scrape down the sides of the bowl with a rubber spatula. Increase the mixer speed to medium and beat 2 minutes more, scraping the sides down again if needed. The batter should look well combined. Pour the batter into the prepared pan, smoothing it out with the rubber spatula. Set the pan aside.

3. Empty the package of pudding mix into a medium-size bowl and whisk in the milk and vanilla until smooth and thickened, 1 to 2 minutes. Pour the pudding over the batter, taking care not to let it touch the sides of the pan. Scatter the chocolate chips evenly over the top. Place the pan in the oven.

4. Bake the cake until it is firm around the edges but still wiggles in the middle, 55 to 60 minutes. A crack will run through the center. Remove the pan from the oven and place it on a wire rack to cool for 20 minutes.

5. Spoon the warm pudding cake into bowls, and top with vanilla or peppermint ice cream.

✹ *Store this cake, covered with aluminum foil, at room temperature for up to 3 days or in the refrigerator for up to 1 week.*

CHOCOLATE-CINNAMON BANANA PUDDING CAKE

Y ou'll love the flavor combination of chocolate, bananas, pudding, and cinnamon in this comforting pudding cake. Serve it warm, with ice cream alongside.

SERVES: 16
PREPARATION TIME: 15 MINUTES
BAKING TIME: 55 TO 60 MINUTES
ASSEMBLY TIME: 2 MINUTES

Vegetable oil spray for misting the pan
1 package (18.25 ounces) plain devil's food
   cake mix
1⅓ cups water
½ cup vegetable oil
1 ripe banana, peeled and mashed (½ cup)
3 large eggs
½ teaspoon ground cinnamon

2 packages (3.4 ounces each) banana
   instant pudding mix
2¾ cups milk
1 teaspoon pure vanilla extract
1 cup semisweet chocolate chips
Vanilla or butter pecan ice cream, for serving

1. Place a rack in the center of the oven and preheat the oven to 350°F. Lightly mist a 13- by 9-inch pan with vegetable oil spray. Set the pan aside.

2. Place the cake mix, water, oil, mashed banana, eggs, and cinnamon in a large mixing bowl. Blend with an electric mixer on low speed for 1 minute. Stop the machine and scrape down the sides of the bowl with a rubber spatula. Increase the mixer speed to medium and beat 2 minutes more, scraping the sides down again if needed. The batter should look well combined. Pour the batter into the prepared pan, smoothing it out with the rubber spatula. Set the pan aside.

3. Empty the packages of pudding mix into a medium-size bowl and whisk in the milk and vanilla until smooth and thickened, 1 to 2 minutes. Pour the pudding over the batter, taking care not to let it touch the sides of the pan. Scatter the chocolate chips evenly over the top. Place the pan in the oven.

4. Bake the cake until it is firm around the edges but still wiggles in the middle, 55 to 60 minutes. A crack will run through the center. Remove the pan from the oven and place it on a wire rack to cool for 20 minutes.

5. Spoon the warm pudding cake into bowls, and top with vanilla or butter pecan ice cream.

✹ *Store this cake, covered with aluminum foil, at room temperature for up to 3 days or in the refrigerator for up to 1 week.*

R

the Cake Mix Doctor says

The riper the banana, the more flavorful this cake will be.

CHOCOLATE SOUFFLÉ PUDDING CAKE

Myriad variations of this cake are out there—in books, on recipe cards, on the Internet, even committed to memory. Most of the scratch versions resemble the Hot Fudge Pudding Cake that was printed in the 1954 *Betty Crocker Cookbook:* a chocolate cake topped with cocoa, brown sugar, and a lot of boiling water before it is baked. Well, this is a quicker version, and it has its own twist— miniature marshmallows that melt into the cake, giving it a soufflé-like quality. Don't be distressed at all the boiling water. It will form a delicious chocolate sauce on the bottom of the pan. Serve this warm.

SERVES: 16

PREPARATION TIME: 10 MINUTES

BAKING TIME: 45 TO 50 MINUTES

Vegetable oil spray for misting the pan

2 cups miniature marshmallows

1 package (18.25 ounces) plain devil's food cake mix

1⅓ cups water

3 large eggs

2 cups (packed) light brown sugar

½ cup unsweetened cocoa powder

3½ cups boiling water

Peppermint ice cream, for serving

1. Place a rack in the center of the oven and preheat the oven to 375°F. Lightly mist a 13- by 9-inch pan with vegetable oil spray. Scatter the marshmallows evenly over the bottom of the pan and set it aside.

2. Place the cake mix, water, and eggs in a large mixing bowl. Blend with an electric mixer on low speed for 1 minute. Stop the machine and scrape down the sides of the bowl with a rubber spatula. Increase the mixer speed to medium and beat 2 minutes more, scraping the sides down again if needed. The batter should look well combined. Pour the batter into the prepared pan, smoothing it out with the rubber spatula. Sprinkle the brown sugar and cocoa powder evenly over the batter. Pour the boiling water over the top. Carefully place the pan in the oven.

3. Bake the cake until it is firm around the edges, is still jiggly in the middle, and the sauce is starting to bubble up around the edges, 45 to 50 minutes. Remove the pan from the oven and place it on a wire rack to cool for 20 minutes.

4. Spoon the warm pudding cake into bowls, and top with peppermint ice cream.

✳ *Store this cake, covered with aluminum foil, at room temperature for up to 3 days or in the refrigerator for up to 1 week.*

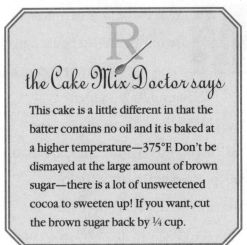

the Cake Mix Doctor says

This cake is a little different in that the batter contains no oil and it is baked at a higher temperature—375°F. Don't be dismayed at the large amount of brown sugar—there is a lot of unsweetened cocoa to sweeten up! If you want, cut the brown sugar back by ¼ cup.

GUATEMALAN WEDDING CAKE

In the 1980s I used to frequent a dessert shop in Atlanta that was appropriately called The Dessert Place. It served huge slices of the most wonderful chocolate layer cakes, poured fashionable coffees before they came into vogue, and served as a late-night hangout for everyone with a sweet tooth. One of their specialties was this layered dessert, which they would make in a large bowl, invert, and then slather with whipped cream. People would order it as the groom's cake for weddings and surround it with fresh flowers.

I had forgotten all about this cake until I heard from Rob Medley, a former pastry chef in Atlanta. He said the recipe began with a chocolate cake mix, which was swabbed with amaretto and layered with a cream cheese and coffee filling. Rob suggested assembling the cake in a 9- or 10-inch loaf pan instead of a bowl. With his guidance and my experimentation I have re-created that cake, and it is one dandy dessert. The loaf is weighted down and chilled for at least 24 hours, and as it compresses, the flavors grow more intense. Sliced and served as is, or with a dollop of whipped cream, this cake comes across as if you had spent a lot of time in the kitchen—but you haven't!

SERVES: 12 TO 16

PREPARATION TIME: 30 MINUTES

BAKING TIME: 32 TO 35 MINUTES

ASSEMBLY TIME: 20 MINUTES

CHILLING TIME: 24 HOURS

CAKE:

Vegetable oil spray for misting the pan

1 package (18.25 ounces) plain devil's food cake mix

1⅓ cups water

½ cup vegetable oil

3 large eggs

FILLING:

1 package (8 ounces) cream cheese, at room temperature

3 tablespoons butter, melted

3 tablespoons strong brewed coffee

¾ cup confectioners' sugar

1 teaspoon pure vanilla extract

½ cup chopped pecans

3 tablespoons amaretto (almond liqueur)

TOPPING:

Sweetened Cream (page 445)

¼ cup grated semisweet chocolate

1. Place a rack in the center of the oven and preheat the oven to 350°F. Lightly mist a 13- by 9-inch pan with vegetable oil spray. Set the pan aside. Line the bottom and up the sides of a 9- to 10-inch loaf pan with waxed paper. Set the loaf pan aside.

2. Place the cake mix, water, oil, and eggs in a large mixing bowl. Blend with an electric mixer on low speed for 1 minute. Stop the machine and scrape down the sides of the bowl with a rubber spatula. Increase the mixer speed to medium and beat 2 minutes more, scraping the sides down again if needed. The batter should look well combined. Pour the batter into the prepared 13- by 9-inch pan, smoothing it out with the rubber spatula. Place the pan in the oven.

3. Bake the cake until it springs back when lightly pressed with your finger, 32 to 35 minutes. Remove the pan from the oven and place it on a wire rack to cool completely, 40 minutes.

4. Meanwhile, prepare the filling: Place the cream cheese, melted butter, brewed coffee, confectioners' sugar, and vanilla in a medium-size mixing bowl. Blend with a wooden spoon until the mixture is combined. Fold in the pecans. Set the filling aside. Reserve the amaretto.

5. When the cake has cooled, run a knife around the edges of the pan and invert the cake onto a cutting board. Carefully slice the cake in half horizontally so you have 2 slabs of cake, each about 1 inch thick. Measure 9 or 10 inches down each slab of cake, depending on which size loaf pan you are using. Cut through the cake crosswise at this mark. Save the cut-off 4-inch ends for patching. Slice each of the 9- or 10-inch slabs of cake into 6 lengthwise strips. You will have 12 strips of cake in all.

6. Arrange 3 strips in the bottom of the prepared loaf pan. Fill in any gaps with leftover cake. Brush the layer with amaretto, then spread one third of the reserved filling on top. Place 3 more strips of cake on top, filling any gaps as needed and pressing down as you work. Brush the cake with amaretto, then spread on another third of the filling. Place three more strips of cake on top, filling any gaps as needed and pressing down as you work. Brush the cake with amaretto, then spread the remaining filling on top. Place the last 3 strips of cake on top, filling any gaps as needed and pressing down as you work. Cover the cake with waxed paper, and place a smaller loaf pan or a small cutting board on top of the terrine. Weight it down with at least 3 pounds of canned goods. Place the weighted-down pan in the refrigerator for 24 hours. The height of the cake should shrink by 2 inches after the weighting-down time is over.

R the Cake Mix Doctor says

As complicated as this recipe may look, it really is not. You just layer in the goodies, weight it down well, chill it long enough, and *voilà*, a fabulous dessert. Make sure you cook the cake long enough, even overbake it, says Rob Medley. This makes it easier to cut into strips. The amaretto and mocha filling will moisten up that dry cake in a jiffy! Should you want to make this as a groom's cake, double the cake recipe, double the filling, and have plenty of Sweetened Cream prepared. Layer the cake, amaretto, and filling in a large mixing bowl, first lining the bowl with waxed paper, then cake strips. Brush the strips with amaretto and spread them with some of the filling. Repeat, beginning with the cake strips, and continue layering until the bowl is filled. Weight down this bombe-shaped cake for 24 hours. Unmold, spread with Sweetened Cream, and decorate with fresh flowers and/or chocolate curls. Spectacular!

7. The next day, prepare the Sweetened Cream. Cover with plastic wrap and place in the refrigerator.

15 Dinner Party Dazzlers

1. Guatemalan Wedding Cake

2. Strawberry Brownie Torte

3. Luscious Lemon White Chocolate Terrine

4. Chocolate Kahlúa Roulade with Espresso Cream Filling

5. Cream Cheese Brownie Pie

6. Key Lime Chocolate Cheesecake

7. Chocolate Brownie Mousse Trifle

8. Little White Chocolate Lemon Drizzle Cakes

9. Raspberry Swirl Brownies

10. White Chocolate Pineapple Upside-Down Cake

11. Chocolate Four-Seasons Wine Cake

12. Darn Good Chocolate Cake with Martha's Chocolate Icing

13. Cappuccino Angel Food Mousse Torte

14. Chocolate Rum Raisin Cake

15. Chocolate Coconut Cream Cake with German Chocolate Cream Cheese Frosting

8. Remove the terrine from the refrigerator, and invert it onto a serving platter. Peel off the waxed paper. Spread the Sweetened Cream on top of the terrine, and garnish with the grated chocolate. (Or if desired, frost the entire terrine with a thin coat of Sweetened Cream and garnish with the grated chocolate.) Slice and serve.

✳ *Store this cake, covered with plastic wrap, in the refrigerator for up to 1 week. Or freeze it, wrapped in foil, for up to 2 months. Thaw the cake overnight in the refrigerator before serving.*

PEAR AND CHOCOLATE TERRINE

Here is another delicious example of how an ordinary cake can become extraordinary. Strips of chocolate cake are layered in a loaf pan with a cream cheese, brandy, and spice mixture, plus spoonfuls of freshly sautéed pears. Make sure the pears are ripe for best flavor, but not too soft or they will fall apart as they cook. Slice and serve as is, with a warm chocolate sauce such as Hot Fudge Sauce (page 456), or Rich Chocolate Glaze (page 449), or with a dollop of Sweetened Cream (page 445).

....

SERVES: 12 TO 16

PREPARATION TIME: 30 MINUTES

BAKING TIME: 32 TO 35 MINUTES

ASSEMBLY TIME: 20 MINUTES

CHILLING TIME: 24 HOURS

....

CAKE:

Vegetable oil spray for misting the pan

1 package (18.25 ounces) plain devil's food cake mix

1⅓ cups water

½ cup vegetable oil

3 large eggs

½ teaspoon ground cinnamon

CREAM CHEESE FILLING:

1 package (8 ounces) cream cheese, at room temperature

3 tablespoons butter, melted

3 tablespoons brandy

⅔ cup confectioners' sugar

½ teaspoon pure vanilla extract

½ teaspoon ground cinnamon

¼ teaspoon ground nutmeg

½ cup chopped pecans

PEAR FILLING:

4 large ripe pears

4 teaspoons butter

4 teaspoons (packed) light brown sugar

1. Place a rack in the center of the oven and preheat the oven to 350°F. Lightly mist a 13- by 9-inch pan with vegetable oil spray. Set the pan aside. Line the bottom and up the sides of a 9- to 10-inch loaf pan with parchment paper (see the Cake Mix Doctor says). Set the loaf pan aside.

2. Place the cake mix, water, oil, eggs, and cinnamon in a large mixing bowl. Blend with an electric mixer on low speed for 1 minute. Stop the machine and scrape down the sides of the bowl with a rubber spatula. Increase the mixer speed to medium and beat 2 minutes more, scraping the sides down again if needed. The batter should look well combined. Pour the batter into the prepared 13- by 9-inch pan, smoothing it out with the rubber spatula. Place the pan in the oven.

3. Bake the cake until it springs back when lightly pressed with your finger, 32 to 35 minutes. Remove the pan from the oven and place it on a wire rack to cool completely, 40 minutes.

4. Meanwhile, prepare the fillings: Place the cream cheese, melted butter, brandy, confectioners' sugar, vanilla, cinnamon, and nutmeg in a medium-size mixing bowl. Blend with a wooden spoon until the mixture is combined. Fold in the pecans. Set the filling aside.

5. For the pear filling, peel, core, and quarter the pears. Carefully slice each quarter into 3 or 4 slivers. Melt 1 teaspoon of the butter in a small skillet over medium heat. Stir in 1 teaspoon of the brown sugar. Place the slivers from 1 pear in the skillet, and sauté until they soften a bit and begin to caramelize, 3 to 4 minutes. Remove the pear slices to a serving plate, and continue with the remaining pears, butter, and brown sugar.

6. When the cake has cooled, run a knife around the edges of the pan and invert it onto a cutting board. Carefully slice the cake in half horizontally so you have 2 slabs of cake, each about 1 inch deep. Measure 9 or 10 inches down each slab of cake, depending on which size loaf pan you are using. Cut through the cake crosswise at this mark. Save the cut-off 4-inch ends for patching. Slice each of the 9- or 10-inch slabs of cake into 6 lengthwise strips. You will have 12 strips of cake in all.

7. Spread one fourth of the sautéed pears evenly over the parchment paper in the bottom of the loaf pan. Pour a little liquid from the pears over them. Spoon one fourth of the cream cheese filling over the pears, spreading it out evenly. Place 3 cake strips over the filling, pressing down gently with your fingers, and fill any gaps with leftover cake. Repeat the layers of pears, cream cheese filling, and cake strips three more times, ending with the cake. Press down as you work.

8. Cover the cake with parchment or waxed paper and place a smaller loaf pan or a small cutting board on top of the terrine. Weight it down with at least 3 pounds of canned goods. Place the weighted-down pan in the refrigerator for 24 hours. The height of the cake should shrink by 2 inches after the weighting-down time is over.

9. The next day, remove the terrine from the refrigerator and invert it onto a serving platter. Peel off the parchment paper. Slice and serve.

R

the Cake Mix Doctor says

Because the pears contain a lot of moisture, waxed paper will get soggy. You will find parchment paper easier to work with in this recipe.

✳ *Store this cake, covered with plastic wrap, in the refrigerator for up to 1 week.*

LUSCIOUS LEMON WHITE CHOCOLATE TERRINE

After one bite, my Aunt Elizabeth wanted this recipe. She didn't believe the cake, with lemon curd and white chocolate sandwiched between, started from a mix. But it did. This winner is a white chocolate and lemon sheet cake that you cool and cut into strips before layering with lemon curd and a quick ganache made of melted white chocolate and heavy cream. Okay, it's not for dieters, but a little bite can't hurt. And it's stunning when served with a spoonful of fresh blueberries or strawberries and curls of white chocolate.

SERVES: 12 TO 16

PREPARATION TIME: 30 MINUTES

BAKING TIME: 35 TO 40 MINUTES

ASSEMBLY TIME: 20 MINUTES

CHILLING TIME: 24 HOURS

CAKE:

Vegetable oil spray for misting the pan

6 ounces white chocolate, coarsely chopped

1 package (18.25 ounces) plain white cake mix

⅔ cup water

⅓ cup vegetable oil

3 large eggs

2 large egg whites

2 tablespoons fresh lemon juice

1 teaspoon grated lemon zest

FILLING:

1 jar (10 ounces) lemon curd, or 1 recipe
Julie's Lemon Curd (page 459)
White Chocolate Ganache (page 444)

TOPPING:

1 cup fresh blueberries or sweetened
sliced fresh strawberries (see
"the Cake Mix Doctor says")

1. Place a rack in the center of the oven and preheat the oven to 350°F. Lightly mist a 13- by 9-inch pan with vegetable oil spray. Set the pan aside. Line the bottom and up the sides of a 9- to 10-inch loaf pan with waxed paper. Set the loaf pan aside.

2. Melt the white chocolate in a small glass bowl in the microwave oven on high power for 1 minute. Remove the bowl from the oven and stir with a small rubber spatula until smooth. (See Melting White Chocolate, page 92.) Let the white chocolate cool slightly.

3. Place the cake mix, water, oil, whole eggs, egg whites, lemon juice, and lemon zest in a large mixing bowl. Pour in the white chocolate. Blend with an electric mixer on low speed for 1 minute. Stop the machine and scrape down the sides of the bowl with

Chocolate-Dipped Fruit

Ever wonder how to make those gorgeous white- or dark-chocolate-dipped strawberries? It's pretty easy. Just chop about 8 ounces of white or semisweet chocolate, place it in a glass bowl, and microwave on high power for 2 to 3 minutes, removing the chocolate from the oven every 20 seconds to stir it. The white chocolate will melt more quickly than the dark chocolate. Or you can carefully melt the chocolate in a saucepan over low heat, stirring constantly.

With your fingers, dip about 24 strawberries—rinsed and dried, with the hulls still attached—halfway into the chocolate. Transfer the berries to a waxed paper–lined tray and allow the chocolate to set, about 30 minutes at room temperature or quicker in the refrigerator. Chill the berries, lightly covered with plastic wrap, until ready to use. They will keep, chilled, for 2 days. You can also dip other fruits in chocolate. Try fresh cherries on the stem, apple wedges, sliced kiwi and star fruit, even pineapple sticks.

a rubber spatula. Increase the mixer speed to medium and beat 2 minutes more, scraping down the sides again if needed. The batter should look well blended. Pour the batter into the prepared 13- by 9-inch pan, smoothing it out with the rubber spatula. Place the pan in the oven.

4. Bake the cake until it is golden brown and springs back when lightly pressed with your finger, 35 to 40 minutes. Remove the pan from the oven and place it on a wire rack to cool completely, 40 minutes.

5. Meanwhile, prepare the fillings: If you are using store-bought lemon curd, spoon it into a small glass bowl and place it in the microwave to warm for 1 minute on high power. Set the bowl aside. If you are preparing Julie's Lemon Curd, do so now. Prepare the White Chocolate Ganache, and set the bowl aside to cool.

6. When the cake has cooled, run a knife around the edges of the pan and invert the cake onto a cutting board. Carefully slice the cake in half horizontally so you have 2 slabs of cake, each about 1 inch thick. Measure 9 or 10 inches down each slab of cake, depending on which size loaf pan you are using. Cut through the cake crosswise at this mark. Save the cut-off 4-inch ends of cake for patching. Slice each of the 9- or 10-inch slabs of cake into 6 lengthwise strips. You will have 12 strips of cake in all.

7. Arrange 3 cake strips on the bottom of the prepared loaf pan. Fill in any gaps with leftover cake. Spread one fourth of the lemon curd over the cake, then drizzle it with one fourth of the ganache. Place 3 more strips of cake on top, filling any gaps as needed and pressing down as you work. Spread the cake with another fourth of the lemon curd and drizzle with another fourth of the ganache. Repeat the layers of cake, lemon curd, and ganache two more times, ending with the ganache and pressing down as you work. Cover the cake with waxed paper and place a smaller loaf pan or a

the Cake Mix Doctor says

To sweeten the berries, sprinkle 1 tablespoon sugar over them, stir, and let sit for 15 to 20 minutes before serving.

If you want to substitute the flavors of lime or orange, it is simple to do: Use lime or orange juice and zest in the cake, and buy or make your own lime or orange curd. Homemade citrus curd is a delicious addition to this cake, and it's easy to prepare if you follow Julie's Lemon Curd recipe (page 459). Poured into a glass jar, citrus curd also makes a wonderful gift.

small cutting board on top of the terrine. Weight it down with at least 3 pounds of canned goods. Place the weighted-down pan in the refrigerator for 24 hours. The height of the cake should shrink by 2 inches after the weighting-down time is over.

8. The next day, remove the terrine from the refrigerator and invert it onto a serv-

ing platter. Peel off the waxed paper. Slice, and serve with a spoonful of berries alongside.

✳ *Store this cake, covered with plastic wrap, in the refrigerator for up to 1 week.*

CHOCOLATE LOVE CAKE

You don't really need a heart-shaped cake to express feelings of admiration for someone. A cake made by you is certainly enough. But when you want that festive presentation—for a Valentine's Day party, a birthday, a coming-home fête—then this is it. The batter is baked in an 8-inch round and an 8-inch square pan. To make a heart, the round layer is cut in half and these semicircles are placed on adjoining sides of the square and covered with frosting. The cake has a wonderfully subtle flavor of cherries. And the frosting . . . well, the frosting is special because it is a whipped ganache: Heavy cream is heated and poured over semisweet chocolate, a cherry liqueur is added if you like, the mixture is chilled, and then it is whipped like cream. Garnish this pretty cake with white and dark chocolate curls, fresh cherries on the stem, even rose petals.

SERVES: 12 TO 16
PREPARATION TIME: 10 MINUTES
BAKING TIME: 30 TO 35 MINUTES
ASSEMBLY TIME: 10 MINUTES

FROSTING:

*Whipped Chocolate Ganache (page 442),
    flavored with kirsch if desired*

CAKE:

*Solid vegetable shortening for greasing
    the pans*
Flour for dusting the pans
*1 package (18.25 ounces) devil's food cake
    mix with pudding*
1 can (21 ounces) cherry pie filling
2 large eggs
1 teaspoon pure almond extract

GARNISH:

White and dark chocolate curls

(see page 250)

1 cup fresh cherries with stems, or

1 cup rose petals

1. Prepare the ganache, adding 1 table-spoon kirsch or other cherry liqueur if desired. Cover the bowl with plastic wrap and place it in the refrigerator to chill for 1 hour.

2. Meanwhile, place a rack in the center of the oven and preheat the oven to 350°F. Generously grease one 8-inch round and one 8-inch square cake pan with solid vegetable shortening, then dust with flour. Shake out the excess flour. Set the pans aside.

3. Place the cake mix, cherry pie filling, eggs, and almond extract in a large mixing bowl. Blend with an electric mixer on low speed for 1 minute. Stop the machine and scrape down the sides of the bowl with a rubber spatula. Increase the mixer speed to medium and beat 2 minutes more, scraping down the sides again if needed. The batter should look well combined. Divide the batter between the prepared pans, smoothing it out with the rubber spatula. Place the pans in the oven side by side.

4. Bake the cakes until they spring back when lightly pressed with your finger, 30

the Cake Mix Doctor says

The storage dilemma with this cake is that it is large and it won't fit in a cake saver, so you have to cover it with waxed paper. It will freeze well unfrosted, if you like: Bake the layers ahead of time, cool, then freeze them for up to 2 months in heavy-duty aluminum foil. Thaw the layers, then arrange and frost as directed.

to 35 minutes. Remove the pans from the oven and place them on wire racks to cool for 10 minutes. Run a sharp knife around the edge of each layer and invert each onto a rack, then invert again onto another rack so that the cakes are right side up. Allow to cool completely, 30 minutes.

5. When the ganache is nearly chilled, place the electric mixer beaters in the refrigerator to chill for 10 minutes. Remove the beaters and the bowl of ganache. Whip the ganache on high speed for 2 to 3 minutes, or until the frosting lightens in color and triples in volume.

6. Place the square cake layer on a large serving platter so that one point faces

How to Make Chocolate Curls

To make curls, you'll need to begin with an 8-ounce block of semisweet or white chocolate purchased from a specialty shop or your local bakery. (Most supermarkets don't stock these large blocks, and you need this size to create ribbon-like curls.) Place the chocolate block on a plate in a warm spot—by a sunny window, at the back of a gas stove, on top of the refrigerator—for about an hour, just to lightly soften it. Then drag a sharp vegetable peeler down the smooth side (no ridges or brand name in it) of the chocolate block in one motion from top to bottom, so you create curls. They will vary in size, but that doesn't matter. Use several handfuls of these curls on top of your frosted cake, then make some more curls to freeze in a zipper-lock bag for up to 1 month. The remaining chocolate block can be wrapped tightly and chilled, then kept in a cool place to use on future desserts.

you. Cut the round cake layer in half, and place the halves on adjoining sides of the square, to form a heart shape. Spread the frosting over the top and sides of the cake with clean, smooth strokes.

7. Scatter the chocolate curls on top of the cake, and the cherries or rose petals around it. Slice and serve.

✳ *Store this cake, covered in waxed paper, in the refrigerator for up to 1 week.*

BROWNIE CHOCOLATE MOUSSE TRIFLE

My friend Kathy Sellers passed along a recipe for a brownie trifle, and it was the beginning of this fabulous recipe in which crumbled brownies are layered with chocolate mousse and whipped topping. Unlike Kathy's recipe, which uses a chocolate mousse mix, I make a super-easy mousse of my own. I also added pecans and chocolate chips to the brownies, but I didn't tinker with the frozen whipped topping. I knew this dessert was going to be so rich, that I needed a sweet and creamy layer that didn't add to the richness in a big way—Cool Whip. If you must, go ahead and whip your own cream for this layer. You'll need about 2 cups.

SERVES: 16

PREPARATION TIME: 25 MINUTES

BAKING TIME: 25 TO 30 MINUTES

CHILLING TIME: 1 HOUR

ASSEMBLY TIME: 10 MINUTES

CHOCOLATE MOUSSE:

1 cup semisweet chocolate chips

1 cup heavy (whipping) cream

BROWNIES:

Vegetable oil spray for misting the pan

1 package (19.8 ounces) brownie mix

8 tablespoons (1 stick) unsalted butter, melted

¼ cup buttermilk or milk

2 large eggs

1 cup semisweet chocolate chips

½ cup chopped pecans

TOPPING:

1 container (12 ounces) frozen whipped topping, thawed

1 cup toffee chips or almond brickle chips

R

the Cake Mix Doctor says

It's tough to tell when brownies are done, and unfortunately they overbake easily. It's even tougher to tell when you scatter chips and nuts on top, because then you can't see the center of the cake and if you stick a toothpick in the cake, it will come up wet with melted chocolate! So use your nose. In about 20 minutes the brownies will smell very good. Let them bake another few minutes, and pull them out of the oven at 25 minutes. Let them go another minute if you are unsure. The nice thing about this dessert is that you can overbake the brownies a bit and not worry because so many delicious things are on top!

One last note: If you want to turn this into a totally decadent confection, drizzle a little Kahlúa or orange-flavored liqueur, such as Cointreau, over the brownies after you crumble them into the dish.

1. For the chocolate mousse, place the chocolate chips in a medium-size mixing bowl and set aside. Place the cream in a small saucepan over medium heat. Bring to a boil, then remove from the heat. Pour the hot cream over the chocolate chips, and with a wooden spoon stir the mixture until the chocolate melts. Place the bowl, uncovered, in the refrigerator to chill completely, 1 hour.

2. Meanwhile, place a rack in the center of the oven and preheat the oven to 350°F. Lightly mist the bottom of a 13- by 9-inch pan with vegetable oil spray. Set the pan aside. Set aside a glass trifle dish or a large glass salad bowl.

3. Place the brownie mix, melted butter, buttermilk, and eggs in a large mixing bowl. Stir with a wooden spoon until all the ingredients are incorporated, about 50 strokes. Pour the batter into the prepared pan, smoothing it out with a rubber spatula. Scatter the chocolate chips and the pecans evenly over the top of the batter. Place the pan in the oven.

4. Bake the cake until the outside 2 inches have formed a crust and it feels firm, 25 to 30 minutes (see "the Cake Mix Doctor says"). Remove the pan from the oven and place it on a wire rack to cool completely, 30 minutes.

5. Meanwhile, place the electric mixer beaters in the refrigerator to chill.

6. Remove the chilled chocolate mixture and the chilled beaters from the refrigerator. Beat the chocolate mixture on medium-high speed until it forms stiff peaks, 1 to 2 minutes, and is quite thick and mousse-like.

7. Cut the pan of brownies into two portions. Crumble one half of the brownies into ½-inch pieces and scatter them evenly over the bottom of the reserved serving dish. Spoon large blobs of the chocolate mousse over the brownie layer, and then use a rubber spatula to spread the mousse out evenly. Spread half of the thawed frozen topping over the mousse, and scatter half of the toffee chips on top. Crumble the remaining brownies and repeat the layers, finishing by scattering the rest of the toffee chips evenly over the top. Cover the dish with plastic wrap and chill until serving time.

8. To serve, spoon the brownie trifle into serving bowls.

✷ *Store the trifle, covered with plastic wrap, in the refrigerator for up to 1 week.*

STRAWBERRY BROWNIE TORTE

W hen strawberries come into season—and you know when this is because the prices drop and they look so irresistible—this is a great dessert to prepare. It's a bit of a twist on the traditional strawberry shortcake, using layers of brownie instead of a sweet biscuit or sponge cake. And the whipped cream, too, *de rigueur* in shortcake, has been tinted chocolate.

....

SERVES: 16

PREPARATION TIME: 25 MINUTES

BAKING TIME: 15 TO 20 MINUTES

ASSEMBLY TIME: 10 MINUTES

....

BROWNIES:

Vegetable oil spray for misting the pan

Flour for dusting the pan

1 package (19.8 ounces) brownie mix

½ cup vegetable oil

¼ cup water

3 large eggs

¼ cup strawberry preserves, at room temperature

CHOCOLATE WHIPPED CREAM:

2 cups heavy (whipping) cream

2 tablespoons unsweetened cocoa powder

2 tablespoons confectioners' sugar, or more as needed

STRAWBERRIES:

1 pint fresh strawberries

1 tablespoon granulated sugar

6 whole strawberries, for garnish

1. Place a rack in the center of the oven and preheat the oven to 350°F. Line the bottom of a 16½- by 11½- by 1-inch jelly-roll pan with waxed or parchment paper. Mist the paper with vegetable oil spray, then dust with flour. Shake out the excess flour. Set the pan aside. Place the electric mixer beaters in the refrigerator to chill.

2. Place the brownie mix, oil, water, and eggs in a large mixing bowl. Stir with a wooden spoon until all the ingredients are incorporated, about 50 strokes. Pour the batter into the prepared pan, smoothing it out with a rubber spatula. Place the pan in the oven.

3. Bake the cake until the outside 2 inches have formed a crust and it feels firm, 15 to 20 minutes. Remove the pan from the oven and place it on a wire rack. While the brownies are still hot, spread the strawberry preserves over them. Let the brownies cool completely, 30 minutes.

4. Meanwhile, prepare the whipped cream: Place the heavy cream, cocoa powder, and confectioners' sugar in a large mixing bowl. Remove the beaters from the refrigerator, and whip the mixture with an electric mixer on high speed for 2 to 3 minutes, or until stiff peaks form. Cover the bowl with plastic wrap and chill until it's time to assemble the torte.

5. Rinse the strawberries and pat them dry. Remove the hulls and slice the berries lengthwise into a small bowl. Toss with the sugar and set aside.

the Cake Mix Doctor says

This is one brownie recipe in which you don't need to worry about overbaking. Even if you slightly overbake them, they will be moistened from the whipped cream and strawberries. It's a little easier to handle the brownie rectangles if they are slightly frozen: Place the 4 pieces of brownie, lightly covered with foil, in the freezer for 30 minutes to firm up.

6. To assemble, cut the pan of brownies crosswise into 4 pieces, cutting through the waxed paper. Carefully place 1 brownie piece on a serving platter. Remove the chocolate whipped cream from the refrigerator. Spread ¾ cup of the whipped cream over the brownie, and top with one third of the strawberries and juice. Repeat the layers of brownie, whipped cream, and berries twice. Top with the last piece of brownie, and either leave as is or frost the torte with any remaining chocolate whipped cream.

7. Garnish the torte with the whole strawberries. Then slice and serve.

✻ *Store this cake, covered with waxed paper or under a glass dome, in the refrigerator for up to 1 week.*

DARK CHOCOLATE ROULADE

WITH CHOCOLATE CREAM FILLING

Since I became the "Cake Mix Doctor," many people have asked me for a variety of different kinds of cake, including one with a chocolate cream filling. When Leah Paley, of Richmond, Virginia, shared her recipe for a chocolate sponge roll, I thought it would be just the right type of cake for the requested cream filling. And so, here it is. This roulade packs serious chocolate flavor and makes a stunning presentation on birthdays and anniversaries. Children love the filling, by the way, which is even more delicious after it has been chilled.

....

SERVES: 16

PREPARATION TIME: 25 MINUTES

BAKING TIME: 15 TO 20 MINUTES

ASSEMBLY TIME: 20 MINUTES

....

Softened butter for greasing the pan

1 package (18.25 ounces) plain dark chocolate fudge cake mix

½ cup water

⅓ cup vegetable oil

4 large eggs

2 tablespoons unsweetened cocoa powder

Chocolate Cream Filling (page 461)

Chocolate Dream Glaze (page 447)

1. Place a rack in the center of the oven and preheat the oven to 350°F. Lightly butter the bottom of a 16½- by 11½- by 1-inch jelly-roll pan, and line it with enough parchment paper to cover the bottom and still have a couple of inches extending at each end. Lightly butter the parchment paper, but do not butter the sides of the pan. Set the pan aside.

2. Place the cake mix, water, oil, and eggs in a large mixing bowl. Blend with an electric mixer on low speed for 1 minute. Stop the machine and scrape down the sides of the bowl with a rubber spatula. Increase the mixer speed to medium and beat 2 minutes more, scraping the sides down again if needed. The batter should look thick and well combined. Pour the batter evenly into the prepared pan, smoothing it out with a rubber spatula. Place the pan in the oven.

3. Bake the cake until it springs back when lightly pressed with your finger and a toothpick inserted in the center comes out clean, 15 to 20 minutes. Remove the pan from the oven and place it on a wire rack while you dust a clean kitchen towel (thin cotton or linen) with the cocoa powder. Immediately invert the pan onto the towel and carefully peel off the parchment that clings to the bottom of the cake. While the cake is still hot, use the towel to help you carefully roll the cake into a jelly roll, or roulade: Begin with the long side next to you and roll away from you. Don't worry if the roulade splits while you are rolling it because you will cover up these blemishes with the filling. Place the roulade, seam side down, wrapped in the kitchen towel or in parchment paper, on the counter to cool for 30 minutes.

4. Meanwhile, prepare the Chocolate Cream Filling. Set it aside.

5. When the cake is cool, you are ready to assemble the roulade. Carefully unroll the cake just enough so that you can spread the inside surface generously with the filling.

Gently roll the cake back into its roulade shape, carefully pulling the kitchen towel out from under it. Place the roulade, seam side down, on a serving platter. Cover it with plastic wrap and place the platter in the refrigerator to chill while you prepare the glaze.

6. Prepare the Chocolate Dream Glaze.

7. Remove the roulade from the refrigerator and spread the glaze to completely cover it, using smooth, clean strokes. Slice and serve.

✱ *Store the roulade, covered in plastic wrap, in the refrigerator for up to 1 week.*

R

the Cake Mix Doctor says

Take care when making roulades, for once you roll up the warm cake in the kitchen towel dusted with cocoa, you must not let it rest more than 30 to 45 minutes before you fill it. Longer than that and it will crack. If you wish, use confectioners' sugar instead of the cocoa to dust the kitchen towel. Either one adds flavor and prevents the cake from sticking to the towel. And be careful not to roll up the towel in the roulade.

CHOCOLATE KAHLÚA ROULADE

WITH ESPRESSO CREAM FILLING

A cross between a roulade and a tiramisù, this is the dessert to prepare when you crave that mocha flavor. A few of us tested this roulade several times to get just the right filling, and we finally settled on adding coffee powder—it provides the right kick but allows the filling to stay firm. Kahlúa is a wonderful addition, brushed onto the baked roulade *and* whisked into the hot glaze.

....

SERVES: 16

PREPARATION TIME: 20 MINUTES

BAKING TIME: 15 TO 20 MINUTES

ASSEMBLY TIME: 20 MINUTES

....

ESPRESSO CREAM FILLING:

1 cup vanilla low-fat yogurt, at room
    temperature
1 package (8 ounces) cream cheese,
    at room temperature
⅓ cup confectioners' sugar
1½ to 2 teaspoons coffee powder
    (see "the Cake Mix Doctor says")
½ teaspoon pure vanilla extract

CAKE:

Softened butter for greasing the pan
1 package (18.25 ounces) plain devil's food
    cake mix
½ cup water
⅓ cup vegetable oil
4 large eggs
½ teaspoon ground cinnamon
2 to 3 tablespoons Kahlúa or other coffee
    liqueur (optional)
2 tablespoons unsweetened
    cocoa powder

CHOCOLATE KAHLUA DREAM GLAZE:

1 cup semisweet chocolate chips

3 tablespoons butter

2 tablespoons light corn syrup

1 tablespoon Kahlúa or other coffee liqueur

1. For the filling, place the yogurt, cream cheese, confectioners' sugar, coffee powder, and vanilla in a medium-size mixing bowl and blend with an electric mixer on low speed for 1 to 2 minutes. The mixture should look well combined. Cover the bowl with plastic wrap and place it in the refrigerator to thicken up.

2. Meanwhile, place a rack in the center of the oven and preheat the oven to 350°F. Lightly butter the bottom of a 16½- by 11½- by 1-inch jelly-roll pan and line it with enough parchment paper to cover the bottom and extend over each end by a couple of inches. Lightly butter the parchment paper, but do not butter the sides of the pan. Set the pan aside.

3. Place the cake mix, water, oil, eggs, and cinnamon in a large mixing bowl. Blend with an electric mixer on low speed for 1 minute. Stop the machine and scrape down the sides of the bowl with a rubber spatula. Increase the mixer speed to medium and beat 2 minutes more, scraping the sides down again if needed. The batter should look thick and well combined. Pour the batter evenly into the prepared pan, smoothing it out with a rubber spatula. Place the pan in the oven.

4. Bake the cake until it springs back when lightly pressed with your finger and a toothpick inserted in the center comes out clean, 15 to 20 minutes. Remove the pan from the oven and place it on a wire rack. Brush it with the Kahlúa, if desired. Dust a clean kitchen towel (thin cotton or linen) with the cocoa powder, and immediately invert the pan onto the towel. Carefully peel off the parchment that clings to the bottom of the cake. While the cake is still hot, use the towel to help you carefully roll the cake into a jelly roll, or roulade. Begin with the long side next to you and roll away from you. Don't worry if the roulade splits while you are rolling it because you will cover up these blemishes

R the Cake Mix Doctor says

To make the coffee powder, begin with 1 tablespoon instant coffee granules. Place these in a food processor and process for 1 minute or until a powder forms. This will make about 2 teaspoons powder.

with the filling. Place the roulade, seam side down, wrapped in the kitchen towel or in parchment paper, on the counter to cool for 30 minutes.

5. When the cake is cool, you are ready to assemble the roulade. Carefully unroll the cake just enough so that you can spread the inside surface generously with the filling. Gently roll the cake back into its roulade shape, carefully pulling the kitchen towel out from under it. Place the roulade, seam side down, on a serving platter. Cover it with plastic wrap and place the platter in the refrigerator to chill while you prepare the glaze.

6. For the glaze, place the chocolate chips, butter, and corn syrup in a large glass bowl. Place in the microwave oven on high power for 1 to 1½ minutes. Remove the bowl and stir with a wire whisk until the butter and chocolate have melted and the glaze is smooth. Whisk in the Kahlúa, and set the bowl aside.

7. Remove the roulade from the refrigerator and spread the glaze to completely cover it, using smooth, clean strokes. Slice and serve.

✱ *Store the roulade, covered in plastic wrap, in the refrigerator for up to 1 week.*

CREAM CHEESE BROWNIE PIE

I love trying Pillsbury Bake-Off winning recipes. When my daughters ask if there is any dessert after dinner, I glibly reply, "Only some million-dollar pie." Is any recipe worth a million dollars? Since that has been the grand-prize kitty for the most recent Bake-Offs, it is a question to ponder. I do recall that the last few winners have contained chocolate—no doubt to justify that premium price tag! This 2000 grand prize–winning recipe comes from Roberta Sonefeld, of Hopkins, South Carolina, and is based on a Pillsbury brownie mix. Leave it to a Southerner to enter a fudge pie recipe in the Bake-Off—fudge pie is sacred stuff south of the Mason-Dixon line. Our grandmothers and mothers made it, we gorged on it at picnics and parties, and now it comes in this streamlined prize-winning cake mix version.

SERVES: 8

PREPARATION TIME: 15 MINUTES

BAKING TIME: 40 TO 45 MINUTES

ASSEMBLY TIME: 2 MINUTES

1 store-bought refrigerated 9-inch pie crust

1 package (8 ounces) cream cheese, at room temperature

3 tablespoons sugar

1 teaspoon pure vanilla extract

3 large eggs

1 package (15.1 ounces) hot fudge swirl deluxe brownie mix

¼ cup vegetable oil

2 tablespoons water

½ cup chopped pecans

1. Place a rack in the center of the oven and preheat the oven to 350°F. Place the pie crust in a 9-inch pie pan. Flute the edges as desired (see "the Cake Mix Doctor says," page 265).

2. Place the cream cheese, sugar, vanilla, and 1 egg in a medium-size mixing bowl. Blend with an electric mixer on low speed until smooth, 1 minute. Set the bowl aside.

3. Set aside the hot fudge packet from the brownie mix (you'll use it for the topping). Place the brownie mix, oil, 1 tablespoon of the water, and the remaining 2 eggs in a large mixing bowl. Beat with a wooden spoon until just incorporated and smooth, about 50 strokes. Spread ½ cup of the brownie mixture in the bottom of the crust. Spoon the cream cheese mixture over this, and carefully spread it over the brownie layer with a rubber spatula. Top with the remaining brownie mixture, spreading it evenly to smooth the top. Sprinkle the pecans on top of the pie. Place the pan in the oven.

4. Bake the pie until the crust is deep golden brown, the center has puffed up, and the nuts have toasted, 40 to 45 minutes. Remove the pan from the oven, and place it on a wire rack to cool for 30 minutes.

5. Before serving, squirt the reserved hot fudge sauce from the packet into a small glass bowl. Place in the microwave oven on high power to warm, 30 seconds. Stir in the remaining 1 tablespoon water. Driz-

What to Drink with Chocolate Cake

Depending on the time of day and the occasion, and possibly the locale, I can think of only three beverages to drink with a slice of chocolate cake. And I know much depends on what type of chocolate cake it is, but speaking in very general terms, here are my choices:

* *Milk.* Suitable any time of the day, on any occasion, and in any venue.

* *Coffee.* Better suited to mornings and after dinner, on any occasion, and in any venue.

* *Port.* Best poured after dinner, on festive occasions, at home—port prices in restaurants are ridiculous!

zle this fudge sauce over the top of the pie. Serve warm, or place in the refrigerator, uncovered, until chilled, 3 hours. Slice and serve.

✳ *Store this pie, covered in aluminum foil, at room temperature for up to 1 day or in the refrigerator for up to 1 week. Or freeze it, wrapped in foil, for up to 2 months. Thaw the pie overnight in the refrigerator before serving.*

the Cake Mix Doctor says

This pie is good with or without the fudge sauce on top. And it is delicious warm, although the Pillsbury recipe calls for chilling it. Actually, there is nothing more delicious than room-temperature fudge pie!

KENTUCKY BOURBON PECAN FUDGE PIE

Down Kentucky way, good cooks know how to combine the flavors of their local bourbon with pecans and chocolate. I remember a Kentucky bourbon chocolate candy that my parents used to eat. It was called Rebecca Ruth's, I think, and you couldn't get the stuff in Nashville—you had to drive across the state line into Kentucky just to buy it (because it was so boozy, I guess!). I recall sneaking a bite once, and finding that it had the strongest taste I could imagine. The flavor was intense bourbon, and obviously not meant for children! This pie is for adults, too, because the bourbon flavor comes sailing through. If you want to tee-total the recipe, simply omit the bourbon and use buttermilk or water instead. It will be a delicious pecan fudge pie, but don't tell the folks in Kentucky!

SERVES: 8
PREPARATION TIME: 10 MINUTES
BAKING TIME: 42 TO 47 MINUTES

1 store-bought refrigerated 9-inch
    pie crust
1 package (19.8 ounces) brownie mix
8 tablespoons (1 stick) unsalted butter,
    melted
¼ cup bourbon, buttermilk, or
    water
2 large eggs
½ cup semisweet chocolate chips
¼ cup finely chopped pecans

1. Place a rack in the center of the oven and preheat the oven to 350°F. Place the pie crust in a 9-inch pie pan. Flute the edges as desired (see "the Cake Mix Doctor says").

2. Place the brownie mix, melted butter, bourbon, and eggs in a large mixing bowl. Beat with a wooden spoon until just incorporated and smooth, about 50 strokes. Pour the batter onto the prepared crust, smoothing the top with a rubber spatula. Sprinkle the chocolate chips and pecans on top of the pie. Place the pie in the oven.

3. Bake the pie until the crust is deep golden brown, the center has puffed up, and the nuts have toasted, 42 to 47 minutes. Remove the pan from the oven, and place it on a wire rack to cool for 30 minutes.

4. Slice and serve.

✳ *Store this pie, covered in aluminum foil, at room temperature for up to 3 days or in the refrigerator for up to 1 week. Or freeze it, wrapped in foil, for up to 2 months. Thaw the pie overnight in the refrigerator before serving.*

the Cake Mix Doctor says

It's easy to make a refrigerated pie crust look homemade. Place it in your own pie pan and gently press it into the pan with your fingertips. If any crust overlaps the edge of the pan, fold it underneath and press down gently to create a clean, even line. Now, create a fluted (ruffled) edge: Place the thumb and index finger of your left hand on the edge of the crust so they form a U shape. With the index finger of your right hand push the edge of the crust gently into that U, creating an indentation. Do this every 2 inches around the crust. Or, to take an easier route, simply press into the edge of the crust with the tines of a fork all the way around.

If the crust on this pie gets too brown for your liking, cover it with strips of aluminum foil, taking care not to cover the pie filling, and let it continue to bake.

Chocolate Angel Food and Chiffon Cakes

• • •

When you take egg yolks and fat out of a cake recipe, you remove a lot of flavor. So what is the allure of angel food cakes? They seem to be just sugar and hot air, as their high egg white ratio drives them upward in the pan. Yet a lot of folks out there are big fans.

In fact, my mother and grandmother would choose angel food before any other cake. They say the key is the cake's delicacy, its ability to satisfy and yet not fill us up, and its spongy texture that sops up juicy peaches and berries. And they're right—it's for those reasons that angel food is a beloved American classic. In fact, at the end of 2000 the *Dallas Morning News* surveyed sixteen cookbook authors and food experts to determine the top cakes of the last century. Angel food was mentioned more than any other cake.

Chocolate angel food? Now this is a slightly different creature. And constructing one used to mystify me until I discovered Dutch-process cocoa powder. Its deep color and rich flavor are just the ingredients to turn an angel food mix into a chocolate angel. Add the flavoring of your choice—apricot, orange, peppermint, coffee—and you have a mighty interesting cake.

But go carefully. The angel food mix is resilient enough to withstand temperature differences, overbaking, and under-baking, but it will not stand up to too much fat. When I folded in yogurt, milk, or ice cream, I tossed those sunken experiments into the garbage. Even too much peppermint oil or dried coconut sent the cake southward. Watch the sugar, too, because angel food mixes are extremely sweet. Yet the juice from the crushed pineapple in the Chocolate Pineapple Angel Food Cake seems to be just the right partner—it doesn't interfere with the cake's ability to build height, but it does cut its inherent sweetness.

As long as you follow my directions, you will bake up a beautiful cake. Take care to just combine the ingredients in the beginning and then beat them for no longer than 1 minute before turning the batter into an ungreased pan. The angel needs the ungreased edges to pull itself up to the highest heights. And to main-tain that height after it has baked, imme-diately turn the pan upside down over a long-neck bottle and let the cake cool in that position for at least an hour.

Many people have asked me what type of pan is best for baking an angel food cake, and I've concluded that the shiny tube pans are best. Some of the nonstick pans have too slippery a sur-face, preventing the cakes from rising as well as they should and—worse—allow-ing the cakes to fall out of the pan while cooling upside down. So the cake doesn't overbrown, set the oven rack one or two positions below the center.

It's not always what you add to the cake batter, but what you do with the angel food cake after it is baked, that cre-ates the impact. Try the Frozen Chocolate Neapolitan Cake or the White Chocolate Angel Mousse Cake to see what I mean.

Have fun with these angelic recipes, like Barbara's Chocolate Marble Angel Food Cake, Chocolate-Swirled Apricot Angel Food Cake, or the Chocolate Coco-nut Macaroon Cake.

And don't forget the angel's cousin, the chiffon. Although light in texture, chiffon cakes contain egg yolks and veg-etable oil. They, too, should be baked in ungreased pans for optimum rise. Whether glazed with white chocolate or enrobed in peppermint frosting, these chiffons, like the angels, offer a light taste as long as you use a light touch when preparing them.

BARBARA'S CHOCOLATE MARBLE ANGEL FOOD CAKE

WITH SHINY CHOCOLATE GLAZE

When Barbara Weindling, of Nashville, Tennessee, is cooking a big meal, she plans on a lighter cake for dessert. This is the angel food cake she bakes every Thanksgiving and for Hanukkah celebrations. And did I mention that it's easy and beautiful as well as low in fat? It looks like a lot more trouble than it is, with that gossamer-thin glaze coating the top and sides. Barbara modestly admits: "I am a from-scratch kind of girl, but one of my family's favorite cakes is doctored."

SERVES: 16

PREPARATION TIME: 10 MINUTES

BAKING TIME: 38 TO 42 MINUTES

ASSEMBLY TIME: 2 MINUTES

1 package (16 ounces) angel food cake mix

1¼ cups water

1 tablespoon Dutch process unsweetened
*   cocoa powder*

Shiny Chocolate Glaze (page 450)

1. Place a rack one position lower than center in the oven (see "the Cake Mix Doctor says"), and preheat the oven to 350°F. Set aside an ungreased 10-inch tube pan.

2. Place the cake mix and water in a large mixing bowl. Beat with an electric mixer on low speed for 30 seconds. Stop the machine and scrape down the sides of the bowl with a rubber spatula. Increase the mixer speed to medium and beat for 1 minute more, scraping the sides down again if needed. The batter should look well combined. Pour half of the batter into a medium-size mixing bowl, and fold the cocoa powder into it until just incorporated. Drop the white and chocolate batters, alternately, by generous tablespoons into the ungreased pan. Smooth the top with the rubber spatula. Place the pan in the oven.

3. Bake the cake until it is lightly browned and the crust feels firm to the touch when lightly pressed with your fin-

ger, 38 to 42 minutes. Remove the pan from the oven and immediately turn it upside down over the neck of a glass bottle. Allow to cool for 1 hour.

4. Remove the pan from the bottle. Run a long, sharp knife around the edge of the cake and invert it onto a rack, then invert it again onto a serving platter so that it is right side up.

15 Cakes to Bake for Your Mom

1. White Chocolate Chiffon Cake with White Chocolate Glaze

2. Chocolate Chiffon Cake with Crushed Peppermint Buttercream Frosting

3. Frozen Chocolate Neapolitan Cake

4. Barbara's Chocolate Marble Angel Food Cake with Shiny Chocolate Glaze

5. Chocolate Cream Cheese Pound Cake

6. Chocolate Macaroon Ring Cake

7. German Chocolate Chip Pound Cake

8. White Chocolate Pound Cake with Strawberries and Warm Lemon Curd Sauce

9. Chocolate Cinnamon Banana Cake with Quick Caramel Frosting

10. Ebony and Ivory Cake

11. My Favorite Birthday Cake

12. White Chocolate Banana-Macadamia Cheesecake

13. Luscious Lemon White Chocolate Terrine

14. Chocolate Love Cake

15. Baby Chocolate Pistachio Cakes

5. Prepare the Shiny Chocolate Glaze. Spoon the glaze over the cooled cake, allowing it to drizzle down the sides. Slice and serve.

✸ *Store this cake in a cake saver at room temperature for up to 1 week. Or freeze it in a cake saver for up to 6 months. Thaw the cake overnight in the refrigerator before serving.*

R/
the Cake Mix Doctor says

Cakes get too brown if you bake them in the center of the oven. Just move the rack a notch or two down from the center, and your cake should rise and brown just fine.

CHOCOLATE-ORANGE ALMOND MARBLE ANGEL FOOD CAKE

I n *The Cake Mix Doctor* I had a recipe for doctoring up angel food batter with orange juice concentrate. Here I take that recipe a step further. Almond flavoring and orange zest are added to the batter, and half of it is also flavored with chocolate. The combination is pleasing to the palate and to the eye. Dollop the batters haphazardly in the pan, or spoon them in neat alternating rows of orange and chocolate— whatever suits your personality! To glaze? A simple chocolate-orange syrup, of course.

SERVES: 16

PREPARATION TIME: 20 MINUTES

BAKING TIME: 38 TO 42 MINUTES

ASSEMBLY TIME: 2 MINUTES

CAKE:

1 package (16 ounces) angel food
     cake mix

1 cup water

¼ cup frozen orange juice concentrate,
     thawed

1 teaspoon pure almond extract

1 teaspoon grated orange zest

2 tablespoons Dutch-process unsweetened
     cocoa powder

GLAZE:

½ cup semisweet chocolate chips

2 tablespoons butter

2 tablespoons light corn syrup

2 teaspoons frozen orange juice
     concentrate, thawed

Angel Food Tips

Mixes have pretty much taken the mystery out of preparing an angel food cake. However, there are still some things you need to know about baking these light-as-a-feather cakes.

- Use an ungreased shiny aluminum pan. The batter needs to grasp the sides of the pan in order to rise. Nonstick slippery surfaces may cause your cake to fall out of the pan when cooling upside down.

- Be sure your mixing bowl and beaters are clean and free of grease.

- Don't overbeat the batter. Combine for just 30 seconds at low speed to moisten the ingredients, then beat for 1 minute at medium to build volume.

- Bake on the next-to-lowest oven rack. You may need to remove the top oven rack, depending on the size of your oven, to allow room for the tube pan.

- Don't underbake the angel. Light-colored batters are done when they turn golden brown. Both light and chocolate batters are done when the crust is cracked and feels firm to the touch when pressed gently with your finger.

- Let the cakes hang upside down to cool. No, this isn't for their bad backs—it is to preserve precious volume. Choose a long-neck bottle, such as a vinegar or wine bottle, that fits inside the center of the tube pan. Or use a metal funnel. After baking, immediately turn the pan upside down over the bottle. Let it cool this way for at least an hour. To unmold, loosen the edges with a long sharp knife and invert the cake onto a rack, and again to right-side-up position on a serving platter.

1. Place a rack one position lower than center in the oven, and preheat the oven to 350°F. Set aside an ungreased 10-inch tube pan.

2. Place the cake mix, water, thawed orange juice concentrate, almond extract, and orange zest in a large mixing bowl. Beat with an electric mixer on low speed for 30 seconds. Stop the machine and scrape down the sides of the bowl with a rubber spatula. Increase the mixer speed to medium and beat for 1 minute more, scraping the sides down again if needed.

The batter should look well combined. Pour half of the batter into a medium-size mixing bowl, and fold the cocoa powder into it until just incorporated. Drop the orange and chocolate batters, alternately, by generous tablespoons into the ungreased pan. Smooth the top with the rubber spatula. Place the pan in the oven.

3. Bake the cake until it is lightly browned and the crust feels firm to the touch when lightly pressed with your finger, 38 to 42 minutes. Remove the pan from the oven and immediately turn it upside down over the neck of a glass bottle. Allow to cool for 1 hour.

4. Remove the pan from the bottle. Run a long, sharp knife around the edge of the cake and invert it onto a rack, then invert it again onto a serving platter so that it is right side up.

5. Prepare the glaze: Place the chocolate chips, butter, and corn syrup in a small saucepan over low heat. Stir until the butter melts, 2 to 3 minutes. Stir in the thawed orange juice concentrate. Immediately spoon the glaze over the cooled cake,

R̸

the Cake Mix Doctor says

You can create a checkerboard effect in this cake: Alternate 4 dollops of chocolate batter with 4 dollops of orange batter in the bottom of the pan. For the second layer of batter, start by spooning a chocolate dollop on top of an orange dollop, then an orange dollop on top of a chocolate dollop, and continue around. Continue with a third layer, alternating the batters again. Although the dollops will bake together and lose some of their definition, you will see a checkerboard pattern when you slice into the cake.

allowing it to drizzle down the sides. Slice and serve.

✱ *Store this cake in a cake saver at room temperature for up to 1 week. Or freeze it in a cake saver for up to 6 months. Thaw the cake overnight in the refrigerator before serving.*

CHOCOLATE PINEAPPLE ANGEL FOOD CAKE

We had fun discussing a non-chocolate version of this recipe in my newsletter. When I first heard about the cake, I tested it in a tube pan (it is an angel food cake, after all). But when I ran it in my newsletter, readers wrote to say they baked it in a 13- by 9-inch pan. I prefer the classic shape, and that's what I suggest here. However, for this book I added dark Dutch-process cocoa powder to the batter, and this miraculous and moist cake took on a whole new identity. You could frost this cake, but I prefer just a dusting of confectioners' sugar.

....

SERVES: 16

PREPARATION TIME: 10 MINUTES

BAKING TIME: 40 TO 45 MINUTES

....

1 package (16 ounces) angel food cake mix

1 can (20 ounces) crushed pineapple in its own juice

¼ cup Dutch-process unsweetened cocoa powder (see "the Cake Mix Doctor says")

1 teaspoon sifted confectioners' sugar, for dusting

1. Place a rack one position lower than center in the oven, and preheat the oven to 350°F. Set aside an ungreased 10-inch tube pan.

the Cake Mix Doctor says

Dutch-process unsweetened cocoa powder can be found in many supermarkets. It is darker in color and smoother in flavor than regular cocoa powder. I like it in angel food cake batters because it is so dark and because it seems to cut through the sweetness of the batter.

2. Place the cake mix, pineapple and juice, and cocoa powder in a large mixing bowl. Beat with an electric mixer on low speed for 30 seconds. Stop the machine and scrape down the sides of the bowl with a rubber spatula. Increase the mixer speed to medium and beat for 1 minute more, scraping the sides down again if needed. The batter should look well combined. Pour the batter into the ungreased pan, smoothing the top with the rubber spatula. Place the pan in the oven.

3. Bake the cake until the crust feels firm to the touch when lightly pressed with your finger, 40 to 45 minutes. Remove the pan from the oven and immediately turn it upside down over the neck of a glass bottle. Allow to cool for 1 hour.

4. Remove the pan from the bottle. Run a long, sharp knife around the edge of the cake and invert it onto a rack, then invert it again onto a serving platter so that it is right side up. Dust with confectioners' sugar, slice, and serve.

✽ *Store this cake in a cake saver at room temperature for up to 1 week. Or freeze it in a cake saver for up to 6 months. Thaw the cake overnight in the refrigerator before serving.*

Angels in a 13- by 9-inch Pan

I can't tell you how many people have e-mailed me about turning all sorts of cakes into sheet cakes in a 13- by 9-inch pan. So I figured I'd be prepared this time and I'd test an angel food cake in this pan. I prepared the Deep Chocolate Almond Angel Icebox Cake (see page 280), poured it into an ungreased 13- by 9-inch pan, and placed it on the center rack in a preheated 350°F oven. The cake baked up beautifully, rising high above the 2-inch sides of the pan, but about the time it was done—35 to 40 minutes—it settled back down a bit. It was still a pretty cake, and since the cake was cooked through, it didn't sink in the center. When you try this with one of the recipes, take care to press the top of the cake to make sure it is crusty and firm. Do not stick a toothpick in the center to check for doneness, or the cake will sink. As soon as the pan is out of the oven and on a rack to cool, run a sharp knife around the edges of the cake to loosen it from the sides. Let the cake cool in the pan for 30 minutes, then remove it with a long, flat metal spatula, as you would with any sheet cake. Then frost it with a buttercream or whipped cream frosting, slice, and serve.

CHOCOLATE-SWIRLED APRICOT ANGEL FOOD CAKE

As long as you are gentle with angel food batter and you keep within the amount of liquid needed in the recipe, you can add wonderful flavors. This cake is a good example of how you can easily flavor the cake with a fruit juice. I add the chocolate flavor with just a simple swirl of chocolate syrup.

SERVES: 16
PREPARATION TIME: 10 MINUTES
BAKING TIME: 45 TO 50 MINUTES
ASSEMBLY TIME: 2 MINUTES

CAKE:

1 can (11.5 ounces) apricot nectar
2 tablespoons water, or as needed
1 package (16 ounces) angel food cake mix
⅓ cup chocolate syrup

GLAZE:

½ cup sugar
4 tablespoons (½ stick) butter or margarine
½ cup semisweet chocolate chips

1. Place a rack one position lower than center in the oven, and preheat the oven to 350°F. Set aside an ungreased 10-inch tube pan.

2. Measure out ⅓ cup of the apricot nectar and set it aside for the glaze. Add water as needed to the remaining apricot nectar so that it measures 1¼ cups. Place the apricot nectar mixture and the cake mix in a large mixing bowl. Beat with an electric mixer on low speed for 30 seconds. Stop the machine and scrape down the sides of the bowl with a rubber spatula. Increase the mixer speed to medium and beat for 1 minute more, scraping the sides down again if needed. The batter should look well combined. Pour the batter into the ungreased pan. Pour the chocolate syrup evenly over the top of the batter, and using a dinner knife, swirl the syrup into the batter, creating a marbled effect. Place the pan in the oven.

3. Bake the cake until it is lightly browned and the crust feels firm to the touch when lightly pressed with your finger, 45 to 50 minutes. Remove the pan from the oven and immediately turn it upside down over the neck of a glass bottle. Allow to cool for 1 hour.

4. Meanwhile, prepare the glaze: Place the sugar, butter, and reserved ⅓ cup apricot nectar in a small saucepan over medium-low heat. Cook, stirring constantly, until the mixture comes to a boil. Let boil for 1 minute, stirring. Then remove the pan from the heat and stir in the chocolate chips until they have melted. Set the glaze aside to cool slightly.

5. Remove the angel food pan from the bottle. Run a long, sharp knife around the edge of the cake and invert it onto a rack, then invert it again onto a serving platter so that it is right side up. Spoon the glaze over the cooled cake, allowing it to drizzle down the sides. Slice and serve.

✳ *Store this cake in a cake saver at room temperature for up to 1 week. Or freeze it in a cake saver for up to 6 months. Thaw the cake overnight in the refrigerator before serving.*

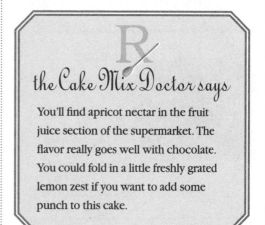

the Cake Mix Doctor says

You'll find apricot nectar in the fruit juice section of the supermarket. The flavor really goes well with chocolate. You could fold in a little freshly grated lemon zest if you want to add some punch to this cake.

CHOCOLATE COFFEE ANGEL FOOD CAKE

Rita Bagby, of Russiaville, Indiana, jokingly says, "When I'm not watching the corn grow, I bake!" This good Midwestern cook sent me one of her favorite recipes, a coffee angel food cake with a coffee buttercream frosting— delicious. I decided to create a mocha variation by adding some cocoa and a pinch of cinnamon—also delicious! The toasted almond slices are pretty scattered on top of the cake; you might save a handful to press into a single row around the bottom of the cake, too. And for a truly festive touch, surround the cake with chocolate-covered coffee beans, if you can get hold of some.

SERVES: 16
PREPARATION TIME: 8 MINUTES
BAKING TIME: 38 TO 42 MINUTES
ASSEMBLY TIME: 5 MINUTES

2 teaspoons instant coffee granules
1¼ cups hot water
1 package (16 ounces) angel food
    cake mix
2 tablespoons Dutch-process unsweetened
    cocoa powder
¼ teaspoon ground cinnamon
½ cup sliced almonds
Coffee Buttercream Frosting (page 416)

1. Place a rack one position lower than center in the oven, and preheat the oven to 350°F. Set aside an ungreased 10-inch tube pan.

2. Stir the instant coffee granules into the hot water in a glass measuring cup until the coffee has dissolved. Place the cake mix, coffee mixture, cocoa powder, and cinnamon in a large mixing bowl. Beat with an electric mixer on low speed for 30 seconds. Stop the machine and scrape down the sides of the bowl with a rubber spatula. Increase the mixer speed to medium and beat for 1 minute more, scraping the sides down again if needed. The batter should look well blended. Pour the batter into the ungreased pan. Smooth the top with the rubber spatula. Place the pan in the oven.

3. Bake the cake until it is lightly browned and the crust feels firm to the touch when lightly pressed with your finger, 38 to 42 minutes. Remove the pan from the oven (leave the oven on), and immediately turn it upside down over the neck of a glass bottle. Allow to cool for 1 hour.

4. Meanwhile, toast the almonds: Place the almonds on a cookie sheet and spread them out well. Place the sheet in the hot oven and toast until the almonds are golden brown, 4 to 6 minutes. Remove the sheet from the oven and let the almonds cool.

5. Run a long, sharp knife around the edge of the cake and invert it onto a rack, then invert it again onto a serving platter so that it is right side up.

6. Prepare the Coffee Buttercream Frosting. Spread the frosting on the top and sides of the cake with smooth, clean strokes. Sprinkle the top with the toasted almond slices. Slice and serve.

✻ *Store this cake in a cake saver at room temperature for up to 3 days or in the refrigerator for up to 1 week. Or freeze it, in a cake saver, for up to 6 months. Thaw the cake overnight in the refrigerator before serving.*

R/

the Cake Mix Doctor says

To give the frosting a true mocha flavor, add 2 tablespoons unsweetened cocoa powder to the butter and sugar, then proceed as directed.

DEEP CHOCOLATE ALMOND ANGEL ICEBOX CAKE

As I spooned into this cake for my second helping, I couldn't decide what part I liked best—the soft, torn pieces of chocolate angel food cake, or the rich ice creams soaked into them, or the chocolate-flavored whipped cream smothering it all! This is a terrific do-ahead company dessert, made by layering and then freezing angel food cake, ice cream, and whipped cream. You can add a drizzle of amaretto or other almond liqueur to dress it up, and garnish it with grated chocolate and toasted almonds if you really want to impress. Or if you are impatient, simply bake the cake—in a 13- by 9-inch pan, *not* a tube pan—and frost it with the whipped cream topping, bypassing the ice cream and the freezing. It's delicious that way, too.

....

SERVES: 16

PREPARATION TIME: 10 MINUTES

BAKING TIME: 35 TO 40 MINUTES

ASSEMBLY TIME: 30 MINUTES

....

CAKE:

1 package (16 ounces) angel food
    cake mix
1¼ cups water
¼ cup Dutch-process unsweetened cocoa
    powder
½ teaspoon pure almond extract

FILLING:

1 pint chocolate almond ice cream
1 pint vanilla ice cream
2 tablespoons amaretto (optional)

CHOCOLATE WHIPPED CREAM:

2 cups heavy (whipping) cream

2 to 3 tablespoons chocolate syrup

⅓ cup grated semisweet chocolate

1. Place a rack one position lower than center in the oven, and preheat the oven to 350°F. Set aside an ungreased 13- by 9-inch pan.

2. Place the cake mix, water, cocoa powder, and almond extract in a large mixing bowl. Beat with an electric mixer on low speed for 30 seconds. Stop the machine and scrape down the sides of the bowl with a rubber spatula. Increase the mixer speed to medium and beat for 1 minute more, scraping the sides down again if needed. The batter should look well combined. Pour the batter into the ungreased pan. Smooth the top with the rubber spatula. Place the pan in the oven.

3. Bake the cake until it is lightly browned and the crust feels firm to the touch when lightly pressed with your finger, 35 to 40 minutes. Remove the pan from the oven and place it on a wire rack. Immediately run a sharp knife around the edges of the cake to separate the cake from the pan. Allow to cool for 30 minutes.

4. Meanwhile, remove the ice cream from the freezer to let it soften. Place clean mixer beaters and a large bowl in the refrigerator to chill.

5. When the cake has cooled, break it into 1-inch pieces. Scatter half of the pieces in the bottom of a clean 13- by 9-inch baking dish. Drizzle a tablespoon of amaretto over the cake if desired. Spoon both of the ice creams, alternately, over the cake pieces. Smooth the ice cream out with a rubber spatula. Cover the ice cream with the remaining cake pieces. Drizzle another tablespoon of amaretto over the cake if desired. Cover the dish with foil and place it in the freezer for 15 minutes.

6. Meanwhile, prepare the chocolate whipped cream: Remove the beaters and bowl from the refrigerator. Pour the cream into the bowl. Using the chilled beaters, beat on high speed for 2 to 3 minutes, or until the mixture thickens to soft peaks. Drizzle the chocolate syrup over the cream. Continue beating on high speed until the cream forms stiff peaks.

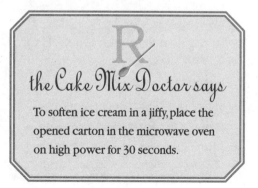

the Cake Mix Doctor says

To soften ice cream in a jiffy, place the opened carton in the microwave oven on high power for 30 seconds.

7. Remove the dish from the freezer. Spread the chocolate whipped cream over the cake mixture, spreading it out to the edges. Cover the dish with foil and return it to the freezer. Let freeze for 1 hour, or until hard.

8. Remove the dish from the freezer 15 minutes before serving. Scatter the grated chocolate on top, and spoon onto serving dishes.

✸ *Store this cake in the freezer for up to 1 week.*

Cool Tips for Building Ice Cream Cakes

- Begin with a completely cooled cake.

- Freeze the cake to make slicing easier.

- Slice the cake with a sharp serrated knife.

- Slice round layers horizontally into halves, angel foods horizontally into three tiers, and loaves horizontally into three or four slices. Cut sheet cakes vertically into three sections.

- Choose ice creams with attractive color contrasts. If the cake is chocolate, choose vanilla, strawberry, or mint chocolate chip ice cream, for example. Alternate colors by placing a different ice cream on top of each layer. Allow at least 1 cup of each flavor ice cream, and up to a pint of each for larger cakes.

- The finished cake takes less time to freeze through if the ice cream is frozen when it is placed on the cake, instead of softened and spread. Remove the ice

cream from its carton and slice it, patching these pieces on the cake until the layer is covered.

- Return the cake to the freezer between layers if the kitchen is warm.

- When the last layer of cake is on top, wrap the cake with foil and freeze until it is firm.

- An hour before serving, prepare the frosting, such as a whipped cream frosting, and coat the top and sides of the cake. Garnish the top of the cake with toasted sliced almonds, maraschino cherry halves, or grated chocolate. Return the cake to the freezer, uncovered, until serving time.

- After serving, place the cake in a cake saver, and return it to the freezer.

- Ice cream cakes will keep for up to a week in the freezer. After that, they tend to lose moisture and dry out.

FROZEN CHOCOLATE NEAPOLITAN CAKE

t is 15°F outside as I am writing this recipe, and the instructions are making me colder. *Brrr!* But this spectacular cake is worth it—tall, bright with ice cream inside, slathered with a sweetened whipped cream frosting, and garnished with toasted almonds and sliced strawberries. It may take a little extra effort, with all the in and out of the freezer to keep the ice cream solid, but you will enjoy it whether the weather is warm or cold!

············

SERVES: 16

PREPARATION TIME: 10 MINUTES

BAKING TIME: 35 TO 40 MINUTES

ASSEMBLY TIME: 2 HOURS

············

CAKE:

1 package (16 ounces) angel food
    cake mix

1¼ cups water

¼ cup Dutch-process unsweetened cocoa
    powder

TOPPING:

1 cup sliced almonds

2 recipes Sweetened Cream (page 445)

1 teaspoon pure almond extract

FILLING:

2 pints strawberry ice cream

1 pint vanilla ice cream

1 cup fresh strawberries, stems left on

1. Place a rack one position lower than center in the oven, and preheat the oven to 350°F. Set aside an ungreased 10-inch tube pan.

2. Place the cake mix, water, and cocoa powder in a large mixing bowl. Beat with an electric mixer on low speed for 30 seconds. Stop the machine and scrape down the sides of the bowl with a rubber spatula. Increase the mixer speed to medium and beat for 1 minute more, scraping the sides down again if needed. The batter should look well combined. Pour the batter into the ungreased pan. Smooth the top with the rubber spatula, and place the pan in the oven.

3. Bake the cake until it is lightly browned and the crust feels firm to the touch when lightly pressed with your finger, 35 to 40 minutes. Remove the pan from the oven (leave the oven on), and immediately turn it upside down over the neck of a glass bottle. Allow to cool for 1 hour.

4. Meanwhile, spread the sliced almonds out on a baking sheet and toast them in the oven until lightly browned, 6 to 7 minutes. Remove the pan from the oven and let the almonds cool.

5. Prepare the 2 recipes of Sweetened Cream, adding the almond extract when you add the confectioners' sugar. Cover the bowl with plastic wrap and place it in the refrigerator to chill.

6. Remove the cake pan from the bottle. Run a long, sharp knife around the edge of the cake and invert it onto a rack, then invert it again onto a plate so that it is right side up. Cover the cake lightly with foil, and place it in the freezer to firm up for 1 hour.

7. Remove the cake from the freezer. With a sharp serrated knife, slice the cake horizontally into four equal layers. Remove 1 pint of the strawberry ice cream from the freezer. Carefully peel off the cardboard carton, and slice the ice cream crosswise into ½-inch-thick slices. Place the bottom layer of cake on a serving platter or cake round, and cover it with flat slices of strawberry ice cream, patching it to cover the entire surface. Use up the entire pint. Place the next layer of cake on top. Cover the cake with the same piece of foil and return it to the freezer for 15 minutes. Cover the remaining two layers of cake with a fresh piece of foil or plastic wrap.

8. Remove the cake from the freezer. Also remove the vanilla ice cream from the freezer. Carefully peel off the cardboard carton, and slice the ice cream crosswise into ½-inch-thick slices. Cover the top of the second cake layer with vanilla slices, patching it to cover the entire surface. Place the next layer of cake on top. Re-cover the cake with the foil and return it to the freezer for 15 minutes.

9. Remove the cake from the freezer. Remove the last pint of strawberry ice cream from the freezer. Carefully peel off the cardboard carton, and slice the ice cream crosswise into ½-inch-thick slices. Cover the top of the third cake layer with strawberry slices, patching it to cover the entire surface. Place the last layer of cake on top. Cover the cake with the same piece of foil and return it to the freezer for 15 minutes.

10. Remove the cake from the freezer. Frost the top and sides of the cake with a layer of the reserved Sweetened Cream, working quickly and using clean, smooth strokes. Garnish the sides of the cake with the toasted almond slices. Cover the cake lightly with waxed paper or place it in a cake saver. Return it to the freezer, preferably overnight.

11. Just before serving, partially slice the strawberries so you can fan them out on their stems. Arrange them on the top of the cake and on the plate around it. Slice and serve.

✳ *Store this cake in a cake saver in the freezer for up to 1 week.*

the Cake Mix Doctor says

Freezing the cooled angel food cake for 1 hour makes it easier to slice it into layers.

WHITE CHOCOLATE ANGEL FOOD MOUSSE CAKE

This cake might appear complicated, but the time is in the assembly. The cake bakes quickly, the white chocolate mousse is fast (really a super-thick cream), and the buttercream frosting is made in minutes—the day ahead, if you like. Yes, you do have to squeeze in 4 hours for the nearly finished cake to chill before you can frost it. The recipe idea and the one for the Cappuccino Angel Food Mousse Torte (page 289) are based on recipes I saw in *Southern Living* magazine many months ago. Garnish this cake with big red strawberries, either plain or dipped in white chocolate, or with

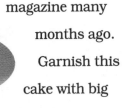

grated white and dark chocolate, lemon slices, or candied citrus (see How to Make Candied Orange Zest, page 228).

SERVES: 16
PREPARATION TIME: 20 MINUTES
BAKING TIME: 20 TO 25 MINUTES
ASSEMBLY TIME: 30 MINUTES
CHILLING TIME: 4 HOURS

Quick White Chocolate Mousse (page 460)
1 package (16 ounces) angel food cake mix
1¼ cups water
1 teaspoon pure vanilla extract
Vanilla Buttercream Frosting (page 412)
1 cup fresh strawberries, for garnish (dipped in white chocolate if desired; see Chocolate-Dipped Fruit, page 245)
1 cup grated white chocolate (see "the Cake Mix Doctor says") for garnish

1. Prepare the Quick White Chocolate Mousse up to the chilling point. While it is chilling over ice, proceed with the cake (remembering to stir the mousse every 5 minutes).

2. Place a rack in the center of the oven and preheat the oven to 350°F. Line three 9-inch round cake pans with waxed or parchment paper.

3. Place the cake mix, water, and vanilla in a large mixing bowl. Beat with an electric mixer on low speed for 30 seconds. Stop the machine and scrape down the sides of the bowl with a rubber spatula. Increase the mixer speed to medium and beat for 1 minute more, scraping the sides down again if needed. The batter should look well combined. Divide the batter among the prepared pans, and smooth the tops with the rubber spatula. Place the pans in the oven; if your oven is not large enough to hold them on one rack, place two pans on the center rack and the third pan in the center of the highest rack.

4. Bake the cakes until they are golden brown and the crust feels firm to the touch when lightly pressed with your finger, 20 to 25 minutes.

5. Meanwhile, place clean mixer beaters in the refrigerator to chill.

6. Remove the pans from the oven and place them on a wire rack to cool for 20 minutes.

7. While the cakes are cooling, remove

R

the Cake Mix Doctor says

An easy way to grate white chocolate is to let a bar come to room temperature, then run it down the largest holes of a cheese grater, being careful not to grate your knuckles! You can also run a sharp vegetable peeler against the bar for larger curls. Make sure you use the side that is smooth, with no ridges or brand name stamped in it.

the chilled beaters from the refrigerator. Remove the Quick White Chocolate Mousse from the ice bath, and with the chilled beaters, beat it on medium-high speed until nearly stiff peaks form. Don't overbeat this mousse.

8. When the cakes have cooled, invert one layer onto a serving platter and peel off the waxed paper. Spread with half of the mousse. Invert a second layer on top, and gently peel off the paper. Spread it with the remaining mousse. Invert the third layer onto one hand, and with your other hand peel off the paper. Place this third layer right side up on top of the cake. Cover the cake with plastic wrap

Standing Tall

I have learned a lot from the television appearances I've made since publication of my first book. The most important thing is that both the cake and I look better if we stand up straight! I'll work on me, but you can work on your cakes, even if they're never going before a camera.

Cakes look best when you raise them up on a cake stand instead of serving them on a plate. They look important up there. They look large. They look ready to eat!

The next time you plan to serve a selection of cakes on a buffet table at a picnic or family gathering, take care to arrange those cakes with height in mind. If the cake is brought on a pretty plate, place that plate on top of a small glass bowl to raise it up. Or find a pretty plant stand and pop that cake plate on top. Have a selection of cake stands available. The layers look best way up in the air, on the highest and widest stands, whereas the Bundt cakes look nicer on shorter stands. Bars and brownies are pretty cut and stacked on a small stand that isn't too wide.

Line the cake stands with lace paper doilies, which you can buy at party stores and most supermarkets. But take care not to frost the cake right on the doily, as smudges are hard to clean up: Either line the doily with waxed paper strips before frosting, or frost the cake on a cardboard round and then transfer this round to the doily-lined stand. Cakes that need glazing should be placed on wider cake stands; some stands have a rim that will catch any glaze runoff.

---

and place in the refrigerator to chill for at least 4 hours.

9. Meanwhile, prepare the frosting, rinse and dry the strawberries (and dip them in white chocolate, if you like).

10. Remove the cake from the refrigerator. Spread the top and sides with the frosting, using smooth, clean strokes.

Garnish with the strawberries and grated white chocolate. Slice and serve.

✳ *Store this cake, under a cake saver or lightly wrapped in plastic wrap, in the refrigerator for up to 1 week.*

CAPPUCCINO ANGEL FOOD MOUSSE TORTE

Here I go again—another seemingly complicated tower of angel food cake. But once you've got the system down—make the white chocolate mousse and chill it, bake the cake, assemble and chill, then frost the cake—that's it. This time we're making rectangular layers out of angel food cake baked in a jelly-roll pan. It makes for a nice, light torte. Coffee is the perfect flavoring for this chocolate log, not only blended right into the angel food batter but folded into the buttercream frosting as well. Serve this after a nice dinner with—what else?—a cup of coffee.

SERVES: 16

PREPARATION TIME: 20 MINUTES

BAKING TIME: 20 TO 25 MINUTES

ASSEMBLY TIME: 30 MINUTES

CHILLING TIME: 4 HOURS

Quick White Chocolate Mousse (page 460)

1 package (16 ounces) angel food cake mix

1¼ cups cold brewed coffee

½ teaspoon ground cinnamon

Coffee Buttercream Frosting (page 416)

1 cup grated semisweet chocolate

1. Prepare the Quick White Chocolate Mousse up to the chilling point. While it is chilling over ice, proceed with the cake (remembering to stir the mousse every 5 minutes).

2. Place a rack in the center of the oven and preheat the oven to 350°F. Line a 16½- by 11½ -inch or 15- by 10-inch jelly-roll pan with parchment or waxed paper. (The larger the pan, the less time the cake will take to bake).

3. Place the cake mix, brewed coffee, and cinnamon in a large mixing bowl. Beat with an electric mixer on low speed for 30 seconds. Stop the machine and scrape down the sides of the bowl with a rubber spatula. Increase the mixer speed to medium and beat for 1 minute more, scraping the sides down again if needed. The batter should look well blended. Pour the batter into the prepared pan. Smooth the top with the rubber spatula. Place the pan in the oven.

4. Bake the cake until it is lightly browned and the crust feels firm to the touch when lightly pressed with your finger, 20 to 25 minutes.

5. Meanwhile, place clean mixer beaters in the refrigerator to chill.

6. Remove the pan from the oven and place it on a wire rack to cool for 30 minutes.

7. While the cake is cooling, remove the chilled beaters from the refrigerator. Remove the Quick White Chocolate Mousse from the ice bath, and with the chilled beaters, beat it on medium-high speed until nearly stiff peaks form. Don't overbeat this mousse.

8. When the cake has cooled, loosen the edges with a knife. Cut the cake lengthwise into thirds with a sharp, serrated knife, cutting through the parchment. Invert one layer onto a serving platter and peel off the paper. Spread with half of the mousse. Place a second layer on top, and spread it with the remaining mousse. Place the third layer of cake on top. Cover the cake with plastic wrap and place it in the refrigerator to chill for at least 4 hours.

9. Meanwhile, prepare the Coffee Buttercream Frosting.

10. Remove the cake from the refrigerator. Spread the top and sides with the frosting, using smooth, clean strokes. Garnish with the grated chocolate. Slice and serve.

✱ *Store this cake, lightly wrapped in plastic wrap, in the refrigerator for up to 1 week.*

the Cake Mix Doctor says

Cinnamon is a subtle way to boost the flavor of coffee.

CHOCOLATE COCONUT MACAROON CAKE

You've heard of fallen chocolate cakes, those cakes that sink when they come out of the oven and reveal a wondrously gooey center when you fork into them? Well, this is the angel food

version. The dried coconut contains just enough oil to make this cake chewy and macaroonlike, but keeps it from rising more than halfway. It's different and delicious, especially when served with a spoonful of vanilla ice cream.

SERVES: 16

PREPARATION TIME: 10 MINUTES

BAKING TIME: 40 TO 45 MINUTES

ASSEMBLY TIME: 2 MINUTES

the Cake Mix Doctor says

Dried coconut is critical to this cake. You can find it where you buy dried fruits and grains at the natural foods store. It gives this cake a chewy, macaroonlike consistency.

1 package (16 ounces) angel food cake mix

1¼ cups water

¼ cup Dutch-process unsweetened cocoa powder

½ cup plus 1 tablespoon dried coconut (see "the Cake Mix Doctor says")

1 tablespoon miniature semisweet chocolate chips

Vanilla ice cream, for serving

1. Place a rack one position lower than center in the oven, and preheat the oven to 350°F. Set aside an ungreased 10-inch tube pan.

2. Place the cake mix, water, cocoa pow-

15 Fast Ways to Jazz up Vanilla Ice Cream

Stir in, refreeze until firm, then serve:

1. Crushed peppermint candy

2. Ground cinnamon

3. Kahlúa or other coffee liqueur

4. Mashed sweetened peaches and toasted chopped pecans

5. Crushed peanut brittle

6. Crème de menthe

7. Chopped fresh pineapple and dark rum

8. Crushed Girl Scout Thin Mint cookies

9. Miniature semisweet chocolate chips and dried coconut

10. Chopped fresh mango and grated lime zest

11. Almond brickle chips

12. Crumbled baked brownies

13. Finely ground coffee powder

14. Orange marmalade

15. Chocolate syrup and toasted slivered almonds

der, and ½ cup dried coconut in a large mixing bowl. Beat with an electric mixer on low speed for 30 seconds. Stop the machine and scrape down the sides of the bowl with a rubber spatula. Increase the mixer speed to medium and beat for 1 minute more, scraping the sides down again if needed. The batter should look well blended. Pour the batter into the ungreased pan. Smooth the top with the rubber spatula. Sprinkle the remaining 1 tablespoon coconut and the chocolate chips evenly over the batter. Place the pan in the oven.

3. Bake the cake until it is lightly browned and the crust feels firm to the touch when lightly pressed with your finger, 40 to 45 minutes. Remove the pan from the oven and immediately turn it upside down over the neck of a glass bottle. Allow to cool for 1 hour.

4. Remove the pan from the bottle. Run a long, sharp knife around the edge of the cake and invert it onto a rack, then invert it again onto a serving platter so that it is right side up.

5. Slice, and serve with vanilla ice cream.

✱ *Store this cake in a cake saver at room temperature for up to 1 week. Or freeze it in a cake saver for up to 6 months. Thaw the cake overnight in the refrigerator before serving.*

WHITE CHOCOLATE CHIFFON CAKE

WITH WHITE CHOCOLATE GLAZE

Adding white chocolate to a batter is tricky. It's so full of fat that you can easily make the cake greasy. The solution is to add extra egg whites, which help in a couple of ways. They produce a higher and lighter cake, and they have a drying effect on the white chocolate. So here is one great cake, topped with a simple and elegant glaze.

SERVES: 16

PREPARATION TIME: 12 MINUTES

BAKING TIME: 50 TO 55 MINUTES

ASSEMBLY TIME: 5 MINUTES

6 ounces white chocolate, coarsely chopped

5 large egg whites

½ teaspoon cream of tartar

1 package (18.25 ounces) plain white cake mix

⅔ cup water

⅓ cup vegetable oil

3 large egg yolks

2 teaspoons pure vanilla extract

White Chocolate Glaze (page 452)

1. Place a rack in the center of the oven and preheat the oven to 325°F. Set aside an ungreased 10-inch tube pan.

2. Melt the white chocolate in a small glass bowl in the microwave oven on high power for 1 minute. Remove the bowl from the oven and stir with a small rubber spatula until it is smooth. (See Melting White Chocolate, page 92.) Let it cool slightly. Set the bowl aside.

3. Place the egg whites and the cream of tartar in a medium-size mixing bowl. Beat with an electric mixer on high speed until stiff peaks form, 2 to 3 minutes. Set the bowl aside.

4. Place the cake mix, water, oil, egg yolks, vanilla, and melted white chocolate in a large mixing bowl, and with the same beaters used to beat the egg whites (no need to clean them), blend with the electric mixer on low speed for 1 minute. Stop the machine and scrape down the sides of the bowl with a rubber spatula. Increase the mixer speed to medium and beat 2 minutes more, scraping the sides down again if needed. The batter will be very thick and should look well blended. Turn the beaten egg whites out on top of the batter, and with the rubber spatula fold the whites into the batter until the mixture is light but well combined (see How to Fold, page 445). Pour the batter into the ungreased pan, smoothing the top with the rubber spatula. Place the pan in the oven.

5. Bake the cake until it is golden brown and springs back when lightly pressed with your finger, 50 to 55 minutes. Remove the pan from the oven and immediately turn it upside down over the neck of a glass bottle. Allow to cool for 1 hour.

6. Remove the pan from the bottle. Run a long, sharp knife around the edge of the cake and invert it onto a rack, then invert it again onto a serving platter so that it is right side up.

7. Prepare the White Chocolate Glaze.

8. Spoon the glaze over the top of the cake, and let it run down the sides. Let the cake rest for 10 minutes, then slice and serve.

✳ *Store this cake, wrapped in aluminum foil or plastic wrap, or in a cake saver, at room temperature for up to 1 week. Or freeze it, wrapped in foil, for up to 6 months. Thaw the cake overnight in the refrigerator before serving.*

the Cake Mix Doctor says

The egg whites will beat to higher peaks if they are at room temperature.

The glaze can be prepared while the cake is cooling. If it cools and hardens too much before you are ready to spoon it over the cake, return it to low heat and stir until it is smooth and pourable.

RASPBERRY SWIRL WHITE CHOCOLATE CHIFFON CAKE

WITH RASPBERRY GLAZE

Frozen raspberries are one of the busy cook's best secrets. Purée them, strain out the seeds, and you have an elegant sauce for any chocolate cake. Or drain the thawed raspberries and use them in this simple chiffon cake. The juice is saved and thickened with a little cornstarch to pour over the cake. This cake is for raspberry lovers. It is bright with raspberry color and flavor.

....

SERVES: 16

PREPARATION TIME: 20 MINUTES

BAKING TIME: 55 TO 60 MINUTES

ASSEMBLY TIME: 5 MINUTES

....

CAKE:

6 ounces white chocolate, coarsely chopped

5 large egg whites

½ teaspoon cream of tartar

1 package (12 ounces) frozen sweetened
    raspberries

1 package (18.25 ounces) plain white
    cake mix

½ cup water

¼ cup vegetable oil

3 large egg yolks

2 teaspoons pure vanilla
    extract

RASPBERRY GLAZE:

¼ cup sugar

1½ teaspoons cornstarch

1 teaspoon fresh lemon juice

1. Place a rack in the center of the oven and preheat the oven to 325°F. Set aside an ungreased 10-inch tube pan.

2. Melt the white chocolate in a small glass bowl in the microwave oven on high power for 1 minute. Remove the bowl from the oven and stir with a small rubber spatula until it is smooth. (See Melting White Chocolate, page 92.) Set the bowl aside.

3. Place the egg whites and cream of tartar in a medium-size mixing bowl. Beat with an electric mixer on high speed until stiff peaks form, 2 to 3 minutes. Set the bowl aside.

4. Drain the raspberries in a fine-mesh sieve or colander set over a small bowl, reserving the juice. Set aside ⅔ cup of the juice for the glaze. Mash the raspberries with a fork until you have about ¾ cup, then strain them through a fine-mesh sieve and drain them again if needed. Measure out ½ cup mashed berries; reserve the remainder for another use.

5. Place the cake mix, water, oil, egg yolks, vanilla, melted white chocolate, and ½ cup mashed raspberries in a large mixing bowl, and with the same beaters used to beat the egg whites (no need to clean them), blend with the electric mixer on low speed for 1 minute. Stop the machine and scrape down the sides of the bowl with a rubber spatula. Increase the mixer speed to medium and beat 2 minutes more, scraping the sides down again if needed. The batter will be very thick and should look well combined. Turn the beaten egg whites out on top of the batter, and with the rubber spatula fold the whites into the batter until the mixture is light but well combined (see How to Fold, page 445). Pour the batter into the ungreased pan, smoothing the top with the rubber spatula. Place the pan in the oven.

6. Bake the cake until it is golden brown and springs back when lightly pressed with your finger, 55 to 60 minutes. Remove the pan from the oven and immediately turn it upside down over the neck of a glass bottle. Allow to cool for 1 hour. (See "the Cake Mix Doctor says")

7. Remove the pan from the bottle. Run a long, sharp knife around the edge of the cake and invert it onto a rack, then invert it again onto a serving platter so that it is right side up.

8. Prepare the glaze: Strain the reserved ⅔ cup raspberry juice to remove any seeds. Place the sugar and cornstarch in a small saucepan and stir. Pour in the raspberry juice and lemon juice, and stir to combine. Place the pan over medium heat, and stir constantly until the mixture boils and thickens slightly, 2 minutes. Remove from the heat, and let the glaze cool in the pan for 15 minutes. It will continue to thicken.

9. Spoon the glaze over the top of the cake, and let it run down the sides. Let the cake rest for 10 minutes, then slice and serve.

✹ *Store this cake, wrapped in aluminum foil or plastic wrap, or in a cake saver, at room temperature for 3 days or in the refrigerator for up to 1 week. Or freeze it, wrapped in foil, for up to 6 months. Thaw the cake overnight in the refrigerator before serving.*

the Cake Mix Doctor says

If you are nervous about turning this cake upside down over a bottle, let it cool in the pan for 20 minutes. Then run a long sharp knife around the edge and invert it onto a rack, then invert it again so that it cools right side up.

CHOCOLATE CHIFFON CAKE

WITH CRUSHED PEPPERMINT BUTTERCREAM FROSTING

Every time I think about making a chiffon cake, I want to put on a certain frilly lime green polka-dot apron that my Aunt Elizabeth gave me. It has that June Cleaver look that you'd expect from a woman who was about to bake such a nostalgic 1960s cake. And if this is retro, then transport me back to that magic decade, for I love the simplicity of this cake, its high stature, and how great it looks with a dusting of confectioners' sugar or a spreading of creamy peppermint frosting. In fact, I'm off to find that apron . . .

SERVES: 16

PREPARATION TIME: 10 MINUTES

BAKING TIME: 60 TO 65 MINUTES

ASSEMBLY TIME: 5 MINUTES

5 large egg whites

½ teaspoon cream of tartar

1 package (18.25 ounces) plain chocolate
   fudge or devil's food cake mix

¾ cup water

½ cup vegetable oil

3 large egg yolks

2 teaspoons pure vanilla extract

Crushed Peppermint Buttercream Frosting
   (page 414)

1. Place a rack in the center of the oven and preheat the oven to 325°F. Set aside an ungreased 10-inch tube pan.

2. Place the egg whites and cream of tartar in a medium-size mixing bowl. Beat with an electric mixer on high speed until stiff peaks form, 2 to 3 minutes. Set the bowl aside.

3. Place the cake mix, water, oil, egg yolks, and vanilla in a large mixing bowl, and with the same beaters used to beat the egg whites (no need to clean them), blend with the electric mixer on low speed for 1 minute. Stop the machine and scrape down the sides of the bowl with a rubber spatula. Increase the mixer speed to medium and beat 2 minutes more, scraping the sides down again if needed. The batter will be very thick and should look well combined. Turn the beaten egg whites out on top of the batter, and with the rubber spatula fold the whites into the batter until the mixture is light but well combined (see How to Fold, page 445). Pour the batter into the ungreased pan, smoothing the top with the rubber spatula. Place the pan in the oven.

4. Bake the cake until it springs back when lightly pressed with your finger, 60 to 65 minutes. Remove the pan from the oven and immediately turn it upside down over the neck of a glass bottle. Allow to cool for 1 hour.

5. Remove the pan from the bottle. Run a long, sharp knife around the edge of the cake and invert it onto a rack, then invert it again onto a serving platter so that it is right side up.

6. Prepare the Crushed Peppermint Buttercream Frosting.

7. Spread the frosting over the top and sides of the cake with smooth, clean strokes. Let the cake rest for 10 minutes, then slice and serve.

✳ *Store this cake in a cake saver at room temperature for 3 days or in the refrigerator for up to 1 week. Or freeze it in a cake saver for up to 6 months. Thaw the cake overnight in the refrigerator before serving.*

R
the Cake Mix Doctor says

Whereas you should bake angel food cakes on a lower rack level, you can bake chiffon cakes on the center rack of the oven. But if in doubt as to which level is correct, bake this cake lower, not higher.

Muffins, Cupcakes, and Little Cakes

• • •

On the train ride from Philadelphia to New York City, I was working feverishly to complete this book manuscript, typing in muffin, cupcake, and little cake recipes on my laptop computer. Jenny Mandel, of Workman Publishing, was sitting next to me, and she would periodically lean over and look at whatever I was typing. "Oooh" was her response to Little White Chocolate Lemon Drizzle Cakes. Another time it was Baby Chocolate Pistachio Cakes and "Aaah." It went on like this for several hours, what with an unexpected delay in New Jersey, and the passengers around us must have thought we had gone mad.

Just mad about muffins, cupcakes, and all those little cakes!

It goes way back, as they say. I like small bites. I would rather graze through an assortment of appetizers than sit down to a massive main course. And this chapter allows you to graze your way through dessert, taking a small portion and saving the rest for later. These smaller cakes are perfect for food writers as well as children, the elderly, and smaller households.

I can't tell you how many requests I had for smaller cakes after *The Cake Mix Doctor* was published. People wanted a slice or two of chocolate cake, but not the entire cake. So with recipes like Triple-Chocolate To-Live-For Muffins, you get that quick chocolate fix, whether it's midmorning or late at night. The rest of the muffins can go into the freezer and stay there until you pull another one out, pop it in the microwave, and get another chocolate fix.

How to turn your favorite cake recipe into muffins or cupcakes? It's possible with almost any recipe, but you'll have the best results if the cake is sturdy in structure, containing 3 to 4 eggs, possibly a package of pudding mix, not too much liquid, and just a few add-ins like chocolate chips and nuts. Yet the only way to know for sure is to just give the recipe a go. I prefer to line muffin pans with paper liners, but you can spray them with a misting of vegetable oil spray. Fill the cups from two-thirds to three-quarters full, and bake at 350°F. The little baked cakes need to rest in the pan for about 5 minutes before you turn them out onto a rack to cool completely. Then eat for instant pleasure or freeze for future gratification!

So, what makes a muffin a muffin and a cupcake a cupcake? Generally, muffins tend to be less sweet and more dense in texture than cupcakes. Because my editor, Suzanne Rafer, begs for consistency, I decided that muffins would be those unfrosted cakes you eat any time of the day, such as the Chocolate Peanut Butter Muffins with Peanut Butter Drizzle, and the Pumpkin German Chocolate Chip Muffins. Cupcakes, on the other hand, would be frosted and festive, perfect for parties. Some of my favorites are the Chocolate Banana Cupcakes with Pineapple Cream Cheese Frosting, the Red Velvet Cupcakes with White Chocolate Cream Cheese Frosting, and the Little White Chocolate Pound Cakes with Quick Caramel Frosting.

"Chocolate is a permanent thing."
—MILTON S. HERSHEY

Not falling into either category are the other little cakes—the miniature loaves, baby Bundts, and baby angel food cakes. (These baby angels are baked in mini angel or tube pans, but their batter may contain whole eggs. So, they're not actually angel food cakes.) You can buy these pans at houseware and cookware stores, and they are so much fun to use. They make beautiful presentations for special occasions—or just any occasion, such as sharing with a friend on a longer-than-planned train ride.

TRIPLE-CHOCOLATE TO-LIVE-FOR MUFFINS

I have a confession to make here, and I know this will come back to haunt me. . . . In response to a late-night urge, I have been known to traipse out to the chest freezer in the garage in my socks, pluck a frozen muffin out of the plastic bag, and munch on it while I fold laundry. Not glamorous stuff, I'll admit, but mighty satisfying. These are precisely the type of sturdy, chunky chocolate muffins you want to live, not die, for. Bake them for adult birthdays, for traveling, for a handy hostess gift, for the bake sale—and for after-hours emergencies.

MAKES 24 MUFFINS
(2 ½ INCHES EACH)
PREPARATION TIME: 10 MINUTES
BAKING TIME: 23 TO 27 MINUTES

24 paper liners for muffin pans (2½-inch size)
1 package (18.25 ounces) plain devil's food
    cake mix
1 package (3.9 ounces) chocolate instant
    pudding mix
1 cup sour cream
½ cup water
½ cup vegetable oil
4 large eggs
1½ cups semisweet chocolate chips
Confectioners' sugar, for dusting (optional)

R the Cake Mix Doctor says

Vary the type of chocolate chips in this easy muffin recipe. Instead of all semi-sweet chips, use half milk chocolate or half white chocolate. You'll love the color variation, and there will be a surprise in every bite!

Chocolate Substitutions

- When the recipe calls for 1 ounce of semisweet chocolate and you have none, add about ½ ounce unsweetened chocolate plus 2⅓ teaspoons sugar, or add 1 tablespoon plus 2 teaspoons unsweetened cocoa powder, 1 tablespoon plus ½ teaspoon sugar, and 1½ teaspoons butter.

- When the recipe calls for semisweet chips and all you have is semisweet bar chocolate, don't run out to the supermarket! If you have a sharp knife, you can make your own. The chips won't be as heat-tolerant as the commercial ones, but they'll work in a pinch. Chop the chocolate into ¼-inch pieces, either by dicing it as you would a block of cheese or by creating chocolate flakes. To make flakes, starting at one end of the chocolate square or block, cut ⅛-inch-thick shavings, using a rocking motion with your knife. Keep this motion going, firmly pressing the chocolate against the knife, until all the chocolate has been shaved into flakes. Use these flakes or the diced chocolate on top of brownies or pies, in cakes, or in frosting or glaze recipes that call for semisweet chocolate chips.

1. Place a rack in the center of the oven and preheat the oven to 350°F. Line 24 muffin cups with paper liners. Set the pans aside.

2. Place the cake mix, pudding mix, sour cream, water, oil, and eggs in a large mixing bowl. Blend with an electric mixer on low speed for 1 minute. Stop the machine and scrape down the sides of the bowl with a rubber spatula. Increase the mixer speed to medium and beat 2 minutes more, scraping the sides down again if needed. The batter should look thick and well combined. Fold in the chocolate chips, making sure they are well distributed throughout the batter. Spoon the batter into the lined muffin cups, filling each liner three quarters of the way full. Place the pans in the oven.

3. Bake the muffins until they spring back when lightly pressed with your finger and a toothpick inserted in the center comes out clean, 23 to 27 minutes. Remove the pans from the oven and place them on wire racks to cool for 5 minutes.

Run a dinner knife around the edges of the muffin liners, lift the muffins up from the bottom of the pan using the end of the knife, and pick them out of the cups carefully with your fingertips. Place them on a wire rack to cool for 15 minutes before serving. Dust with confectioners' sugar, if desired.

✳ *Store the muffins, wrapped in aluminum foil or plastic wrap, or in a cake saver, at room temperature for up to 1 week. Or freeze them, wrapped in foil, for up to 6 months. Thaw the muffins overnight on the counter before serving.*

PUMPKIN GERMAN CHOCOLATE CHIP MUFFINS

Not too long ago I was shopping for peaches at my favorite produce market here in Nashville, my stomach rumbling from hunger, and at the checkout counter I spotted some huge and tempting pumpkin chocolate chip muffins. Chocolate in the morning? You bet. I'll never forget that first taste experience of pumpkin plus chocolate. Sheer heaven. Pumpkin provides substance and moisture, so you don't need to add oil. Chocolate comes through with flavor. And a smidgen of cinnamon seals the deal.

MAKES 24 MUFFINS
(2½ INCHES EACH)
PREPARATION TIME: 10 MINUTES
BAKING TIME: 20 TO 25 MINUTES

24 paper liners for muffin pans (2½-inch size)
1 package (18.25 ounces) plain German chocolate cake mix
1 can (15 ounces; 1¾ cups) pumpkin
2 large eggs
1 teaspoon pure vanilla extract
1 teaspoon ground cinnamon
1 cup semisweet chocolate chips

1. Place a rack in the center of the oven and preheat the oven to 350°F. Line 24 muffin cups with paper liners. Set the pans aside.

2. Place the cake mix, pumpkin, eggs, vanilla, and cinnamon in a large mixing bowl. Blend with an electric mixer on low speed for 1 minute. Stop the machine and scrape down the sides of the bowl with a rubber spatula. Increase the mixer speed to medium and beat 2 minutes more, scraping the sides down again if needed. The batter should look thick and well combined. Fold in the chocolate chips, making sure they are well distributed

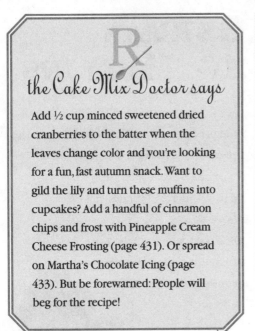

Add ½ cup minced sweetened dried cranberries to the batter when the leaves change color and you're looking for a fun, fast autumn snack. Want to gild the lily and turn these muffins into cupcakes? Add a handful of cinnamon chips and frost with Pineapple Cream Cheese Frosting (page 431). Or spread on Martha's Chocolate Icing (page 433). But be forewarned: People will beg for the recipe!

throughout the batter. Spoon the batter into the lined muffin cups, filling each liner two thirds of the way full. Place the pans in the oven.

3. Bake the muffins until they spring back when lightly pressed with your finger and a toothpick inserted in the center comes out clean, 20 to 25 minutes. Remove the pans from the oven and place them on wire racks to cool for 5 minutes. Run a dinner knife around the edges of the muffin liners, lift the muffins up from the bottom of the pan using the end of the knife, and pick them out of the cups carefully with your fingertips. Place them on a wire rack to cool for 15 minutes before serving.

✳ *Store the muffins, wrapped in aluminum foil or plastic wrap, or in a cake saver, at room temperature for up to 1 week. Or freeze them, wrapped in foil, for up to 6 months. Thaw the muffins overnight on the counter before serving.*

MEXICAN CHOCOLATE CINNAMON MUFFINS

Chocolate and cinnamon have long been paired in Mexican cooking. They are natural companions, as shown in this easy muffin recipe using cinnamon chips and miniature chocolate chips. Not only do they create music for the mouth, but they offer an elaborate symphony for the nose as the chocolate and cinnamon smells waft through your kitchen. Bake these muffins when you want to surprise someone. They're festive, fun, and sure to be gobbled up!

MAKES 24 MUFFINS
(2½ INCHES EACH)

PREPARATION TIME: 10 MINUTES

BAKING TIME: 23 TO 27 MINUTES

24 paper liners for muffin pans
    (2½-inch size)
1 package (18.25 ounces) plain devil's food
    cake mix
1 package (3.9 ounces) chocolate instant
    pudding mix
1 cup sour cream
½ cup water
½ cup vegetable oil
4 large eggs
1 cup miniature semisweet chocolate chips
1 cup cinnamon chips

1. Place a rack in the center of the oven and preheat the oven to 350°F. Line 24 muffin cups with paper liners. Set the pans aside.

R
the Cake Mix Doctor says

For a dressy look, dust these muffins with confectioners' sugar just before serving.

2. Place the cake mix, pudding mix, sour cream, water, oil, and eggs in a large mixing bowl. Blend with an electric mixer on low speed for 1 minute. Stop the machine and scrape down the sides of the bowl with a rubber spatula. Increase the mixer speed to medium and beat 2 minutes more, scraping the sides down again if needed. The batter should look thick and well combined. Fold in the chocolate chips and cinnamon chips, making sure they are well distributed throughout the batter. Spoon the batter into the lined muffin cups, filling each liner three quarters of the way full. Place the pans in the oven.

3. Bake the muffins until they spring back when lightly pressed with your finger and a toothpick inserted in the center comes out clean, 23 to 27 minutes. Remove the pans from the oven and place them on wire racks to cool for 5 minutes. Run a dinner knife around the edges of the muffin liners, lift the muffins up from the bottom of the pan using the end of the knife, and pick them out of the cups carefully with your fingertips. Place them on a wire rack to cool for 15 minutes before serving.

✳ *Store the muffins, wrapped in aluminum foil or plastic wrap, or in a cake saver, at room temperature for up to 1 week. Or freeze them, wrapped in foil, for up to 6 months. Thaw the muffins overnight on the counter before serving.*

CHOCOLATE SURPRISE MUFFINS

My friend Martha Bowden created these fun muffins, modeled after a muffin with a surprise inside that her mother used to bake. I, too, remember making muffins with a filling—for me it was a teaspoon of jam—when I was little. In this version, what hides inside is a creamy, almost cheesecake-like filling studded with chocolate chips. Yum!

....

MAKES 24 MUFFINS
(2½ INCHES EACH)
PREPARATION TIME: 20 MINUTES
BAKING TIME: 23 TO 27 MINUTES

....

R

the Cake Mix Doctor says

These are delicious covered with the Shiny Chocolate Glaze (page 450). You only need half of the glaze recipe.

FILLING:

1 package (8 ounces) cream cheese,
*   at room temperature*
⅓ cup sugar
1 teaspoon pure vanilla extract
1 large egg
1 cup miniature semisweet chocolate chips

CAKE:

24 paper liners for muffin pans
*   (2½-inch size)*
1 package (18.25 ounces) plain devil's food
*   cake mix*
1⅓ cups water
½ cup vegetable oil
3 large eggs

15 Cakes the Kids Will Want to Bake for You

1. Cookies and Cream Cake

2. Incredible Mocha Melted Ice Cream Cake with Chocolate Marshmallow Frosting

3. Easy Hershey Bar Swirl Cake

4. Milky Way Swirl Cake

5. Chocolate Surprise Muffins

6. Chocolate Peanut Butter Muffins with Peanut Butter Drizzle

7. Easy Chocolate Poke Cake

8. Marcia's Easy Chocolate Toffee Crunch Poke Cake

9. Banana Split Fudge Cake

10. Chocolate Strawberry Cheesecake

11. Chocolate Soufflé Pudding Cake

12. Chocolate Love Cake

13. Fudge Snowtops

14. Quick Peanut Butter Kiss Cookies

15. Chocolate Mint Brownies

1. Place the cream cheese and sugar in a large mixing bowl. Beat with an electric mixer on low speed until combined, 30 seconds. Add the vanilla and egg. Beat another 30 seconds on low, or until the egg is incorporated. Stir in the chocolate chips. Set the filling aside.

2. Place a rack in the center of the oven and preheat the oven to 350°F. Line 24 muffin cups with paper liners. Set the pans aside.

3. Place the cake mix, water, oil, and eggs in a large mixing bowl. Blend with an electric mixer on low speed for 1 minute. Stop the machine and scrape down the sides of the bowl with a rubber spatula. Increase the mixer speed to medium and beat 2 minutes more, scraping the sides down again if needed. The batter should look thick and well combined. Spoon the batter into the lined muffin cups, filling each liner two thirds of the way full. Spoon a heaping teaspoon of the filling onto the center of each muffin. The filling will sink into the batter as the muffins bake. Place the pans in the oven.

4. Bake the muffins until they spring back when lightly pressed with your finger, 23 to 27 minutes. Remove the pans from the oven and place them on wire racks to cool for 5 minutes. Run a dinner knife around the edges of the muffin liners, lift the muffins up from the bottom of the pan using the end of the knife, and pick them out of the cups carefully with your fingertips. Place them on a wire rack to cool for 15 minutes before serving.

✳ *Store the muffins, wrapped in aluminum foil or plastic wrap, or in a cake saver, at room temperature for up to 1 week. Or freeze them, wrapped in foil, for up to 6 months. Thaw the muffins overnight in the refrigerator before serving.*

LOADED GERMAN CHOCOLATE CREAM CHEESE MUFFINS

Like the Chocolate Surprise Muffins, these have secret contents of cream cheese and chocolate . . . plus coconut and pecans. And like the Chocolate Surprise Muffins, you spoon the filling onto the batter just before the muffins go in the oven. The filling sinks into these gooey muffins. I made these for my daughter's sixth birthday party in the school cafeteria. I thought the kids might whine because there wasn't any frosting on top. They did whine, but because I brought only one apiece!

MAKES 24 MUFFINS
(2½ INCHES EACH)
PREPARATION TIME: 20 MINUTES
BAKING TIME: 23 TO 27 MINUTES

FILLING:

1 package (8 ounces) cream cheese,
    at room temperature
⅓ cup sugar
1 teaspoon pure vanilla extract
1 large egg
½ cup miniature semisweet chocolate chips
½ cup sweetened flaked coconut
¼ cup finely chopped pecans

CAKE:

24 paper liners for muffin pans
    (2½-inch size)
1 package (18.25 ounces) plain German
    chocolate cake mix
1¼ cups water
⅓ cup vegetable oil
3 large eggs

R

the Cake Mix Doctor says

Some children refuse to eat dark chocolate; they favor the milder flavor and lighter color of the German mix. If nuts are an issue, just omit them. And if the birthday boy or girl insists on frosting, go with Fluffy Chocolate Frosting (page 408), perfect for licking off the top!

1. Place the cream cheese and sugar in a large mixing bowl. Beat with an electric mixer on low speed until combined, 30 seconds. Add the vanilla and egg. Beat another 30 seconds on low, or until the egg is incorporated. Stir in the chocolate chips, coconut, and pecans. Set the filling aside.

2. Place a rack in the center of the oven and preheat the oven to 350°F. Line 24 muffin cups with paper liners. Set the pans aside.

3. Place the cake mix, water, oil, and eggs in a large mixing bowl. Blend with an electric mixer on low speed for 1 minute. Stop the machine and scrape down the sides of the bowl with a rubber spatula. Increase the mixer speed to medium and beat 2 minutes more, scraping the sides down again if needed. The batter should look thick and well combined. Spoon the batter into the lined muffin cups, filling each liner two thirds of the way full. Spoon a tablespoon of filling onto the center of each muffin. Place the pans in the oven.

4. Bake the muffins until they spring back when lightly pressed with your finger, 23 to 27 minutes. Remove the pans from the oven and place them on wire racks to cool for 5 minutes. Run a dinner knife around the edges of the muffin liners, lift the muffins up from the bottom of the pan using the end of the knife, and pick them out of the cups carefully with your fingertips. Place them on a wire rack to cool for 15 minutes before serving.

✳ *Store the muffins, wrapped in aluminum foil or plastic wrap, or in a cake saver, at room temperature for up to 1 week. Or freeze them, wrapped in foil, for up to 6 months. Thaw the muffins overnight in the refrigerator before serving.*

CHOCOLATE PEANUT BUTTER MUFFINS

WITH PEANUT BUTTER DRIZZLE

I thought about naming these "Melt-in-Your-Mouth" peanut butter muffins, but I figured I'd get into all kinds of legal trouble toying with that phrase. So I'll stick to just what they are: chocolate muffins studded with peanut butter and chocolate chips, and drizzled with just a smidgen of melted peanut butter. They're not only my kind of muffin to pack on a long car trip, they're also great for lunch boxes and for shipping off to the college dorm.

MAKES 24 TO 28 MUFFINS
(2½ INCHES EACH)
PREPARATION TIME: 15 MINUTES
BAKING TIME: 22 TO 25 MINUTES
ASSEMBLY TIME: 2 MINUTES

CAKE:

*24 to 28 paper liners for muffin pans
    (2½-inch size)*

*1 package (18.25 ounces) plain devil's food
    cake mix*

*1 package (3.9 ounces) chocolate instant
    pudding mix*

1½ cups buttermilk

½ cup creamy peanut butter

½ cup vegetable oil

4 large eggs

1 cup peanut butter chips

½ cup semisweet chocolate chips

PEANUT BUTTER DRIZZLE:

⅔ cup creamy peanut butter

1 tablespoon confectioners' sugar

One Muffin Recipe, Three Different Pans

Here is how you can begin with one muffin recipe—the Chocolate Peanut Butter Muffins, for example—and bake them in three different size pans:

- **For little Bundt muffins/cupcakes.** About ½ cup of batter goes into each of these little Bundt pans, which measure about 2 inches across. You can make about 36 of these little fluted cupcakes, and they take from 18 to 20 minutes at 350°F.

- **For standard muffins/cupcakes.** These measure from 2½ inches to 3 inches across. You can make 24 to 28 of these muffins, and they take from 22 to 25 minutes at 350°F.

- **Miniature muffins/cupcakes.** These are 2 inches or less in diameter. A muffin recipe will yield from 4 to 5 dozen of these tiny muffins. They need just 12 to 15 minutes at 350°F.

1. Place a rack in the center of the oven and preheat the oven to 350°F. Line 28 muffin cups with paper liners. Set the pans aside.

2. Place the cake mix, pudding mix, buttermilk, peanut butter, oil, and eggs in a large mixing bowl. Blend with an electric mixer on low speed for 1 minute. Stop the machine and scrape down the sides of the bowl with a rubber spatula. Increase the mixer speed to medium and beat 2 minutes more, scraping the sides down again if needed. The batter should look thick and well combined. Fold in the peanut butter chips and chocolate chips, making sure they are well distributed throughout the batter. Spoon the batter into the lined muffin cups, filling each liner three quarters of the way full (you will get between 24 and 28 muffins; remove the empty liners, if any). Place the pans in the oven.

3. Bake the muffins until they spring back when lightly pressed with your finger and a toothpick inserted in the center comes out clean, 22 to 25 minutes. Remove the pans from the oven and place them on wire racks to cool for 5 minutes. Run a dinner knife around the edges of the muffin liners, lift the muffins up from the bottom of the pan using the end of the knife, and pick them out of the cups carefully with your fingertips. Place them on a wire rack to cool for 15 minutes before serving.

4. For the drizzle, place the peanut butter and sugar in a small microwave-safe bowl. Microwave at high power until the peanut butter is just melted, for 30 seconds. Stir to combine well. With a dinner knife, drizzle this glaze over the top of the muffins. Let the muffins rest for 10 minutes before serving.

✳ *Store the muffins, wrapped in aluminum foil or plastic wrap, or in a cake saver, at room temperature for up to 1 week. Or freeze them, wrapped in foil, for up to 6 months. Thaw the muffins overnight on the counter before serving.*

R
the Cake Mix Doctor says

If you love the combination of peanut butter, chocolate, and bananas, add a mashed banana to the batter and reduce the peanut butter to ¼ cup.

CINNAMON-CHOCOLATE ANGEL FOOD MUFFINS

Who says muffins have to be loaded with fat? These trim little gems are based on angel food cake mix, which is free of fat. You just add Dutch-process cocoa, which is deep and dark in color but mellow in flavor, a smidgen of cinnamon, and water to make the mix rise, and *voilà!* Delicious, guilt-free muffins that rise high and crack beautifully on top, perfect for gifts or for serving alongside some sweetened fresh strawberries.

MAKES 28 MUFFINS
(2½ INCHES EACH)

PREPARATION TIME: 10 MINUTES

BAKING TIME: 15 TO 18 MINUTES

*28 paper liners for muffin pans
    (2½-inch size)*

1 package (16 ounces) angel food cake mix

1¼ cups water

*¼ cup Dutch-process unsweetened cocoa
    powder*

½ teaspoon ground cinnamon

1. Place a rack in the center of the oven and preheat the oven to 350°F. Line 28 muffin cups with paper liners. Set the pans aside.

2. Place the cake mix, water, cocoa, and cinnamon in a large mixing bowl. Beat with an electric mixer on low speed for 1 minute. Stop the machine and scrape down the sides of the bowl with a rubber spatula. Increase the mixer speed to medium and beat 1 minute more, scraping the sides down again if needed. The batter should look well combined. Spoon the batter into the lined muffin cups, filling each liner two thirds of the way full. Place the pans in the oven.

3. Bake the muffins until they are firm

on top and spring back when lightly pressed with your finger, 15 to 18 minutes. Remove the pans from the oven and place them on wire racks to cool for 5 minutes. Run a dinner knife around the edges of the muffin liners, lift the muffins up from the bottom of the pan using the end of the knife, and pick them out of the cups carefully with your fingertips. Place them on a wire rack to cool for 15 minutes before serving.

✳ *Store the muffins, wrapped in aluminum foil or plastic wrap, or in a cake saver, at room temperature for up to 1 week. Or freeze them, wrapped in foil, for up to 6 months. Thaw the muffins overnight on the counter before serving.*

R
the Cake Mix Doctor says

If you like, go ahead and frost these muffins. I would choose the Shiny Chocolate Glaze (page 450), Martha's Chocolate Icing (page 433), or for something totally pristine, the Chocolate Ganache (page 441). But you can't go on touting how heart-healthy these muffins are if you frost them!

This recipe shows Dutch-process cocoa at its finest. The dark color deepens the angel food cake batter, and the smooth flavor nicely rounds out what can often be a too-sweet cake.

WHITE CHOCOLATE MUFFINS

WITH CINNAMON STREUSEL

Just right for sharing with friends over a cup of hot tea, the secret ingredient in these rich, buttery little cakes is no secret at all— white chocolate. Some people may say you can't taste white chocolate and therefore they don't care for it, but in baking it can make a real difference. White chocolate adds flavor and a nice, rich crumb to these muffins, making them closely resemble a from-scratch pound cake. And with the cinnamon and pecan streusel sprinkled on top, they bake up fragrant and slightly crunchy.

MAKES 24 MUFFINS
(2½ INCHES EACH)

PREPARATION TIME:
15 MINUTES

BAKING TIME:
20 TO 25 MINUTES

CAKE:

24 paper liners for muffin pans
   (2½-inch size)
6 ounces white chocolate, coarsely chopped
6 tablespoons (¾ stick) butter
1 package (18.25 ounces) plain white
   cake mix
¾ cup milk
3 large eggs
1 teaspoon pure vanilla extract

CINNAMON STREUSEL:

⅓ cup finely chopped pecans
1 tablespoon light brown sugar
½ teaspoon ground cinnamon

1. Place a rack in the center of the oven and preheat the oven to 350°F. Line 24 muffin cups with paper liners. Set the pans aside.

2. Place the white chocolate and the butter in a small saucepan over low heat. Stir constantly until both melt and the mixture is smooth, 3 to 4 minutes. Let cool slightly.

3. Place the cake mix, milk, eggs, vanilla, and white chocolate mixture in a large mixing bowl. Blend with an electric mixer on low speed for 1 minute. Stop the machine and scrape down the sides of the bowl with a rubber spatula. Increase the mixer speed to medium and beat 2 minutes more, scraping the sides down again if needed. The batter should look thick and well combined. Set the batter aside.

4. For the streusel, combine the pecans, brown sugar, and cinnamon in a small bowl. Stir well.

5. Spoon the batter into the lined muffin cups, filling each liner no more than two thirds of the way full. Sprinkle ½ teaspoon of the streusel mixture on top of each muffin. Place the pans in the oven.

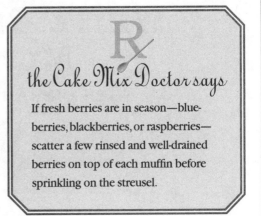

the Cake Mix Doctor says

If fresh berries are in season—blueberries, blackberries, or raspberries—scatter a few rinsed and well-drained berries on top of each muffin before sprinkling on the streusel.

6. Bake the muffins until they spring back when lightly pressed with your finger and a toothpick inserted in the center comes out clean, 20 to 25 minutes. Remove the pans from the oven and place them on wire racks to cool for 5 minutes. Run a dinner knife around the edges of the muffin liners, lift the muffins up from the bottom of the pan using the end of the knife, and pick them out carefully with your fingertips. Place them on a wire rack to cool for 15 minutes before serving.

❋ *Store the muffins, wrapped in aluminum foil or plastic wrap, or in a cake saver, at room temperature for up to 1 week. Or freeze them, wrapped in foil, for up to 6 months. Thaw the muffins overnight on the counter before serving.*

CHOCOLATE CHERRY CHIP CUPCAKES

WITH MARTHA'S CHOCOLATE ICING

The first time I tasted Choco-late-Covered Cherry Cake for *The Cake Mix Doctor,* I remarked that it would make great cupcakes. The cake batter combines cherry pie filling and a little almond flavor with a devil's food mix, and it is one of the moistest chocolate cakes I have ever tasted. Fast forward. . . . I am testing the cupcake and muffin chapter for this book. My sister Susan is visiting from Atlanta, and I bake these fragrant cupcakes and top them with an easy cooked chocolate icing that hardens while the cupcakes cool. Needless to say, after three cupcakes Susan demands the recipe to take home!

MAKES 24 CUPCAKES
(2 1/2 INCHES EACH)
PREPARATION TIME: 10 MINUTES
BAKING TIME: 20 TO 25 MINUTES
ASSEMBLY TIME: 5 MINUTES

24 paper liners for muffin pans
    (2½-inch size)
1 package (18.25 ounces) plain devil's food
    cake mix or devil's food cake mix
    with pudding
1 can (21 ounces) cherry pie filling
2 large eggs
1 teaspoon pure almond extract
1 cup semisweet chocolate chips
Martha's Chocolate Icing (page 433)

1. Place a rack in the center of the oven and preheat the oven to 350°F. Line 24 muffin cups with paper liners. Set the pans aside.

2. Place the cake mix, cherry pie filling, eggs, and almond extract in a large

Filling Cupcake Pans

Cathi Williams, of Powhatan, Virginia, was searching for a gizmo to help her fill muffin cups neatly. Our readers came to the rescue with these great ideas:

• The ice cream scoop with lever: It pushes the cake batter out. You can use a smaller cookie scoop for miniature muffins.

• A 4-cup measuring cup: It has a pour spout for easy filling.

• A ladle.

• Or, don't worry about different-size cupcakes or muffins. Kids don't care!

mixing bowl. Blend with an electric mixer on low speed for 1 minute. Stop the machine and scrape down the sides of the bowl with a rubber spatula. Increase the mixer speed to medium and beat 2 minutes more, scraping the sides down again if needed. The batter should look thick and well combined, with pieces of broken-up cherries throughout. Fold in the chocolate chips, making sure they are well distributed throughout the batter. Spoon the batter into the lined muffin cups, filling each liner three quarters of the way full. Place the pans in the oven.

3. Bake the cupcakes until they spring back when lightly pressed with your finger and a toothpick inserted in the center comes out clean, 20 to 25 minutes. Remove the pans from the oven and place them on wire racks to cool for 5 minutes. Run a

dinner knife around the edges of the cupcake liners, lift the cupcakes up from the bottom of the pan using the end of the

R the Cake Mix Doctor says

If you think kids will be squeamish about these cherries, don't fret. The cherries blend into the batter, making an incredibly moist cake with a faint cherry taste—and one that needs no oil. If you want more cherry taste, fold in ½ cup chopped maraschino or fresh cherries. These cupcakes are elegant enough for dinner parties and are just right for Valentine's Day or Presidents' Day parties at school.

knife, and pick them out of the cups carefully with your fingertips. Place them on a wire rack to cool for 15 minutes before frosting.

4. Meanwhile, prepare Martha's Chocolate Icing.

5. With a long metal spatula, spread a heaping tablespoon of icing onto each cupcake until smooth. Let the cupcakes rest for 10 minutes before serving.

✳ *Store the cupcakes, wrapped in aluminum foil or plastic wrap, or in a cake saver, at room temperature for up to 1 week. Or freeze them, wrapped in foil, for up to 6 months. Thaw the cupcakes overnight on the counter before serving.*

CHOCOLATE SOUR CREAM CUPCAKES

WITH TEN DIFFERENT BUTTERCREAM FROSTINGS

Please don't take the title of this recipe too literally—I don't want you to spread ten different types of frosting onto each cupcake. I just want to show you how versatile the little chocolate cupcake is when spread with your choice of frosting. Think of this as a frosting for every mood, like searching for a radio station as you drive home. Will it be country, classical, or rock? Or just the news? Only you have control of that radio dial, and of the choice of frosting!

....

MAKES 22 TO 24 CUPCAKES
(2½ INCHES EACH)

PREPARATION TIME: 10 MINUTES

BAKING TIME: 20 TO 25 MINUTES

ASSEMBLY TIME: 5 MINUTES

....

22 to 24 paper liners for muffin pans
   (2½-inch size)
1 package (18.25 ounces) devil's food cake
   mix with pudding
¾ cup water
1 cup sour cream
½ cup vegetable oil
3 large eggs
1 teaspoon pure vanilla extract
Your Choice of Ten Frostings
   (see Ten Toppers, facing page)

R
the Cake Mix Doctor says

Cupcakes can be frozen with frosting. But they freeze better if frozen without frosting because the frosting becomes watery as the cupcakes thaw. Besides, frosting is easy enough to assemble once those frozen cupcakes have come to room temperature.

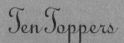

Ten Toppers

1. Orange-Cocoa Cream Cheese Frosting (page 429)

2. Chocolate Sour Cream Frosting (page 410)

3. Vanilla Buttercream Frosting (page 412)

4. Crushed Peppermint Buttercream Frosting (page 414)

5. Lemon Buttercream Frosting, ½ recipe (page 419)

6. Cinnamon-Chocolate Cream Cheese Frosting (page 423)

7. Fluffy Chocolate Frosting (page 408)

8. White Chocolate Cream Cheese Frosting (page 425)

9. Pineapple Cream Cheese Frosting, ½ recipe (page 431)

10. Fresh Peach Buttercream Frosting (page 418)

1. Place a rack in the center of the oven and preheat the oven to 350°F. Line 24 muffin cups with paper liners. Set the pans aside.

2. Place the cake mix, water, sour cream, oil, eggs, and vanilla in a large mixing bowl. Blend with an electric mixer on low speed for 1 minute. Stop the machine and scrape down the sides of the bowl with a rubber spatula. Increase the mixer speed to medium and beat 2 minutes more, scraping down the sides again if needed. The batter should look well combined. Spoon the batter into the lined muffin cups, filling each liner three quarters of the way full. (You will get between 22 and 24 cupcakes; remove the empty liners, if any.) Place the pans in the oven.

3. Bake the cupcakes until they spring back when lightly pressed with your finger and a toothpick inserted in the center comes out clean, 20 to 25 minutes. Remove the pans from the oven and place them on wire racks to cool for 5 minutes. Run a dinner knife around the edges of the cupcake liners, lift the cupcakes up from the bottom of the pan using the end of the knife, and pick them out of the cups carefully with your fingertips. Place them on a wire rack to cool for 15 minutes before frosting.

4. Meanwhile, prepare the frosting of your choice.

5. Spread the tops of the cupcakes with frosting, and serve.

✱ *Store these cupcakes, in a cake saver or under a glass dome, for up to 3 days at room temperature or in the refrigerator for up to 1 week. Or freeze them, in a cake saver, for up to 6 months. Thaw the cupcakes overnight in the refrigerator before serving.*

CHOCOLATE BANANA CUPCAKES

WITH PINEAPPLE CREAM CHEESE FROSTING

When you combine bananas and chocolate, you've got a winner. One of my favorite doctoring tricks is to begin a chocolate cake with mashed banana in the bowl. The banana adds moisture and flavor, and the riper the banana the better. Kids and adults love these cupcakes, and the frosting is so terrific that you can't help licking it off before you take a bite!

....

MAKES 22 TO 24 CUPCAKES
(2½ INCHES EACH)

PREPARATION TIME:
10 MINUTES

BAKING TIME:
20 TO 25 MINUTES

ASSEMBLY TIME:
5 MINUTES

....

*22 to 24 paper liners for muffin pans
(2½-inch size)*

2 ripe bananas, sliced (¾ cup)

*1 package (18.25 ounces) plain devil's food
cake mix*

1 cup buttermilk

½ cup vegetable oil

3 large eggs

1 teaspoon pure vanilla extract

*½ recipe Pineapple Cream Cheese Frosting
(page 431)*

℞

the Cake Mix Doctor says

Since these cupcakes need only half a recipe of the Pineapple Cream Cheese Frosting, you will need to cut the frosting recipe in half.

1. Place a rack in the center of the oven and preheat the oven to 350°F. Line 24 muffin cups with paper liners. Set the pans aside.

2. Place the banana slices in a large mixing bowl. Blend with the electric mixer on low speed for 30 seconds or until they are mashed. Add the cake mix, buttermilk, oil, eggs, and vanilla. Blend with the electric mixer on low speed for 1 minute. Stop the machine and scrape down the sides of the bowl with a rubber spatula. Increase the mixer speed to medium and beat 2 minutes more, scraping the sides down again if needed. The batter should look thick and well combined. Spoon the batter into the lined muffin cups, filling each liner two thirds of the way full. (You will get between 22 and 24 cupcakes; remove the empty liners, if any.) Place the pans in the oven.

3. Bake the cupcakes until they spring back when lightly pressed with your finger and a toothpick inserted in the center comes out clean, 20 to 25 minutes. Remove the pans from the oven and place them on wire racks to cool for 5 minutes. Run a dinner knife around the edges of the cupcake liners, lift the cupcakes up from the bottom of the pan using the end of the knife, and pick them out of the cups carefully with your fingertips. Place them on a wire rack to cool for 15 minutes before frosting.

4. Meanwhile, prepare half a recipe of the Pineapple Cream Cheese Frosting.

5. With a long metal spatula, spread a heaping tablespoon of frosting on each cupcake until smooth. Serve.

✳ *Place these cupcakes, uncovered or in a cake saver, in the refrigerator until the frosting sets, 20 minutes. Then store them, in a cake saver or under a glass dome, at room temperature for up to 3 days or in the refrigerator for up to 1 week. Or freeze them, wrapped in aluminum foil or in a cake saver, for up to 6 months. Thaw the cupcakes overnight in the refrigerator before serving.*

ORANGE SWIRL CHOCOLATE CUPCAKES

WITH ORANGE-COCOA CREAM CHEESE FROSTING

Left alone, marble cake mixes are pretty ho-hum. But here is a way to jazz one up using orange juice and grated orange zest. In fact, this makes one terrific cupcake for Halloween parties because the colors of the finished cupcake are orange and dark brown. If you're feeling festive, decorate the top of each cupcake with a miniature candy pumpkin or a few candy corns.

MAKES 24 CUPCAKES
(2½ INCHES EACH)
PREPARATION TIME: 20 MINUTES
BAKING TIME: 18 TO 22 MINUTES
ASSEMBLY TIME: 5 MINUTES

24 paper liners for muffin pans
  (2½-inch size)
1 package (18.25 ounces) plain fudge marble
  cake mix
1⅓ cups fresh orange juice
⅓ cup vegetable oil
3 large eggs
1 teaspoon grated orange zest
Orange-Cocoa Cream Cheese Frosting
  (page 429)

1. Place a rack in the center of the oven and preheat the oven to 350°F. Line 24 muffin cups with paper liners. Set the pans aside.

2. Place the cake mix, orange juice, oil, and eggs in a large mixing bowl. Blend with the electric mixer on low speed for 1 minute. Stop the machine and scrape down the sides of the bowl with a rubber spatula. Increase the mixer speed to medium and beat 1½ minutes more, scraping the sides down again if needed. The batter should look thick and well combined. Measure out 1 cup of the batter and put it in a small mixing bowl. Add the orange zest to the remaining batter in the large bowl. Mix on low speed for 30 seconds. Add the chocolate package from the cake mix to the smaller amount of batter and mix on low until just combined, 30 seconds.

3. Spoon the plain orange batter into the lined muffin cups, filling each liner two thirds of the way full. Spoon a heaping teaspoon of the chocolate batter on top of each cupcake. With a dinner knife, swirl the chocolate batter into the orange batter, creating a marbled effect. Place the pans in the oven.

4. Bake the cupcakes until they spring back when lightly pressed with your finger, 18 to 22 minutes. Remove the pans from the oven and place them on wire racks to cool for 5 minutes. Run a dinner knife around the edges of the cupcake liners, lift the cupcakes up from the bottom of the pan using the end of the knife, and pick them out of the cups carefully with your fingertips. Place them on a wire rack to cool for 15 minutes before frosting.

5. Meanwhile, prepare the Orange-Cocoa Cream Cheese Frosting.

the Cake Mix Doctor says

You can control the darkness of the frosting by using either regular or Dutch-process cocoa powder. The regular makes a lighter brown frosting, whereas the Dutch-process cocoa creates a darker, more intimidating Halloweeny color.

6. With a long metal spatula, spread a heaping tablespoon of frosting on each cupcake until smooth. Serve.

✳ *Place these cupcakes, uncovered or in a cake saver, in the refrigerator until the frosting sets, 20 minutes. Then store them, in a cake saver or under a glass dome, at room temperature for up to 3 days or in the refrigerator for up to 1 week. Or freeze them, wrapped in aluminum foil or in a cake saver, for up to 6 months. Thaw the cupcakes overnight in the refrigerator before serving.*

RED VELVET CUPCAKES

WITH WHITE CHOCOLATE
CREAM CHEESE FROSTING

There might be only a few staid occasions when these cupcakes wouldn't seem appropriate, mostly because of their vivid fire-engine-red color. But on Valentine's Day, the Fourth of July, Christmas, and especially for birthday parties, these cupcakes are downright fun. And, skeptics, once you taste a bite of their tangy German chocolate flavor and the creamy richness of the white chocolate frosting, you will wonder why you ever disapproved! Red Velvet Cake is a staple in the South and is finding a following in other regions as well.

MAKES 24 CUPCAKES
(2½ INCHES EACH)
PREPARATION TIME: 10 MINUTES
BAKING TIME: 20 TO 25 MINUTES
ASSEMBLY TIME: 5 MINUTES

24 paper liners for muffin pans
    (2½-inch size)
1 package (18.25 ounces) German chocolate
    cake mix with pudding
1 cup sour cream
½ cup water
¼ cup vegetable oil
3 large eggs
1 bottle (1 ounce) red food coloring
1 teaspoon pure vanilla extract
White Chocolate Cream Cheese Frosting
    (page 425)

1. Place a rack in the center of the oven and preheat the oven to 350°F. Line 24 muffin cups with paper liners. Set the pans aside.

2. Place the cake mix, sour cream, water,

oil, eggs, food coloring, and vanilla in a large mixing bowl. Blend with an electric mixer on low speed for 1 minute. Stop the machine and scrape down the sides of the bowl with a rubber spatula. Increase the mixer speed to medium and beat 2 minutes more, scraping the sides down again if needed. The batter should look well combined. Spoon the batter into the lined muffin cups, filling each liner two thirds of the way full. Place the pans in the oven.

3. Bake the cupcakes until they spring back when lightly pressed with your finger, 20 to 25 minutes. Remove the pans from the oven and place them on wire racks to cool for 5 minutes. Run a dinner knife around the edges of the cupcake liners, lift the cupcakes up from the bottom of the pan using the end of the knife, and pick them out of the cups carefully with your fingertips. Place them on a wire rack to cool for 15 minutes before frosting.

4. Meanwhile, prepare the White Chocolate Cream Cheese Frosting.

5. With a long metal spatula, spread a heaping tablespoon of frosting on each cupcake until smooth. Serve.

✱ *Place these cupcakes, uncovered or in a cake saver, in the refrigerator until the frosting sets, 20 minutes. Then store them, in a cake saver or under a glass dome, at room temperature for up to 3 days or in the refrigerator for up to 1 week. Or freeze them, wrapped in aluminum foil or in a cake saver, for up to 6 months. Thaw the cupcakes overnight in the refrigerator before serving.*

the Cake Mix Doctor says

If you want to crank up the red color, add another bottle of food coloring. Be forewarned, however, that using a German chocolate cake mix instead of the traditional white mix means the cupcakes will have much more flavor but will be less brilliant in color. For a stellar look, top the frosted cupcakes with whole fresh raspberries.

RASPBERRY-PEACH WHITE CHOCOLATE CUPCAKES

WITH LEMON BUTTERCREAM FROSTING

Fresh raspberries and peaches are a mighty fine duo, and when they are folded into a rich white chocolate–enhanced cake batter, well, the results are as delicious as you might expect. I made these cupcakes for a neighbor who had just had a new baby, and although I also brought over a pan of meat loaf, some mashed potatoes, and green beans, it was the cupcakes she thanked me for first! You can serve these soft and delicate cupcakes as is or frosted with a light lemon buttercream. For a special occasion, top with candied citrus zest (see page 228).

MAKES 24 CUPCAKES
(2½ INCHES EACH)
PREPARATION TIME: 10 MINUTES
BAKING TIME: 20 TO 25 MINUTES
ASSEMBLY TIME: 5 MINUTES

24 paper liners for muffin pans
(2½-inch size)
6 ounces white chocolate, finely chopped
6 tablespoons (¾ stick) butter, cut into pieces
1 package (18.25 ounces) plain white cake mix
1 cup milk
3 large eggs
1 teaspoon pure vanilla extract
1 cup fresh raspberries
½ cup peeled, chopped fresh peaches, well drained
½ recipe Lemon Buttercream Frosting (page 419)

Fitting Muffin Pans in the Oven

When your oven isn't wide enough to place two muffin pans side by side on one rack, you'll have to stagger them. Place one pan on the right side of the center rack and one pan on the left side of the rack one notch higher. Watch the higher pan, as it will bake and brown more quickly.

1. Place a rack in the center of the oven and preheat the oven to 350°F. Line 24 muffin cups with paper liners. Set the pans aside.

2. Place the white chocolate and the butter in a small saucepan over low heat. Cook, stirring, until both have melted, 3 to 4 minutes. Let cool slightly.

3. Place the cake mix, milk, eggs, vanilla, and white chocolate mixture in a large mixing bowl. Blend with the electric mixer on low speed for 1 minute. Stop the machine and scrape down the sides of the bowl with a rubber spatula. Increase the mixer speed to medium and beat 2 minutes more, scraping the sides down again if needed. The batter should look well combined. Fold in the raspberries and peaches. Spoon the batter into the lined muffin cups, filling each liner two thirds of the way full. Place the pans in the oven.

4. Bake the cupcakes until they spring back when lightly pressed with your finger and a toothpick inserted in the center comes out clean, 20 to 25 minutes. Remove the pans from the oven and place them on wire racks to cool for 5 minutes. Run a dinner knife around the edges of the cupcake liners, lift the cupcakes up from the bottom of the pan using the end of the knife, and pick them out of the cups carefully with your fingertips. Place them on a wire rack to cool for 15 minutes before frosting.

5. Meanwhile, prepare half a recipe of the Lemon Buttercream Frosting.

6. With a long metal spatula, spread a heaping tablespoon of frosting on each cupcake until smooth. Serve.

❋ *Place these cupcakes, uncovered or in a cake saver, in the refrigerator until the frosting sets, 20 minutes. Then store them, in a cake saver or under a glass*

the Cake Mix Doctor says

This is a rich and tender cake batter because of the fat from the butter and white chocolate, and because of the sugar in the white chocolate and the cake mix. Make sure that those peaches aren't watery—drain them well. If the fruit is especially ripe and juicy, cut back on the milk by ¼ cup.

As a time-saver, melt the butter and white chocolate in the microwave oven on high power for about a minute. Stir until all the white chocolate has melted.

Instead of frosting these cupcakes, you can serve them as is or top them with finely chopped pecans just before baking.

dome, at room temperature for up to 3 days or in the refrigerator for up to 1 week. Or freeze them, wrapped in aluminum foil or in a cake saver, for up to 6 months. Thaw the cupcakes overnight in the refrigerator before serving.

LITTLE WHITE CHOCOLATE POUND CAKES

WITH QUICK CARAMEL FROSTING

These are remarkable little cakes, not only because they are rich and sturdy enough to mimic from-scratch pound cake, but also because they don't taste heavy. The extra egg whites not only add volume but also seem to counterbalance the fat in the white chocolate. Baked in muffin pans, these are cupcakes gone uptown! Topped with the warm caramel frosting that sets in a minute, these cupcakes are what you carry over to the new neighbor or prepare for the school bake sale. Everyone will swoon over the frosting, and just wait until they bite into the white chocolate cake . . .

MAKES 20 TO 22 CUPCAKES
(2½ INCHES EACH)
PREPARATION TIME: 10 MINUTES
BAKING TIME: 20 TO 25 MINUTES
ASSEMBLY TIME: 5 MINUTES

20 to 22 paper liners for muffin pans
   (2½-inch size)
6 ounces white chocolate, finely chopped
1 package (18.25 ounces)
   plain yellow
   cake mix
⅔ cup water
⅓ cup vegetable oil
3 large eggs
2 large egg whites
2 teaspoons pure vanilla extract
Quick Caramel Frosting (page 440)

1. Place a rack in the center of the oven and preheat the oven to 350°F. Line 22 muffin cups with paper liners. Set the pans aside.

2. Melt the white chocolate in a small

glass bowl in the microwave oven on high power for 1 minute. Remove the bowl from the oven and stir with a small rubber spatula until it is smooth. (See Melting White Chocolate, page 92.) Let it cool slightly.

3. Place the cake mix, water, oil, whole eggs, egg whites, vanilla, and melted white chocolate in a large mixing bowl. Blend with the electric mixer on low speed for 1 minute. Stop the machine and scrape down the sides of the bowl with a rubber spatula. Increase the mixer speed to medium and beat 2 minutes more, scraping the sides down again if needed. The batter should look well combined.

4. Spoon the batter into the lined muffin cups, filling each liner two thirds of the way full. (You will get between 22 and 24 cupcakes; remove the empty liners, if any.) Place the pans in the oven.

5. Bake the cupcakes until they spring back when lightly pressed with your finger and are golden brown, 20 to 25 minutes. Remove the pans from the oven and place them on wire racks to cool for 5 minutes. Run a dinner knife around the edges of the cupcake liners, lift the cupcakes up from the bottom of the pan using the end of the knife, and pick them out

of the cups carefully with your fingertips. Place them on a wire rack to cool for 15 minutes before frosting.

6. Meanwhile, prepare the Quick Caramel Frosting.

7. Ladle a couple of tablespoons of warm frosting over each cupcake, and with a long metal spatula, spread the frosting until smooth. Let the cupcakes rest for 10 minutes, then serve.

✱ *Place these cupcakes in a cake saver or under a glass dome and store at room temperature for up to 1 week. Or freeze them, wrapped in aluminum foil or in a cake saver, for up to 6 months. Thaw the cupcakes overnight in the refrigerator before serving.*

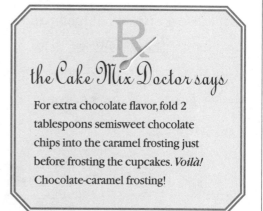

the Cake Mix Doctor says

For extra chocolate flavor, fold 2 tablespoons semisweet chocolate chips into the caramel frosting just before frosting the cupcakes. *Voilà!* Chocolate-caramel frosting!

LITTLE CHOCOLATE ALMOND CREAM CHEESE CAKES

WITH MARTHA'S CHOCOLATE ICING

Based on one of my favorite chocolate pound cake recipes, this simple method for making cupcakes is sure to please. I have made these in the 2-inch cupcake-size Bundt pans (12 cups to the pan) as well as the slightly larger miniature Bundt pans. Whatever the size of the pan, this little cake turns out moist and memorable. These gems are delicious as is, or even better when frosted with a spoonful of shiny chocolate icing.

MAKES 24 BUNDT CUPCAKES
(2 INCHES EACH)
PREPARATION TIME: 8 MINUTES
BAKING TIME: 14 TO 17 MINUTES
ASSEMBLY TIME: 5 MINUTES

Vegetable oil spray for misting the pans
1 package (18.25 ounces) plain butter recipe
 fudge cake mix
1 package (8 ounces) cream cheese, at room
 temperature
½ cup water
½ cup vegetable oil
¼ cup sugar
4 large eggs
1 teaspoon pure almond extract
Martha's Chocolate Icing (page 433)

R

the Cake Mix Doctor says

One trick to this recipe is that the cream cheese needs to be soft, at room temperature, in order for the batter to blend evenly with no lumps. Don't worry if your cream cheese is still in the refrigerator! Just unwrap it and place it on a microwave-safe plate. Microwave at high power for 30 seconds, or until soft.

If you want to bake these cakes in the 4-inch miniature Bundt pans, fill them two thirds full and bake for 18 to 20 minutes. One recipe makes about 12 miniature Bundt cakes.

1. Place a rack in the center of the oven and preheat the oven to 350°F. Lightly mist the Bundt cupcake pans with vegetable oil spray. Set the pans aside.

2. Place the cake mix, cream cheese, water, oil, sugar, eggs, and almond extract in a large mixing bowl. Blend with an electric mixer on low speed for 1 minute. Stop the machine and scrape down the sides of the bowl with a rubber spatula. Increase the mixer speed to medium and beat 2 minutes more, scraping the sides down

again if needed. The batter should look well combined. Spoon the batter into the prepared pans, filling each cup two thirds of the way full. Place the pans in the oven.

3. Bake the cupcakes until they spring back when lightly pressed with your finger, 14 to 17 minutes. Remove the pans from the oven and place them on a wire rack to cool for 10 minutes. Then run a sharp knife around the edge of each cupcake and invert them onto a rack to cool for 20 minutes more.

4. Meanwhile, prepare Martha's Chocolate Icing.

5. Spoon warm icing over each cupcake, and use a long metal spatula to smooth the icing. Let the cupcakes rest for 20 minutes, then serve.

✳ *Store these cupcakes, wrapped in aluminum foil or plastic wrap, or in a cake saver, at room temperature for up to 1 week. Or freeze them, wrapped in foil, for up to 6 months. Thaw the cupcakes overnight in the refrigerator before serving.*

LITTLE WHITE CHOCOLATE LEMON DRIZZLE CAKES

When this book was in the testing phase, these cakes appeared in a beautiful color photograph in the *Washington Post.* A photographer had come to the house to take a photo of me, and he couldn't help but notice these little lemon cakes cooling on the kitchen counter. It didn't seem to matter that this recipe didn't appear in *The Cake Mix Doctor.* Garnished with sprigs of mint and fresh berries, they certainly were stunning on that silver platter! I am just glad that no one requested a recipe I wasn't able to share. Until now! The miniature angel cakes are baked 6 to a pan. But as angelic as they are, they are not angel food—this batter contains egg yolks.

MAKES 12 MINIATURE ANGEL CAKES
(4 INCHES EACH)
PREPARATION TIME:
10 MINUTES
BAKING TIME:
20 TO 25 MINUTES
ASSEMBLY TIME:
2 MINUTES

CAKES:

Vegetable oil spray for misting the pans
Flour for dusting the pans
6 ounces white chocolate, finely chopped
1 package (18.25 ounces) plain yellow
*   cake mix*
½ cup fresh lemon juice, from 4 large lemons
½ cup vegetable oil
⅓ cup water
4 large eggs
2 teaspoons grated lemon zest

Little Pans: How Much Batter Should You Use?

- For the Nordic Ware Bundtlette (1-cup capacity), use ¾ cup batter (makes 12).

- For the Nordic Ware Bundt cupcake (½-cup capacity), use ¼ cup batter (makes 24).

- And for the Nordic Ware Angelette (1-cup capacity), use ¾ cup batter (makes 12).

- One recipe of cake mix batter will fill about 6 miniature (6-inch) loaf pans.

LEMON DRIZZLE:

1 cup confectioners' sugar, sifted

2 tablespoons fresh lemon juice

1 teaspoon grated lemon zest

1. Place a rack in the center of the oven and preheat the oven to 350°F. Lightly mist 12 miniature (4-inch) angel pans with vegetable oil spray, then dust with flour. Shake out the excess flour. Set the pans aside.

2. Melt the white chocolate in a small glass bowl in the microwave oven on high power for 1 minute. Remove the bowl from the oven and stir with a small rubber spatula until it is smooth. (See Melting White Chocolate, page 92.) Let it cool slightly.

3. Place the cake mix, lemon juice, oil, water, eggs, lemon zest, and melted white chocolate in a large mixing bowl. Blend with an electric mixer on low speed for 1 minute. Stop the machine and scrape down the sides of the bowl with a rubber spatula. Increase the mixer speed to medium and beat 2 minutes more, scraping the sides down again if needed. The batter should look well combined. Spoon the batter into the prepared pans, filling each pan two thirds of the way full. Place the pans in the oven.

4. Bake the cakes until they spring back when lightly pressed with your finger, 20 to 25 minutes. Remove the pans from the oven and place them on a wire rack to cool for 10 minutes. Run a sharp knife around the edge of each cake, and invert them onto a rack. Invert again and allow to cool completely, 20 minutes.

5. Meanwhile, prepare the Lemon Drizzle: Place the confectioners' sugar in a small mixing bowl and whisk in enough of the

R

the Cake Mix Doctor says

Vary the batter in this recipe by using a
white cake mix instead of yellow. And
vary it once again by using fresh lime
juice and zest in the cake and the drizzle.
This recipe is amazingly adaptable!

lemon juice to make the glaze smooth and
easy to spoon. Fold in the zest.

6. Spoon the drizzle over each cake,
allowing it to run down the middle and
sides. Let the cakes rest for 20 minutes
before serving.

✳ *Store these little cakes, wrapped in aluminum foil or plastic wrap, or in a cake
saver, at room temperature for up to 1 week.
Or freeze them, wrapped in foil, for up to
6 months. Thaw the cakes overnight in the
refrigerator before serving.*

BABY CHOCOLATE PISTACHIO CAKES

A classic recipe in *The Cake Mix Doctor* is the chocolate and pistachio Bundt cake. That recipe also works well as little cakes, such as these miniature Bundts. It's a little fussy layering the chocolate chips and pecans in the bottom of the pans, then the two batters, but the consolation is that this recipe makes 12 cakes! You don't need to serve them at one time—they freeze for up to 6 months. For a fancier presentation with not a lot of work, spoon a little vanilla ice cream on each cake and drizzle chocolate syrup over the top.

MAKES 12 MINIATURE BUNDT CAKES
(4 INCHES EACH)
PREPARATION TIME: 25 MINUTES
BAKING TIME: 20 TO 25 MINUTES
ASSEMBLY TIME: 5 MINUTES

Vegetable oil spray for misting the
    pans
Flour for dusting the pans
½ cup chopped pecans or pistachios
½ cup semisweet chocolate chips
1 package (18.25 ounces) plain white
    cake mix
1 package (3.4 ounces) pistachio
    instant pudding mix
⅓ cup sugar
1 cup water
½ cup vegetable oil
4 large eggs
½ cup chocolate syrup

1. Place a rack in the center of the oven and preheat the oven to 350°F. Lightly mist 12 miniature (4-inch) Bundt pans with vegetable oil spray, then dust with flour. Shake out the excess flour. Sprinkle

Ode to Chocolate Chips

They were first sold in grocery stores in 1939, six years after Massachusetts innkeeper Ruth Wakefield baked the first chocolate chip cookie by accident. She didn't want to wait for the chunk of semisweet chocolate to melt, so she figured she'd just chop it up and fold it into her cookie dough. And the rest is history. Chocolate chips are old enough to be senior citizens. And I cannot imagine baking, or even life, without them. Why do I love chocolate chips the way I do?

- Because they're easy. Stick your hand in the bag for a midafternoon snack, or pour them on top of a last-minute batch of brownies.

- Because they're bold. Heat doesn't scare these tough chips. They don't melt away in a hot oven. No, they soften and leave little pools of chocolate, should you be so lucky as to bite into them while they are warm, and then they firm up into solid chunks when they're left to cool.

- Because they're everywhere. Chocolate chips are sold in every supermarket in every state in the nation. They are as accessible as the apple. While no doubt not as good for our teeth, they have made brownies and chocolate chip cookies more American than apple pie.

- Because they're not perfect. They're temperamental at times, sinking to the bottom of the cake if the batter is too thin, or seizing up if some liquid creeps into the pot when you're trying to melt them. And yet they fold into sensuous mousses, frostings, and glazes. A chocolate ganache made with semisweet chocolate chips not only pulls together like a dream, it also isn't bitter, as ganache can be with a darker chocolate.

I love chocolate chips because they are like confetti at the dawn of a New Year, like popcorn at the movies, like rice at a wedding. They are a constellation of earnest chocolate flavor to savor every day.

the pecans and chocolate chips evenly in the bottom of the pans. Set the pans aside. **2.** Place the cake mix, pudding mix, sugar, water, oil, and eggs in a large mixing bowl. Blend with an electric mixer on low speed for 1 minute. Stop the machine and scrape down the sides of the bowl with a rubber spatula. Increase the mixer speed to medium and beat 2 minutes more. The batter should look thick and well combined. Transfer 1 cup of the batter to a small bowl, add the chocolate syrup, and stir until the mixture is well combined. Set the small bowl aside.

3. Pour the remaining batter into the prepared pans. Pour the chocolate batter over the top to form a second layer. Place the pans in the oven.

4. Bake the cakes until they spring back when lightly pressed with your finger, 20 to 25 minutes. Remove the pans from the oven and place them on wire racks to cool for 15 minutes. Run a sharp knife around the edges of the cakes, and invert them onto a rack to cool completely, 15 minutes more.

5. To serve, slide the cakes onto a serving platter.

R the Cake Mix Doctor says

You can make these little cakes smaller, as 2½-inch cupcakes; the baking time will be slightly shorter. Frost them with a spoonful of Martha's Chocolate Icing (page 433). You can also use a yellow cake mix. And to turn this into a spectacular dessert, spoon Hot Fudge Sauce (page 456) over the cakes just before serving.

✳ *Store these cakes, wrapped in aluminum foil or plastic wrap, or in a cake saver, at room temperature for up to 1 week. Or freeze them, wrapped in foil, for up to 6 months. Thaw the cakes overnight in the refrigerator before serving.*

STACY'S MINI CHOCOLATE CHIP LOAVES

I am frequently asked how to turn a pound cake recipe into miniature loaves. The recipes that do this best are sturdy cakes such as this one—cakes with 4 eggs and often a package of instant pudding. One recipe will yield about 6 miniature loaves. Stacy Ross, of Nashville, Tennessee, was the originator of this family-favorite recipe. I told Stacy that I have reduced the amount of vegetable oil in her recipe, but I don't think she likes me messing with a good thing! And she's probably right, so for both the purists out there and those looking for a way to cut the fat, I've given a range for the vegetable oil and you can decide. Cutting back on the oil doesn't change the flavor, but it does make the loaves less tender.

MAKES 6 MINI LOAVES
(6 INCHES EACH)
PREPARATION TIME: 15 MINUTES
BAKING TIME: 35 TO 40 MINUTES

Vegetable oil spray for misting the
*   pans*
Flour for dusting the pans
1 bar (4 ounces) German chocolate
1 package (18.25 ounces) plain yellow
*   cake mix*
1 package (3.4 ounces) vanilla instant
*   pudding mix*
1 cup whole milk
¾ to 1 cup vegetable oil (see headnote)
4 large eggs
1 cup semisweet chocolate chips

1. Place a rack in the center of the oven and preheat the oven to 350°F. Lightly mist six 6-inch loaf pans with vegetable oil spray, then dust with flour. Shake out the excess flour. Set the pans aside.

2. Grate the chocolate using a food processor or hand grater until it is finely grated. Set the grated chocolate aside.

3. Place the cake mix, pudding mix, milk, oil, and eggs in a large mixing bowl. Blend with an electric mixer on low speed for 1 minute. Stop the machine, fold in the grated chocolate, and scrape down the sides of the bowl with a rubber spatula. Increase the mixer speed to medium and beat 2 minutes more, scraping the sides down again if needed. Fold in the chocolate chips. The batter should look well combined, and the chocolate chips should be evenly distributed. Pour the batter into the prepared pans, dividing it equally. Place the pans in the oven.

4. Bake the loaves until they spring back when lightly pressed with your finger, 35 to 40 minutes. Remove the pans from the oven and place them on wire racks to cool for 10 minutes. Run a long, sharp knife around the edges of each loaf, invert them onto your hand, then invert again onto the rack so that they are right side up. Allow the loaves to cool completely, 20 minutes. Then serve.

✳ *Store these miniature loaves, wrapped in aluminum foil or plastic wrap, or in a cake saver, at room temperature for up to 1 week. Or freeze them, wrapped in foil, for up to 6 months. Thaw the loaves overnight in the refrigerator before serving.*

R
the Cake Mix Doctor says

Try this recipe with a German chocolate cake mix and use miniature chocolate chips. This is a glorious, adaptable recipe, but one that is very rich. Because it is so rich, it keeps well and freezes well, making it perfect for gift giving.

MINI GERMAN CHOCOLATE BANANA LOAVES

My children love miniature anything—toys, cookies—and these loaves are just their size. The German chocolate has a softer flavor than devil's food, making it perfect for many children who don't like the taste of dark chocolate. (They don't live in our house!) Plus, kids love cinnamon, and these loaves contain cinnamon chips, an easy add-in at the end of the recipe. And to please the parents, I've squeezed some healthy bananas into the batter, which makes the loaves not only better for you, but fragrant and moist.

MAKES 6 MINI LOAVES
(6 INCHES EACH)
PREPARATION TIME: 10 MINUTES
BAKING TIME: 30 TO 35 MINUTES

Vegetable oil spray for misting
the pans
Flour for dusting the pans
2 ripe bananas, sliced (¾ cup)
1 package (18.25 ounces) plain German
chocolate cake mix
1 cup buttermilk
½ cup vegetable oil
3 large eggs
1 teaspoon pure vanilla extract
1 cup cinnamon chips

1. Place a rack in the center of the oven and preheat the oven to 350°F. Lightly mist six 6-inch loaf pans with vegetable oil spray, then dust with flour. Shake out the excess flour. Set the pans aside.

2. Place the banana slices in a large mixing bowl. Blend with an electric mixer on low speed for 30 seconds or until they are mashed. Add the cake mix, buttermilk, oil, eggs, and vanilla. Blend with the electric mixer on low speed for 1 minute. Stop the machine and scrape down the sides of the bowl with a rubber spatula. Increase the mixer speed to medium and beat

2 minutes more, scraping the sides down again if needed. Fold in the cinnamon chips. The batter should look well combined, and the cinnamon chips should be evenly distributed. Pour the batter into the prepared pans, dividing it equally. Place the pans in the oven.

3. Bake the loaves until they spring back when lightly pressed with your finger, 30 to 35 minutes. Remove the pans from the oven and place them on wire racks to cool for 10 minutes. Run a long, sharp knife around the edges of each loaf, invert them onto your hand, then invert again onto a rack so that they are right side up. Allow the loaves to cool completely, 20 minutes. Then serve.

✻ *Store these miniature loaves, wrapped in aluminum foil or plastic wrap, or in a cake saver, at room temperature for up to 1 week. Or freeze them, wrapped in foil, for up to 6 months. Thaw the loaves overnight in the refrigerator before serving.*

the Cake Mix Doctor says

To dress up these simple loaves, drizzle them with the Cinnamon Chip Glaze (page 454). The recipe is also delicious when made with a really dark chocolate cake mix, such as the chocolate fudge cake mix.

Cookies, Bars, and Brownies

• • •

Don't think this chapter is low priority just because it is positioned at the back of the book. In fact, you could say I've saved the best for last because making a bar or cookie or brownie is so simple and fast. You can squeeze it in between other tasks, like roasting a chicken or sorting laundry or finishing up the chapter on layer cakes!

Of all the cookies in my first book, it was the chocolate cookies that I found myself making time and time again. So, I wasn't surprised to find myself looking forward to creating the recipes for this chapter. Like, for example, the Chocolate Chunk Walnut Chewies and the Chocolate Cinnamon Chip Chewies, which have become favorites in our house. They can be made in bulk, baked, and stashed in the freezer for later parties, bake sales, and lunch boxes. Other new favorites this go-around include the Fudge Snowtop and its cousin the Almond Chocolate Chip Fudge Snowtop. These most excellent cookies contain, of all ingredients, a container of thawed whipped topping. My children love to watch them puff up like snowy hilltops as they bake. They, too, freeze well.

The bars, as well, are both comforting and decadent to eat. We are partial to the Peanut Butter Chocolate Bars in the first book, so I had to include them this time—in a variation using chunky peanut butter. They are so deliciously rich! My new favorites include the Chocolate Hello Dollies, a takeoff on a

1960s favorite down South; Joy of Almond Bars, so named because they resemble a famous candy bar; and Sarah's Chocolate Peppermint Sticks, a delightfully thin bar made by a Texas cake decorator named Sarah Goodenough (yes, that is her real name!).

....

"What use are cartridges in battle? I always carry chocolate instead."

—George Bernard Shaw

....

People are amazed that something as sophisticated as biscotti can be started with cake mix. You bet! Stir in dried cherries, chopped almonds, chocolate flakes, and hazelnuts and you have biscotti perfect for dunking into hot coffee in your own kitchen or wrapping as gifts for your friends.

And then there are the brownies. Now, I have a slight confession to make. Up until this book, I never bought a package of brownie mix because scratch brownies are so simple to prepare. Yet I wanted to explore the mixes to find out if they really made simple even simpler and whether you could doctor them up into fabulous brownies that tasted as if they were made from scratch. The answers are yes and yes. My delicious results lie in this chapter, and I think differently about brownie mixes now. Just try the Pecan Chip Buttermilk Brownies, the Marbled Cream Cheese and Kahlúa Brownies, the Chocolate Mint Brownies, the Banana Black Walnut Brownies. . . . Heck, all the brownies are yummy. I would not have included them if they weren't!

FUDGE SNOWTOPS

Cleveland, Ohio, writer Phillip Iannarelli first wrote asking me for a certain cookie recipe he was trying to remember from his past, and then as we began exchanging e-mails, Phillip recalled that the recipe given to him many years ago con-

tained a cake mix, 2 eggs, and 4 ounces of Cool Whip. I took it from there, and here are the results: cookies that puff up and then crack like white tundra. They taste like chewy brownies, so Phillip and I settled on the name Fudge Snowtops.

....
MAKES: 5 DOZEN 2-INCH COOKIES
PREPARATION TIME: 5 MINUTES
BAKING TIME: 10 TO 12 MINUTES
....

1 package (18.25 ounces) plain devil's food
    cake mix
2 large eggs
1¾ cups thawed frozen whipped topping
½ cup confectioners' sugar, sifted

1. Place the cake mix, eggs, and whipped topping in a large mixing bowl. Blend with an electric mixer on low speed for 30 seconds. Stop the machine and scrape down the sides of the bowl with a rubber spatula. Increase the mixer speed to medium and beat 1 to 2 minutes more, or until the dough is smooth and thick. Cover the bowl with plastic wrap and place it in the refrigerator to chill for 30 minutes.

the Cake Mix Doctor says

If you want to offer the Snowtops in a non-fudge variation as well, make a batch with yellow or white cake mix. If your kitchen is warm, keep the extra dough—whether fudge, yellow, or white—in the refrigerator between batches.

2. Place a rack in the center of the oven and preheat the oven to 350°F. Set aside two ungreased cookie sheets.

3. Spoon the confectioners' sugar into a shallow dish. Remove the dough from the refrigerator. Spoon out teaspoonfuls of the batter and gently roll them into balls between your palms. Place these balls in the dish of confectioners' sugar and roll them around with your fingertips until they are coated with sugar. Coat only as many cookies as you'll bake at one time. Place the balls about 2 inches apart on the ungreased cookie sheets. Place the sheets in the oven. (If your oven cannot accommodate both cookie sheets on the center rack, place one on the top rack and one on the center rack and rotate them halfway through the baking time.)

4. Bake the cookies until they puff up and are firm around the edges but still soft in the middle, 10 to 12 minutes. Remove the sheets from the oven. Let the cookies rest on the cookie sheets for 2 minutes. Then use a metal spatula to transfer them to wire racks and allow them to cool completely, 15 minutes.

5. Repeat the process with the remaining cookie dough.

✳ *Store the cookies in an airtight container at room temperature for up to 1 week. Or freeze them, wrapped in foil and placed in a plastic freezer bag, for up to 3 months. Thaw the cookies overnight on the counter before serving.*

ALMOND CHOCOLATE CHIP FUDGE SNOWTOPS

When I tasted the Fudge Snowtops (page 352), I immediately blurted out, "These are incredible," then wondered how they would taste with lots of almond flavor. So it goes with recipe testing—you're constantly on the lookout for another successful variation. The addition of almond extract, finely chopped almonds, and miniature chocolate chips turns the plain Snowtop into a party atop a Snowtop!

MAKES: 5 DOZEN 2-INCH COOKIES
PREPARATION TIME: 5 MINUTES
BAKING TIME: 10 TO 12 MINUTES

1 package (18.25 ounces) plain devil's food
    cake mix
2 large eggs
1¾ cups thawed frozen whipped topping
½ teaspoon pure almond extract
¼ cup miniature chocolate chips
¼ cup finely chopped almonds
½ cup confectioners' sugar, sifted

1. Place the cake mix, eggs, whipped topping, and almond extract in a large mixing bowl. Blend with an electric mixer on low speed for 30 seconds. Stop the machine and scrape down the sides of the bowl with a rubber spatula. Increase the mixer speed to medium and beat 1 to 2 minutes more, or until the dough is smooth and thick. Fold in the chocolate chips and chopped almonds until well incorporated. Cover the bowl with plastic wrap and place it in the refrigerator to chill for 30 minutes.

2. Place a rack in the center of the oven and preheat the oven to 350°F. Set aside two ungreased cookie sheets.

3. Spoon the confectioners' sugar into a

shallow dish. Remove the dough from the refrigerator. Spoon out teaspoonfuls of the batter and gently roll them into balls between your palms. Place these balls in the dish of confectioners' sugar and roll them around with your fingertips until they are coated with sugar. Coat only as many cookies as you'll bake at one time. Place the balls about 2 inches apart on the ungreased cookie sheets. Place the sheets in the oven. (If your oven cannot accommodate both cookie sheets on the center rack, place one on the top rack and one on the center rack and rotate them halfway through the baking time.)

4. Bake the cookies until they puff up and are firm around the edges but still soft in the middle, 10 to 12 minutes. Remove the sheets from the oven. Let the cookies rest on the cookie sheets for 2 minutes. Then use a metal spatula to transfer them to wire racks and allow them to cool completely, 15 minutes.

5. Repeat the process with the remaining cookie dough.

R

the Cake Mix Doctor says

These cookies are easy enough to remove from the cookie sheet, but if you want to make cookie removal truly a breeze, invest in a nonstick Silpat mat. This is a flexible baking mat made of glass fibers coated with silicone. It fits right on your cookie sheet, and the cookies do not stick to the pan. The Silpat is found at Williams-Sonoma stores, among others.

✳ *Store the cookies in an airtight container at room temperature for up to 1 week. Or freeze them, wrapped in foil and placed in a plastic freezer bag, for up to 3 months. Thaw the cookies overnight on the counter before serving.*

Some Cookie Baking Tips
(or, what your mother never told you and you had to learn on your own . . .)

- Cookie dough needs to just pull together. Unlike cake batters, it doesn't need beating.

- Cookie dough can be made, covered with plastic wrap, and chilled for up to 1 day in advance of baking.

- Cookie dough can be frozen in a sturdy plastic container for up to 2 months. Let it thaw in the refrigerator, then bring it to room temperature.

- Line cookie sheets with parchment paper or special baking liners, such as the Silpat liner, for easy removal and cleanup.

- Drop cookie dough onto cold baking sheets using a soupspoon or, for larger cookies, using a small ice cream scoop.

- If the cookie sheets are warm, let them cool on the counter or under cold running water before dropping dough onto them.

- Rolled cookies should be placed on cold baking sheets and then, ideally, placed in the refrigerator for 5 minutes so the cookie shapes can set. This is especially important when baking in a hot kitchen.

- Shiny aluminum pans will trigger browning and crispness on the bottom of a cookie. And this adds to a cookie's flavor. Insulated pans, on the other hand, prevent browning.

- Don't let cookies rest on the sheet for more than 1 minute after they have been pulled from the oven. They will continue to cook on the hot surface, and the longer they remain, the more difficult they are to remove.

- Use a metal spatula to transfer cookies to a wire rack to cool.

- Store cooled cookies in airtight metal tins if you want them to stay crisp, or in plastic containers if you want them to stay soft and chewy.

- Cooled baked cookies may also be frozen in zipper-lock bags for up to 6 months.

CHOCOLATE CHUNK WALNUT CHEWIES

This is a great chocolate cookie recipe not only because it is a cinch to throw together but also because these cookies bake up chewy and moist, just like a brownie. Instead of the usual chocolate chips, I fold in larger chunks of semisweet chocolate. And what better accompaniment to those chunks than chopped walnuts? Unless, that is, you hail from Georgia or Texas, then by all means use pecans!

MAKES: 4 DOZEN 2-INCH COOKIES
PREPARATION TIME: 10 MINUTES
BAKING TIME: 10 TO 12 MINUTES

*1 package (18.25 ounces) plain
 devil's food cake mix*
8 tablespoons (1 stick) butter, melted
¼ cup (packed) light brown sugar
2 large eggs
2 teaspoons pure vanilla extract
*1 cup coarsely chopped semisweet
 chocolate*
¾ cup finely chopped walnuts

1. Place a rack in the center of the oven and preheat the oven to 350°F. Set aside two ungreased cookie sheets.

2. Place the cake mix, melted butter, brown sugar, eggs, and vanilla in a large mixing bowl. Blend with an electric mixer on low speed for 1 minute. The dough will be smooth and thick. Fold in the chocolate until well distributed.

3. Drop heaping teaspoons of the dough 2 inches apart on the ungreased cookie sheets. Sprinkle a little of the walnuts on top of each cookie. Place the sheets in the oven. (If your oven cannot accommodate both cookie sheets on the center rack, place one on the top rack and one on the center

R/

the Cake Mix Doctor says

You can buy chocolate chunks in the bag at the grocery store, or if you want to use the semisweet chocolate on your pantry shelf, just get out a sharp knife and a cutting board. Chop the chocolate into ½-inch pieces, scraping all the shavings into the mixing bowl as well. In a hurry? Fold the walnuts into the dough instead of sprinkling them on top.

I love to sprinkle nuts right on top of cookies and brownies before they go into the oven. Not only does this save time, but it allows the nuts to toast, which deepens the flavor of the cookie.

rack and rotate them halfway through the baking time.)

4. Bake the cookies until they have set but are still a little soft in the center and the walnuts have toasted, 10 to 12 minutes. Remove the sheets from the oven. Let the cookies rest on the cookie sheets for 2 minutes. Then use a metal spatula to transfer them to wire racks and allow them to cool completely, 20 minutes.

5. Repeat the process with the remaining cookie dough.

❋ *Store the cookies, wrapped in aluminum foil or in an airtight container, at room temperature for up to 1 week. Or freeze them, wrapped in foil and placed in a plastic freezer bag, for up to 3 months. Thaw the cookies overnight on the counter before serving.*

CHOCOLATE CINNAMON CHIP CHEWIES

The test kitchen at Hershey's concocted this recipe using the chocolate cookie I created with their new cinnamon chips mixed in. It's a winner. Cinnamon goes so well with chocolate, and these special cookies make a nice gift around the holidays. For an added touch, drizzle them with Cinnamon Chip Glaze.

MAKES: 4 DOZEN 2-INCH COOKIES
PREPARATION TIME: 10 MINUTES
BAKING TIME: 8 TO 10 MINUTES
ASSEMBLY TIME: 2 MINUTES

Vegetable oil spray for misting the pans
1 package (18.25 ounces) plain devil's food
    cake mix
⅓ cup water

4 tablespoons (½ stick) butter, melted
1 large egg
1 cup cinnamon chips
½ cup chopped pecans
Cinnamon Chip Glaze (page 454)

1. Place a rack in the center of the oven and preheat the oven to 350°F. Lightly mist two cookie sheets with vegetable oil spray. Set the pans aside.

2. Place the cake mix, water, melted butter, and egg in a large mixing bowl. Blend with an electric mixer on low speed for

℞

the Cake Mix Doctor says

Hershey's cinnamon chips should be in supermarkets nationwide by now. They come in a 10-ounce bag that yields 1⅔ cups. Use 1 cup in the cookie dough, then use the remaining ⅔ cup to make the glaze.

1 minute. Stop the machine and scrape down the sides of the bowl with a rubber spatula. Increase the speed to medium and beat for 1 minute more. The dough will be smooth and thick. Fold in the cinnamon chips and the pecans until well distributed.

3. Drop heaping teaspoons of the dough 2 inches apart on the prepared cookie sheets. Place the sheets in the oven. (If your oven cannot accommodate both cookie sheets on the center rack, place one on the top rack and one on the center rack and rotate them halfway through the baking time.)

4. Bake the cookies until they have set but are still a little soft in the center, 8 to 10 minutes. Remove the sheets from the oven. Let the cookies rest on the cookie sheets for 2 minutes. Then use a metal spatula to transfer them to wire racks and allow them to cool completely, 20 minutes.

5. Repeat the process with the remaining cookie dough.

6. Meanwhile, prepare the Cinnamon Chip Glaze. Drizzle over the cooled cookies.

✳ *Store the cookies, wrapped in aluminum foil or in an airtight container, at room temperature for up to 1 week. Or freeze them, wrapped in foil and placed in a plastic freezer bag, for up to 3 months. Thaw the cookies overnight on the counter before serving.*

QUICK PEANUT BUTTER KISS COOKIES

This cookie recipe has been around for a long time in a from-scratch version; here is how to make the cookie quickly using a cake mix. It's perfect for bake sales and gift giving, when you need a big bunch of cookies all at once. P.S.: Children can help in the production—unwrapping the candy, pressing the Kiss into place, and of course eating them! One 13-ounce bag will give you enough Kisses.

MAKES:
6 DOZEN 1-INCH COOKIES

PREPARATION TIME:
20 MINUTES

BAKING TIME:
8 TO 10 MINUTES

1 package (18.25 ounces) plain butter recipe golden cake mix
1 can (14 ounces) sweetened condensed milk
1 cup creamy peanut butter
1 large egg
1 teaspoon pure vanilla extract
72 Hershey's Kisses, unwrapped

1. Place a rack in the center of the oven and preheat the oven to 350°F. Set aside two ungreased cookie sheets.

2. Place the cake mix, sweetened condensed milk, peanut butter, egg, and vanilla in a large mixing bowl. Blend with an electric mixer on low speed for 1 to 1½ minutes. The dough will be thick and will come together in a ball.

3. Pinch off pieces of the dough and roll them into 1-inch balls. Place them 1 inch apart on the ungreased cookie sheets. Place the sheets in the oven. (If your oven cannot accommodate both cookie sheets on the center rack, place one on the top rack and one on the cen-

the Cake Mix Doctor says

For a crunchy texture, use chunky
peanut butter instead of smooth.

ter rack and rotate them halfway
through the baking time.)

4. Bake the cookies until they puff up
and lightly brown, 8 to 10 minutes. The
cookies will still be soft, and you don't
want to overbake them. Remove the pans
from the oven, and immediately place a
chocolate Kiss in the center of each cookie
and press it down lightly. Let the cookies
rest on the sheet for 1 minute. Then use a
metal spatula to transfer them to wire
racks and allow them to cool completely,
15 minutes.

5. Repeat the process with the remaining
cookie dough.

✳ *Store these cookies, in a cake saver or
in a plastic container, at room temperature
for up to 1 week. Or freeze them, wrapped
in foil, for up to 6 months. Thaw the cookies
overnight on the counter before serving.*

DEVIL'S FOOD HEARTS

Seems like a dangerous thought—that the devil might have something to do with your heart. But rest assured, the only danger with this cookie is that you might want to eat too many! Use a plain devil's food cake mix, one without pudding inside. Add only butter, an egg, and a little vanilla and you have a wonderful chocolate dough that can be rolled thin and cut into shapes. I chose hearts and decorated them with different shades of pink icing for Valentine's Day, but you could just as easily cut them into pumpkins and pipe on some orange frosting for Hal-loween. Or if you don't want to wait for a holiday, just sprinkle on some granulated sugar before they go into the oven.

....

MAKES: 5 DOZEN 2½-INCH COOKIES
PREPARATION TIME: 20 MINUTES
BAKING TIME: 8 TO 12 MINUTES

....

1 package (18.25 ounces) plain devil's food
    cake mix
12 tablespoons (1½ sticks) unsalted butter,
    at room temperature
1 large egg
1½ teaspoons pure vanilla extract
Flour for rolling out the cookies
¼ cup sugar (optional)

1. Place the cake mix, butter, egg, and vanilla in a large mixing bowl. Blend with an electric mixer on low speed for 1 minute. The dough will be thick and will come together into a ball. Cover the bowl with plastic wrap and place it in the refrigerator to chill for at least 3 hours, or preferably overnight.

the Cake Mix Doctor says

Rolled cookies are a different creature from drop cookies. The dough needs to be cold, so work with only a quarter of it at a time, leaving the rest in the refrigerator. Place the dough on a floured work surface and pound it with a wooden rolling pin until it is shaped like a disk. Then, reflouring the surface and the rolling pin as needed, roll the dough gradually but quickly until it is ¼ inch thick. Flip the dough over as you work, so it doesn't stick on the bottom. Work from the center to the edge, rolling in one direction only, not back and forth.

When the dough is the right thickness, flour your cookie cutter and press it down firmly on the dough. Cut out the entire round of dough, making sure your cuts are close together. Run a floured long metal spatula underneath the dough to loosen the cookies and transfer them to an ungreased cookie sheet. If your kitchen is warm, let the cookies chill on the cookie sheet in the refrigerator for 5 minutes before placing it in the hot oven. Always place cookie dough on cool baking sheets so the cookies don't spread during baking. If the cookie sheet just came out of the oven, hold it under cold running water to cool it off. Then pat it dry before baking the next batch.

2. Remove the dough from the refrigerator. Dust a work surface with flour. Assemble your cookie cutters, a long metal spatula (to help transfer the cookie dough to the sheets), and a metal pancake spatula (for removing the cookies from the sheets).

3. Place a rack in the center of the oven and preheat the oven to 350°F. Set aside two ungreased cookie sheets.

4. Working with a quarter of the dough at a time, and keeping the remaining dough in the refrigerator, place the dough on the floured surface and pound and roll it out to ¼-inch thickness (see "the Cake Mix Doctor says"). Cut the dough into the desired shapes and transfer them to the ungreased cookie sheets, using the long metal spatula. If you are not going to frost the cookies (see the box on the facing page), sprinkle them with granulated sugar. Place the cookie sheets in the oven. (If your oven cannot accommodate both cookie sheets on the center rack, place one on the top rack and one on the center rack and rotate them halfway through the baking time.)

5. Bake the cookies until they puff up and then sink back, 8 to 12 minutes. Remove the sheets and let the cookies rest on the cookie sheets for 1 minute.

Decorating with Icing

Feeling festive? Use my favorite icing to decorate these cookies: Stir together 1 cup confectioners' sugar and 2 tablespoons milk. Add enough food coloring to tint the icing to the desired hue, taking care to add only a drop at a time (a little coloring goes a long way). The icing needs to be thick enough so it will set up but thin enough to work its way through a squeeze bottle. (Before you begin, buy a couple of plastic squeeze bottles at a restaurant supply store or discount store. You can fill these with different shades of icing, which will make your decorating mess-free!) Pour the icing into the squeeze bottle with the aid of a funnel or by using a tablespoon. Squeeze designs on the cooled cookies—outlining them, drawing stripes, creating a plaid pattern with two colors, splashing polka dots, you name it. Or spread the frosting all over the cookie, using a dinner knife. For an added touch, dust the wet icing lightly with colored sugar sprinkles. Let the cookies rest for at least 1 hour before you pack them away, so the icing can set.

Then use the spatula to transfer them to wire racks and allow them to cool completely and get crisp, 15 minutes.

6. Repeat the rolling, cutting, and baking process with the remaining dough.

✳ *Store these cookies, in a cake saver or in a metal tin, at room temperature for up to 1 week. Or freeze them, wrapped in foil, for up to 6 months. Thaw the cookies overnight on the counter before serving.*

CHOCOLATE COOKIE SANDWICHES

A ngeleen Geddes, of Osceola, Iowa, was listening to WHO radio in Des Moines when I was on the air, and she sent me this recipe, which really belongs to her sister in St. Louis. That's something a sister would do, isn't it? These are soft cookie sandwiches that you can fill with whipped cream, ice cream, or even the Chocolate Cream Filling (page 461). Her husband likes to take them to work because they're less messy than a slice of frosted cake. But fill them with ice cream, roll them in miniature chocolate chips or sprinkles, and they can be pretty messy and good!

....

MAKES: 20 COOKIE SANDWICHES
PREPARATION TIME: 15 MINUTES
BAKING TIME: 8 TO 10 MINUTES
ASSEMBLY TIME: 10 MINUTES

....

COOKIE:

1 package (18.25 ounces) plain devil's food cake mix
⅓ cup vegetable oil
2 large eggs

FILLING:

1 pint vanilla ice cream, or ice cream of your choice

1. Place a rack in the center of the oven and preheat the oven to 350°F. Set aside two ungreased cookie sheets.

2. Place the cake mix, oil, and eggs in a large mixing bowl. Blend with an electric mixer on low speed for 1 to 1½ minutes. The dough will be smooth and thick. Spoon out teaspoons of the dough and place them 2 inches apart on the ungreased cookie sheets. Place the sheets in the oven. (If your oven cannot accommodate both cookie sheets on the center rack, place one on the top rack and one on the center rack and rotate them halfway through the baking time.)

3. Bake the cookies until they puff up and are firm around the edges but are still soft in the middle, 8 to 10 minutes. Remove the sheets from the oven and immediately flatten each cookie with a metal spatula. Let the cookies rest on the cookie sheets for 2 minutes. Then use the spatula to transfer them to wire racks and allow them to cool completely, 15 minutes.

4. Repeat the process with the remaining cookie dough.

5. For the ice cream filling, remove the ice cream from the freezer for about 15 minutes to soften slightly. To fill the cookies, place a tablespoon of ice cream on the flat side of one cookie and sandwich it with a second cookie, flat side in. Wrap each cookie sandwich in plastic wrap and freeze until hard, 30 minutes.

✷ *Store the cookie sandwiches in an airtight container in the freezer for up to 3 months.*

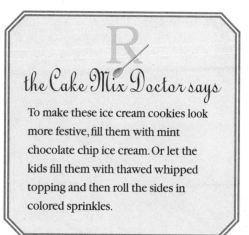

the Cake Mix Doctor says

To make these ice cream cookies look more festive, fill them with mint chocolate chip ice cream. Or let the kids fill them with thawed whipped topping and then roll the sides in colored sprinkles.

CHUNKY CHOCOLATE PEANUT BUTTER BARS

The Peanut Butter Chocolate Bars in *The Cake Mix Doctor* were an instant hit. We baked those bars on press stops and for book signings from coast to coast, and they remain a countrywide favorite. When I tried the recipe with chunky peanut butter, I found the bars had just the right amount of crunch. The original recipe called for pecans as well, but I omitted them here. Another winner!

MAKES: 48 BARS

PREPARATION TIME: 20 MINUTES

BAKING TIME: 25 TO 30 MINUTES

1 package (18.25 ounces) plain yellow
    cake mix
1 cup chunky peanut butter
8 tablespoons (1 stick) butter, melted
2 large eggs
2 cups semisweet chocolate chips
1 can (14 ounces) sweetened condensed
    milk
2 tablespoons butter
1 cup frozen unsweetened grated
    coconut, thawed, or sweetened
    flaked coconut
2 teaspoons pure vanilla extract

1. Place a rack in the center of the oven and preheat the oven to 325°F. Set aside an ungreased 13- by 9-inch baking pan.

2. Place the cake mix, peanut butter, melted butter, and eggs in a large mixing bowl. Blend with an electric mixer on low speed for 1 minute. Stop the machine and scrape down the sides of the bowl with a rubber spatula. The mixture will be satiny and thick. Reserve 1½ cups of the mixture for the topping. Transfer the remaining mixture to the pan. Using your

the Cake Mix Doctor says

These bars can be baked, sliced, and then frozen in a plastic container. If you need a last-minute gift or a potluck dessert, remove the plastic container from the freezer and let the bars thaw en route!

fingertips, press the mixture evenly over the bottom of the pan so that it reaches the sides. Set aside.

3. For the filling, place the chocolate chips, condensed milk, and 2 tablespoons butter in a medium-size heavy saucepan over low heat. Stir and cook until the chocolate is melted and the mixture is well combined, 3 to 4 minutes. Remove the pan from the heat and stir in the coconut and vanilla until well distributed. Pour the chocolate mixture over the crust, and spread it evenly with the rubber spatula so that it reaches the sides of the pan. Using your fingertips, crumble the reserved crust mixture and scatter it evenly over the chocolate. Place the pan in the oven.

4. Bake the cake until it is light brown, 25 to 30 minutes. Remove the pan from the oven and place it on a wire rack to cool for 30 minutes.

5. Cut the cake into 48 bars. Remove the bars from the pan with a metal spatula, and serve.

✳ *Store these bars, covered in plastic wrap or aluminum foil, at room temperature for up to 3 days or in the refrigerator for up to 1 week. Or freeze them, wrapped in foil, for up to 6 months. Thaw the bars overnight on the counter before serving.*

JOY OF ALMOND BARS

This recipe needs to come with a disclaimer—actually, a couple of disclaimers: Do not prepare if you are thinking of dieting. Do not prepare unless you have at least two dozen people to feed. Now that that's settled, let's get on with the good news: This recipe is outstanding,  loved by both children and adults. Combining the great flavors of chocolate, coconut, almond, and more chocolate, the results are delicious and indeed resemble a candy bar with a similar name.

....

MAKES: 48 BARS

PREPARATION TIME: 35 MINUTES

BAKING TIME: 15 TO 20 MINUTES

ASSEMBLY TIME: 5 MINUTES

....

CAKE:

Vegetable oil spray for misting the pan

Flour for dusting the pan

*1 package (18.25 ounces) plain devil's food
    cake mix*

1⅓ cups water

½ cup vegetable oil

3 large eggs

COCONUT FILLING:

1 can (13 ounces) evaporated milk

1 cup sugar

24 large marshmallows

*1 package (12 ounces) frozen unsweetened
    grated coconut, thawed*

CHOCOLATE TOPPING:

1½ cups sugar

8 tablespoons (1 stick) butter

2 cups semisweet chocolate chips

1 teaspoon pure vanilla extract

½ cup sliced almonds

1. Place a rack in the center of the oven and preheat the oven to 350°F. Lightly mist two 13- by 9-inch baking pans with vegetable oil spray, then dust with flour. Shake out the excess flour. Set the pans aside.

2. Place the cake mix, water, oil, and eggs in a large mixing bowl. Blend with an electric mixer on low speed for 1 minute. Stop the machine and scrape down the sides of the bowl with a rubber spatula. Increase the mixer speed to medium and beat for 2 minutes more, scraping down the sides again if needed. The batter should look thick and well combined. Divide the batter between the prepared pans, smoothing it out with the rubber spatula. Place the pans in the oven.

3. Bake the cakes until they spring back when lightly pressed with your finger, 15 to 20 minutes. Remove the pans from the oven and place them on wire racks to cool for 20 minutes.

4. Meanwhile, prepare the filling: Measure out 1 cup of the evaporated milk; set the rest aside for the topping. Place the 1 cup evaporated milk and the sugar in a medium-size saucepan over medium-high heat, and stir constantly until it comes to a boil, 7 to 8 minutes. Remove the pan from the heat and stir in the marshmallows until they melt, returning them to low heat if needed. Fold in the coconut and set aside.

5. For the topping, place the remaining ⅔ cup evaporated milk and the sugar in a medium-size saucepan over medium-high heat, and stir constantly until it comes to a boil, 4 to 5 minutes. Remove the pan from the heat and stir in the butter, chocolate chips, and vanilla until melted. Fold in the almonds. Place the pan over low heat to keep the mixture pourable.

6. To assemble the bars, divide the coconut filling between the two cakes, and spread it out with a metal spatula so that it reaches the edges of the pans. Immediately pour on the chocolate topping and spread it out with a metal spatula so that it reaches the edges. Place the cakes, uncovered, in the refrigerator to set, 2 hours.

7. Cut the cakes into bars—I cut them large, to get 24 bars per pan—and serve.

✳ *Store these bars, covered in plastic wrap or aluminum foil, at room temperature for up to 3 days or in the refrigerator for up to 1 week. Or freeze them, wrapped in foil, for up to 6 months. Thaw the bars overnight on the counter before serving.*

---

the Cake Mix Doctor says

It may seem strange to bake this cake in two pans, but you will see that you need the space in the pans to layer on the filling and then the topping.

GERMAN CHOCOLATE LEMON CRUMB SQUARES

L
emon squares are pretty sacred down South, and I know some people will not like me tampering with a good thing—especially mixing it with chocolate! But here is a quick and easy way to make a light and refreshing bar that's perfectly suited for picnics, luncheons, gifts, or just tucking into a brown paper sack. The intense lemon flavor comes from the zest, but you could also use lemon oil, found at cookware stores. These bars freeze well, and you can serve them partially frozen for a lemony chocolate icebox bar.

MAKES: 48 BARS
PREPARATION TIME: 12 MINUTES
BAKING TIME: 25 TO 30 MINUTES

1 package (18.25 ounces) German chocolate
    cake mix with pudding
2 large eggs
⅓ cup vegetable oil
1 package (8 ounces) cream cheese,
    at room temperature
½ cup sugar
2 tablespoons fresh lemon juice
2 teaspoons grated lemon zest

R
the Cake Mix Doctor says

Instead of using a pudding-in-the-mix
German chocolate cake mix, you can
use a plain German chocolate mix and
add a small package of vanilla, chocolate, or lemon instant pudding.

1. Place a rack in the center of the oven and preheat the oven to 350°F. Set aside an ungreased 13- by 9-inch baking pan.

2. Place the cake mix, 1 egg, and the oil in a large mixing bowl. Blend with an electric mixer on low speed for 1 to 1½ minutes. Stop the machine and scrape down the sides of the bowl with a rubber spatula. The mixture will be thick and crumbly. Reserve 1 cup of the mixture for the topping. Transfer the remaining mixture to the pan. Using your fingertips, press it evenly over the bottom and ½ inch up the sides of the pan. Set the pan aside.

3. For the filling, place the cream cheese in a medium-size mixing bowl and blend with the electric mixer on medium speed until light and fluffy, 1 minute. Stop the machine and add the remaining egg and the sugar, lemon juice, and zest. Blend on low speed until just incorporated, 30 seconds. Pour the lemon filling over the crust, and spread it out evenly with the rubber spatula so that it reaches the sides of the pan. Using your fingertips, crumble the reserved crust mixture and scatter it evenly over the filling. Place the pan in the oven.

4. Bake the cake until it is light brown, 25 to 30 minutes. Remove the pan from the oven and place it on a wire rack to cool for 30 minutes.

5. Cut the cake into bars and serve.

✳ *Store these bars, covered in plastic wrap or aluminum foil, at room temperature for up to 3 days or in the refrigerator for up to 1 week. Or freeze them, wrapped in foil, for up to 6 months. Thaw the bars overnight on the counter before serving, or serve them partially frozen as an icebox bar.*

CHOCOLATE HELLO DOLLIES

A bar cookie similar to this was all the rage when I was growing up. This is a crispy chocolate cake mix version of that cookie, and one that takes only 10 minutes to prepare and less than 30 minutes to bake. This bar has all the goodies—butterscotch chips, chocolate chips, coconut, and chopped pecans or walnuts. It's so scrumptious, your mouth will greet it with a big welcoming "Hello!"

MAKES: 48 BARS

PREPARATION TIME: 10 MINUTES

BAKING TIME: 25 TO 30 MINUTES

1 package (18.25 ounces) devil's food cake mix with pudding

8 tablespoons (1 stick) butter, at room temperature, cut into 8 pieces

1 cup butterscotch chips

1 cup semisweet chocolate chips

1 cup sweetened flaked coconut

1 cup chopped pecans or walnuts

1 can (14 ounces) sweetened condensed milk

1. Place a rack in the center of the oven and preheat the oven to 350°F. Set aside an ungreased 15- by 10-inch jelly-roll pan.

2. Place the cake mix and butter in a large mixing bowl. Cut the butter into the cake mix with two knives or a pastry blender until the mixture is crumbly. Sprinkle this mixture over the bottom of the jelly-roll pan and press it into the pan with your fingertips to form a crust.

3. Sprinkle the top of the crust evenly with the butterscotch chips, chocolate chips, coconut, and nuts. Pour the sweetened condensed milk evenly over all the ingredients. Place the pan in the oven.

4. Bake the bars until they are lightly browned and bubbly all over, 25 to 30 minutes. Remove the pan from the oven and place it on a rack to cool for 30 minutes. Cut into bars.

✳ *Store these bars, covered in plastic wrap or aluminum foil, at room temperature for up to 5 days. Or freeze them, wrapped in foil, for up to 6 months. Thaw the bars overnight on the counter before serving.*

R

the Cake Mix Doctor says

If the butter is soft, the process of cutting it into the cake mix will go a lot faster. And yes, you can substitute stick margarine for the butter.

SARAH'S CHOCOLATE PEPPERMINT STICKS

This was the last recipe I tested for this book, and maybe in some way I was saving the best for last! I met Sarah Goodenough (isn't that a wonderful name?) at a cake-decorating show in Detroit. A cake baker from Arlington, Texas, she mentioned that she had been doctoring cake mixes for some time and told me that her signature recipe was for a bar cookie she called Peppermint Sticks. I jotted down a few of the ingredients, and then I tracked Sarah down at home later to help me fill in the gaps. She makes a crust layer using a German chocolate mix, layers on a peppermint-flavored buttercream, then pours over a bitter chocolate glaze. Well, I thought these bars were heavenly warm, but once I chilled them and the chocolate set, they tasted just like those patty-shaped chocolate peppermint candies. Wow, do those Texans know how to bake!

....

MAKES: 48 "STICKS" (2¼ BY 1 INCH)
PREPARATION TIME: 20 MINUTES
BAKING TIME: 20 TO 23 MINUTES

....

1 package (18.25 ounces) plain German chocolate cake mix

2 large eggs

¼ cup vegetable oil

1 tablespoon water

2 cups confectioners' sugar, sifted

2 tablespoons half-and-half or whole milk

4 tablespoons butter (½ stick), 2 tablespoons at room temperature

½ teaspoon pure peppermint extract

2 ounces unsweetened chocolate, coarsely chopped

R
the Cake Mix Doctor says

To save time, use two 1-ounce packets of premelted unsweetened chocolate (found in the baking aisle) in the glaze; melt the butter and combine it with the chocolate.

Sarah prevents her cake from developing a crust around the edges by attaching wet terry-cloth baking strips to the outside of the pan. This helps the cake layer to bake flat all the way across. These strips are sold where you find cake-decorating supplies.

Take care not to overbake the cake layer in this recipe. It needs to be chewy.

Sarah and her family have had fun tinting the peppermint filling in this recipe to suit the season. She adds a drop or two of green food coloring for St. Patrick's Day, a drop or two of red and yellow to make orange for Halloween, but she wouldn't advise you to add yellow alone: "One time my daughter added yellow and the filling came out looking like mustard!"

1. Place a rack in the center of the oven and preheat the oven to 350°F. Set aside an ungreased 13- by 9-inch pan.

2. Place the cake mix, eggs, oil, and water in a large mixing bowl. Blend with an electric mixer on low speed until the dough is well combined, 1 minute. Transfer the batter to the ungreased pan and smooth it evenly to the sides with a rubber spatula. Place the pan in the oven.

3. Bake the cake layer until it puffs up and cracks and the edges look crusty, 20 to 23 minutes. Don't overbake this layer; it should look jiggly when you shake the pan. Remove the pan from the oven and place it on a rack to cool for 10 minutes. Set aside.

4. For the filling, place the confectioners' sugar, half-and-half, 2 tablespoons room-temperature butter, and peppermint extract in a medium-size mixing bowl. Blend with an electric mixer on low speed to incorporate, 30 seconds. Increase the mixer speed to medium and beat until fluffy, 1½ minutes. Spread this filling thinly over the warm cake, using a long metal spatula or dinner knife to reach the edges. Let the cake rest until the filling forms a thin crust on top, 10 minutes.

5. Meanwhile, prepare the glaze: Melt the chocolate and remaining 2 tablespoons butter in a small glass bowl in the microwave oven on high power for 45 seconds, and stir until the chocolate has melted. Pour this warm chocolate glaze over the cake, and spread it with the metal spatula or dinner knife until it reaches the edges.

6. Slice the cake and serve warm, or cover the pan with aluminum foil and chill until firm, 2 to 3 hours, then slice and serve.

✳ *Store these bars, covered in plastic wrap or aluminum foil, in the refrigerator for up to 1 week. Or freeze them, wrapped in foil, for up to 3 months. Thaw the bars overnight in the refrigerator before serving.*

ORANGE-CHOCOLATE BISCOTTI WITH ALMONDS

I n *The Cake Mix Doctor*, I did not know whether to place the biscotti in the "This Can't Contain Cake Mix" chapter or with the other cookies and bars. I am sure it was a  surprise at first for readers to see biscotti made with cake mix, but once you see how easy they are to make, you'll understand why they are so popular. The orange is a natural partner for the chocolate cake batter here.

MAKES: 18 BISCOTTI

PREPARATION TIME: 15 MINUTES

BAKING TIME: 30 TO 35 MINUTES
FOR FIRST BAKING, 10 MINUTES
FOR SECOND

RESTING TIME IN OVEN:
30 TO 40 MINUTES

1 package (18.25 ounces) plain devil's food cake mix

8 tablespoons (1 stick) butter, melted

2 large eggs

1 cup all-purpose flour

½ cup finely chopped almonds

2 teaspoons grated orange zest

¼ teaspoon orange oil or extract (optional)

1. Place a rack in the center of the oven and preheat the oven to 350°F. Line a baking sheet with parchment paper and set it aside.

2. Place the cake mix, melted butter, eggs, flour, almonds, orange zest, and orange oil, if desired, in a large mixing bowl. Blend with an electric mixer on low speed until well blended, 3 to 4 minutes. The dough will be thick and come together into a ball. Transfer it to the prepared baking sheet. With floured hands, shape the dough into a rectangle about 14 inches long by 4 inches wide by ½ inch thick. Mound the dough so it is slightly higher in the center. Place the baking sheet in the oven.

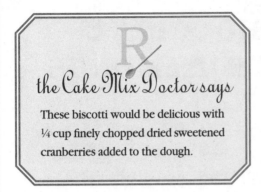

the Cake Mix Doctor says

These biscotti would be delicious with ¼ cup finely chopped dried sweetened cranberries added to the dough.

3. Bake the biscotti rectangle until it feels firm when lightly pressed with your finger and a toothpick inserted in the center comes out clean, 30 to 35 minutes. Remove the baking sheet from the oven and let the biscotti cool for 10 minutes. Leave the oven on.

4. Cutting on the baking sheet, use a sharp, serrated knife to slice the rectangle on the diagonal into 1-inch-thick slices. Carefully turn these slices onto their sides, using the slicing knife to arrange them on the same baking sheet. Return the baking sheet to the oven.

5. Bake the biscotti for 10 minutes. Turn the oven off, and let the biscotti remain in the oven until they are crisp, 30 to 40 minutes more. Remove the baking sheet from the oven, transfer the biscotti to a rack, and allow them to cool completely, 2 hours.

✹ *Store the biscotti in an airtight container at room temperature for up to several weeks.*

CHOCOLATE BISCOTTI
WITH WHITE CHIPS AND SWEET CHERRIES

These biscotti are a visual treat, the white chocolate chips contrasting with the dark chocolate cake. And they are delicious dunked into a cup of Darjeeling or a steaming cappuccino.

MAKES: 18 BISCOTTI

PREPARATION TIME: 15 MINUTES

BAKING TIME: 30 TO 35 MINUTES
FOR FIRST BAKING,
10 MINUTES FOR SECOND

RESTING TIME IN OVEN:
30 TO 40 MINUTES

1 package (18.25 ounces) plain devil's food
   cake mix
8 tablespoons (1 stick) butter, melted
2 large eggs

1 cup all-purpose flour
½ cup white chocolate chips
¼ cup finely chopped dried sweetened
   cherries
½ teaspoon pure almond extract

1. Place a rack in the center of the oven and preheat the oven to 350°F. Line a baking sheet with parchment paper and set it aside.

2. Place the cake mix, melted butter, eggs, flour, white chocolate chips, cherries, and almond extract in a large mixing bowl. Blend with an electric mixer on low speed until well blended, 3 to 4 minutes. The dough will be thick and come together into a ball. Transfer it to the prepared baking sheet. With floured hands, shape the dough into a rectangle about 14 inches long by 4 inches wide by ½ inch thick. Mound the dough so it is slightly higher in the center. Place the baking sheet in the oven.

3. Bake the biscotti rectangle until it feels firm when lightly pressed with your finger and a toothpick inserted in the center comes out clean, 30 to 35 minutes.

Remove the baking sheet from the oven and let the biscotti cool for 10 minutes. Leave the oven on.

4. Cutting on the baking sheet, use a sharp, serrated knife to slice the rectangle on the diagonal into 1-inch-thick slices. Carefully turn these slices onto their sides, using the slicing knife to arrange them on the same baking sheet. Return the baking sheet to the oven.

5. Bake the biscotti for 10 minutes. Turn the oven off, and let the biscotti remain in the oven until they are crisp, 30 to 40 minutes more. Remove the baking sheet from the oven, transfer the biscotti to a rack, and allow them to cool completely, 2 hours.

✻ *Store the biscotti in an airtight container at room temperature for up to several weeks.*

the Cake Mix Doctor says

If any white chocolate chips fall out when you slice the biscotti, just gently press them back into the slice before it is turned on its side and the pan is returned to the oven.

CHOCOLATE CINNAMON BISCOTTI

WITH CHOCOLATE FLAKES AND HAZELNUTS

Chocolate and cinnamon talk to each other in this dandy of a biscotti. You can be drinking the most ordinary cup of tea, coffee, or sweet wine, but if you dunk this biscotti into the cup or glass, ordinary no more! The chocolate flakes are made by simply running a sharp knife quickly down the side of a bar of semisweet chocolate, as if you were slicing an onion.

....

MAKES: 18 BISCOTTI

PREPARATION TIME:
15 MINUTES

BAKING TIME:
30 TO 35 MINUTES FOR FIRST
BAKING, 10 MINUTES FOR SECOND

RESTING TIME IN OVEN:
30 TO 40 MINUTES

....

1 package (18.25 ounces) plain
German chocolate cake mix
8 tablespoons (1 stick) butter,
melted
2 large eggs
1 cup all-purpose flour
½ cup finely chopped hazelnuts (see "the
Cake Mix Doctor says")
¼ cup flaked or grated semisweet
chocolate
½ teaspoon ground cinnamon

1. Place a rack in the center of the oven and preheat the oven to 350°F. Line a baking sheet with parchment paper and set it aside.

2. Place the cake mix, melted butter, eggs, flour, hazelnuts, chocolate flakes, and cinnamon in a large mixing bowl. Blend with an electric mixer on low speed until well blended, 3 to 4 minutes. The dough will be thick and come together into a ball. Transfer it to the prepared baking sheet. With floured hands, shape the dough into a rectangle about 14 inches long by 4 inches wide by ½ inch thick. Mound the dough so it is slightly higher in the center. Place the baking sheet in the oven.

3. Bake the biscotti rectangle until it feels firm when lightly pressed with your finger and a toothpick inserted in the center comes out clean, 30 to 35 minutes. Remove the baking sheet from the oven and let the biscotti cool for 10 minutes. Leave the oven on.

4. Cutting on the baking sheet, use a sharp, serrated knife to slice the rectangle on the diagonal into 1-inch-thick slices. Carefully turn these slices onto their sides, using the slicing knife to arrange them on the same baking sheet. Return the baking sheet to the oven.

5. Bake the biscotti for 10 minutes. Turn the oven off, and let the biscotti remain in the oven until they are crisp, 30 to 40 minutes more. Remove the baking sheet from the oven, transfer the biscotti to a rack, and allow them to cool completely, 2 hours.

✳ *Store the biscotti in an airtight container at room temperature for up to several weeks.*

R

the Cake Mix Doctor says

Hazelnuts are also called filberts or cobnuts. To remove their bitter brown skin, heat them on a baking sheet at 350°F for 10 to 15 minutes, or until the skin starts to flake. Remove the nuts from the pan and rub them vigorously with a clean kitchen towel to remove all the skin. Then proceed with your recipe.

PECAN CHIP BUTTERMILK BROWNIES

This is possibly the easiest and the most basic brownie in this chapter, and when you read it, you will wonder why I bothered to write such a simple recipe. When you taste them, you'll see that the secret is in the chips and nuts that are sprinkled on top before baking. The chips melt nicely and the pecans toast lightly. My son, John, eats these still frozen, whereas his sisters, Kathleen and Litton, reheat them for 10 to 15 seconds in the microwave and then spoon vanilla ice cream on top.

....

MAKES: 24 SQUARES
PREPARATION TIME: 7 MINUTES
BAKING TIME: 20 TO 25 MINUTES

....

Vegetable oil for misting
  the pan
1 package (19.8 ounces)
  brownie mix
8 tablespoons (1 stick) unsalted
  butter, melted
⅓ cup buttermilk
2 large eggs
1 teaspoon pure vanilla extract
½ cup semisweet chocolate chips
½ cup finely chopped pecans

R

the Cake Mix Doctor says

You can use a larger package of brownie mix—21 to 21.5 ounces— in this recipe. It may need a few tablespoons more buttermilk but otherwise will substitute well. And it may take 2 to 3 minutes longer to bake. The success lies in taking care not to overbake these brownies.

1. Place a rack in the center of the oven and preheat the oven to 350°F. Lightly mist the bottom of a 13- by 9-inch pan with vegetable oil spray. Set the pan aside.

2. Place the brownie mix, melted butter, buttermilk, eggs, and vanilla in a large mixing bowl. Stir with a wooden spoon until all the ingredients are incorporated and the batter lightens in texture, 50 strokes. Pour the batter into the prepared pan and spread it out evenly with a rubber spatula. Scatter the chocolate chips and pecans evenly over the top. Place the pan in the oven.

3. Bake the brownies until the outer 2 inches form a crust and a toothpick inserted in this area comes out clean, 20 to 25 minutes. Remove the pan from the oven and place it on a rack to cool for 30 minutes.

4. Cut the brownies into 24 squares.

✳ *Store these brownies, covered in plastic wrap or aluminum foil, at room temperature for up to 5 days. Or freeze them, wrapped in foil, for up to 6 months. Thaw the brownies overnight on the counter before serving.*

JESSICA'S CARAMEL CHOCOLATE BROWNIES

Jessica Brown, of Chandler, Arizona, sent me this wonderful recipe, and it has become a favorite at my house. She says it has made its way around her home state of Kentucky, and that something similar to it won a blue ribbon at the Kentucky State Fair many years ago. Jessica

has tweaked the recipe through the years to arrive at this basic formula. You can add 1 to 2 cups of the chocolate chips, depending on how rich you want these brownies to be. And I think the nuts add a nice crunch, which balances out the gooey sweetness of the brownies' center.

MAKES: 24 SQUARES
PREPARATION TIME: 15 MINUTES
BAKING TIME: 28 TO 30 MINUTES

Vegetable oil spray for misting the pan
1 package (18.25 ounces) plain German
   chocolate cake mix
12 tablespoons (1½ sticks) butter, at room
   temperature
1 can (5 ounces) evaporated milk
1 bag (14 ounces) caramels (45 small
   caramels), unwrapped
1 to 2 cups semisweet chocolate chips
   (see headnote)
1 cup chopped walnuts or pecans (optional)

the Cake Mix Doctor says

Sizes of caramel bags vary, so it's best to count the candies. There are about 45 in a 14-ounce bag; a 9¼-ounce bag contains about 30.

15 Dark and Devilish Halloween Cakes

1. Pumpkin Spice German Chocolate Cheesecake

2. Chocolate Midnight Cake with Vanilla Buttercream Frosting

3. Dark Chocolate Sheet Cake with Fresh Orange Cream Cheese Frosting

4. Dark Chocolate Roulade with Chocolate Cream Filling

5. Chocolate Carrot Cake with Pineapple Cream Cheese Frosting

6. Orange Swirl Chocolate Cupcakes with Orange-Cocoa Cream Cheese Frosting

7. Chocolate-Orange Almond Marble Angel Food Cake

8. Chocolate-Swirled Apricot Angel Food Cake

9. Orange-Chocolate Biscotti with Almonds and Cranberries

10. Jessica's Caramel Chocolate Brownies

11. German Chocolate Sheet Cake with Rocky Road Frosting

12. Chocolate-Orange Cream Cheese Pound Cake with Fresh Orange Drizzle

13. Darn Good Chocolate Cake with Martha's Chocolate Icing

14. Black Russian Cake

15. Pumpkin German Chocolate Chip Muffins

1. Place a rack in the center of the oven and preheat the oven to 350°F. Lightly mist the bottom of a 13- by 9-inch pan with vegetable oil spray. Set the pan aside.

2. Place the cake mix, butter, and ⅓ cup of the evaporated milk in a large mixing bowl. Blend with an electric mixer on low speed for 1 minute. The batter will be thick and well combined. Turn half of the batter into the prepared pan, smoothing it out with a rubber spatula. Place the pan in the oven.

3. Bake the cake layer until it puffs up but is still soft, 6 minutes. Remove the pan from the oven. Leave the oven on.

4. Place the caramels in a medium-size saucepan with the remaining ⅓ cup evaporated milk. Stir and cook over medium-low heat until the caramels melt and the mixture is smooth and thick, 4 to 5 minutes. Remove the pan from the heat and pour the hot caramel mixture over the cake layer. Scatter the chocolate chips evenly on top. Dollop teaspoonfuls of the remaining cake batter at random over the chocolate chips. Scatter the nuts on top of the batter, if desired. Place the pan in the oven.

5. Bake until the batter on top lightly browns and a crust forms around the edges of the pan, 22 to 24 minutes. The brownies should still be a little soft in the center. Remove the pan from the oven and place it on a wire rack to cool completely, 30 minutes.

6. Slice and serve the brownies. To make slicing easier, chill the brownies for 1 hour first.

✳ *Store these brownies, covered with plastic wrap or aluminum foil, at room temperature for up to 3 days or in the refrigerator for up to 1 week. Or freeze them, wrapped in foil, for up to 6 months. Thaw the brownies overnight on the counter before serving.*

CHERRY CHEESECAKE BROWNIES

Yummy. That's about all that needs to be said about this brownie. Sandwiched inside is a creamy cheese-cake center that leaves you asking, "Is this a brownie or a cheesecake?" It's both.

....

MAKES: 24 SQUARES
PREPARATION TIME: 15 MINUTES
BAKING TIME: 25 TO 30 MINUTES

....

CHEESECAKE FILLING:

2 small packages (3 ounces each)
    cream cheese, at room
    temperature
5 tablespoons butter, at room temperature
⅓ cup sugar
2 large eggs
1 teaspoon pure vanilla extract

BROWNIES:

Vegetable oil spray for misting the pan
1 package (19.8 ounces) brownie mix
⅓ cup vegetable oil
¼ cup water
2 large eggs
⅓ cup chopped dried sweetened cherries
½ cup miniature semisweet chocolate chips

1. Prepare the filling: Place the cream cheese, butter, sugar, eggs, and vanilla in a large mixing bowl and blend with an electric mixer on low speed, or with a wooden spoon, until the mixture is smooth and well combined. Set the bowl aside.

℞

the Cake Mix Doctor says

You need to grease only the bottom of the pan when making brownies. Dried sweetened cherries can be found at natural foods markets and gourmet stores.

How to Turn a Brownie Mix into a Pie

A 9-inch pie crust will hold one recipe of brownies made with a 19.8-ounce or smaller brownie mix. Pour the batter into an unbaked crust, and bake at 350°F until the outside edges are quite firm and the center is still soft, about 45 minutes. The crust may darken quite a bit as the pie bakes through, so you may need to cut strips of aluminum foil and place them around the edges to shield the crust from overbrowning. Let the pie cool well—even chill it—before slicing. Brownie pies should be soft in the center. Serve with whipped cream or vanilla ice cream.

2. Place a rack in the center of the oven and preheat the oven to 350°F. Lightly mist the bottom of a 13- by 9-inch pan with vegetable oil spray. Set the pan aside.

3. Place the brownie mix, oil, water, and eggs in a large mixing bowl. Stir with a wooden spoon until all the ingredients are incorporated and the batter lightens in texture, 50 strokes. Fold in the dried cherries until they are well incorporated. Pour half of the batter into the prepared pan and spread it out evenly with a rubber spatula. Spread the cream cheese filling over the batter, using the rubber spatula. Dollop the remaining brownie batter over the filling, and swirl it into the filling with a dinner knife to create a marbled effect. Scatter the chocolate chips evenly on the top. Place the pan in the oven.

4. Bake the brownies until they are lightly browned and the outer 2 inches form a crust, 25 to 30 minutes. Remove the pan from the oven and place it on a rack to cool for 30 minutes. Cut the brownies into 24 squares.

✳ *Store these brownies, covered with plastic wrap or aluminum foil, at room temperature up to 3 days or in the refrigerator for up to 1 week. Or freeze them, wrapped in foil, for up to 6 months. Thaw the brownies overnight on the counter before serving.*

MARBLED CREAM CHEESE AND KAHLÚA BROWNIES

Much like the Cherry Cheesecake Brownies (page 390), these brownies rely on a layer of cream cheese filling, but they also turn to the wonderful flavor of Kahlúa for an added kick. My husband took these brownies to the office and everyone clamored for more . . . and demanded the recipe! For a child-friendly version, use vanilla instead of Kahlúa in the filling, and use water instead of Kahlúa in the brownies.

MAKES: 24 SQUARES
PREPARATION TIME: 15 MINUTES
BAKING TIME: 27 TO 32 MINUTES

CHEESECAKE FILLING:

1 package (8 ounces) cream cheese, at room temperature
5 tablespoons butter, at room temperature
¼ cup sugar
1 large egg
1 tablespoon Kahlúa or other coffee liqueur

BROWNIES:

Vegetable oil spray for misting the pan
1 package (19.8 ounces) brownie mix
⅓ cup vegetable oil
¼ cup Kahlúa or other coffee liqueur
2 large eggs
½ cup miniature semisweet chocolate chips (optional)

1. Prepare the filling: Place the cream cheese, butter, sugar, egg, and Kahlúa in a large mixing bowl and blend with an electric mixer on low speed, or with a wooden spoon, until the mixture is smooth and well combined. Set the bowl aside.

2. Place a rack in the center of the oven and preheat the oven to 350°F. Lightly mist

prepared pan and spread it out evenly with a rubber spatula. Spread the cream cheese filling over the top of the batter, and using a dinner knife, swirl it into the batter to create a marbled effect. Scatter the chocolate chips evenly over the top if desired. Place the pan in the oven.

4. Bake the brownies until they are lightly browned and the outer 2 inches form a crust, 27 to 32 minutes. Remove the pan from the oven and place it on a wire rack to cool for 30 minutes. Cut the brownies into 24 squares.

✳ *Store these brownies, covered with plastic wrap or aluminum foil, at room temperature for up to 3 days or in the refrigerator for up to 1 week. Or freeze them, wrapped in foil, for up to 6 months. Thaw the brownies overnight on the counter before serving.*

R the Cake Mix Doctor says

An easy trick that makes removing brownies a breeze is to line the 13- by 9-inch pan with aluminum foil, letting some foil hang over the sides of the pan. Lightly mist the bottom of the foil with vegetable oil spray, then proceed with the recipe.

---

the bottom of a 13- by 9-inch pan with vegetable oil spray. Set the pan aside.

3. Place the brownie mix, oil, Kahlúa, and eggs in a large mixing bowl. Stir with a wooden spoon until all the ingredients are incorporated and the batter lightens in texture, 50 strokes. Pour the batter into the

CHOCOLATE WALNUT BROWNIES

Jackie Garza, of Monterey, California, e-mailed the newsletter looking for a brownie recipe that started not with a brownie mix, but with a chocolate cake mix. (After all, when you're in the mood for brownies, you may have only a regular cake mix on hand.) Several readers quickly responded and I used the recipes as inspiration to come up with this one based on a devil's food cake mix. I increased the amount of butter to make the brownies richer and added vanilla. The generous scoop of walnuts makes the brownies deserving of their name. These are wonderfully chewy squares—delicious served warm with ice cream.

R the Cake Mix Doctor says

Here are a couple of thoughts: You will notice that not all of the brownie recipes call for dusting the pan with flour. I find it is easier to remove a brownie from the pan if the pan has been dusted with flour, but it isn't always needed. In this recipe, however, the brownies are thinner and chewier, so do flour the pan first for easy removal.

········

MAKES: 24 SQUARES

PREPARATION TIME: 10 MINUTES

BAKING TIME: 20 TO 25 MINUTES

········

Vegetable oil for misting the pan

Flour for dusting the pan

1 package (18.25 ounces) devil's food cake
    mix with pudding

5 tablespoons butter, melted

⅓ cup milk

1 large egg

Brownie Pizza

What do a round shallow pan plus a brownie mix equal? A brownie pizza, that's what! Just lightly mist a 12-inch round pizza pan with vegetable oil spray, then pour in your favorite brownie batter made with 3 eggs. Bake at 350°F for about 20 to 25 minutes, or until the brownie springs back in the center when touched. You want a springy brownie, not too gooey, or you won't be able to pick up a slice. Remove the pan from the oven and place it on a wire rack. Immediately top the pizza with semisweet chocolate chips, butterscotch chips, milk chocolate chips, white chocolate chips, toffee chips, sliced fresh strawberries . . . the list is endless. Arrange the toppings as if you were topping individual pieces of pizza, or scatter them randomly over the top. Slice the pizza and serve warm. Or let the brownie cool for 20 minutes, spread it with whipped cream or thawed whipped topping, and then scatter with toppings. To transport to a party, place the pizza in a clean pizza box lined with waxed paper.

1 teaspoon pure vanilla extract

1 cup semisweet chocolate chips

¾ cup finely chopped walnuts

1. Place a rack in the center of the oven and preheat the oven to 350°F. Lightly mist the bottom of a 13- by 9-inch pan with vegetable oil spray and dust it with flour. Shake out the excess flour. Set the pan aside.

2. Place the cake mix, melted butter, milk, egg, and vanilla in a large mixing bowl. Blend with an electric mixer on low speed for 30 seconds. Stop the machine and scrape down the sides of the bowl with a rubber spatula. Increase the mixer speed to medium and beat 1 to 2 minutes more, or until the batter is smooth and very thick. Stir in the chocolate chips and walnuts. Turn the batter into the prepared pan and press it into place with a fork or your fingertips. Don't worry if it doesn't reach all the way to the sides of the pan, because it will expand as the pan heats. Place the pan in the oven.

3. Bake the brownies until they puff up in the center and are firm around the edges, 20 to 25 minutes. Remove the pan from the oven and place it on a wire rack to cool for 20 minutes. The brownies will fall slightly, becoming thin and chewy as they cool. Slice into squares.

✳ *Store these brownies, covered in plastic wrap or aluminum foil, at room temperature for up to 5 days. Or freeze them, wrapped in foil, for up to 6 months. Thaw the brownies overnight on the counter before serving.*

Brownie Tips and Tricks

For something as simple as a brownie mix, buying one can be terribly confusing. Unlike traditional two-layer cake mixes, where the size of the box is pretty consistently 18.25 ounces, brownie mixes range from well under a pound to nearly a pound and a half! And it's difficult to find a mix that is just mix because the boxes are crammed with packets of things to add.

• Choose the biggest box of mix with the fewest add-in ingredients.

• The back of the box will offer you two methods of preparation: using 2 eggs for a more fudgy brownie or 3 eggs for a more cakey brownie. Choose the former if you like a wetter taste texture, but choose the latter if you are adding bananas, cream cheese, or other wet ingredients.

• Blend brownie batter using a wooden spoon, not an electric mixer (unless you are making brownies using a cake mix). Overbeating makes the batter tough, so you just want to mix the ingredients until they come together and lighten. This takes about 50 strokes around the bowl.

• Use butter instead of oil for a richer flavor. Use unsalted butter because the mix itself is salty.

• Use buttermilk instead of water if you have it on hand.

• Don't overbake brownie mixes! They should be pulled from the oven when they become fragrant, when the outside 2 inches have formed a crust, and always before the recommended time on the back of the box. Most brownies from a mix will be done in 25 minutes at 350°F. Brownies baked in insulated pans will take 5 minutes longer.

SUNDAY FUDGE CAKE

WITH CREAMY CHOCOLATE FROSTING

This recipe doesn't have a fancy bone in it. The brownies are uncomplicated and nut-free, for people with allergies or folks who just don't like crunch. And the frosting—how I love this little bit of frosting, which is creamy and goes on nice and thin. Chill the brownies after frosting to make slicing easier. Make this cake on Saturday for Sunday lunch. And it's just right for packing in a tailgate picnic in the fall or for picnics in the park in the spring.

MAKES: 24 SQUARES
PREPARATION TIME: 10 MINUTES
BAKING TIME: 23 TO 27 MINUTES

BROWNIES:

Vegetable oil spray for misting the pan
Flour for dusting the pan
1 package (19.8 ounces) brownie mix
8 tablespoons (1 stick) unsalted butter, melted
⅓ cup water
2 large eggs
1 teaspoon pure vanilla extract

CREAMY CHOCOLATE FROSTING:

3 tablespoons butter, at room temperature
3 tablespoons unsweetened cocoa powder
1 tablespoon light corn syrup
1 teaspoon pure vanilla extract
1 cup confectioners' sugar, sifted
2 tablespoons milk

1. Place a rack in the center of the oven and preheat the oven to 350°F. Lightly mist the bottom of a 13- by 9-inch pan with vegetable oil spray and dust it with flour. Shake out the excess flour. Set the pan aside.

R

the Cake Mix Doctor says

If you want to add nuts, why not sprinkle on lightly toasted almond slices after you frost the brownies?

2. Place the brownie mix, melted butter, water, eggs, and vanilla in a large mixing bowl. Stir with a wooden spoon until all the ingredients are incorporated and the batter lightens in texture, 50 strokes. Pour the batter into the prepared pan, smoothing it out with a rubber spatula. Place the pan in the oven.

3. Bake the brownies until the outer 2 inches have formed a crust and feel firm, 23 to 27 minutes. Remove the pan from the oven and place it on a wire rack to cool completely, 30 minutes.

4. Meanwhile, prepare the frosting: Place the butter, cocoa powder, corn syrup, and vanilla in a medium-size mixing bowl. Beat on low speed with an electric mixer until combined, 1 minute. Stop the machine, and scrape down the sides with a rubber spatula. Add the confectioners' sugar and the milk. Beat on low speed to incorporate the sugar, 30 seconds. Then increase the speed to medium and beat until lightened and fluffy, 1 minute more.

5. Spread the frosting thinly over the top of the cooled brownies with a metal spatula. Cover the pan with plastic wrap or aluminum foil, and place in the refrigerator to chill for 1 hour, if possible. Slice and serve.

✸ *Store these brownies, covered with plastic wrap or aluminum foil, at room temperature for up to 3 days or in the refrigerator for up to 1 week. Or freeze them, wrapped in foil, for up to 6 months. Thaw the brownies overnight on the counter before serving.*

TEXAS SHEET CAKE

A takeoff on the famous buttermilk chocolate sheet cake made with a pan frosting and pecans, this brownie is compact and thinner, so it's more like a bar than a cake. The frosting is so easy, but make sure you toast the pecans well and chop them coarsely so there are some big pieces. Add a little salt to those toasted pecans for a delicious contrast to the sweet chocolate frosting.

MAKES: 24 SQUARES

PREPARATION TIME:
10 MINUTES

BAKING TIME:
20 TO 25 MINUTES

BROWNIES:

Vegetable oil spray for misting the pan
Flour for dusting the pan
1 package (18.25 ounces) German chocolate cake mix with pudding
5 tablespoons butter, melted
⅓ cup milk
1 large egg
1 teaspoon pure vanilla extract

TOASTED PECAN PAN FROSTING:

1 heaping cup pecan halves
¼ teaspoon salt (optional)
8 tablespoons (1 stick) butter
4 heaping tablespoons unsweetened cocoa powder
⅓ cup milk
3½ to 4 cups confectioners' sugar, sifted

1. Place a rack in the center of the oven and preheat the oven to 350°F. Lightly mist the bottom of a 13- by 9-inch pan with vegetable oil spray and dust it with flour. Shake out the excess flour. Set the pan aside.

2. Place the cake mix, melted butter, milk, egg, and vanilla in a large mixing bowl. Blend with an electric mixer on low speed for 30 seconds. Stop the machine and scrape down the sides of the bowl with a rubber spatula. Increase the mixer speed to medium and beat 1 to 2 minutes more, or until the batter is smooth and very thick. Turn the batter into the prepared pan and press it into place with a fork or your fingertips. Don't worry if it doesn't reach all the way to the sides of the pan because it will expand as the pan heats. Place the pan in the oven.

3. Bake the brownies until puffed up in the center and firm around the edges, 20 to 25 minutes. Remove the pan from the oven and place it on a wire rack to cool for 20 minutes. Leave the oven on. The brownies will fall slightly, becoming thin and chewy as it cools.

4. Meanwhile, prepare the frosting: Place the pecans in a foil pie pan and place it in the oven. Let them toast until deep brown, 5 to 6 minutes. Remove the pan from the oven and let the pecans cool. Lightly sprinkle them with salt if desired. When they are cool, chop coarsely.

5. Place the butter in a medium-size saucepan over medium-high heat. Stir until the butter has melted. Remove the pan from the heat. Stir in the cocoa powder until completely dissolved. Then stir in the milk. Pour in the confectioners' sugar, a little at a time, and stir until the frosting is smooth and satiny. Fold in the pecans.

6. Pour the frosting over the top of the cooled brownies, and spread it to the edges with a metal spatula. Let the frosting set on the cake for 20 minutes or, better yet, chill the brownies for 1 hour. Then slice into squares.

✳ *Store these brownies, covered with plastic wrap or aluminum foil, at room temperature for up to 5 days or in the refrigerator for up to 1 week. Or freeze them, wrapped in foil, for up to 6 months. Thaw the brownies overnight on the counter before serving.*

the Cake Mix Doctor says

If you sprinkle 1½ cups of miniature marshmallows over the brownies before you pour on the frosting, this could be called a Mississippi Mud Cake. Or opt for the Rocky Road Frosting (page 438), with the marshmallows already in the frosting.

CHOCOLATE MINT BROWNIES

I t's not often that a pan of brownies lasts for any considerable time at my house. But when I made these, I had also tested some chocolate layer cakes. What with the selection of desserts, there were leftovers. And thank goodness for that! Allowing the brownies to sit overnight gave the peppermint flavor a chance to seep from the candy pieces into the brownies. The next day, when we bit into the brownie, we got a little peppermint flavor tease. But when we bit right into the candy, it was full-throttle peppermint!

MAKES: 24 SQUARES
PREPARATION TIME: 15 MINUTES
BAKING TIME: 25 TO 30 MINUTES

24 chocolate-covered peppermint-cream-
    filled candies (1½-inch size),
    such as York Peppermint Patties
    (see "the Cake Mix Doctor says")
Vegetable oil spray for misting the pan
1 package (19.8 ounces) brownie mix
8 tablespoons (1 stick) unsalted butter,
    melted
¼ cup buttermilk
3 large eggs
1 teaspoon pure vanilla extract

1. Remove the wrappers from the peppermint candies. Set the candy aside.

2. Place a rack in the center of the oven and preheat the oven to 350°F. Lightly mist the bottom of a 13- by 9-inch pan with vegetable oil spray. Set the pan aside.

3. Place the brownie mix, melted butter, buttermilk, eggs, and vanilla in a large mixing bowl. Stir with a wooden spoon until all the ingredients are incorporated and the batter lightens in texture, 50 strokes. Pour half of the batter into the prepared pan and spread it out evenly with a rubber spatula. Arrange the peppermint candies in rows of six across and four down on the top of the batter, spacing them evenly. Pour the remaining batter on top of the peppermints, spreading it with the rubber spatula to completely cover them. Place the pan in the oven.

4. Bake the brownies until the top swells up slightly and they are just beginning to pull away from the sides of the pan, 25 to 30 minutes. Remove the pan from the oven and place it on a wire rack to cool for 30 minutes.

5. Cut the brownies into 24 squares, making sure there is a piece of candy in each square.

✳ *Store these brownies, covered in plastic wrap or aluminum foil, at room tem-*

R

the Cake Mix Doctor says

York Peppermint Patties come in 5.3-ounce bags. You will need two bags for this recipe—and if luck is with you, you might have a couple extra candies to nibble on while you bake! The candy bakes up hard in this recipe. If you don't like this texture, coarsely chop the patties and then scatter them over the first layer of batter.

perature for up to 5 days. Or freeze them, wrapped in foil, for up to 6 months. Thaw the brownies overnight on the counter before serving.

BANANA BLACK WALNUT BROWNIES

Black walnuts harvested from your own trees are a lot of work, but delicious. I remember my father silently gathering the green walnuts from the hillside, letting them cure through the fall in plastic barrels in the basement until they turned black as coal, and then shooing eager squirrels out of the basement so they didn't raid his stash. But this was just the beginning. By wintertime, we removed the messy black hulls, which stained our hands and clothes, and my father would crack those walnuts purposefully with a hammer on the basement's cold, hard concrete floor. We heard about people driving their cars back and forth over black walnuts just to loosen the hull and split the shell, but that was too reckless for my dad. When a fire was going in the fireplace, we'd sit around and pick out and eat the sweet meat inside. Black walnuts might have been work (much like raising children), but their flavor was sweet and pronounced, unlike any other food. I hope you enjoy them in this easy banana-chocolate brownie. You don't need to harvest your own—you can buy black walnuts at the natural foods store.

MAKES: 24 SQUARES
PREPARATION TIME: 12 MINUTES
BAKING TIME: 20 TO 25 MINUTES

Vegetable oil spray for misting the pan

1 ripe banana, peeled and mashed (½ cup)

1 package (19.8 ounces) brownie mix

8 tablespoons (1 stick) unsalted butter, melted

¼ cup water or buttermilk

3 large eggs

1½ cups semisweet chocolate chips

½ cup finely chopped black walnuts

1. Place a rack in the center of the oven and preheat the oven to 350°F. Lightly mist the bottom of a 13- by 9-inch pan with vegetable oil spray. Set the pan aside.

2. Place the mashed banana, brownie mix, melted butter, water, and eggs in a large mixing bowl. Stir with a wooden spoon until all the ingredients are incorporated and the batter lightens in texture, 50 strokes. Pour the batter into the prepared pan and spread it out evenly with a rubber spatula. Scatter the chocolate chips and black walnuts evenly on top. Place the pan in the oven.

3. Bake the brownies until the outer 2 inches form a crust and a toothpick inserted in this area comes out clean, 20 to 25 minutes. Remove the pan from the oven and place it on a wire rack to cool for 30 minutes.

4. Cut the brownies into 24 squares. They will mellow in flavor if left to rest for 2 hours.

❋ *Store these brownies, covered in plastic wrap or aluminum foil, at room temperature for up to 5 days. Or freeze them, wrapped in foil, for up to 6 months. Thaw the brownies overnight on the counter before serving.*

the Cake Mix Doctor says

If you can't find black walnuts, substitute English walnuts. They're delicious, too! Remember that the riper the banana, the more flavor it will have. And don't overbake these brownies. Let them cool thoroughly before slicing or you will think they have not cooked through.

RASPBERRY SWIRL BROWNIES

Nothing could be easier than doctoring up a box of brownie mix by swirling in some raspberry jam and a few chocolate chips. But let me tell you, these humble brownies taste mighty sophisticated! Look for the seedless raspberry jam in the supermarket, preferably the kind made with all fruit juice and less sugar.

MAKES: 24 SQUARES
PREPARATION TIME: 10 MINUTES
BAKING TIME: 23 TO 27 MINUTES

Vegetable oil spray for misting the pan
1 package (19.8 ounces) brownie mix
8 tablespoons (1 stick) unsalted butter,
   melted
⅓ cup water
2 large eggs
1 teaspoon pure vanilla extract
½ cup seedless raspberry jam
¼ cup semisweet chocolate chips
½ cup finely chopped pecans (optional)

1. Place a rack in the center of the oven and preheat the oven to 350°F. Lightly mist the bottom of a 13- by 9-inch pan with vegetable oil spray. Set the pan aside.

2. Place the brownie mix, melted butter, water, eggs, and vanilla in a large mixing bowl. Stir with a wooden spoon until all the ingredients are incorporated and the batter lightens in texture, 50 strokes. Pour the batter into the prepared pan, smoothing it out with a rubber spatula. Drop the raspberry jam by teaspoonfuls onto the batter, and with a dinner knife swirl the jam into the batter. Scatter the chocolate chips and the pecans evenly over the top. Place the pan in the oven.

3. Bake the brownies until the outer 2 inches have formed a crust and feel firm, 23 to 27 minutes. Remove the pan from the oven and place it on a wire rack to cool completely, 30 minutes.

4. Slice and serve the brownies.

✳ *Store these brownies, covered with plastic wrap or aluminum foil, at room temperature for up to 3 days or in the refrigerator for up to 1 week. Or freeze them, wrapped in foil, for up to 6 months. Thaw the brownies overnight on the counter before serving.*

R

the Cake Mix Doctor says

Instead of raspberry jam, swirl in ½ cup of orange marmalade before baking; omit the chocolate chips and cover with the Creamy Chocolate Frosting.

Frostings

· · ·

I f you think you can spread canned frosting on your glorious cake, just wait a minute. My mother has always said that you can get away with cake mix cake, but your frosting must be home-made. And I believe that she's right.

So, in this chapter you'll find all the toppings and fillings that you'll need to bedeck that gorgeous chocolate cake. You have creamy frostings made with butter and cream cheese, serious and sophisti-cated ganache made from heavy cream, a sour cream frosting that tastes scrump-tious spread on anything, as well as but-tercream frostings flavored with lemon, peach, even peppermint. To keep one foot firmly in my grandmother's kitchen, as well, I've included some cooked frostings that I call icings. They're a snap to prepare on top of the stove, but taste so delicious, it'll seem as if you've been cooking all day.

When frosting seems too much, go for a glaze—smooth, spreadable, and especially easy. Try the lighter Shiny Chocolate Glaze, the Chocolate Cinnamon Glaze, the Milk Chocolate Glaze, and even the luxurious White Chocolate Glaze that is out of this world spooned over white chocolate cake.

I have found that when making toppings and fillings, there is room for variation, depending on how much con-fectioners' sugar you add, how long you beat the frosting, or what temperature it is before it goes on the cake. It takes a little practice to know when a frosting is the right consistency to spread, or when a glaze is just the right thickness that it will cloak the cake and not run over the sides of the plate. Don't be afraid to ad-just these things as you prepare your frostings and sauces. And be sure to enjoy every frosted bite!

FLUFFY CHOCOLATE FROSTING

The most versatile of any frosting, use this creamy, wonderful chocolaty stuff to frost just about any cupcake, layer cake, or sheet cake. The version here has a stronger, more distinctly chocolate flavor than the one in *The Cake Mix Doctor*. The secret is in the boiling water, which wakes up the taste of cocoa. My children squabbled to get the first lick from the bowl!

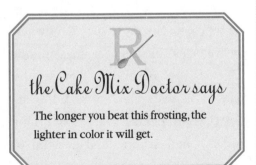

the Cake Mix Doctor says

The longer you beat this frosting, the lighter in color it will get.

MAKES 3 CUPS, ENOUGH TO FROST
A 2- OR 3-LAYER CAKE
OR 30 CUPCAKES

PREPARATION TIME: 10 MINUTES

⅔ cup unsweetened cocoa powder

6 tablespoons boiling water, plus additional
    if needed

8 tablespoons (1 stick) butter, at room
    temperature

3 cups confectioners' sugar, sifted, plus
    additional if needed

1 teaspoon pure vanilla extract

1. Place the cocoa powder in a large mixing bowl and pour the boiling water over it. Stir with a wooden spoon or rubber spatula until the cocoa comes together into a soft mass. Add the butter and blend with an electric mixer on low speed until the mixture is soft and well combined, 30 seconds. Stop the machine. Place the confectioners' sugar and vanilla in the bowl, and beat with the mixer on low speed until the sugar is incorporated, 1 minute. Increase the mixer speed to medium and beat until

Why Sift Confectioners' Sugar?

It may seem like an unnecessary step to sift confectioners' sugar before folding it into your favorite frosting, but if that sugar has lumps in it, and it invariably does, all the mixing in the world will not remove them. You can grate chocolate on top of the cake to disguise the lumps of sugar, or cover them with chopped nuts, but it would have been easier just to sift the sugar first.

The easiest way to sift confectioners' sugar is to place a large fine-mesh strainer or sieve over a medium-size mixing bowl and pour the measured sugar into the strainer; shake the strainer for a minute or two, and you'll have the sifted sugar in the bowl, ready for your recipe.

If you want to reduce the number of lumps in your confectioners' sugar, buy the sugar packaged in a bag rather than in a box. Reseal the bag tightly with a plastic bag clip or a piece of tape.

Always check the way the recipe describes the measurement of sugar: whether it is "3 cups confectioners' sugar, sifted," which means to measure, then sift, or "3 cups sifted confectioners' sugar," in which case the sugar needs to be sifted and then remeasured.

the frosting lightens and is fluffy, 2 minutes more. Add more boiling water, a teaspoon at a time, or more confectioners' sugar, a tablespoon at a time, if the frosting is too thick or too thin to your liking.

2. Use the frosting to frost the top and sides of the cake or cupcakes of your choice.

CHOCOLATE SOUR CREAM FROSTING

I love the Fluffy Chocolate Frosting, but this new kid on the block, a result of sheer experimentation and luck, has stolen my heart! It is much like a basic chocolate pan frosting in that you begin with melted butter and cocoa, but what makes it so luxurious to eat and so pleasurable to work with is the addition of sour cream. Try this frosting on the Chocolate Sour Cream Marble Cake (page 46), the Ever-So-Moist Chocolate Cake (page 37), burned toast, soda crackers, you name it!

MAKES 3 CUPS, ENOUGH TO FROST
A 2- OR 3-LAYER CAKE
OR 30 CUPCAKES
PREPARATION TIME: 10 MINUTES

8 tablespoons (1 stick) butter, cut into
    8 pieces
⅔ cup unsweetened cocoa powder
3 cups confectioners' sugar, sifted
⅓ cup sour cream
1 teaspoon pure vanilla extract

1. Melt the butter in a small saucepan over low heat or melt it in a large glass bowl in the microwave oven on high power for 45 seconds.

the Cake Mix Doctor says

If you make this frosting with regular cocoa, it will have a lighter chocolate color than if you make it with Dutch-process cocoa. It is perfect for contrasting with deep-chocolate layers.

2. Place the melted butter in a large mixing bowl and add the cocoa powder. Whisk until smooth. Add the confectioners' sugar alternately with the sour cream, blending with an electric mixer on low speed for 1 to 1½ minutes, or

until incorporated. Stop the machine and add the vanilla. Increase the mixer speed to medium and beat until light and fluffy, 1 minute more.

3. Use the frosting to frost the top and sides of the cake or cupcakes of your choice.

VANILLA BUTTERCREAM FROSTING

This is the first from-scratch frosting I ever made, and through the years I have changed and perfected it. I think the frosting works best when you add a cup of the confectioners' sugar up front, then add the rest alternately with the liquid. Cranking up the mixer speed incorporates some air and makes the frosting lighter. Use this frosting when you want the chocolate cake layers to shine, or when you're serving folks who aren't that crazy about chocolate. It's just right for the Chocolate Midnight Cake (page 55), Debbie's Dazzling Red Velvet Cake (page 88), or any of the cupcakes.

MAKES 3½ CUPS, ENOUGH TO FROST A 2- OR 3-LAYER CAKE

PREPARATION TIME: 5 MINUTES

8 tablespoons (1 stick) butter, at room temperature

2 teaspoons pure vanilla extract

4 cups confectioners' sugar, sifted

3 to 4 tablespoons milk

R

the Cake Mix Doctor says

Pure vanilla extract adds a lot to this basic frosting. Go ahead and add a full tablespoon (3 teaspoons) if you are crazy about vanilla. And shop around when it comes to purchasing vanilla. Try some of the fun, more upscale vanillas at specialty shops. But if you want the best price around on plain and simple pure vanilla, shop at the warehouse wholesale clubs for the 16-ounce bottles.

1. Place the butter, vanilla, and 1 cup of the confectioners' sugar in a large mixing bowl. Blend with an electric mixer on low speed to incorporate, 30 seconds. Add the remaining confectioners' sugar alternately with 3 tablespoons milk, 1 tablespoon at a time, blending with the mixer on low speed. Add another 1 tablespoon milk if the frosting seems too stiff. Increase the mixer speed to medium and beat until light and fluffy, 1 minute more.

2. Use to frost the top and sides of the cake of your choice.

CRUSHED PEPPERMINT BUTTERCREAM FROSTING

Pretty with crushed peppermint candy folded in, this frosting can be spread on the Chocolate Chiffon Cake (page 298) and the Chocolate Sour Cream Cupcakes (page 324). Then make the results even prettier by topping the cake or cupcakes with more crushed candy. The easiest way to crush hard candy is to place it in a clean kitchen towel, fold the ends over to enclose it, then whack the towel several times with a rolling pin. This is how my grandmother used to crush ice, long before there was a button on the freezer door. It relieves a lot of stress, too!

....

MAKES 3½ CUPS, ENOUGH TO FROST
A 2- OR 3-LAYER CAKE
OR 36 CUPCAKES

PREPARATION TIME: 10 MINUTES

....

8 tablespoons (1 stick) butter, at room temperature
½ teaspoon pure peppermint extract
3½ cups confectioners' sugar, sifted
3 to 4 tablespoons milk
½ cup crushed peppermint candy

R
the Cake Mix Doctor says

During the winter holidays you can find chocolate peppermint sticks in the stores. They are a fun substitute, crushed and added to this recipe instead of the regular peppermints.

1. Place the butter, peppermint extract, and 1 cup of the confectioners' sugar in a large mixing bowl. Blend with an electric mixer on low speed to incorporate, 30 seconds. Add the remaining confectioners' sugar alternately with 3 tablespoons milk, 1 tablespoon at a time, blending with the mixer on low speed. Add another 1 tablespoon milk if the frosting seems too stiff. Increase the mixer speed to medium and beat until light and fluffy, 1 minute more. Fold in the peppermint candy.

2. Use to frost the top and sides of the cake or cupcakes of your choice.

COFFEE BUTTERCREAM FROSTING

T his recipe comes from Rita Bagby, of Russiaville, Indiana, and it is delicious on her Chocolate Coffee Angel Food Cake (page 278). It is also good with chocolate added, for a mocha twist. To dress up the sides of the cake, press toasted almond slices lightly into this frosting. The flavors of almond and coffee are a pleasant match.

the Cake Mix Doctor says

For a mocha variation, add 2 tablespoons unsweetened cocoa along with the confectioners' sugar.

MAKES 3½ CUPS, ENOUGH TO FROST A 2- OR 3-LAYER CAKE

PREPARATION TIME: 10 MINUTES

¼ cup whole milk

2 tablespoons instant coffee granules

8 tablespoons (1 stick) butter, at room temperature

4 cups confectioners' sugar, sifted, plus additional if needed

1. Pour the milk into a small glass bowl and heat in the microwave oven on high power for 30 seconds, or until very hot. Stir in the coffee granules until they dissolve. Set the mixture aside.

2. Place the butter in a large mixing bowl. Blend with an electric mixer on low speed until fluffy, 30 seconds. Stop the machine and add 1 cup of the confectioners' sugar. Blend with the mixer on low speed until the sugar is

Letting Cakes Rest Before Serving

Cakes are like roasted chicken—they are easier to slice if left to rest. Now, the cake certainly doesn't need as much resting time as a chicken does, but it helps if after frosting or glazing, you let it rest at room temperature for at least 10 to 20 minutes before slicing.

incorporated, 30 seconds. Alternating, add the coffee mixture and the rest of the sugar, beating on low speed until smooth. Add more sugar if the frosting seems thin. Increase the mixer speed to medium and beat until lightened, 1 to 2 minutes more.

3. Use to frost the top and sides of the cake of your choice.

FRESH PEACH BUTTERCREAM FROSTING

You get better frosting if you use ripe summer peaches. So, if you've frozen sweetened peaches for use all year long, now's the time to pull them out of the freezer. Spread this yummy frosting liberally on the White Chocolate Peach Cake (page 90), or for an unexpected treat on the Ever-So-Moist Chocolate Cake (page 37).

the Cake Mix Doctor says

It's tricky adding fruit purées to buttercream frostings. You must add just a little—3 to 4 tablespoons—or the frosting will have too much liquid and no amount of confectioners' sugar will thicken it. Use the best peaches, real butter, not margarine, and pure vanilla extract, not imitation vanilla.

MAKES 3½ CUPS, ENOUGH TO FROST A 2- OR 3-LAYER CAKE

PREPARATION TIME: 10 MINUTES

8 tablespoons (1 stick) butter, at room temperature

3¾ cups confectioners' sugar, sifted

3 to 4 tablespoons puréed fresh or thawed frozen peaches

½ teaspoon pure vanilla extract

1. Place the butter in a large mixing bowl. Blend with an electric mixer on low speed until fluffy, 30 seconds. Stop the machine and add the confectioners' sugar, 3 tablespoons peach purée, and vanilla. Blend with the mixer on low speed until the sugar is incorporated, 1 minute. Increase the speed to medium and beat until light and fluffy, 1 minute more. Blend in another 1 tablespoon peach purée if the frosting seems too stiff.

2. Use to frost the top and sides of the cake of your choice.

LEMON BUTTERCREAM FROSTING

This is a pretty frosting, whether spread onto the Raspberry-Peach White Chocolate Cupcakes (page 333), the Chocolate Sour Cream Cupcakes (page 324), or the Little White Chocolate Pound Cakes (page 336). Lemon is a versatile flavoring, suitable for any time of the year. Always use fresh lemon juice and zest.

MAKES 3½ CUPS, ENOUGH TO FROST A 2- OR 3-LAYER CAKE OR 30 CUPCAKES

PREPARATION TIME: 10 MINUTES

8 tablespoons (1 stick) butter, at room temperature

4 cups confectioners' sugar, sifted

2 to 3 tablespoons milk

1 tablespoon fresh lemon juice

1 teaspoon grated lemon zest

R the Cake Mix Doctor says

When lemons are cold, they don't like to give up much juice. To make a refrigerated lemon juicier, warm it under hot tap water before slicing and juicing.

1. Place the butter and 1 cup of the confectioners' sugar in a large mixing bowl. Blend with an electric mixer on low speed to incorporate, 30 seconds. Add the remaining confectioners' sugar alternately with 2 tablespoons milk, 1 tablespoon at a time, and the lemon juice, blending with the mixer on low. Stir in the lemon zest. Add another 1 tablespoon milk if the frosting seems too stiff. Increase the mixer speed to medium and beat until light and fluffy, 1 minute more.

2. Use to frost the top and sides of the cake or cupcakes of your choice.

CREAM CHEESE FROSTING

I used to think that cream cheese frostings were too heavy, but now I have discovered this lighter version, using part cream cheese and part butter. The addition of cream cheese makes a frosting less sweet and is a nice complement to cakes, especially chocolate. This is just the right frosting for Debbie's Dazzling Red Velvet Cake (page 88), the Chocolate Midnight Cake (page 55), and the Chocolate Carrot Cake (page 177).

MAKES 3½ CUPS, ENOUGH TO FROST
A 2- OR 3-LAYER CAKE
PREPARATION TIME: 5 MINUTES

1 package (8 ounces) cream cheese, at room
    temperature
8 tablespoons (1 stick) butter, at room
    temperature
3¾ cups confectioners' sugar, sifted, plus
    additional if needed
2 teaspoons pure vanilla extract

1. Place the cream cheese and butter in a large mixing bowl. Blend with an electric mixer on low speed until combined, 30 seconds. Add the confectioners' sugar, a little at a time, blending with the mixer on low speed until the sugar is well incorporated, 1 minute. Add more sugar as needed to make the frosting spreadable. Add the vanilla, then increase the mixer speed to medium and blend until the frosting is fluffy, 1 minute more.

2. Use this frosting to frost the top and sides of the cake or cupcakes of your choice.

R
the Cake Mix Doctor says

To save fat and calories, use reduced-fat cream cheese. Make sure your cream cheese is soft before beginning this frosting. If it is cold, unwrap the package, remove the foil, and place the cream cheese on a plate in the microwave oven on high for 20 to 30 seconds. Don't substitute margarine for the butter, however.

GERMAN CHOCOLATE CREAM CHEESE FROSTING

When I was developing the recipe for the Chocolate Coconut Cream Cake (page 167), I thought it made sense to come up with a cream cheese frosting that contained German chocolate as well. This is a silky smooth, beautiful frosting, and it would be spectacular on any of the German chocolate sheet cakes, the German Chocolate Cake (page 66), or the German Chocolate Spice Cake (page 69).

MAKES 3½ CUPS, ENOUGH TO FROST
A 2- OR 3-LAYER CAKE
OR A 13- BY 9-INCH CAKE

PREPARATION TIME: 10 MINUTES

*1 bar (4 ounces) German chocolate, coarsely
    chopped*
*1 package (8 ounces) cream cheese, at room
    temperature*
1 tablespoon milk
1 teaspoon pure vanilla extract
4 cups confectioners' sugar, sifted

1. Place the chocolate in a small glass bowl in the microwave oven, and melt on high power for 1½ minutes. Stir until all the chocolate has melted, and set the bowl aside.

2. Place the cream cheese in a large mixing bowl. Blend with an electric mixer on low speed until well combined, 30 seconds. Stop the machine. Add the melted chocolate, and blend with the mixer on low speed until the chocolate is incorporated, 30 seconds. Add the milk, vanilla, and 3½ cups of the confectioners' sugar, and blend on low speed until the sugar is incorporated, 30 seconds. Add more sugar as needed to make the frosting spread- able. Increase the mixer speed to medium and blend until the frosting is fluffy, 1 minute more.

3. Use to frost the top and sides of the cake of your choice.

the Cake Mix Doctor says

This is too much frosting to frost just the top of a sheet cake. Invert the cake onto a serving platter and frost the sides, too.

CINNAMON-CHOCOLATE CREAM CHEESE FROSTING

Whenever I make up this frosting, I can't decide what to do first— slather it on the Chocolate Pumpkin Spice Cake (page 195) or pop a big spoonful into my mouth! Flavored with dark Dutch-process cocoa and ground cinnamon, it is a perennial as far as I am concerned, delicious on any dark chocolate layer cake or cupcake in this book.

R the Cake Mix Doctor says

To lighten the color of this frosting, use regular unsweetened cocoa powder. Cream cheese frostings are a snap to prepare the day ahead—just chill and then let come to room temperature while the cake bakes.

MAKES 3½ CUPS, ENOUGH TO FROST
A 2- OR 3-LAYER CAKE

PREPARATION TIME: 5 MINUTES

1 package (8 ounces) cream cheese, at room temperature

8 tablespoons (1 stick) butter, at room temperature

½ cup Dutch-process unsweetened cocoa powder

1 teaspoon ground cinnamon

1 teaspoon pure vanilla extract

4 cups confectioners' sugar, sifted

1. Place the cream cheese and the butter in a large mixing bowl. Blend with an electric mixer on low speed until well combined, 30 seconds. Stop the machine. Add the cocoa powder, cinnamon, vanilla, and 3¾ cups of the confectioners' sugar. Blend with the mixer

Leaning Tower of Cake

*I*f the weather is really warm, the cake is warm, and the frosting is gooey and warm, well, you have just the right combination for . . . a leaning tower of cake! Don't let this happen. When I tested the layer cake chapter, it was summertime, and I learned to use the freezer to my advantage. (Pastry chefs do this.) Place the bottom layer of the cake on a cardboard round and frost the top of it; then place it in the freezer to firm up for a few minutes. Pull the layer out, place the top layer on, frost the top and sides of the entire cake, then return the cake to the freezer to firm up for a few more minutes. Remove the cake, and store it as the recipe suggests.

Another trick in hot weather is to assemble the layer cake with bottoms facing each other so the cake doesn't slide. Place the first layer bottom side up on the plate and frost it; then place the second layer bottom side down on top of the first layer, and frost it. Frost the top and sides of the cake as you normally would.

on low speed until the ingredients are moistened, 30 seconds. Add more sugar if the frosting seems too thin. Increase the speed to medium and beat until the frosting is fluffy, 2 minutes more.

2. Use to frost the top and sides of the cake of your choice.

WHITE CHOCOLATE CREAM CHEESE FROSTING

This recipe begs repeating. It is one of my favorites from *The Cake Mix Doctor*, and it is just perfect for all the white chocolate cakes in this book. It's also delicious on any of the dark chocolate layer cakes or chocolate cupcakes. Add a few drops of food coloring, and it turns red, green, or orange for holiday parties.

MAKES 3 CUPS, ENOUGH TO FROST
A 2- OR 3-LAYER CAKE

PREPARATION TIME: 10 MINUTES

6 ounces white chocolate, coarsely
    chopped

1 package (8 ounces) cream cheese, at
    room temperature

4 tablespoons (½ stick) butter, at room
    temperature

1 teaspoon pure vanilla extract

3 cups confectioners' sugar, sifted

1. Place the white chocolate in a small glass bowl in the microwave oven on high power for 1 minute. Remove the bowl from the oven and stir with a wooden spoon or a rubber spatula until it is smooth. (See Melting White Chocolate, page 92.) Set the chocolate aside to cool.

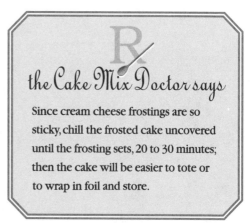

the Cake Mix Doctor says

Since cream cheese frostings are so sticky, chill the frosted cake uncovered until the frosting sets, 20 to 30 minutes; then the cake will be easier to tote or to wrap in foil and store.

2. Place the cream cheese and butter in a large mixing bowl. Beat with an electric mixer on low speed until well combined, 30 seconds. Stop the machine. Add the melted white chocolate and blend on low speed until just combined, 30 seconds. Add the vanilla and 2½ cups of the confectioners' sugar, and blend on low speed until the sugar is incorporated, 30 seconds more. Add more sugar as needed to make the frosting spreadable. Increase the mixer speed to medium and beat until the frosting is fluffy, 1 minute more.

3. Use to frost the top and sides of the cake of your choice.

LEMONY WHITE CHOCOLATE CREAM CHEESE FROSTING

This frosting for the Lemon Lovers' White Chocolate Cake (page 93) is also delicious on a basic angel food cake. One medium lemon will yield about 1 tablespoon juice and 1 teaspoon zest.

....

MAKES 3 CUPS, ENOUGH TO FROST A
2- OR 3-LAYER CAKE

PREPARATION TIME: 10 MINUTES

....

6 ounces white chocolate, coarsely chopped

*1 package (8 ounces) cream cheese, at room
     temperature*

*4 tablespoons (½ stick) butter, at room
     temperature*

1 tablespoon fresh lemon juice

1 teaspoon grated lemon zest

3 cups confectioners' sugar, sifted

1. Place the white chocolate in a small glass bowl in the microwave oven on high power for 1 minute. Remove the bowl from the oven and stir with a wooden spoon or a rubber spatula until it is smooth. (See Melting White Chocolate, page 92.) Set the chocolate aside to cool.

2. Place the cream cheese and butter in a large mixing bowl. Beat with an electric mixer on low speed until well combined, 30 seconds. Stop the machine. Add the lemon juice, lemon zest, and melted white chocolate, and blend on low speed until just combined, 30 seconds. Add the confectioners' sugar and blend on low speed until the sugar is incorporated, 30 seconds. Increase the mixer speed to medium and beat until the frosting is fluffy, 1 minute more.

3. Use to frost the top and sides of the cake of your choice.

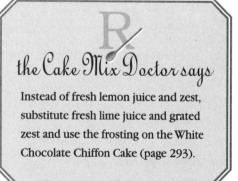

the Cake Mix Doctor says

Instead of fresh lemon juice and zest, substitute fresh lime juice and grated zest and use the frosting on the White Chocolate Chiffon Cake (page 293).

FRESH ORANGE CREAM CHEESE FROSTING

Since my grandmother always made a fresh orange layer cake for Christmas Eve, I am partial to any cake with an orange frosting. This frosting is easy to prepare, using ingredients you likely have on hand. It dresses up the Dark Chocolate Sheet Cake (page 197) as well as the White Chocolate Wedding Cake (page 207).

....

MAKES 3 CUPS, ENOUGH TO FROST A 2- OR 3-LAYER CAKE OR A 13- BY 9-INCH CAKE

PREPARATION TIME: 10 MINUTES

....

1 package (8 ounces) cream cheese, at room temperature

8 tablespoons (1 stick) butter, at room temperature

3 cups confectioners' sugar, sifted

2 tablespoons fresh orange juice

1 tablespoon grated orange zest

1. Place the cream cheese and butter in a large mixing bowl. Blend with an electric mixer on low speed until well combined, 30 seconds. Add the confectioners' sugar, a little at a time, blending with the mixer on low speed until the sugar is well combined, 1 minute. Add the orange juice and zest to the mixture. Increase the mixer speed to medium and beat until the frosting lightens and is fluffy, 1 minute more.

2. Use to frost the top and sides of the cake of your choice.

R
the Cake Mix Doctor says

No fresh oranges? Good carton orange juice will do, especially if it contains pulp. Just omit the orange zest; or if you have a lemon, add 1 teaspoon grated lemon zest instead. For a totally grown-up cake, use half orange juice and half Grand Marnier or another orange liqueur.

ORANGE-COCOA CREAM CHEESE FROSTING

Bob Showalter, of Duncan, South Carolina, who loves to bake cakes, sent me this frosting recipe one spring. He had been frosting my devil's food cakes with it, and he promised that the chocolate and orange combination would taste very European. Bob was right. And adding that orange liqueur helps, too! This frosting is superb on the Chocolate Orange Cake (page 81); or omit the liqueur and frost the Orange Swirl Chocolate Cupcakes (page 329) for the children's school parties.

....

MAKES 3½ CUPS, ENOUGH TO FROST
A 2- OR 3-LAYER CAKE
OR 36 CUPCAKES

PREPARATION TIME: 10 MINUTES

....

1 package (8 ounces) cream cheese, at room temperature

4 tablespoons (½ stick) butter, at room temperature

¼ cup unsweetened cocoa powder

1 teaspoon pure orange extract

3¾ cups confectioners' sugar, sifted

1 to 2 tablespoons orange liqueur, such as Grand Marnier, Cointreau, or Triple Sec

R the Cake Mix Doctor says

If you don't want to add alcohol to this recipe, use orange juice instead. And for a powerful flavor punch, instead of orange extract try ½ teaspoon orange oil. This is a highly concentrated flavor distilled from the zest of many, many oranges. It is expensive, and if you can locate it at a specialty shop, enjoy it and use it sparingly.

Citrus Oils

It's tricky to incorporate flavors into frostings. You need only 3 to 4 tablespoons of liquid, total, in most buttercream frostings and often none at all in cream cheese frostings, so how to pass along an interesting flavor? Opt for orange, lemon, or peppermint extract. Or try a citrus oil. Boyajian, of Norwood, Massachusetts, produces orange, lemon, and lime oils. The oil is made by cold-pressing the rind of the fruit, much like pressing olives to make fine olive oil. These oils are pricey, but they pack a lot of flavor into just $\frac{1}{2}$ teaspoon. And oils are a good substitute should you not want to add grated zest to a frosting or glaze.

1. Place the cream cheese and butter in a large mixing bowl. Blend with an electric mixer on low speed until fluffy, 30 seconds. Stop the machine and add the cocoa powder, orange extract, confectioners' sugar, and 1 tablespoon orange liqueur. Blend with the mixer on low speed until the sugar is well combined, 1 minute. Increase the speed to medium and beat until light and fluffy, 1 minute more. If the frosting seems too stiff, blend in another 1 tablespoon liqueur.

2. Use to frost the top and sides of the cake or cupcakes of your choice.

PINEAPPLE CREAM CHEESE FROSTING

hen the frosting is important—when you want your cake to make a big impression—then this is the one to use. Spread it on Chocolate Banana Cupcakes (page 327), Chocolate Sour Cream Cupcakes (page 324), and sheet cakes like the Chocolate Carrot Cake (page 177) and the Chocolate Rum Raisin Cake (page 188). It has a faint island flavor, and in the depths of winter it will have you dreaming of the beach.

....

MAKES 4 CUPS, ENOUGH TO FROST
A 2- OR 3-LAYER CAKE,
A 13- BY 9-INCH CAKE,
OR 36 CUPCAKES

PREPARATION TIME: 10 MINUTES

....

1 can (8 ounces) crushed pineapple
    in its own juice, well drained
1 package (8 ounces) cream cheese,
    at room temperature
8 tablespoons (1 stick) butter, at room
    temperature
4 cups confectioners' sugar,
    sifted
½ teaspoon ground
    cinnamon (optional)

R. the Cake Mix Doctor says

This recipe makes a lot of frosting. You will need only about half a recipe to frost most cupcake recipes. And the cinnamon flavor is totally optional—you may not want to add it if there is cinnamon in the cake you are frosting.

Pack the well-drained pineapple into a ⅓-cup measure. Set it aside.

2. Place the cream cheese and butter in a large mixing bowl. Blend with an electric mixer on low speed until combined, 30 seconds. Add the confectioners' sugar, a little at a time, blending with the mixer on low speed until the sugar is combined, 1 minute. Add the reserved pineapple and the cinnamon, if desired. Increase the mixer speed to medium and beat until the frosting lightens and is fluffy, 1 minute more.

3. Use to frost the top and sides of the cake or cupcakes of your choice.

MARTHA'S CHOCOLATE ICING

Smoother and sleeker than a frosting, more substantial than a glaze, this generous chocolate coating, which is briefly cooked, brings glory to the category of "icing." Pour it over Bundt cakes, spread it on cupcakes and sheet cakes, or just spoon it on top of vanilla ice cream. It was Martha Bowden and her mother, Shirley Hutson, who shared their cherished recipe with me.

....

MAKES 1½ CUPS, ENOUGH TO FROST A BUNDT OR TUBE CAKE, 24 CUPCAKES, OR A 13- BY 9-INCH CAKE

PREPARATION TIME: 8 MINUTES

....

1 cup granulated sugar
5 tablespoons butter
⅓ cup whole milk
1 cup semisweet chocolate chips

1. Place the sugar, butter, and milk in a medium-size saucepan over medium-high heat. Stir until the mixture comes to a boil, 3 to 4 minutes. Still stirring, let the mixture boil until the sugar dissolves, 1 minute. Remove the pan from the heat.

2. Stir in the chocolate chips, and continue to stir until the mixture is smooth and the chocolate has melted.

3. Spread the icing over the cooled cake or cupcakes of your choice.

R℞
the Cake Mix Doctor says

This icing thickens up as it sits. Hot from the stove, it can be spooned over Bundt cakes—the icing will trickle down the sides. It can be poured on top of sheet cakes and spread with a metal spatula to reach the edges. But wait until it thickens up a bit before icing cupcakes, so the precious icing will be firm enough to stay on top.

CHOCOLATE PAN FROSTING

If you enjoyed this frosting recipe in my first book, you will notice that the quantities have changed slightly. That's because people said they wanted more of this fudgy frosting—enough for a thick coat instead of a thin one—and I can't blame them! Spread Chocolate Pan Frosting onto layer cakes while it is still warm. It will set up as it cools.

MAKES 4 CUPS, ENOUGH TO FROST
A 2- OR 3-LAYER CAKE

PREPARATION TIME: 10 MINUTES

12 tablespoons (1½ sticks) butter
½ cup unsweetened cocoa powder
½ cup whole milk
5½ cups confectioners' sugar, sifted

R the Cake Mix Doctor says

When working with warm frostings, it's important to have your tools at hand. You will need a ladle for spooning some of the frosting over the first layer of cake. Use a thin metal spatula (not a pancake flipper!) to spread the frosting to the edges. Place the second layer on top of the first and now spoon on more frosting. This will be the top of the cake (unless it's a three-layer cake), so either make clean, smooth strokes or wiggle the spatula back and forth for a decorative rippled look. Now to the sides: If the frosting starts to harden, place the pan back over low heat and stir until it is soft again. With the metal spatula, transfer the frosting bit by bit to the sides of the cake, first making a thin coat to seal in the crumbs, then a thicker coat to cover the first. *Voilà!*

1. Melt the butter in a medium-size saucepan over low heat, 2 to 3 minutes. Stir in the cocoa powder and milk. Cook another minute, stirring, until the mixture thickens and just begins to come to a boil. Remove the pan from the heat. Stir in 5 cups of the confectioners' sugar, adding more if needed, until the frosting is thickened and smooth and the consistency of hot fudge sauce.

2. Ladle the warm frosting liberally over the top of a cooled cake of your choice, spreading it with a metal spatula so that it reaches the edges of the cake. Spread the sides of the cake with more frosting, smoothing it out with a long metal spatula as you go. It will harden as it cools. Work quickly because this frosting goes on best while still warm.

PERFECT CHOCOLATE FROSTING

As a newspaper food editor, I used to cringe when I saw words like "perfect" in a recipe because, after all, food is subjective. What is perfect to me might not be to you. But I really

must call this frosting perfect. If you follow this recipe to the letter, you will make the most satiny, delicious chocolate frosting imaginable. And yes, it does call for a whole cup of butter. No wonder it tastes so good and spreads on so easily!

....

MAKES 3½ CUPS, ENOUGH TO FROST
A 2- OR 3-LAYER CAKE

PREPARATION TIME: 15 MINUTES

....

1 cup semisweet chocolate chips
½ cup half-and-half
1 cup (2 sticks) butter, cut into tablespoons
2½ cups confectioners' sugar, sifted

1. Place a large mixing bowl full of ice in the kitchen sink.

2. Place the chocolate chips, half-and-half, and butter in a medium-size saucepan over medium heat. Stir the mixture constantly until the chips and butter melt and the mixture thickens, 5 to 6 minutes. Do not let it boil. Remove the pan from the heat.

R
the Cake Mix Doctor says

Since you need to beat the frosting with an electric mixer while it is still in the saucepan, use a pan without a nonstick coating, which might chip. And remember to always measure confectioners' sugar first, then sift it, unless the recipe calls for "sifted confectioners' sugar."

3. Whisk the confectioners' sugar into the mixture until it becomes smooth. Then, place the saucepan in the bowl of ice, taking special care not to let any of the ice water spill into the saucepan. Beat the mixture with an electric mixer set on low speed until the frosting thickens and is satiny and fudgelike in appearance, 4 to 5 minutes.

4. Spread onto the cake of your choice. The frosting will stiffen up as it sets. If it gets too hard to spread, simply place the saucepan back over low heat and stir until it reaches spreading consistency.

ROCKY ROAD FROSTING

Use this on the German Chocolate Sheet Cake (page 66), as well as the Dark Chocolate Sheet Cake (page 197). It is also delicious on cupcakes such as the Chocolate Sour Cream Cupcakes (page 324).

MAKES 1½ CUPS, ENOUGH TO FROST
A 13- BY 9-INCH CAKE
OR 24 CUPCAKES

PREPARATION TIME: 10 MINUTES

1 cup sugar

5 tablespoons butter

⅓ cup whole milk

1 cup semisweet chocolate chips

¾ cup chopped dry-roasted peanuts

¾ cup miniature marshmallows

1. Place the sugar, butter, and milk in a small saucepan over medium-low heat and cook, stirring constantly, until the mixture comes to a boil, 3 to 4 minutes. Boil, stirring constantly, for 1 minute. Remove the pan from the heat, add the chocolate chips, and stir until they are melted.

2. Let the pan rest off the heat to cool slightly but not completely, 3 to 4 minutes. Fold in the peanuts and marshmallows until they are well combined and the heat from the frosting begins to melt the marshmallows.

3. Turn the frosting out onto a cooled sheet cake, then spread evenly with a spatula until the frosting covers the entire cake. Or spread on cooled cupcakes.

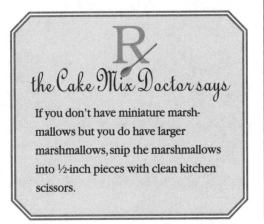

R
the Cake Mix Doctor says

If you don't have miniature marshmallows but you do have larger marshmallows, snip the marshmallows into ½-inch pieces with clean kitchen scissors.

CHOCOLATE MARSHMALLOW FROSTING

Use this wonderful frosting on the Incredible Mocha Melted Ice Cream Cake (page 114) and other pound cakes when you want a chocolate topping that tastes great, looks elegant, and transports well.

....

MAKES 1½ CUPS, ENOUGH TO FROST
A BUNDT CAKE, TUBE CAKE,
13- BY 9-INCH CAKE,
OR 24 CUPCAKES, OR TO THINLY
FROST A 2-LAYER CAKE

PREPARATION TIME: 10 MINUTES

....

the Cake Mix Doctor says

This frosting needs to be spread on while it is warm, so have your cake ready before getting the frosting started. If it gets hard, return it to low heat and stir until it is spreadable again.

2 cups confectioners' sugar

½ cup unsweetened cocoa powder

¾ cup marshmallow creme

4 tablespoons (½ stick) butter

¼ cup whole milk

1 teaspoon pure vanilla extract

1. Sift the sugar and cocoa powder together into a large mixing bowl. Set the bowl aside.

2. Place the marshmallow creme, butter, and milk in a medium-size heavy saucepan over medium-low heat. Stir until the butter and marshmallow creme have melted, 2 to 3 minutes. Remove the pan from the heat. Pour the sugar-cocoa mixture over the marshmallow mixture. Add the vanilla and stir until the frosting is smooth and satiny.

3. Use to frost the cake or cupcakes of your choice.

QUICK CARAMEL FROSTING

Just because this is a chocolate book, don't think for a minute that I would snub my favorite caramel frosting! It is so good covering the Chocolate Cinnamon Banana Cake (page 58), the Little White Chocolate Pound Cakes (page 336), and the White Chocolate Chiffon Cake (page 293). Chocolate and caramel are natural partners. The beauty of this recipe is that you start out with brown sugar so you don't have to go through the laborious step of caramelizing white granulated sugar.

MAKES 3 CUPS, ENOUGH TO FROST
A 2- OR 3-LAYER CAKE

PREPARATION TIME: 10 MINUTES

8 tablespoons (1 stick) butter
½ cup (packed) light brown sugar
½ cup (packed) dark brown sugar

R the Cake Mix Doctor says

If the frosting hardens, place the pan back over low heat and stir until it softens up. And when measuring the brown sugar, be sure to pack the sugar down into the cup measure.

¼ cup whole milk
2 cups confectioners' sugar, sifted
1 teaspoon pure vanilla extract

1. Place the butter and both brown sugars in a medium-size heavy saucepan over medium heat. Cook, stirring, until the mixture comes to a boil, about 2 minutes. Add the milk, stir, and bring the mixture back to a boil. Then remove the pan from the heat. Add the confectioners' sugar and vanilla. Beat with a wooden spoon until the frosting is smooth.

2. Use immediately (while still warm) to frost the cake of your choice.

CHOCOLATE GANACHE

Ganache tastes like it is a lot more trouble to prepare than it is. It is the ultimate chocolate frosting for those who love the taste of dark bitter chocolate. Spread it on the cake just as it is beginning to thicken. Unlike pan frostings, ganache will not set up hard. It will continue to have a wet look and a soft texture.

MAKES 1¾ CUPS, ENOUGH
TO THINLY FROST
A 2- OR 3-LAYER CAKE
PREPARATION TIME: 5 MINUTES

¾ cup heavy (whipping) cream
8 ounces semisweet chocolate, coarsely
    chopped
1 tablespoon liqueur of your choice (optional)

1. Place the cream in a small heavy saucepan over medium heat and bring to a boil, stirring. Meanwhile, place the chopped chocolate (or semisweet chocolate chips; see "the Cake Mix Doctor says") in a large stainless-steel mixing bowl. Remove the cream from the heat, and pour it over the chocolate. Stir with a wooden spoon until the chocolate is melted. Stir in the liqueur if desired.

2. To use this ganache as a glaze, let it stand at room temperature for 10 minutes before spooning it over a cooled cake. To use the ganache as a frosting, let it stand for 30 minutes at room temperature, or chill it for 10 minutes, until it has thickened enough to spread with a metal spatula.

R
the Cake Mix Doctor says

To save chopping, and if you like a slightly sweeter ganache, use 1⅓ cups semisweet chocolate chips instead of the chopped chocolate.

You can even make this ganache in the food processor: Process the chocolate until it is broken into small pieces; then, with the machine running, pour the hot cream into the feed tube and continue to process until the ganache is smooth.

WHIPPED CHOCOLATE GANACHE

You've seen this gorgeous fluffy frosting on wedding cakes and other fancy cakes, and while this recipe may look more elaborate than others, it is quite simple to prepare. You just chill and then whip the chocolate ganache as you would whip cream. What results is a frosting that is lighter in color than other chocolate frostings, and often with pretty streaks of dark chocolate. You can begin with semisweet bar chocolate, semisweet chocolate chips, or even miniature Hershey's Kisses. Should you like a sweeter frosting, taste the ganache before you whip it, and add up to ¼ cup confectioners' sugar as it is being whipped.

MAKES 3 CUPS, ENOUGH TO FROST
A 2- OR 3-LAYER CAKE

PREPARATION TIME: 15 MINUTES
CHILLING TIME: 30 MINUTES

¾ cup heavy (whipping) cream
8 ounces semisweet chocolate, coarsely
    chopped, or 1⅓ cups semisweet
    chocolate chips, or 1¾ cups miniature
    Hershey's Kisses
1 tablespoon liqueur of your choice (optional)

1. Place the cream in a small heavy saucepan over medium heat, and bring to a boil, stirring. Meanwhile, place the chocolate in a large stainless-steel mixing bowl.

2. Remove the cream from the heat, and pour it over the chocolate. Stir with a wooden spoon until the chocolate is melted. Stir in the liqueur if desired.

3. Place the bowl, uncovered, in the refrigerator to chill for at least 30 minutes, or preferably 1 hour. Place the electric mixer beaters in the refrigerator to chill.

4. Remove the bowl and beaters from the refrigerator. Using the chilled beaters, whip the ganache on high speed for 2 to 3 minutes, or until the frosting lightens in color and triples in volume. Spread on the cake of your choice. Store leftover frosted cake in the refrigerator.

the Cake Mix Doctor says

Tiny dark flecks will appear when the chocolate is melted and chilled, creating an attractive contrast to the overall pale color of the frosting. I like to prepare ganache in a stainless-steel bowl because the metal cools down quickly, unlike glass or ceramic bowls, which tend to retain the heat.

WHITE CHOCOLATE GANACHE

I am stretching things a bit to call this frosting a ganache, as it is not as thick and rich as the dark chocolate version. It takes twice as much white chocolate as dark to make a ganache, but the taste is spectacular, and the consistency is delicate and transparent. Buy the best white chocolate you can, making sure it contains cocoa butter. Drizzle this into the Luscious Lemon White Chocolate Terrine (page 244), or spoon it over Little Chocolate Almond Cream Cheese Cakes (page 338) for a memorable topping.

MAKES 1¾ CUPS, ENOUGH
TO THINLY FROST A BUNDT CAKE
OR A 2-LAYER CAKE

PREPARATION TIME: 5 MINUTES

¾ cup heavy (whipping) cream

1 pound white chocolate, coarsely chopped

1. Place the cream in a small heavy saucepan over medium heat, and bring to a boil, stirring. Meanwhile, place the chopped white chocolate in a large stainless-steel mixing bowl.

2. Remove the cream from the heat, and pour it over the white chocolate. Stir with a wooden spoon until the white chocolate is melted.

3. To use this ganache as a glaze, let it stand at room temperature for 10 minutes before spooning over a cooled cake.

R the Cake Mix Doctor says

To make whipped white chocolate ganache, chill the bowl of ganache, uncovered, in the refrigerator for 30 minutes to 1 hour. With chilled beaters, whip it on medium speed until thickened, 2 minutes. Spread between chocolate cake layers for a rich and surprising filling.

SWEETENED CREAM

There's nothing fancy about this recipe—heavy cream is whipped with a little sugar and vanilla for flavoring—and yet it is so delicious. Use it on top of or between layers of many cakes in this book.

MAKES 2 CUPS, ENOUGH TO
GENEROUSLY FILL OR
THINLY FROST A 2-LAYER CAKE,
A BUNDT CAKE, A TUBE CAKE,
OR A 13- BY 9-INCH CAKE
PREPARATION TIME: 4 MINUTES

1 cup heavy (whipping) cream
¼ cup confectioners' sugar, sifted, or to
    taste
½ teaspoon pure vanilla extract or pure
    almond extract

How to Fold

If you're just coming to baking, to you "folding" might refer to card tables, or cards, or worse, laundry! But when it has to do with baking, folding is the down-across-up-over motion used to incorporate whipped cream or beaten egg whites into heavier ingredients without losing the precious air in the batter. To fold properly, as needed for the chiffon cakes or the Cookies and Cream Cake (page 61), turn the beaten egg whites or whipped cream out of the bowl on top of the heavier ingredients. Using a rubber spatula and, beginning at the back of the bowl, gently cut down through the whipped cream or egg whites and the batter, across the bottom of the bowl, and up to the side nearest you. Rotate the bowl a quarter turn after every few strokes. Fold until the batter as a whole lightens in color and texture, and no traces of whipped cream or egg whites remain.

R

the Cake Mix Doctor says

Cream will whip best if the beaters and bowl are chilled. You can do this in the refrigerator for 10 to 15 minutes, or in the freezer for just a few minutes.

1. Chill a large, clean mixing bowl and electric mixer beaters in the freezer for a few minutes while you assemble the ingredients.

2. Pour the cream into the chilled bowl, and beat with the electric mixer on high speed until it thickens, 1½ minutes. Stop the machine and add the confectioners' sugar and the vanilla extract. Beat the cream on high speed until stiff peaks form, 1 to 2 minutes more.

3. Use to frost the cake of your choice.

CHOCOLATE DREAM GLAZE

This glaze goes on like a dream because of the corn syrup. It coats the Dark Chocolate Roulade (page 256) easily, and is delicious on any angel food cake, Bundt cake, or cupcakes.

....

MAKES 1 CUP, ENOUGH
TO FROST THE TOP
OF A BUNDT CAKE, ROULADE,
TUBE CAKE, OR 24 CUPCAKES
PREPARATION TIME: 5 MINUTES

....

1 cup semisweet chocolate chips
4 tablespoons (½ stick) butter
2 tablespoons light corn syrup

1. Place the chocolate chips, butter, and corn syrup in a large glass bowl and place in the microwave oven on high power for 1 to 1½ minutes. Remove the bowl from the oven and stir with a wire whisk until the

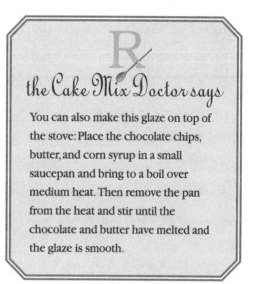

the Cake Mix Doctor says

You can also make this glaze on top of the stove: Place the chocolate chips, butter, and corn syrup in a small saucepan and bring to a boil over medium heat. Then remove the pan from the heat and stir until the chocolate and butter have melted and the glaze is smooth.

butter and chocolate have melted and the glaze is smooth and spreadable.

2. Use to frost the cake or cupcakes of your choice.

MILK CHOCOLATE GLAZE

Those of you who don't like dark chocolate will love the subtle flavor of this creamy glaze, especially on the Milk Chocolate Cherry Pound Cake (page 122). It is also good poured over any dark chocolate pound cake or angel food cake.

....

MAKES ¾ CUP, ENOUGH TO FROST THE TOP OF A BUNDT OR TUBE CAKE

PREPARATION TIME: 5 MINUTES

....

4 bars (1.55 ounces each) milk chocolate

¼ cup confectioners' sugar, sifted

1 teaspoon pure vanilla extract

¼ cup whole milk or heavy (whipping) cream

1. Break up the milk chocolate bars into 1-inch pieces, then place them in a medium-size glass bowl. Microwave them at medium power for 2½ to 3 minutes, stirring until smooth. Or melt the chocolate in a small saucepan over low heat, stirring constantly, until smooth, 2 to 2½ minutes. Stir in the confectioners' sugar, vanilla, and milk. Mix the frosting until it is smooth.

2. Spoon this glaze over the cake of your choice.

R
the Cake Mix Doctor says

Toasted sliced almonds are delicious when pressed into this glaze while it is still warm.

RICH CHOCOLATE GLAZE

You can't beat baking chocolate for that rich, intense kick you need in a quick stir-together glaze. The ingredients for this fast topping are most likely close at hand—semisweet chocolate, butter, confectioners' sugar, and milk. It pulls together in 5 minutes and is delicious on the Boston Cream Pie Cake (page 135) and Rick's Chocolate Rum Bundt Cake (page 151).

MAKES 1/2 CUP, ENOUGH TO FROST THE TOP OF A BUNDT OR TUBE CAKE

PREPARATION TIME: 5 MINUTES

2 ounces semisweet chocolate, coarsely chopped
1 tablespoon butter
1/2 cup confectioners' sugar, sifted
3 tablespoons milk

1. Place the chocolate and butter in a small saucepan over low heat. Stir and cook until both of them melt and the mixture is smooth, 3 to 4 minutes. Remove the pan from the heat, and whisk in the confectioners' sugar and milk until smooth.

2. Spoon the glaze on top of the cake of your choice. Let it set on the cake for 10 minutes before serving.

the Cake Mix Doctor says

This glaze is better when made with whole milk, but it will work just fine with any type of milk you've got in the refrigerator. For more flavor, add a teaspoon of pure vanilla extract.

SHINY CHOCOLATE GLAZE

When the glaze needs to be both a head-turner and light on fat, choose this topping. It's just right for the Good-for-You Chocolate Pound Cake (page 111) and angel food cakes. The glaze gets its intense chocolate flavor from the chocolate chips and its shine from the corn syrup.

MAKES 1 CUP, ENOUGH TO FROST
THE TOP OF A BUNDT OR TUBE CAKE
PREPARATION TIME: 5 MINUTES

1 cup semisweet chocolate chips
2 tablespoons margarine or butter
5 tablespoons light corn syrup
2½ teaspoons water

the Cake Mix Doctor says

You can use butter or margarine in this recipe. Add just enough water to make this glaze spoonable or pourable, but not too thin.

1. Place the chocolate chips, margarine, and corn syrup in a small saucepan over low heat and stir until the chocolate and margarine melt, 2 minutes. Add the water, ½ teaspoon at a time, until the glaze is of a pouring consistency.

2. Spoon or pour this glaze over the cake of your choice.

CHOCOLATE CINNAMON GLAZE

I can't imagine not loving this recipe—it brings together two great flavors, chocolate and cinnamon. Spoon the glaze over any cake, but keep it in mind especially for the Chocolate Banana Pound Cake (page 130).

MAKES 1 1/2 CUPS, ENOUGH TO FROST
A BUNDT CAKE, TUBE CAKE,
24 CUPCAKES,
OR A 9- BY 13-INCH CAKE

PREPARATION TIME: 10 MINUTES

1/2 cup sugar

5 tablespoons butter

1/4 cup milk

3 tablespoons unsweetened cocoa powder

2/3 cup cinnamon chips

1 teaspoon pure vanilla extract

1. Place the sugar, butter, and milk in a medium-size saucepan over medium-high heat. Stir until the butter melts and the mixture comes to a boil, 3 to 4 minutes. Still stirring, let the mixture boil for 1 minute. Remove the pan from the heat.

2. Stir in the cocoa powder, cinnamon chips, and vanilla until the cinnamon chips are melted and the glaze is smooth. Stir, and let the glaze cool for a few minutes, until it thickens slightly.

3. Spoon this glaze over the cake or cupcakes of your choice.

R *the Cake Mix Doctor says*

Cinnamon chips are found next to the chocolate chips in the baking aisle.

WHITE CHOCOLATE GLAZE

If there is a better glaze for the White Chocolate Chiffon Cake (page 293), or for any chocolate pound cake, than this simple glaze made with white chocolate chips, you'll have to write and let me know. It is thick enough to coat the top of the cake, but it is thin enough not to dominate its flavor.

MAKES 1 CUP, ENOUGH TO FROST
THE TOP OF A POUND CAKE
PREPARATION TIME: 8 MINUTES

¼ cup milk
5 tablespoons butter
½ cup sugar
1 cup white chocolate chips

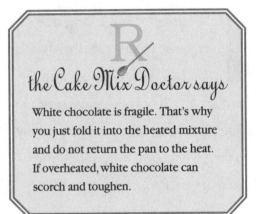

R

the Cake Mix Doctor says

White chocolate is fragile. That's why you just fold it into the heated mixture and do not return the pan to the heat. If overheated, white chocolate can scorch and toughen.

1. Place the milk, butter, and sugar in a small saucepan over medium heat. Heat, stirring constantly, until the mixture comes to a boil, 2 to 3 minutes. Continue boiling and stirring until the butter is melted, 1 minute more. Remove the pan from the heat, add the white chocolate chips, and stir until they are melted.

2. Allow this glaze to cool in the pan for 5 minutes, then spoon it over the cake of your choice.

FRESH ORANGE DRIZZLE

When you crave that citrusy, unmistakable orange flavor, stir together this easy drizzle. It's wonderful over pound cakes, especially the Chocolate-Orange Cream Cheese Pound Cake (page 105).

....

MAKES 1 CUP, ENOUGH TO FROST
THE TOP OF A BUNDT OR TUBE CAKE

PREPARATION TIME: 5 MINUTES

....

1 cup confectioners' sugar, sifted

1 to 2 tablespoons fresh orange juice

1 teaspoon grated orange zest, or

¼ teaspoon orange extract

the Cake Mix Doctor says

If you don't like the raw taste of confectioners' sugar, bring the ingredients to a simmer over low heat, then allow to cool, and spoon over the cake.

1. Place the confectioners' sugar in a small mixing bowl and whisk in enough orange juice to make the glaze smooth and spoonable. Fold in the zest or extract.

2. Spoon the glaze over the cooled cake of your choice, letting it drizzle down the sides and into the center of the cake. Let the cake rest for 10 minutes before slicing.

CINNAMON CHIP GLAZE

This easy glaze was developed by the Hershey's kitchens for their cinnamon chips. Drizzle it over the Chocolate Cinnamon Chip Chewies (page 359) or the Mini German Chocolate Banana Loaves (page 348).

MAKES ABOUT ENOUGH FOR
7 DOZEN COOKIES OR 6 MINI LOAVES
PREPARATION TIME: 2 MINUTES

⅔ cup cinnamon chips
1½ teaspoons solid vegetable shortening

1. Place the cinnamon chips and the shortening in a small glass bowl in the microwave oven on high power. Heat until the chips have just melted, 30 seconds. Remove the bowl from the oven and stir the glaze until it is smooth. Or melt the chips and shortening in a small saucepan over low heat, stirring constantly, 1½ to 2 minutes.

2. Drizzle this glaze with a dinner knife, or pour it into a clean plastic squirt bottle and squirt in squiggly lines over the cookies or cake.

R
the Cake Mix Doctor says

Do not use butter or margarine in this recipe—only vegetable shortening.

SIMPLE SUGAR GLAZE

When you don't want any-thing fussy or anything chocolate, here is what the Cake Mix Doctor ordered! It couldn't be simpler—just sugar and milk. Spoon it over Kathy's Choco-late Chocolate Chip Cake (page 118), or try the coffee variation (see "the Cake Mix Doctor says").

MAKES 1 CUP,
ENOUGH TO FROST THE TOP
OF A BUNDT OR TUBE CAKE
PREPARATION TIME: 2 MINUTES

1 cup confectioners' sugar, sifted
1 to 2 tablespoons milk

1. Place the confectioners' sugar in a small mixing bowl and whisk in enough milk to make the glaze smooth and spoonable.

2. Spoon the glaze over the cake of your choice. Let the cake rest for 10 minutes before slicing.

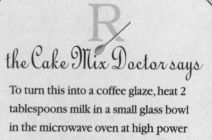

the Cake Mix Doctor says

To turn this into a coffee glaze, heat 2 tablespoons milk in a small glass bowl in the microwave oven at high power for 30 seconds. Stir in 1 tablespoon instant coffee powder until it dissolves. Pour this over 1½ cups confectioners' sugar (sifted of course), and whisk until the glaze is smooth.

HOT FUDGE SAUCE

Every ice cream cake should be blanketed in hot chocolate sauce, right? Here is just the right sauce for those special desserts, ice cream sundaes, and Martha's Chocolate Cherry Ice Cream Cake (page 78).

MAKES 2 CUPS, ENOUGH FOR
12 SERVINGS OVER ICE CREAM CAKE

PREPARATION TIME: 7 MINUTES

1 cup heavy (whipping) cream
⅓ cup light corn syrup
2 cups semisweet chocolate chips

the Cake Mix Doctor says

For an easy peppermint fudge sauce,
add 1 teaspoon peppermint extract.

1. Place the cream and corn syrup in a medium-size saucepan over medium-high heat. Bring just to a boil, stirring constantly, 2 to 3 minutes. Stir in the chocolate chips until they are melted and the sauce is smooth.

2. Spoon the warm sauce over ice cream cake or ice cream.

WARM LEMON CURD SAUCE

My children were invited to a ladies' luncheon hosted by my mother and her sisters. Let's just say that there was a lot of fidgeting going on as those two restless girls had to sit still during lunch. But when a soft yellow cake with a warm lemon puddinglike sauce was served for dessert, you would have thought they had been tranquilized. They savored each and every bite of that cake and its warm, comforting sauce, and I remembered that moment and that sauce! It is so easy to spoon this atop pound cake, gingerbread, or

ice cream, or just when you want to leave your guests speechless.

MAKES 1½ CUPS, ENOUGH
FOR 16 SERVINGS

PREPARATION TIME: 10 MINUTES

¾ cup sugar

2 tablespoons cornstarch

1 cup water

1 large egg

4 tablespoons (½ stick) butter

2 teaspoons grated lemon zest

2 tablespoons fresh lemon juice

1. Place the sugar and cornstarch in a medium-size saucepan. Whisk in the water. Place the pan over medium-high heat and cook, whisking constantly, until the mixture just begins to boil, 4 to 5 minutes. Remove the pan from the heat.

2. Using a fork, lightly beat the egg in a small mixing bowl. Spoon in 2 tablespoons of the hot sugar mixture and beat vigorously with the whisk to incorporate. Spoon in another 2 tablespoons of the hot mixture and beat vigorously again.

3. Place the saucepan back over medium heat, and pour the beaten egg mixture into the pan, whisking constantly. Let the mixture boil for 1 minute, whisking. The mixture will be thick. Remove the pan from the heat, and stir in the butter, lemon zest, and lemon juice until they are incorporated.

4. Spoon this warm sauce over cake or ice cream.

✻ *Store this sauce in a glass jar in the refrigerator for up to 2 weeks. Reheat it on top of the stove over low heat or in the microwave at medium power for 1 to 2 minutes.*

R

the Cake Mix Doctor says

Substitute lime juice and zest, or orange juice and zest, and you change the flavor of the sauce.

JULIE'S LEMON CURD

My friend Julie Buchanan, of Higham Ferrers, England, shared this recipe with me many years ago. It is a dandy, and while it takes a little time to prepare, it is far more delicious than the lemon curd sold in grocery stores.

MAKES 1⅓ CUPS
PREPARATION TIME: 20 MINUTES
COOKING TIME: 5 TO 7 MINUTES

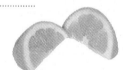

2 large lemons
¾ cup sugar
2 large eggs
6 tablespoons (¾ stick) unsalted butter, melted and slightly cooled

1. Scrub the lemons well with soap and water, then dry them. Grate the zest; you should have about 1 tablespoon. Cut the lemons in half and juice them, removing the seeds; you should have about ¼ cup juice. Place the juice and the zest in a medium-size mixing bowl. Whisk in the sugar and eggs, and beat until well combined, 2 minutes. Whisk in the melted butter until incorporated.

2. Pour the lemon mixture into a medium-size heavy saucepan set over medium heat. Whisk constantly until the mixture gradually thickens and comes to a boil, 5 to 7 minutes. Remove the pan from the heat. Continue to whisk the lemon curd off the heat until it cools down, 4 to 5 minutes.

3. Strain the lemon curd through a fine-mesh sieve to remove the zest, if desired. Pour it into a glass bowl or jar, cover with plastic wrap or a lid, and refrigerate.

✻ *Lemon curd will keep in the refrigerator for up to 1 week.*

R the Cake Mix Doctor says

To extract as much juice as possible from lemons, roll them against a hard surface, like a table or the kitchen counter, with your palm. Or place them in the microwave oven on high power for 50 seconds. Then juice them.

QUICK WHITE CHOCOLATE MOUSSE

Just two ingredients are needed for this easy mousse—white chocolate and heavy cream. To speed up the time it takes for the white chocolate to melt, chop it first. The mixture will thicken as it cools over the ice bath. Then all you need to do is whip it until it forms stiff peaks, like whipped cream. Use this in the White Chocolate Angel Food Mousse Cake (page 286).

....

MAKES 5 CUPS
PREPARATION TIME: 40 MINUTES

....

1¾ cups heavy (whipping) cream
1 pound white chocolate, coarsely chopped

1. Place the heavy cream in a small heavy saucepan over low heat, and heat, stirring occasionally, until it is steaming hot but not boiling. Place the white chocolate in a large stainless-steel mixing bowl. Pour

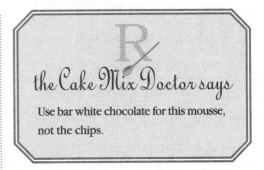

the Cake Mix Doctor says

Use bar white chocolate for this mousse, not the chips.

the hot cream over the white chocolate and stir until all the white chocolate has melted and the mixture is smooth.

2. Fill a larger glass or stainless-steel bowl with ice, and place it in the sink. Rest the bowl of mousse on top of the ice. Let it chill for 30 minutes, stirring every 5 minutes to loosen the chilled mousse around the edges. At the end of the chilling time, the mixture should be the consistency of custard.

3. Beat the mousse at medium speed with an electric mixer until it lightens and then forms stiff peaks. This will take 3 to 4 minutes. Don't overbeat. Cover the bowl with plastic wrap and chill until needed.

CHOCOLATE CREAM FILLING

My children can't get enough of this filling, especially after it has been chilled. I am sure that's because it is ooey-gooey and chocolaty and sweet! Use this filling in the middle of the Dark Chocolate Roulade (page 256) and the Chocolate Cookie Sandwiches (page 366).

MAKES 3 CUPS

PREPARATION TIME:
10 TO 12 MINUTES

½ cup semisweet chocolate chips

8 tablespoons (1 stick) butter, at room
    temperature

1 jar (7 ounces) marshmallow creme

½ teaspoon pure vanilla extract

1½ cups sifted confectioners' sugar

1. Place the chocolate chips in a medium-size glass bowl and place in the microwave oven on high power for 1 minute.

Remove the bowl and stir the chips with a wooden spoon until they are melted.

2. Add the butter, marshmallow creme, and vanilla to the chocolate. Beat with an electric mixer on low speed until well combined, 1 minute. Stop the machine and scrape down the sides of the bowl with a rubber spatula. Add the confectioners' sugar and beat on low speed to incorporate, 30 seconds. Then increase the speed to medium and beat for 1 minute, or until light and fluffy. The filling will be quite thick.

3. Use this filling with the cake layers, sandwich cookies, or roulade of your choice.

R

the Cake Mix Doctor says

Notice that this recipe calls for sifting the confectioners' sugar first, before measuring.

Conversion Table

Liquid Conversions

U.S.	Imperial	Metric
2 Tb	1 fl oz	30 ml
3 Tb	1½ fl oz	45 ml
¼ cup	2 fl oz	60 ml
⅓ cup	2½ fl oz	75 ml
⅓ cup + 1 Tb	3 fl oz	90 ml
⅓ cup + 2 Tb	3½ fl oz	100 ml
½ cup	4 fl oz	125 ml
⅔ cup	5 fl oz	150 ml
¾ cup	6 fl oz	175 ml
¾ cup + 2 Tb	7 fl oz	200 ml
1 cup	8 fl oz	250 ml
1 cup + 2 Tb	9 fl oz	275 ml
1¼ cups	10 fl oz	300 ml
1⅓ cups	11 fl oz	325 ml
1½ cups	12 fl oz	350 ml
1⅔ cups	13 fl oz	375 ml
1¾ cups	14 fl oz	400 ml
1¾ cups + 2 Tb	15 fl oz	450 ml
2 cups (1 pint)	16 fl oz	500 ml
2½ cups	20 fl oz (1 pint)	600 ml
3¾ cups	1½ pints	900 ml
4 cups	1¾ pints	1 liter

Weight Conversions

U.S.	Metric	U.S.	Metric
½ oz	15 g	7 oz	200 g
1 oz	30 g	8 oz	250 g
1½ oz	45 g	9 oz	275 g
2 oz	60 g	10 oz	300 g
2½ oz	75 g	11 oz	325 g
3 oz	90 g	12 oz	350 g
3½ oz	100 g	13 oz	375 g
4 oz	125 g	14 oz	400 g
5 oz	150 g	15 oz	450 g
6 oz	175 g	1 lb	500 g

Oven Temperatures

Fahrenheit	Celsius Gas Mark		Fahrenheit	Celsius Gas Mark	
250	½	120	400	6	200
275	1	140	425	7	220
300	2	150	450	8	230
325	3	160	475	9	240
350	4	180	500	10	260
375	5	190			

Note: Reduce the temperature by 20°C (68°F) for fan-assisted ovens.

Approximate Equivalents

1 stick butter = 8 Tb = 4 oz = ½ cup

1 cup all-purpose presifted flour or dried bread crumbs = 5 oz

1 cup granulated sugar = 8 oz

1 cup (packed) brown sugar = 6 oz

1 cup confectioners' sugar = 4½ oz

1 cup honey or syrup = 12 oz

1 cup grated cheese = 4 oz

1 cup dried beans = 6 oz

2 large eggs = about 2 oz = about ¼ cup

1 egg yolk = about 1 Tb

1 egg white = about 2 Tb

Please note that all conversions are approximate but close enough to be useful when converting from one system to another.

Chocolate Cake Glossary

• • •

Baker's: A brand of chocolate, first made in 1764 in a small mill near Dorchester, Massachusetts, by John Hannon, an Irish-American chocolatier, and James Baker, a physician who financed him. It was originally called the Hannon Chocolate Company. Baker took over the business after Hannon was lost at sea in 1779 en route to buy cacao beans. The business was named the Walter Baker Chocolate Company in 1824, when it was operated by Baker's grandson, Walter Baker. Baker's is now owned by Kraft Foods, Inc.

Baking chocolate: Unsweetened or bitter chocolate used in both cake batters and frostings.

Bittersweet chocolate: When sugar and a little cocoa butter are added to baking chocolate. Can be substituted for semisweet. Sweetness differs slightly among brands, and some may be called "extra bittersweet."

Bloom: White dots or streaks or a dull gray appearance that form on the surface of chocolate after it has been stored in too warm conditions and the cocoa butter separates. This doesn't mean it is spoiled, and the bloom will disappear when the chocolate is melted. Also a sugar bloom that occurs when the chocolate has gotten damp, which causes the chocolate to turn grainy. Chocolate with sugar bloom should be discarded.

Boston cream pie: A classic American dessert that is more like a cake than a pie. It is said to have originated at the Parker House Hotel in Boston. Layers of yellow sponge cake are filled with a vanilla pastry cream or pudding and then all is covered in a shiny chocolate glaze.

Nuggets of Chocolate History

Chocolate has progressed from a primitive potion enjoyed by Aztec royalty, to a luxurious drink sipped solely by wealthy Europeans, to a mainstream foodstuff enjoyed by ordinary people. Whether chocolate appears in the form of baking cocoa, or in a cake mix, or in a milk chocolate candy bar, it transports the eater to someplace sublime.

Here are a few interesting notes about chocolate's colorful history:

• It was first brought to Europe in 1528 by the Spanish explorer Hernando Cortez, who had learned about chocolate from the Aztecs in Mexico—specifically Emperor Montezuma, who reportedly downed goblets of frothy drinking chocolate laced with dried chile peppers. The Aztecs ground the cacao beans with corn kernels and seasoned them with vanilla, honey, flower petals, chiles, and other spices. Christopher Columbus is said to have brought back the first cacao beans, from his fourth visit to the New World, but they were overlooked in favor of other treasures.

• The word "chocolate" is Mexican (from the Mayan and Nahuatle languages) in origin. It refers to "water" and "foam," for early chocolate was consumed only as a beverage.

• Chocolate's popularity, mostly as a beverage, swept across Europe, but only after the Spanish added sugar to it to make it more palatable.

• In 1657 chocolate was introduced into England as a beverage, served in a "chocolate house." It was only afforded by the wealthy, and it was said to be so expensive that it was like "drinking money."

• The first American chocolate factory was opened in 1764 near Dorchester, Massachusetts, by Irish-American John Hannon and his business partner, Dr. James Baker.

• In 1828 Dutch chocolate maker Conrad J. van Houten patented a method for pressing the fat from roasted cacao beans. The pressed mass was dried and then ground into cocoa powder, the forerunner of our instant cocoa. He found that by adding cocoa butter to the ground cocoa, along with some sugar, the mixture could be molded and cooled in forms. *Voilà!* Chocolate candy.

Brownies: The dense and fudgy squares first thought to have appeared in print in 1897 in the Sears, Roebuck catalogue. The story goes that a forgetful cook left the baking powder out of a chocolate cake recipe, and *voilà!* Success! Brownies are a cinch to make from scratch, and you can have fun turning box brownie mixes into fabulous treats. They are usually described as either "fudgy" or "cakey," with the latter containing more egg.

Cacao: The name of the tropical evergreen tree whose beans are dried, partially fermented, and processed to make chocolate, cocoa butter, and cocoa powder. Interestingly, the taller trees like banana, coconut palm, and rubber that grow next to cacao trees and shade them from the sun are called "cacao mothers." The word was corrupted to form "cocoa," the term we use today to describe the powdered chocolate.

Cadbury: The largest British chocolate manufacturer, known around the world. It was named for John Cadbury, who opened a shop in Birmingham, England, in 1822 and sold coffee, tea, and drinking chocolate. Cadbury would later use Dutch machinery to press out all the cocoa butter from chocolate paste and create the first pure cocoa powder in Britain. Cadbury produced chocolates for the mass market. Up until that time, chocolate had been a luxury item enjoyed only by the wealthy. A little more than four decades later (1868), his son, Richard Cadbury, would place chocolates in a box and start a trend that continues each and every Valentine's Day.

Candy bars: When liquid chocolate is poured into molds and filled with nuts, fruits, toffee, and other goodies, it is our beloved candy bar.

Chocolate chips: Tiny pieces of chocolate formulated to tolerate heat and not lose their shape.

Chocolate liquor: The thick ground center of the roasted cacao beans. Present in dark chocolates but not in white chocolate.

Cocoa butter: The ivory-colored fat in cacao beans. It is extracted during the process of making chocolate, then added back to make chocolate richer and smoother. It is also used in the cosmetic and pharmaceutical industries because it is solid at room temperature but liquefies with body heat. Cocoa butter contributes flavor and creaminess to chocolate.

Cocoa powder: Unsweetened cocoa powder is what is produced when the cacao beans are roasted and ground, the cocoa butter has been removed, and the remaining chocolate paste is dried and processed.

Compound chocolate: When chocolate is made with a fat other than cocoa butter. It doesn't have the glossy shine of real chocolate. It is chewy and won't melt in your mouth.

Compound coatings: Compound chocolate with some cocoa butter added. Also called summer coatings. They are popular in making candy.

Dark chocolate: Chocolate that is bittersweet or semisweet.

Devil's food cake: A reddish-brown chocolate cake that has been an American classic for more than 100 years. So named because of its color, which comes from the reddish-brown cocoa powder. Also has been called "Satan cake."

Dutch-process cocoa powder: Cocoa that has been treated with an alkaline solution, making it more mellow in flavor and darker in color than regular unsweetened cocoa powder.

Fudge: A creamy and soft chocolate candy, usually containing nuts. "Fudge" has become an adjective describing rich and creamy chocolate desserts.

Ganache: A frosting or filling made by pouring hot cream over chopped semisweet chocolate. As the chocolate melts, the frosting thickens up and can be spread over cakes. It can also be refrigerated until chilled and then whipped and spread onto cakes.

German, or German's, chocolate: A sweet chocolate containing milk, sugar, and vanilla, named after Samuel German, an employee of the Walter Baker Chocolate Company in Boston in the mid-1800s. It resembles milk chocolate. It is sold today as Baker's German Sweet Chocolate. Often the possessive "s" is dropped and it is called just "German chocolate."

German chocolate cake: Another classic American dessert—a layer cake made with German chocolate and a thick, sweet cooked frosting containing pecans and coconut. (See German Chocolate Cake, page 66.)

Hershey's: A name synonymous with chocolate in the United States. Named for its creator, Milton S. Hershey, a caramel maker who made his fortune adding milk to chocolate. The company is located in

Candy Bars and War

Nothing seems more peaceful than nibbling on a chocolate candy bar. But the candy bar has also played a role in our country's wartime efforts.

At Hershey, production of the popular Kisses has been interrupted only once since they were introduced in 1907. Kisses were not produced between 1942 and 1949 because the silver foil used to wrap them was rationed during and after World War II, and because the equipment was needed to make the chocolate paste for military ration bars.

During World War II, Hershey produced more than 3 billion ration bars for the U.S. military around the world. To increase their shelf life, these candy bars contained no cocoa butter. They were boosted with thiamine hydrochloride (a source of vitamin B_1) to ward off beriberi. The result was a candy bar—called the Field Ration D—that had all the flavor of boiled potatoes, designed so the soldiers would eat them only when they were on the verge of starvation.

But the flavor returned, for in 1943 the Army asked Hershey to come up with a candy bar that tasted better and was heat-resistant. Hershey's Tropical Chocolate Bar was born, and it not only fed servicemen around the globe but ended up in outer space. In July 1971, Apollo 15 astronauts carried along these specially designed chocolate bars.

The most recent "war bar" was developed in 1990, after the Army expressed interest in a heat-resistant bar that tasted like commercially available chocolate. Hershey's Desert Bars, made with pure milk chocolate, were sent to Saudi Arabia for taste tests a few months later.

Hershey, Pennsylvania, and is one of the world's largest chocolate manufacturers, most famous for the milk chocolate bar (since 1900) and the foil-wrapped Hershey's Kisses (since 1907).

Mars: Another well-known American chocolate candy bar manufacturer, founded by Frank and Ethel Mars in 1911. The company is now a snack food and pet food giant, best known for

M&Ms and the Snickers, Milky Way, and Twix bars.

Milk chocolate: When sugar and milk solids are added to baking chocolate.

Mocha: The name for the combination of coffee and chocolate in recipes.

Nestlé: A household word when it comes to chocolate chips and candy bars. Nestlé is a massive multinational food company that originated in 1867.

Semisweet chocolate: Like bittersweet chocolate, semisweet chocolate is made by adding cocoa butter and a little sugar to baking chocolate. The two are interchangeable in recipes. Some of the brands contain milk solids to smooth out the flavor.

Tunnel of Fudge Cake: A wildly popular Pillsbury Bake-Off winner (1966), this walnut-studded chocolate Bundt cake had a ribbon of fudge frosting running through it. The center was made by using a dry frosting mix that is no longer manufactured. Many renditions of this cake have been born, using pudding mix or by undercooking the cake so that the center is still gooey when you slice into it.

Turtles: Candy made by covering pecan halves with caramel and then a coating of chocolate. "Turtle" has become a description for a chocolate dessert that contains pecans and caramel.

White chocolate: A confection usually made from cocoa butter pressed from the cacao bean, along with sugar, butterfat, milk solids, lecithin, and flavorings. However, some white chocolate is made with vegetable oil and not cocoa butter.

Bibliography

• • •

Beranbaum, Rose Levy. *The Cake Bible.* New York: William Morrow and Company, 1988.

Bloom, Carole. *All About Chocolate: The Ultimate Resource for the World's Favorite Food.* New York: Macmillan, 1998.

Byrn, Anne. *Food Gifts for All Seasons.* Atlanta: Peachtree Publishers, 1996.

Coe, Sophie D., and Michael D. Coe. *The True History of Chocolate.* New York: Thames and Hudson, 1996.

Corriher, Shirley O. *CookWise: The Hows and Whys of Successful Cooking.* New York: William Morrow and Company, 1997.

Fuchs, Ronald D. *You Said a Mouthful! Wise and Witty Quotations About Food.* New York: St. Martin's Press, 1996.

Haughton, Natalie. *365 Great Chocolate Desserts.* New York: HarperCollins, 1991.

Herbst, Sharon Tyler. *Never Eat More Than You Can Lift.* New York: Broadway Books, 1997.

Mariani, John. *The Dictionary of American Food & Drink.* New Haven, CT: Ticknor & Fields, 1983.

Pépin, Jacques. *The Short-Cut Cook.* New York: William Morrow and Company, 1990.

Sokolov, Raymond. *Why We Eat What We Eat: How Columbus Changed the Way the World Eats.* New York: Simon & Schuster, 1991.

Teubner, Christian. *The Chocolate Bible.* New York: Penguin Putnam, 1997.

Trager, James. *The Food Chronology: A Food Lover's Compendium of Events and Anecdotes, from Prehistory to the Present.* New York: Henry Holt and Company, 1995.

Index

• • •